A Celebration of Poets

California
Grades 7-9
Spring 2009

A Celebration of Poets
California
Grades 7-9
Spring 2009

An anthology compiled by Creative Communication, Inc.

Published by:

1488 NORTH 200 WEST • LOGAN, UTAH 84341
TEL. 435-713-4411 • WWW.POETICPOWER.COM

All rights reserved. No part of this book may be reproduced or transmitted in any form or by any means, electronic or mechanical without written permission of the author and publisher.

Copyright © 2009 by Creative Communication, Inc.
Printed in the United States of America

ISBN: 978-1-60050-294-1

FOREWORD

Earlier this year I received a phone call from an individual who was sending in a poem written by a friend's son. Through the conversation it was revealed that the person I was talking to was the author, poet and playwright, John Tobias. His poem, "Reflections on a Gift of Watermelon Pickle Received from a Friend Called Felicity" is one of my favorite poems. Starting with the line "During that summer, when unicorns were still possible..." his poem takes me back to all the magical summers that I had where anything could happen. I was given a treat in that Mr. Tobias recited his poem and related the story that inspired it. What I gained most from the conversation was that the inspiration for any writing may seem to come from an event, but it is really written from a lifetime of experiences.

I also received a letter this spring from a young lady who was published in one of our anthologies in 1999. Now a published author working on her second novel, she took the time to write and thank Creative Communication for giving her the start for her writing career. The poets in this anthology are beginning writers. Yet, as they continue in their writing, the experience of being a published author will hopefully be an inspiration to them. As they gain a lifetime of experiences, I hope they will continue to write and share themselves through poetry.

As you read each student's poem, realize that every famous author started somewhere. I hope that I will continue to receive letters from authors who relate that we were the first place they were published. Will one of these authors become famous? Anything is possible.

I hope you enjoy this anthology and the poets who share their lives through words.

Thomas Worthen, Ph.D.
Editor
Creative Communication

WRITING CONTESTS!

Enter our next POETRY contest!

Enter our next ESSAY contest!

Why should I enter?
Win prizes and get published! Each year thousands of dollars in prizes are awarded throughout North America. The top writers in each division receive a monetary award and a free book that includes their published poem or essay. Entries of merit are also selected to be published in our anthology.

Who may enter?
There are four divisions in the poetry contest. The poetry divisions are grades K-3, 4-6, 7-9, and 10-12. There are three divisions in the essay contest. The essay divisions are grades 3-6, 7-9, and 10-12.

What is needed to enter the contest?
To enter the poetry contest send in one original poem, 21 lines or less. To enter the essay contest send in one original non-fiction essay, 250 words or less, on any topic. Each entry must include the student's name, grade, address, city, state, and zip code, and the student's school name and school address. Students who include their teacher's name may help their teacher qualify for a free copy of the anthology. Contest changes and updates are listed at www.poeticpower.com.

How do I enter?

Enter a poem online at:
www.poeticpower.com

or

Mail your poem to:
   Poetry Contest
   1488 North 200 West
   Logan, UT 84341

Enter an essay online at:
www.studentessaycontest.com

or

Mail your essay to:
   Essay Contest
   1488 North 200 West
   Logan, UT 84341

When is the deadline?
Poetry contest deadlines are August 18th, December 3rd, and April 13th. Essay contest deadlines are October 15th, February 17th, and July 15th. Students can enter one poem and one essay for each spring, summer, and fall contest deadline.

Are there benefits for my school?
Yes. We award $15,000 each year in grants to help with Language Arts programs. Schools qualify to apply for a grant by having 15 or more accepted entries.

Are there benefits for my teacher?
Yes. Teachers with five or more students published receive a free anthology that includes their students' writing.

For more information please go to our website at **www.poeticpower.com**, email us at editor@poeticpower.com or call 435-713-4411.

TABLE OF CONTENTS

POETIC ACHIEVEMENT HONOR SCHOOLS	1
LANGUAGE ARTS GRANT RECIPIENTS	5
GRADES 7-8-9	9
TOP POEMS	10
HIGH MERIT POEMS	20
INDEX	213

Spring 2009 Poetic Achievement Honor Schools

Teachers who had fifteen or more poets accepted to be published

The following schools are recognized as receiving a "Poetic Achievement Award." This award is given to schools who have a large number of entries of which over fifty percent are accepted for publication. With hundreds of schools entering our contest, only a small percent of these schools are honored with this award. The purpose of this award is to recognize schools with excellent Language Arts programs. This award qualifies these schools to receive a complimentary copy of this anthology. In addition, these schools are eligible to apply for a Creative Communication Language Arts Grant. Grants of two hundred and fifty dollars each are awarded to further develop writing in our schools.

Bethany Lutheran School
    Vacaville
        Cathy Hays*

Blessed Sacrament School
    Los Angeles
        Bunnee Blum
        Salvador Callela
        Joy Gillett

Carmel Valley Middle School
    San Diego
        Michelle Challis-Hall*

Challenger School – Ardenwood
    Newark
        Rebecca Arnold*

Citrus Hills Intermediate School
    Corona
        Ellen Cleveland*
        Jennifer Fleuette*
        Mary Maiden-Umbarger*

Corpus Christi School
    San Francisco
        Theodore R. Langlais*

Crenshaw Arts/Tech Charter High School
    Los Angeles
        Paige Cooper*

Dorris-Eaton School
    Walnut Creek
        Brad Breilein
        Maggi Brown
        Mary Dickens*
        Claudia Fredriksson*
        Deeni Schoenfeld

Emek Hebrew Academy
    Sherman Oaks
        Kristin Thompson*

Fountain Valley High School
    Fountain Valley
        Patricia Muñoz*

A Celebration of Poets – California Grades 7-9 Spring 2009

Henry T Gage Middle School
Huntington Park
Petra Jones*

Holy Family Catholic School
Citrus Heights
Sherry Moniz*
Sharon Murray*

Islamic School of San Diego
San Diego
Aisha Boulil*

John Adams Middle School
Los Angeles
Linda Bolibaugh*

Kadima Heschel West Middle School
West Hills
Barbara Hudock*

La Joya Middle School
Visalia
Debbie Patton*

Las Flores Middle School
Las Flores
Laurie Cummings*

Linfield Christian School
Temecula
Pat Heckert*
Desirae Jesse
Dr. Ruth Young

Lucerne Valley Jr/Sr High School
Lucerne Valley
Cindy Lazenby
Linda Schlenz*

Madrona Middle School
Torrance
Mr. Berube
Colleen Poelvoorde*

McCabe Elementary School
El Centro
Sandra Ross*

Monte Vista Christian School
Watsonville
Mrs. Marsh
Janice Renard*

Odyssey Charter School
Altadena
Gurupreet Khalsa*

Packinghouse Christian Academy
Redlands
Theresa J. Moore*

Palm Desert Charter Middle School
Palm Desert
Julie Davis
Nanette Davis-Kirchhevel
Kristin Wagner

Redlands High School
Redlands
Ms. Gibson
Joshua Murguia*

Richard Merkin Middle Academy
Los Angeles
Brandon Bell*

Robert C Fisler School
Fullerton
Elizabeth Ellison*

Rolling Hills Country Day School
Rolling Hills Estates
Debby Corette*
Peggy Johns-Campbell*

Santa Rosa Technology Magnet School
Camarillo
Michelle Bennett*

St Alphonsus School
    Los Angeles
        Margaret Kirby*

St Cyprian School
    Sunnyvale
        Denise Brady
        Breigh Zack*

St Helen Catholic Elementary School
    South Gate
        Bernadette Windsor*

St John's Parish Day School
    Chula Vista
        Connie Walker*

St Mary of Assumption School
    Santa Maria
        Ellen Muldoon*

St Timothy School
    Los Angeles
        Sally David*

St Victor Elementary School
    San Jose
        Victoria Hinkle*

The Mirman School
    Los Angeles
        Dr. Julia Candace Corliss*
        Bonnie Muler*
        Wendy Samson*
        Mrs. Walker*

Thornton Jr High School
    Fremont
        Latanya White*

University Preparatory School
    Redding
        Andy Hedman
        Mr. Kaukonen
        Sally vonDachenhausen

Valley Christian High School
    San Jose
        Katie Issacs
        Judy Marc*

Yolo Middle School
    Newman
        Anne Reiswig*

Language Arts Grant Recipients 2008-2009

After receiving a "Poetic Achievement Award" schools are encouraged to apply for a Creative Communication Language Arts Grant. The following is a list of schools who received a two hundred and fifty dollar grant for the 2008-2009 school year.

Acushnet Elementary School, Acushnet, MA
Benton Central Jr/Sr High School, Oxford, IN
Bridgeway Christian Academy, Alpharetta, GA
Central Middle School, Grafton, ND
Challenger Middle School, Cape Coral, FL
City Hill Middle School, Naugatuck, CT
Clintonville High School, Clintonville, WI
Coral Springs Middle School, Coral Springs, FL
Covenant Classical School, Concord, NC
Coyote Valley Elementary School, Middletown, CA
Diamond Ranch Academy, Hurricane, UT
E O Young Jr Elementary School, Middleburg, NC
El Monte Elementary School, Concord, CA
Emmanuel-St Michael Lutheran School, Fort Wayne, IN
Ethel M Burke Elementary School, Bellmawr, NJ
Fort Recovery Middle School, Fort Recovery, OH
Gardnertown Fundamental Magnet School, Newburgh, NY
Hancock County High School, Sneedville, TN
Haubstadt Community School, Haubstadt, IN
Headwaters Academy, Bozeman, MT
Holden Elementary School, Chicago, IL
Holliday Middle School, Holliday, TX
Holy Cross High School, Delran, NJ
Homestead Elementary School, Centennial, CO
Joseph M Simas Elementary School, Hanford, CA
Labrae Middle School, Leavittsburg, OH
Lakewood High School, Lakewood, CO
Lee A Tolbert Community Academy, Kansas City, MO
Mary Lynch Elementary School, Kimball, NE
Merritt Secondary School, Merritt, BC
North Star Academy, Redwood City, CA

Language Arts Grant Winners cont.

Old Redford Academy, Detroit, MI
Prairie Lakes School, Willmar, MN
Public School 124Q, South Ozone Park, NY
Rutledge Hall Elementary School, Lincolnwood, IL
Shelley Sr High School, Shelley, ID
Sonoran Science Academy, Tucson, AZ
Spruce Ridge School, Estevan, SK
St Columbkille School, Dubuque, IA
St Francis Middle School, Saint Francis, MN
St Luke the Evangelist School, Glenside, PA
St Matthias/Transfiguration School, Chicago, IL
St Robert Bellarmine School, Chicago, IL
St Sebastian Elementary School, Pittsburgh, PA
The Hillel Academy, Milwaukee, WI
Thomas Edison Charter School - North, North Logan, UT
Trinity Christian Academy, Oxford, AL
United Hebrew Institute, Kingston, PA
Velasquez Elementary School, Richmond, TX
West Frederick Middle School, Frederick, MD

Grades 7-8-9

Note: The Top Ten poems were finalized through an online voting system. Creative Communication's judges first picked out the top poems. These poems were then posted online. The final step involved thousands of students and teachers who registered as online judges and voted for the Top Ten poems. We hope you enjoy these selections.

Top Poem Grades 7-8-9

I Heard It in a Dream

A silver throng of latent song,
Where ballads fall from trees,
And dance upon the ariose dawn,
Cascading their reprise,

I look beyond the sea of glass,
Where dreams are wont to stray,
And sit in thought, upon the grass,
Of places far away,

Of Flame and Shadow deftly vied,
Denied his baneful throne,
Of ancient dragon's noble stride,
In halls beneath the stone,

The rising of a subtle fire,
In fey celestial gleam,
A melody upon a lyre,
I heard it in a dream.

Eric Bernard, Grade 9
Sky Mountain Charter School

Top Poem Grades 7-8-9

Moments

In all my thirteen years of living,
I have seen things, heard things,
felt things, some won't even remember.
I've seen a hummingbird,
who could have flown faster than a Ferrari,
land on a branch of a blooming tree and rest.
I've watched a black widow
spend hours and hours on a perfect, silk web
and abandon it to help another spin a replica.
I've heard a mother sing to her child at night
whose eyes are permanently crossed
and whose mouth is twisted into a fallen branch.
We see these things every day,
but we forget them because we're too busy,
too selfish, and too obnoxious to remember these moments,
these precious, timeless moments.
As a result, the next generation
believes that these times don't exist.
I tell those who don't remember, who don't know,
these things do exist.
We just don't take notice.

Claire Garcia, Grade 8
Canyon Hills Jr High School

Top Poem Grades 7-8-9

Another Moment of Life

Like the soft whisper of a breeze,
life slips past me,
Memories of the past fade,
as time moves on.

Childhood is but a sweet fog,
cherished, yet forgotten,
The future seems to stretch so wide,
yet looking back from the other side,
A few steps is all I've walked.

Life is short and often bittersweet,
Easy to forget or hard to remember,
We say childhood was the best,
'cause our hundred years stretched on,
but in one blink, we stood,
Innocence gone with the wind.

So hold the memories close,
with all your might,
Cherish every second,
Another moment of life,
joins the breeze…

Kaitlin Hearn, Grade 8
Yuba Environmental Science Charter Academy

Top Poem Grades 7-8-9

Sea of Time

Everyday people sail
the sea of time.
Unable to stop the currents,
we drift by.
Once in a while, the land of rest appears
But slips away like snakes
Sailing and sailing until
there is no more to sail.
As pilgrims sailed to America,
people sail to find
their land of hopes and dreams.
Sometimes misled by illusions
up in the horizon.
But people keep sailing,
roaming the sea of time.
When darkness descends
all sailors rest in peace.
When dawn ascends
a new journey of new sailors begins.
To find their land of hopes and dreams
among the vast openness of the sea of time.

Hee Jae Jung, Grade 8
Carmel Valley Middle School

Top Poem Grades 7-8-9

Hurt…

My neck hurts from holding my head up high
Whispering worthless wishes into the hopeful sky
My lips hurt from faking smiles
This dark road goes on for miles
My eyes hurt from witnessing evil in this life
Thousands of lives ended with a slash of a bloody knife
My ears hurt from blasting my music so loud
My head so low, avoiding the dangerous crowd
And truth be told my hands are cold
From writing down the truth
And my broken soul is evidential proof
That you never know what you got 'til it's gone
And my life is a messy picture, perfectly drawn
My dangling legs hurt from trying to find my way
In a rundown world, where I have no say
Tonight my throat hurts from swallowing my pride
Meanwhile, I'm trying to forget the long nights I've cried
The skipping rocks drown at the depth of the sea
As the wild beasts stampede and roam ever so free
So don't step on a daisy while searching for a rose
Because the frightening soul rests in the one you chose

Yasmine Kahly, Grade 8
Thornton Jr High School

Top Poem Grades 7-8-9

A Caged Protection

The picture I see illustrates a moment of my past,
That's hard to imagine, to remember,
My former self, my memories that resemble dreams, to see me as the stranger in the picture,
It's as if the girl in the photo is imprisoned,
Trapped in a cage and unaware of the bars that surround her,
Blindfolded from pain, not noticing the world beyond her prison,
Outside her realm, living with no fear
She seemed to be glowing with joy and delight, with no worries, no anxiety
But time passed, and slowly, the doors of her cage unlocked,
She cautiously crept out; she finally obtained her freedom,
Gained awareness of the horrors in the world,
But, also the enchanting moments, wonderful friendships and daring adventures,
Sometimes the world became so cruel and unfair,
That she wished to hide back in her cage, to be shielded from others, to be blocked from harm,
But the knowledge of the world that she had acquired,
It beckoned to her; that bittersweet taste of freedom is far more
Precious and beautiful, exquisite and alluring
Than the cage that protected, yet did not prepare her
For life.

Fangfei Li, Grade 8
John F Kennedy Middle School

Top Poem Grades 7-8-9

Midnight Solitude

Under the moonlight, the ocean glimmers,
Stirring pool of green and blue shimmers.
Waves crash against the stationary rocks,
As I stroll by the shore on my late night walks.

Midnight fog arrives, enclosing me,
No more can I see the scenery.
But I know the ocean waits patiently,
For the haze to dissipate and set me free.

I now can see my ocean again,
Waves rolling high every now and then,
Tossing and turning to each side,
Moving along on its solemn ride.

What reassurance I have gained,
To see my ocean has not changed.
Still that same old soothing royal blue,
That silvery twinkle that makes it look new.

My ocean and I must now part,
Its warmth and comfort will stay in my heart.
Its crashing sound and its bluish glow,
Call me through its silent echo.

Brinda B. Perumal, Grade 7
Challenger School – Ardenwood

Top Poem Grades 7-8-9

Dear Dad

Dear Dad,
I miss all the good times we shared together
I'll remember those times forever
I miss hunting and fishing too
I miss all the time I spent with you
That cold day when you passed
Haunts me every day
The dark ghost who haunts my memories
I was young when I watched
You were in a deep sleep
And wouldn't awake
I was scared hoping it was fake
I watched the medics take you away
Through my tear shrouded eyes
I waited hoping and hoping things would work out
The later it got the more I started to doubt
Now you're gone and all I want is that day undone
I love you and all the time we shared
Good bye
Your loving son
TJ

Timothy J. Ryan, Grade 8
C K Price Middle School

Top Poem Grades 7-8-9

Slow But Steady Beeping

"I'm sorry ma'am, but he won't make it through the night"
These words echoing in her mind, as she cries out her plight
She enters the room and stands next to his hospital bed
Scared and alone, the silence thunders in her head

How will she raise three young children on her own?
She wonders why God has abandoned her and left her alone
The slow beeps on the heart monitor fill her heart with pain
The slow beeps on the heart monitor gradually drive her insane

At last she falls asleep but in the morning awakes in fear
Dreading walking into his room, afraid of what she might hear
As she nears the door, she notices she is walking to the beat
Of a slow but steady beeping coming from the room of her sweet

A few days later, the doctor gives her the awaited report
His surgery was a success and with minimal distort
The doctor praises the surgeons for their great precision
But notes to her that the cancer took away most of his vision

She paid no mind to his speech, for the first line reran through her mind
Praising God for forgiving her, and responding merciful and kind
Beside last night's puddle of tears and used-tissue pile
She stands overlooking her husband with love and a smile

David Sanchez, Grade 9
Valley Christian High School

Top Poem Grades 7-8-9

Peace

I returned to the keys of my childhood
And everything I played suddenly became true.
The reminiscent room was a capsule,
Reuniting me with the Innocence of long ago.
And I played on…
The music flowed out,
Like a river, eager to become the ocean again.
The ivory once manipulated by experts
Was now at my hands once more.
And I humbly played on…
So I painted my picture on the Silence of those walls,
Adding to the hidden works of many before.
A life of devotion was now realized.
I was at Peace within.
And I played on…
The last chord diminished, my heart Content.
The work was complete.
My sonic stanzas rested Unheard within that room.
And then I closed my eyes, smiled, remembered,
And my Soul played on…

Troy Wollman, Grade 9
Vasquez High School

My Niece

Right now you're in your mom's belly
So happy and content
And even though we haven't met
I already love you with no extent
And when you're born in July
I will surely cry
Because you are my niece
A part of my new heart

Jeanine Ramos, Grade 8
McCabe Elementary School

The Helping Shoes

The wonderful shoes that have no fears
Remind me of sweat and tears.
The shoes that go with me
And help me run in PE.
When I wear these shoes in the gym
They help me touch the basketball rims.
During PE in the sun
These shoes start to run.
When I put on these shoes
I feel that I can't lose.
These shoes have once been fine
Pushing me to the finish line.

Daniel Huynh, Grade 9
Fountain Valley High School

Graduation Speech

I wait in my seat
For my classmate to finish.
I wait and think back
To the memories of years ago.

I think about our trips,
Our parties and shows.
I think back to times
Of simpler struggles.

Struggles that are like nothing
To what I have now
Struggles that include
High school, adapting and change.

Life has new meaning.
It's not all fun and games.
It's now more difficult,
It's now more demanding.

I hear the clapping audience
Echo of the dark church walls.
I rise out of my seat
To recite my graduation speech.

Devon Hunt, Grade 8
Carden School of Sacramento

Oh What Fun a Circus Is

Oh what fun a circus is, the cheering and clapping and smiles.
They are full of excitement hoping to see it go on for miles.

All the colors and the splendor, the fun and the joy.
All the games and puzzles, glad to win a toy.

A grand variety of foods, the popcorn, peanuts, and pie.
Appealing to all senses, but so expensive to buy.

Magicians and their magic, suspense in the spectators' eyes.
They are keen for the finale and then, oh! Off comes the disguise.

Trapezes, stilt men, and acrobats jumping through hoops and rings.
Tightrope walkers, clowns, and fire-eaters, the sound of the crowd rings.

The elephants, tigers, and bears with their trainers they perform.
Amazing and unique and never dull or lukewarm.

The enjoyment and delight, the smiles and the laughter.
Oh what a pleasure, to think about it after.

Becca Koval, Grade 9
La Reina High School

No Answer

Told you everything, poured my heart out to you,
Yet you crushed me, threw me down;
No real answer,

Do you even care? I'm not sure…
Yet you say you do — just not that way, but you did that to me…
Did you even think before you threw me down?

Before it all I contemplated; taking in all the risks;
You might never talk to me again, but I did,
And you crushed me without a second thought,

But all you said was that we could never be…
Do you want us to be? Never even tried,
How do you know what could happen?

No real answer given, left my head spinning,
Tried once — twice,
Yet no answers appear to me —

Alicia Loh, Grade 7
Home School

Pursuit of Happiness

I'm trapped in a world of unexpressed feelings
In a prison of love and hatred
Jumping in a pool filled with death and despair
Running in a meadow of division and slavery
Locked in the chambers of greediness and selfishness
Coming to the end of your life recognizing the regrets in your past
This is what our world has become!!!

Daniel Daly, Grade 7
Holy Family Catholic School

Cold

You're walking in the rain
It's cold but you don't care
All you can think about is your broken heart
Why did he do it? Those are the only words in your head
People stare
You don't care
Why? What?
Brokenhearted
You see a bench
You sit there and are numb
Sit there and stay there
Forever.

Emily Garrett, Grade 8
Santa Rosa Technology Magnet School

Music

Music is highly entertaining,
sometimes heart-aching

So many different types of music,
hip-hop, classic, country, R&B, other genres.

Some music makes me feel so sad,
but most of the time music makes me glad!

Everyone can dance or play
or sing-along with an enjoyable song

Some songs have a catchy rhythm and beat,
and that is when I start to move my feet!

Whenever I listen to a fun song I love,
it feels like floating on a cloud above

Music is always what I think about,
music is what I can never live without!

Janessa Madarang, Grade 7
Corpus Christi School

My Friends

How much do your friends mean to you?
'Cause I know they mean a lot to me.
I know that you love them too,
Just ask yourself, then you'll see.

They remind me of all the good times we had
When I'm away from them it makes me sad.
All the secrets and stories that have been told
All the memories that I can hold.

My heart dances when we're together
I hope that it will stay like this forever.
I love them with all my heart.
I know that we won't break apart.

Mai Khanh Nguyen, Grade 9
Fountain Valley High School

Music

Music is a song from the heart
Music expresses feeling
Music can be joyful and uplifting
Music can be sorrowful and depressing
Music can tell about a wonderful time in life
Music can explain a dramatic event that occurred
Music can be for worship
Music can be for dancing
Music can be for pleasure
Music can be for entertainment
Music can be played in any form
Music can be written in any style
No matter how music is written, played, sung or
expressed, it is heard throughout our world and
brings us together in surprising ways.

Nicole Peternel, Grade 7
Monte Vista Christian School

Sunny Mornings

I woke up this morning
And the clouds had gone far away
The shining sun was out
The birds on wires were chirping wildly

I was feeling great today
I felt as if I was refreshed
The gloom was washed away
And happiness was filling up the morning

As I spent the day
Doing nothing except for playing video games
Then when I went outside
The sun had gone very far away

This goes to show that
When you have a nice sunny day
Don't waste your valuable time
Playing video games for the whole morning

Weston Goldberg, Grade 7
Santa Rosa Technology Magnet School

Oak Tree

An oak tree,
the leaves so bright,
catching the wind that surrounds it.

The branches so long,
majestic they are,
reaching to the gates of heaven.

Its roots so fine,
almost never ending,
crawling to bring peace to the fiery depths of hell.

Sebastian Cosentino, Grade 7
Holy Family Catholic School

Auburn

Red robins chirping a friendly melody
Outside my front window
The fall sky filled with myriad color
Leaves fly through the sky
Like a bumble bee
Collecting pollen from the carnations

The redwoods stand so tall
A soldier at his post
In front of the auburn sky

The light of the dazzling sun
Glinting a ruby in the sky
Make the river Hawaiian punch
Rainbow fish jump
Their scales flicker in the sunlight

As the day moves on into the night
Foxes creep into their dens
Under the great red oak
Where couples have traveled
To engrave their names
Pronounce their love to the world
Earth transforms into the shade of Jupiter
Dafna Black, Grade 8
Emek Hebrew Academy

Between the Covers

Nestled
Between the covers
Of a well-worn book,
I prepare myself for the journey.

Whoosh! Thrust into the pages
Between the covers,
I meander about
Exploring the world of action.

The story
Of characters
To be loved, cherished, and followed
Unfolds between the covers.

I'm lost in the tale
Between the covers
Of fantasies and dreams,
Battles and conflicts.

A hidden world lies
Between the covers —
A world that whispers
"Come and be a part."
Annaliese Miller, Grade 8
Rolling Hills Country Day School

Acting

"To be or not to be"
This would apply to me
The ground my stage
Bound to the page

To feel different than you act
To put on a face
From place to place

To laugh on que
To cry on command
How to say a line
From time to time

Acting is more than
Fun and play
Some people do it every day.
Annalea R. Fusci, Grade 8
Santa Rosa Technology Magnet School

The Storm

It was dark that day
Raining, cars driving
Cars passed
Back and forth
They came his way
He had drunk a little
But not enough
There was a rock
He was coming
Coming fast
He couldn't do
Much about it
All we did
Was cry about it

I was five
I won't forget him
He was always with me
He still is
The storm has passed
But I still need him

I miss you dad.
Luis Carmona, Grade 8
La Joya Middle School

Jack-O-Lantern

It shines in the night,
Oh so bright,
Scaring and staring,
All through the night
On Halloween night,
The night of fright.
Drew Smith, Grade 8
Citrus Hills Intermediate School

Ode to Friends

They are there
to help,
to listen,
to support you.

A friend will
understand your words
A friend will
include you everywhere.

A friend that wants
you to be their slave,
A friend that wants
to threaten you or

A friend that makes
you do bad things,
A friend that wants
to dominate you

IS NOT A REAL FRIEND!
Juanita Loza, Grade 8
La Joya Middle School

Desire

If there is something to desire
There is something to recall
If there is something to recall
There is something to regret
If there is something to regret
There was nothing to desire
Caylen Nealy, Grade 8
Richard Merkin Middle Academy

Pizza Pie

I have to make a pizza pie
I will make the crust out of rye
None of it can be dry
If it is I just might cry

Now let's talk about the toppings
As long as they're not animal droppings
Maybe I'll add pepperoni popping
I'll ad some fish if they're not flopping

Now how about the cheese
Gooey cheddar if you please
I'll drive the car with my mom's keys
To go and get some gooey cheese

Now I have
Just enough stuff
To make a pizza
For Mr. McGruff
Quinten Kelley, Grade 7
Santa Rosa Technology Magnet School

Scene at the River

The bridge in the greenish blue river
It stands so still
The pine trees behind it waving to and fro
The grass that moves like the deep blue sea
Little person with a black dress
Thinking about flying
Flying high into the air
But can't because of gravity
The white puffy clouds
Sometimes blocking the sun
But not this time
Because this time it's clear as day
The last but not least
The rocks in the river
Blocking the water
But the water gets past

Stephen Shaw, Grade 8
Daniel Savage Middle School

Ode to Flowers

The gardens filled with a diversity of flowers,
that blossoms beautifully in the spring.
From white to purple, and green to blue,
the different, unique scent they all have.
The red rose petal as delicate as a lock of hair,
from weddings to parties or dances to ceremonies,
we use them to decorate our homes.
The lily in the small, swampy pond,
with lots of tall trees and a big yellow sun,
there are many brown logs as well as green frogs.
The tall, purple mountains,
the dry, yellow deserts,
the flowers are located around the world,
from top to bottom,
and side to side.

Jasmine Wong, Grade 8
Madrona Middle School

Midsummer Night's Dream of Love

True love of lovers never flow with ease
Instead it sieges right through the problems
In this case it interrupts the others in haze
But more the struggles, more loves are bloomed
Lysander drives Hermia's love with haste
And juggles her love in the will of Puck
Pyramus visits his Thisbe fast paced
But gets murdered in his way out of luck
Then Hermia gets his love back in trust
And soon, Thisbe dies to be with him again
Though the two has died, all has gained their lust
Their chain of love has maintained and remained
Their love is like a coffee, it's bittersweet
But everyone drinks it as if it's sweet

Sukjin Bae, Grade 8
John Adams Middle School

My Salvation

My destiny is named. My fate is imminent,
And my soul has been claimed. My sentence prominent.

Am I to be sold as a piece of meat?
Instead of something bold and rid of defeat?

Yes, I am bought. Sold and sought out
By greedy gents. And to an unknown land I am sent.

Whipped to move, whipped to still.
Stripped of groove, stripped of free will.

I once had freedom. I once was my own master,
Of a different kingdom. Now I march ever faster.

Moving to somewhere new, where I know I will die.
'Tis sad, but it is true. In the yard my body will eternally lie.
Eternity is distant, foreboding and without mercy.
Its position consistent. It will never moving be.

The end, is the end.
Around the bend, is my salvation.

Elaina Ahmed, Grade 9
Fountain Valley High School

Unexplainable

I'm sitting here thinking and wondering what to write about…
Candy? I'm not in the mood.
Friends? I'll do that later.
Family? Is incomplete.
Love? I'm just a kid, don't know much about that.
Problems? There's too many.
Decisions? Are just too hard.
So why do I have so much going through my head?
'Cause what I feel can't be written on paper.
Dreams are what I think and illusions are what I see.
My feelings inside are so *unexplainable*,
I just wish you were able to hear the voice inside my head,
and see what is going on inside my mind.
I sometimes feel blind
Because I see what others can't find in sight.
I guess nothing seems to be real,
In this so called world I'm living in.

Rut Flores, Grade 8
Richard Merkin Middle Academy

Finding You

Finding you…you're the one that I waited for
And now that I found you, I've changed into who I now am
Something no one else could be
Whenever we talk, you're the only person I hear
Everyone else just goes away
You and I have our own little world
Now that I found you, I'm not alone in this wide world…

Ivan Cardenas, Grade 7
Corpus Christi School

We Stand Together

Throughout the many years
We've seen many tears
We've changed for the good
Done more than most would
We stand together
All that we've come through
We are free me and you
All of us are one
Yet the change still is not done
We stand together
Though many war
We may still be sore
Our hearts may not be healed
But our freedom is sealed
We stand together
The red the white and the blue
They stand for me and you
Our flag must fly high
And our freedom never die
AMERICA

Briana Johnson, Grade 9
Lucerne Valley Jr/Sr High School

Ligada

Hope has stitches,
each stitch connects us together,
each one holds us together
Every knot,
every connection
from one piece to this piece
makes all the difference
But, the stitch can fall apart,
or it can be torn
Let each stitch,
every knot
cover us
with Hope.

Madeleine Scroggin, Grade 8
La Joya Middle School

In the Night

When the people are asleep
I'm awake
smelling
tasting
the night's peace
feeling like I own the world
watching the moon
and stars going by
waiting
for the next
person to realize
that the night
isn't so bad

Steven Erhard, Grade 7
Bethany Lutheran School

Imaginary Band

I walk down the street, listening to the beat of the basketball.
An imaginary trumpet appears to blare out notes,
then a percussion bass starts to hit a G chord.
Finally a lone guitar is heard over all other sounds,
a symphony of magical melody is formed.
The imaginary band brings tears to my eyes and a smile to my face,
as it slowly fades away.

Xavier Dedenbach, Grade 7
Holy Family Catholic School

Your Ghostly Presence

I'm staring out a dark window, and a tear streams down my face.
Ghostly arms are wrapped around me, but it's just an empty space.

When you left, it feels, my world collapsed, now I can only dream of the past.
We had a fair share of yelling and fights, But I will never forget that one last night.

Me screaming your name as I watched you in pain, But I told them to stop.
When you weren't breathing I knew you were leaving, and my heart began to drop.

Now all that's left is a sorrow memory burned deep into my mind.
And now you think after all this time, I would leave the past behind.

But yet some nights When I'm all alone I hear your angel-like whisper.
Is my imagination playing with my head? Cause my heart is still broken, blistered.

When you left, it feels like I left too. I cannot live without standing next to you,
As many tears I cry you won't come back
But my whole world fell apart, left me in the black,
Cold darkness of the real world.

Gabby Gibson, Grade 8
Citrus Hills Intermediate School

I Don't Understand

I don't understand
Why the flowers bloom in the dawn of spring
Why the world is filled with ignorance
Why people make stupid choices
Most of all…I don't understand why lovers cheat.

"Why did you kiss her?! You don't even know her!"
"I thought you loved me, not anyone else!"
"What's so special about her anyway?!"
"I thought I was yours and you were mine!"
"I don't need your excuses, lies, or sympathy,
I'm done with you; enjoy the rest of your life with her and your guilt!"

I feel better, but now I'm scarred for life.
Our love for each other was incredible and now it's gone forever.
We will never get it back no matter who we date.
Just remember one thing…
"Roses are red, violets are blue, I will NEVER EVER forgive you!"

Myriam Uribe, Grade 8
La Mesa Middle School

Remember

Remember that time five summers ago
When we were playing in the street?
With my dog and my cat, and your old pet rat,
And no shoes on our feet.

Remember how red our feet were,
When we went back in my home?
Our feet were so red, my mom would've sworn,
That our feet had almost shone.

Remember when you had to move away,
And we had to say goodbye?
I'll never forget that very sad day,
And sometimes I still cry.

You'll always be in my memory,
Your face I'll always remember.
And I'll never forget that horrible day,
On the 2nd of September.

Daniel Heim, Grade 8
McCabe Elementary School

Unicorns

Majestic unicorns prancing in the meadow
Their unihorns are yellow
They frolic and play
In the gorgeous pink hay

Sabrina Zimmer, Grade 8
McCabe Elementary School

Definitions of Depression

Every time I look at myself in the mirror.
I begin to hate more and more.
Oh what a sin,
That should be illegal

Always the wrong person.
Always the wrong time.
I am the one creating this silent hell.
I am the creator!
I would like to scream to the world.
Only myself is causing this.

I feel so hopeless.
The life I live is so useless.
I stay in the darkness

Like a vampire wearing the cloak of pitch black,
Of darkness and despair.
Thirsting for prey to feed on.

I am the definition of depression.
What happened to living the life I love?
Loving the life I live.

Sarangua Ganzorig, Grade 8
Presidio Middle School

Causes of Love

Going against the rules for love makes me feel sad
I see love as a way of happiness
The authority of others cause me to be mad
I feel like I live in a world of doubtness
Enjoy being with others, I get bored
I want to be like a butterfly lost in a garden
Lost with that person to enjoy life more
Going against the rules breaks my heart in fragments
But money does not make me feel different
Others think I am fortunate to be comfortable
The sentiment of love does not make me indifferent
Feeling like a caged bird that is unsuitable
   Love makes me happy, love makes me disobedient
   Love me unpeaceful and not radiant

Jocelyn Lopez, Grade 8
John Adams Middle School

I Don't Understand

I don't understand
Why people are driven to succeed beyond their capacity
Why success is measured only by a grade
Why memorization is the only way to do well

But most of all
Why competing means pushing others down
Why it costs friendships and love
Why it tears lives apart

What I understand most is
Why children must learn
Why children must believe
Why we are the leaders of tomorrow

Elyse Kedzie, Grade 8
Dorris-Eaton School

The Reason I Fall Once Again

The reason I fall,
is to pursue something great in my life

The reason I let go,
is to earn greater things

The reason I cry,
is to learn how to be my own comforter

The reason I sing,
is to experience the importance of things I have

The reason I live,
is to pursue an everlasting dream that never wears out

The reason I fall once again,
is to learn how to pick myself back up.

Mike Mun, Grade 8
Robert C Fisler School

The Games Before Halloween

It was a hyped game before Halloween,
The Celtics were dressed in their green,
As their team was playing at home,
Fans were about to leave with a groan

Their opponents were not unfamiliar,
As they were defeated by them before,
The Celtics really wanted to win,
So they could even up the score,

The Lakers were #1 in the West,
The Celtics were #2 in the East,
They were facing Kobe Bryant,
A superstar who was a beast,

Coach of the Celtics looked scared,
His team was about to be slaughtered,
And after the game, nobody would care,
About the team…
Who would always wear faded old green.

Ricky Gore, Grade 8
Robert C Fisler School

Fill Me Up

Fill me up to my top,
With good things,
No, no, no, keep going, don't stop.

Fill me up with sunshine,
Don't give me any dark nights,
Some moonlight sounds fine.

Fill me up with smiles,
Frowns won't do,
More expressions of all styles.

Fill me up with love,
No heartache please,
More, to help me rise above.

Fill me up to my top,
With the best things in life,
Don't let anything drop.

Monica Macedo, Grade 9
Valley Christian High School

Nice/Mean

Nice,
fun, friends,
laughing, sharing, caring,
sweet, calm, grumpy, rude,
bully, angry, lonely,
frustrating, hurtful,
Mean

Eden Moalem, Grade 7
Kadima Heschel West Middle School

Life is a Perpetual Way of the World

Born into the expansive world without knowing how to communicate or walk
Cold, blinded, and confused
Your parents feeding you strange things
Showing you off to friends, family, and colleagues like a trophy
Before you know it, you're a walking and talking teenager
Your parents sending you to school every day
Going through a weird stage in your life that your mom calls puberty
Your parents are now divorced
Living with your mom
Mom starts giving you your space
An adult
A degree in business
Buying a home
A huge investment
Getting coffee in the morning, before going to work
A tough day
Death
Sadness, spreading throughout the family tree
Funeral
Emptiness, nothingness, blank
Life

Tyler Hickerson, Grade 8
Adaline E Kent Middle School

Parents

My parents are my best supporter in my life
When I need support they're always there for me
They always tell me what is wrong and right so I don't fall in a hole
When I fall they help me get back up again
They always tell me be who you are don't be other people
When I need help they put their stuff aside first and help me first
They rather sleep late then me getting a bad grade
Parents are your best supporters in your world.

Winnie Chen, Grade 7
Purple Lotus International Institute

Fragile Eggshell Mind

Spirits infuse the body of the young boy
Mixing his very existence with that of theirs
He wants to help, but he cannot
They are already gone
He watches as the bodies of the fallen become harder and harder to see
The sirens fade away into nothingness
The boy turns, face streaked with tears, not entirely his own
He had been fractured
His soul cut up into tiny pieces
He would never be the same again
He cried his lamentations into the air
Though no one could hear him
No one other than the spirits inside his body
He was changed
Never to remain the same
Yet never to change
And he could never pull them away

Adan Overcash, Grade 8
Coronado Middle School

The Ice Cream Man
Hi kids what kind of ice cream would you like?
That will be $1.50
Thank you have a great day
I hope that I get a lot of ice cream sold
I need to pay my bills
Hey, what would you like to buy
Sorry, I ran out of that one
But I have one just like it
But in a cup
Would you like that one instead?
That will be $2.00
Hope to see you kids again
It is hot
I'm going home
I'm tired too

Linda Reynoso, Grade 7
Daniel Savage Middle School

My Lucky Singlet
It was just a silky singlet
For my big wrestling matches
For protection
Against hard double legs and low singles

Every Sunday, same place same time
I would put on my singlet for the championship tie
Always nervous as I stepped on the mat
But I always knew where my head had to be

Third round…I was down by one
It was a good thing that I knew what had to be done
Just a quick High C is what I had to do
Then the ref finally gave me two

End of the third round
All black and blue
The ref raised my hand
This trophy is for you

Jason Cone, Grade 8
Robert C Fisler School

What Moms Are
Moms are the best part of life.
They are guardian angels
sent from heaven to take care
of us. They love their children
and will even die for them.
Moms cherish their children just
like valuable treasures.
But most importantly, moms
bring joy and happiness into
this world. Moms make the world a
better place. I love my mom and she is my all.

Annabel Rhee, Grade 8
Gretchen Whitney High School

Yosemite
Majestic mountains all along the windy road.
Trees like skyscrapers, reaching to the clouds.
The rocks watch over everything like silent protectors
The valley is alive, it's Yosemite.

Loads of natural wonders everywhere you turn.
Just from the wildlife you can learn
The views are amazing, the wildlife is grazing
The valley is alive, it's Yosemite.

The days are warm the nights are cold
Driving in the car, you start to see something amazing unfold
I cannot even compare how amazing it is there
The valley is alive, it's Yosemite.

The trees are abundant, everywhere you go
It is so amazing it makes you just say "whoa"
It is so filled with peace, it makes you cease,
And look at the wonders that make up Yosemite.

Nathan McCabe, Grade 8
Sacred Heart School

A Day in My Tree
As I climb up my tree to my secret place,
I think of the scope I received last week.
I can't wait to try it,
To spy like a thief,
To look out at the sea towards the island of dreams.
As I haul myself up into my tree,
I see my scope gleaming brightly in the sun.
When I finally got up I ran to the scope,
I peered through the lens and what did I see?
Not a bird not a tree,
But a flag in the breeze.
50 stars gleamed on a background of blue,
Red and white clash like a mini war too.
It screamed out freedom, equality, and justice for you.
I'll go back to my tree, tomorrow for sure,
Why I'll see the flag waving every day
And I'll know where I am,
America,
And I'll remember my scope,
From which I spied that flag first!

Haley Henson, Grade 8
St Cyprian School

Yellow Drooping Flowers
Fifteen yellow drooping flowers
Oh so sad if only they had one more chance,
One more chance not to be so droopy,
And not be in a dull background
One more chance to be bright and shine as the sun to be bright,
And shine as the sun to be in the light
To shine just one more time.

Georgiana Apostu, Grade 7
Daniel Savage Middle School

Jour de Nuit

Through the bleak red dawn, early in breaking, shines the vague dim light, glowing, awaiting.
Of one so bright in passion a score, of our hopes and high futures that will be galore.

The wild gold rays beat upon the low, as biting the rich upon their goals.
Glimmering the same all throughout, the desolate land without a doubt.

The sun is clear upon the air, when a soot figure is cast on the brilliant flare.
Consuming it so with such deep desire, with a pristine white ring to truly admire.

The light of light in many ways, showing no cease in its endless praise,
To shine out the evident lust, in the high and quick flecking celestial dust,

No ordinary being can sing, the beseeching old rhythm in perfect sync,
With that the luminary sphere creates, in the soul of the living, soul of the fear.

As the sun with the moon, and the light with the eclipse,
We show what we are, by the good, and bad, and the bliss.

Ivan Salazar, Grade 8
Walter F Dexter Middle School

Saved

You've not saved one but you've saved two, as you preached about the world you knew.
Everything seen in a different light, she tried to keep up with all her might.
Among a sea of faces, perhaps invisible — perhaps unseen, but nevertheless inspired to search for higher things.
She was moved, and remained faithful — she would not bow to the world.
How blind he is, does he not see? The girl whose life he's changed.
For he's saved not one but two instead.
The world is turning, its meaning losing, but as it changes he'll remain the same.
To her he's always brilliant, yet never vain.

Katie Shao, Grade 9
Oliver Wendell Holmes Jr High School

Basketball

Dribble, dribble, shoot, shoot, drive the ball to the hoop
This is what my coach is yelling from the sideline. It is a really close game.
My team has slight advantage because we are home
As every shot my team makes, the crowd erupts into an uproar.
As they cheer, this gets my adrenaline pumping.
It increases my ambition to win the game even more.
As I dribble up and down the court crossing people up.
Then I go for the jump shot. Swish! As the crowd cheers for me once again.
Tic-tock as the game clock goes. One minute left before the game is over.
Hustling up and down the court. Time to play defense now.
As a player comes dribbling up to me. Tries to shake me, but it's not working.
As he goes for the jump shot, I jump as high as I can to get the block.
But it barely just goes over my fingertips into the net.
Tic-tock the clock says, I have 30 seconds left. Now we're on offense, time to do it all again
The game is now tied, and everyone is chanting RJ in unison.
As I hold the ball for the last shot just over half-court.
Everyone is counting 10, 9, 8, 7 I make my move, trying to shake the defender.
He fortunately give me enough space to pop a "three"
I capitalize on it, take the shot as the clock expires and my shot goes in.
The crowd and my team rush onto the court. One after another I get a "good game" and a hug.
My coach says congrats to me. As this is the last game of the season. Leaving the crowd happy.

Robert Dela Cruz, Grade 7
St Victor Elementary School

The 4 Elements

Fire, Earth, Air, and Water
Fire the light that gives us faith
Fire the warmth in our lives
Fire the hope in the darkness
Fire, Earth, Air, and Water

Fire, Earth, Air, and Water
Earth that which we build our foundations on
Earth that which makes us solid
Earth that which gives birth to all
Fire, Earth, Air, and Water

Fire, Earth, Air, and Water
Air that which blows us on our way
Air that which is our silent guide in lives
Air that which speaks of our freedom
Fire, Earth, Air, and Water

Fire, Earth, Air, and Water
Water the cooling wave in our everyday lives
Water that which gives and destroys lives
Water the healing powers of the earth
Fire, Earth, Air, and Water

Brandon Sit, Grade 7
St Victor Elementary School

The Sun Knows

The sun knows how to make friends
Warming you up on a sunny day
Being friendly to the trees
Offering sunshine to the bees.
The sun knows how to comfort you
When it sees you under a weeping willow.
The sun knows how to retire at night
When the rest of us are tired and happy
The sun knows how to be the sun.

Alondra Avila-Diaz, Grade 7
Yolo Middle School

Door to My Future

The doorway to my future opens up
I see all the things that happen to me
I am drinking hot green tea from a cup
A man beside me is walking, who is he?
He has short brown hair and a gorgeous smile
He leans, whispering something in my ear
I laugh and stare at his eyes for awhile
A child tugs on my arm and pulls in near
My face is filled with compassion and joy
I realize this is my family
My child is the one who is beside me, Roy
We are all spending time, happily
There is no hatred in the open air
This is my future that I want to share

Rachel Park, Grade 8
Madrona Middle School

Lonely

Sitting
There.
A girl, alone.
Her team
Chatters
Without her.

She stands,
Walks, and tries to join their closed circle.
Another girl
Arrives —
Walks in —
Stands in front of her.

The shy girl bites her lip,
Turns,
Walks away.

Katherine Corn, Grade 8
Carmel Valley Middle School

Click Click

A fantastic frenzy of food and fun is about to begin!
It's Friday at 4:00 P.M.
We pull in the driveway, and the hunt is on!
I race in setting my bulging, bursting backpack aside.
My stomach rumbles and rages like a roaring lion.

I smell the warm inviting scent of popcorn.
I immediately go in for the kill, and
It tastes like buttery goodness.
I scarf down bananas, chips, water, and
Whatever my ravenous hands can grasp.

Then I leap upstairs like a cheetah seeking its prey.
At last I pounce upon my keyboard,
I admire the keyboard with desire.
Click *click* click *click* click

When my stomach starts growling again,
I know the words will come…*"John, dinner!"*
I am downstairs at the table like a flash of lightning.
After dinner I return to my e-l-e-c-t-r-o-n-i-c-s
Click *click* click *click* click

John Lahammer, Grade 7
Rolling Hills Country Day School

Prometheus in Solitude

F reedom, the one thing that escapes my grasp
E ternity, the time of my sentence
T ied to my mountain for bestowing fire;
T ry as I might my fetters never break, an
E ternal chain that will not
R upture, freedom within sight, yet always out of touch

Christopher Ashdown, Grade 7
The Mirman School

Ode to Puppies

O puppies!
Do your little tails
ever stop wagging?
Only Mommy can calm,
your whimpers.
How I love the smell
of your sweet puppy breath.
I love to watch you tumble and play,
then collapse in weariness
after a long day.
You were born without sight,
or the ability to hear,
with each passing day you
grow, and change, and appear.
The world becomes big and amazing
to you with each passing day.
O puppies!! O puppies!!
How I love you so!!
The saddest day of all,
is when we have to let you go!!!

Katie Merrill, Grade 7
Linfield Christian School

The Decline of Radio

Born out of boom
sweeping the market
continuance of speech
broadcasts and real time
survival of the newest
irony of sorts
in came television
out went the auditory box
time continues
music still plays
in cars and in showers
places of seclusion
the program is obsolete
talk and songs only
overcome by the future
indeed the glory's over
traces don't linger
history is lost
few can tell
of the tales
been had

Jessica R. W. Sullivan, Grade 9
Fairfield Academy

Sickness

Fe **E** ling fatigued
the s **N** eezing and coughing
will **N** ot retreat
    U nable to sleep or leave bed
lay **I** ng here, waiting

Jonathan Burns, Grade 7
The Mirman School

Peace

Bombs bursting
Missiles launching
People dying
War is beginning
Conflict is rising!
Why can't we live in peace and harmony?
Why is this the issue!?
Why can't we live hand in hand?
Put our differences aside and care for each other
What is wrong with working together,
With each of our unique talents and abilities?
Because maybe not in this generation…or the next…but sooner or later
We will need to work together
Save our environment and the world
The first step to this is…
Peace

Karena Phan, Grade 7
Holy Family Catholic School

Moving On

What is a heart without a soul?
A soul without a heart?
A heart with cuts and tears, does that mean a strong soul?
A heart that beats in tune with a smile, is it fake?
Is this a happiness that really exists?
I see a heart that is bruised and broken, covered in bandages.
But still beating…this person feels pain but knows how to move on.
Loving something that is not available, crying for something not there,
Yearning for something that can't return the feeling,
These are signs of a weak soul.
This is the sign of a person who has not moved on and been strong.
The question is: have you moved on?

Molly Swain, Grade 7
Orinda Intermediate School

The Test

'Twas a Thursday night, and all was at rest,
Except for 48 children preparing for the test.
Their pens and pencils were like chicken feet scratching away,
Their stomachs churning, burning, and cowering with fear of the very next day.
The next morning as they got up and into the shower,
They thought, *"My life's going to be over in only six hours."*
At recess, the studied with all their hearts.
Trying predict what would be the hardest part.
Then the bell went singing away.
The musical notes spelling D-O-O-M-S-D-A-Y.
The teacher snorted at this odd caper.
"How could so much misery be caused by a piece of paper?"
As he passed back the results,
Happy smiles turned into sulks.
Soon the students realized that there was not need to fuss.
After all, everyone received an A+!

Roman Del Rio, Grade 7
Rolling Hills Country Day School

The Exciting Horse Day

My very first horse show is suddenly here;
That day seems so very clear.
Getting up so very early, hoping to be all ready to go
Having the horse and gear on with the trailer we tow.
Towing the trailer for miles, feeling till the end,
Hopefully being here before the show begins.
Enter in the ring filled with fear,
The judge approaches saying, "Just pros here."
We sure did have a workout; it was beautiful, smooth and free
Keeping calm, I hope that's the winning key.
I was placed up high with the top riders of that day;
It was really fun coming this way.
I don't mind doing it again next week;
I'll grab a brochure and take a quick peek.
Back to towing the trailer for hours again,
Leaving the fun show from start to end.
My excited mind is calm now, no need to fear
I'll remember this show, very crystal clear.

Sarah Mendoza, Grade 7
The Classical Academy

You and Me

Every day every second there is
Only one thought, of you and me being together
The last sight I saw you
The last time I touched you
That last moment we spent together
Was priceless and unforgettable
The time I needed a friend to talk to
You were always there
You're there to pick me up if I fall
The last hug you gave me
The last kiss you gave me
My heart just stopped there.

Alina Ahmed, Grade 8
Citrus Hills Intermediate School

Ode to My Mother

Thanks to my mother,
who has never left my side.

Thanks to the love,
she never stops shedding.
Because of that love,
I never stop growing.

Oh dear mother will you help till night,
She says "Yes I will, for I am your mother
and I love you day or night."
My mother helps me so I can become a big girl.

No matter what I will always love her,
and she will always love me.

Rachita Rawal, Grade 8
Robert C Fisler School

I Will Wait

At school, at home, at the beach, all around,
I can never stop thinking about you;
The laughs we had shared still ring with great sound
As I lie in bed and think of a few.
Whether we were meant to be together,
Will always be a mystery to me,
But know this; I will love you forever;
So why have you left me, I cannot see;
Was it something I did, something I said?
Without you I'm in a state of distress,
All of my sorrow has gone to my head;
Will you please save me from my frightful mess!
So come to me now, it is getting late,
And until the end of time, I will wait.

Christian Halvorsen, Grade 8
Las Flores Middle School

Me

I was hiding
I wanted to disappear
I wanted to vanish
I thought I was unloved when I found out my own
Mother wanted to send me away
I felt so unloved I cried all night
Without realizing that this was my light
And this could help me reach the heights
So here I am to this day
And knowing now that even if it doesn't seem like it
I'm loved
And…
There is no better feeling

Shayna Goldstein, Grade 8
Jack Weaver - Oak Grove School

Candy

Candy is sweet,
Candy is a delight to eat,
It makes a great treat.

Candy comes in all shapes, sizes, and flavors
Some are even sharp like razors
But they are all tasty to me.

There are chocolate ones; fruity ones;
Spicy ones; chewy ones
And even gooey ones.
But most of all I like the juicy ones.

Although candy is bad for your teeth
It makes you get up and jump on your feet!
Yes, candy is awesome
But it doesn't make the world blossom.
So next time think twice before you munch
Or you might have to go to the dentist a bunch!

André Brisbane, Grade 7
Holy Family Catholic School

Baby Lines

There was a crack on the floor
When my brother was born.

Long and web-like
Across the hospital tiles
Gurgles, in my ear
Eyes on the weaving path.

The solid line peeling back
A world of dust underneath.
Intently crouched over,
Sweaty brows all around.

Quiet murmurs of concern,
White, clean tied shoes,
I stare at that crack in the floor
Until a flash of red splatter.

Phebe Hong, Grade 9
Santa Rosa High School

Remorsing the Dream

I slept, I thought.
You were there in my dream,
I ran to you, I opened my arms
but I walked right past you.
I gnashed my teeth of anger,
I did not want that.

You looked hurt and sad.
"I'm sorry I will change that,"
is what you said.
I miss you, how could I do such a thing?
Nonetheless, in a dream.

I will sleep again tonight,
I shall shed blood of him I walked to,
no I will not.
It would waste too much time
to leave you for that.
I will throw my arms around you,
embrace you, kiss you,
tell you how I missed you.
You will only stare,
you remembered my dream.

Keely Craig, Grade 9
Calvin Christian School

The Blue Phenomenon

The sky is blue, so large and vast,
You never know what it will cast,
Puffy clouds in silky skies
Or thunderbolts with ghostly cries,
Some days blazing, some days freezing,
All the while, ever-pleasing.

Louis Napoles, Grade 8
Chino Valley Christian School

The Sea Watcher's Kingdom

The Sea Watcher's kingdom was luscious and gay,
For there are markets, and houses, and temples
Out on the cliff, the sea will spray,
For in the Sea Watcher's kingdom there are foods called truffles.
If worse comes to worse, the Sea Watcher will fight,
Even if it means his own fragile life.
He might lose everything, even his sight.
With his battle cry he wins with the thrust of his knife.
At the end of the hard battle he claims his prize —
The sword of the now dead General Slye.
From the people came a sound that was not so nice
But that sound surely did turn into a soft little cry
As they looked and saw all of the lives lost,
As the soft, frothy snow turned into hard, icy frost.

Drew Hitchman, Grade 7
Yolo Middle School

Rosa Parks

I saw a youthful Rosa Parks find her seat on the bus
I didn't know that the simplest act could create such a fuss
I heard the bus driver yelling at her to give up her seat
Rosa didn't budge and would not admit defeat.

Rosa knew she would be fine, she was sure
Where there was hate there must be a cure
She couldn't just give up, she had only one shot
Her actions soon sparked the Montgomery Bus Boycott.

With Civil Rights leaders she did collaborate
As everything began to come together, she knew this was her fate
Parks eventually received many honors like the Congressional Gold
With her courage, people who have been losing hope became bold.

Though some people were simply not willing to let her lead
She was widely honored for her gracious deeds
I read the newspaper where her death was the front page story
Rosa Parks will go down into history with all of her glory.

Keren Nichole Reimann, Grade 9
Lucerne Valley Jr/Sr High School

To Disneyland…

I remember going on a long bus ride.
I remember stopping at a lot of fast food restaurants.
I remember a bunch of sleepy students on the bus.
I remember the misty and foggy roads.
I remember arriving at a big house.
I remember sleeping in a big room with everyone.
I remember my friend's dog, Princess, sitting on my mom's comb.
I remember the late night swim.
I remember the Space Mountain.
I remember the nighttime fireworks.
I remember driving a little car through a passageway.
I remember the long buy ride.
I remember coming back with a smile.

Raymond Cao, Grade 9
Purple Lotus International Institute

Spring Friendship

Spring is the beginning of new life
Birds are singing, flowers are blooming.
Happy times are looming, all is right

Sun shines brightly, days are long,
Nights go quickly, then comes dawn.
Winter has passed, life is waking up,
Time to step out, and try to keep up.

Spring blossoms with friendships that are changing
People move on and leave you dangling
New friends are made, old ones are gone
It makes you want to sing a song
How to remain the same with so much change?

Spring has come, summer is near
The season brings joy each year
Have to change to make life right
Soon I will see the morning light!

Monica Zuniga, Grade 8
Madrona Middle School

Fyre

One person stands at the gate. Watching
The pyre grows higher as the dawn breaks like the sea
Sirens sound, but no one answers them. Watching
Lights mix, panic melts like the moonlight in the morning
He thinks of things lost, of things he will miss or want
His thoughts show fear, and selfish misunderstanding
He walks away slowly; the light behind him grows brighter
Nothing matters anymore, he knows now. Watching
He knows that fire isn't bad; it recreates the sun and its beauty
Fire is life, light, and love. It is wrongly used, and it twists itself
Sadness overcomes, love comforts the pain. Watching
Neither man nor the universe knows exactly what fire is for.
Fire is life, light, and love.

Doran DiStefano, Grade 7
Santa Rosa Technology Magnet School

The Prettiest Girl in the World

Skin that is light and hair that is curled,
From my first glance I sensed a connection,
Your beauty unsurpassed by the known world,
I looked in your eyes; I saw perfection.
The prettiest thing I ever will find,
You had my attention right from the start,
And I cannot get you out of my mind,
You kindled my fire; you beat my heart.
I give you my all, my all that I've got,
Oh most gorgeous woman God ever made,
Cheerful and awesome, you're right on the dot,
Your bright disposition will never fade.
And I can offer a little romance,
So may I take you to the eighth grade dance?

Scott Phillips, Grade 8
Las Flores Middle School

That's When I Know

I walk outside…
The sweet aromas of roses fill the air
The grass is wet and cold beneath my feet
The air is fresh and chilly but I do not care
I scurry to the other side of the garden
And climb up the mammoth tree
I get caught on a branch
Its sharp end pokes me on the top of my hand
It bleeds a deep red blood
Then I get up to my nook I sit there
Staring…Staring…Staring…
Clearing my head
I pick an orange off the tree
I peel it open
The juice stings my cut
It is okay
I pop the small slice into my mouth
Its tart juice fills my palate
The sun is now out the grass is now dry
That's when I know,
I am ready for the day ahead of me

Elizabeth Goldsmith, Grade 7
Brentwood School

Dancing

Under the stage lights twinkle, twinkle;
Feeling so wonderfully
Moving like no one is watching.
Looking so beautiful;
A bouquet of flowers are waiting for you when you are done.
Beautiful like you;
The roses are so red; red as your lips.
When you go on stage again;
the lights twinkle, twinkle,
So does your face, when you go on stage.

Alex Wilson, Grade 7
Citrus Hills Intermediate School

Run Away

The little girl ran as fast as she could
Quickening each step through the little wood,
She had to get away, she knew that she should
Run away from it all, running away for good.

Remembering why she was running, she quickened her pace
Trying to forget the memories, trying to forget his face,
But she knew that she couldn't, her nightmares had said
For the memories still dwelled, dwelled in her head.

She knew she should stop, her body screamed her to
But the memories kept her going, all the way through,
As she ran through the darkness, her knees gave way
Her chest reached the ground, and that's where it stayed.

Annaliese Engelhardt, Grade 8
Carden School of Sacramento

Gone
He waved his final goodbye,
we all couldn't believe it,
but it hit me the hardest.

I couldn't hold the tears in,
he shut the door,
I started to sob,
I couldn't watch him go.

I left to my room,
it was just too devastating,
I continued to weep,
wanting him to stay.

It burned to find out,
but I glared through the window,
hoping he was there,
and he was not,
Gone!
Jake Modesitt, Grade 8
La Joya Middle School

I Was Afraid To…
When I first saw you,
I was afraid to meet you.
When I first met you,
I was afraid to kiss you.
When I first kissed you,
I was afraid to love you.
When I first loved you,
I was afraid to lose you.
When I first lost you,
I was afraid to love you again.
When I loved you again,
I was afraid to see you.
When I saw you again,
I was afraid to talk to you.
When I talked to you again,
I was afraid to ask you out.
When I asked you out,
I was afraid you would say, "No."
When you said, "Yes,"
I was very happy.
You said, "I will love you forever!"
Anna Marie Garcia, Grade 8
Chico Jr High School

Night Sky
The night takes all of the energy
out of me and makes me tired.
The night takes this energy
and puts it in all the stars
to brighten them in the pitch,
black, dark, night sky.
Kiersten Gallagher, Grade 7
Bethany Lutheran School

Friends
Friends
x6
Daniela, Clarissa, Kailin, Kacee
Anaisa and Cynthia too.
They all do something different for me:
1. makes me smile
2. keeps me strong
3. never doubts me
4. makes me never take the wrong path
5. always helps me with math
6. makes me laugh
I know when I am really sick
they will bring me flowers.
When I cry they'll say it's ok,
tomorrow is a new day.
Friendship
a never ending story
always filled with glory.
Friends
x7…soon.
Nicole Perezgrovas, Grade 8
McCabe Elementary School

Iron Spirit
Cool to the touch
Dead in spirit
I yearn for the blow
For the clash, for the strike
For me to be whole

Steel upon iron
Wrought upon stone
My maker is working
Is toiling, is laboring
Is giving me life

The hammer strikes
The anvil shakes
The blacksmith's heart pounds
It beats, it strains
It pulsates with vitality

Alas, I am complete
Bare iron no more
I now have life
Have purpose, have meaning
Have spirit
Julien Bloch, Grade 8
Palm Desert Charter Middle School

The Sun
The sun is so hot
You feel it on a warm day
Its rays heat the air.
Reed Miller, Grade 7
Holy Family Catholic School

Flag
Represents our country.
Colored red, white and blue.
The stars represent the states
Remembering Veterans of the wars,
Filled with emotion in our state.
We all have respect for our country.
Chris Cheng, Grade 7
St Alphonsus School

Falling Snow
This winter
will not be like the last.
I will let the snow fall freely,
creating a white cotton blanket
over the world.

This winter
I will not step
on the soft powdery snow
making a brown dirty footstep
over the pristine white blanket.

This winter I will
touch it, feel it,
and let it cool my hands,
but the snow won't easily slip
through my fingers.

This time,
I will cherish the memories
forever
creating a bright yellow sun
along with the falling snow.
Shayna Farzan, Grade 8
Emek Hebrew Academy

Metamorphosis
It starts as a little crush
Not knowing what it's going to be
It grows and grows
Eventually rolling up
Waiting to see
What the crush may be
It forms and forms
As the relationship grows
Time passes by
And finally it comes
To let loose
And whip open
To spread its wings
And become something
Ugly
Or become something
Beautiful
Melissa De La Mora, Grade 8
La Joya Middle School

Love Is Difficult

Love always has its difficulties
Love doesn't always last the whole lifetime
Love is both, sweet as caramel candies
And bitter as a fresh-squeezed lemon lime
Love can last a lifetime full of joy
Love can be as big as the universe
But when you are not truly in love
You will suffer greatly for the immerse
You really love. Love isn't a game,
You don't always lose or envision.
Sometimes you regret your reference frame
But you have to accept their collisions.
No matter what love difficulty
You experience, live life happily.

Josefina Castillo, Grade 8
John Adams Middle School

Weekend Work

On normal days I wake up early,
But this is no normal day.
This is a day away from school,
A day for catch up and fun.

But for me, it is another workday.
I become the rooster of the house,
Up early to greet the flaming, fiery, furnace,
Shining upon the earth.

I pull out not only pen and paper but also a laptop,
For I feel the urge to chat with my friends while doing algebra.
With the subdued machine-gun salvo of the keyboard,
School becomes a minor priority.

Stealthily, a figure appears on the staircase,
Creeping up next to me as silently as the early morning tide.
I turn and see my parents,
And I realize that I have spent the entire morning chatting,
When I could have finished my schoolwork.

Austin Schoff, Grade 8
Rolling Hills Country Day School

Earth Shivering

Earth shivering
On a cold day
Its big blue jacket
Not helping enough
People crying from the cold
Wanting heat
The Earth feels that the people are not taking care of him
While the people are thinking the opposite
The solution is to take care of each other
Earth sweating
On a hot day!

Salman Ali, Grade 8
Islamic School of San Diego

Picture This

I was searching for my dream horse.
Searching through hundreds of pictures, losing my course.
Finally, I saw the right picture.
I knew that we would be the perfect mixture.
His mane was flowing and his coat was glowing.
I knew we had to meet.
So I would bring him a treat.
When I first saw him, it was love at first sight.
I wanted to hug him with all my might.
It was meant to be.
He's the horse for me.
When I ride him,
We are one.
He is so much fun.
I love him with all my heart.
I never want us to part.
It's destiny we are together.
I will take care of him forever.

Anna Mascaro, Grade 7
Santa Rosa Technology Magnet School

Nastia Liukin

Born in Moscow in 1989
To two loving parents
Who were Olympic and world champions.
She has the gymnast gene.

Speaks fluent English and Russian.
Attended Southern Methodist University
As a business major
The international kind.

Individual all around
Olympic Gold Medallist
Gymnastics, the uneven bars
Twelve years old, on the Junior National Team.

Michael Pina, Grade 9
Lucerne Valley Jr/Sr High School

Secret Treasure

There is a priceless treasure I have found.
One you cannot buy or find in a store.
It's something more precious than sight or sound.
Anyone can have it, the rich or poor.
Keeps families together and friendships strong.
It is hard to find but easy to lose.
It makes your heart leap and break out in song.
Wanted more than money or stylish shoes.
Not always perfect, not a fairy tale.
Some do not know what they have discovered.
This gift will not survive with betrayal.
But soon, this secret will be uncovered.
Now what could this treasure possibly be?
This gift is the love found in you and me.

Danielle Shinmoto, Grade 8
Las Flores Middle School

War

War is red
It sounds like a command
It tastes like soap
And smells like methane
It looks dead
It makes me feel sad

Nicholas Stanton, Grade 8
Citrus Hills Intermediate School

My Father

My father is a great man
who takes care of me
when mom's away at work —
he is a good man
who has fun with me
and cares for me so much.
My father
makes me very happy
when we do things
together.

Mario Zamora, Grade 7
Corpus Christi School

The Sad Woman

Look how beautiful she is
Doesn't she look cute with red hair
But she's sad
She looks like she wants to leave
As in running away
She's lost someone close to her
She wants to help people
She feels like she's hurt so many people
She wants to give needs to the wounded
She doesn't want it to happen again

Samantha Fredrickson, Grade 8
Daniel Savage Middle School

Impatient

I have to have it.
It smells as if brownies
Are baking in the oven
Waiting to be consumed.
You can hear it
Screeching in your mind
Waiting to be heard.
Seen in milky,
Dark, glorious, chocolate,
As if it were hypnotizing
Your taste buds.
Easily gorged,
Like dark black ink
Staining a fresh white piece of paper.
It dwells inside you
And cannot be devoured.

Ignacio Cervantes, Grade 8
St Alphonsus School

My Light

My world is like a windmill.
It never stops spinning.
Hour by hour, day by day.
It just keeps spinning.
My world is in a dark shadow.
But there is always that one speck of light that slows the spinning down,
that wakes me up and gets me through the day.
That little light is so small, but yet so big.
It picks me up when I'm down, spins me around when I'm looking the wrong way.
That light is growing on me.
I'm becoming immune to it.
It's my light!
No one else's!
So I must let it shine.

Brandi Perez, Grade 7
Blessed Sacrament School

Dragon in the Night

As the light fades from the treetops and the stars begin to sing,
A dragon uncurls in the darkness and spreads his majestic wings.
The land around him is deserted, his cave is dark and remote,
As fire erupts from within him, from his glorious muscled throat.
He leaps into the darkness and soars up to the moon,
As he twists and twirls upward, the winds begin to croon:
"Oh, dagger toothed and sharp of claw, this hunter reigns the sky,
And to the earth, he spirals down, oh, watch this hunter fly!"
His teeth were as white as ivory, his eyes had a wild light,
As he twisted and turned in the blackness and flew in the velvet night.
Such grace he carried with him, for his enormous size,
And this was the most beautiful sight to be seen by a pair of human eyes.
Dragons of every color, hatchling and giant alike,
Could be seen in all of their splendor, on this most wonderful night.
As the eastern sky is lighted, it shows the coming day,
The dragon then flies homeward, back to his warm black cave.
As the dragon lay still and sleeping, the night was very long,
The sun is rising upward, the winds finish their song:
"Oh, mighty hunter flies at night to hide himself away!
By day he dreams of many things until the daylight fades!"

Allison Deoudes, Grade 7
Monte Vista Christian School

Seven Rings

Seven rings,
three of gold, and four of silver
protected by a frozen pool, in a dark cave,
of gold and of silver
seven shackles, each one a vice, but shiny and appealing as they are
of gold and silver
man, in his selfish way, shattered the ice, took all seven rings
of gold and of silver
and flashed his prize to a world, where all that mattered was
gold and silver

Santiago Quintana, Grade 8
Carmel Valley Middle School

High Merit Poems – Grades 7, 8 and 9

My Friend Moon

Round like a white balloon
You circle in the sky
Pure like sugar
Your crystals shine and shine
Yellow cheese forever
Your tastiness I see
Croissant-looking crescents
Appear before me
Whenever you are light
You're always with me
At night you're lonely as
A star in space
But in daylight you have a big red friend to play with
Moon you are mysterious
Like the aurora lights in the north
In the morning you vanish
But in the afternoon you come to visit me
Well I guess it's time to go, nice seeing you

Marco Morales, Grade 8
Longfellow Spanish Immersion Magnet School

Nature's End

The wind whispers in my ear
Many things I can hear
Birds singing their notes
Fluffing their feathery coats
The sun sets, opening for me an orange and pink canvas
The lake ripples
Forming a smile with dimples
Flowers blooming yellow, pink, and red
Beautiful messages to the eyes they send
This is at Nature's End

Layla Elmi, Grade 7
Islamic School of San Diego

A World of Imprisonment

Gotta stay strong, so I don't lose my mind
And gotta be tough, 'cause the world don't accept my kind
I was born a thug and always been different
Life's hard when you're brown and lyrically gifted
I'll be sittin' on the block in my Padres cap
Be wishin' I could write another rap
But it's like my hands are paralyzed
And the crimes from my past got me mesmerized
I take a glance at myself, and what do I see?
Who I used to think was me based on my affiliations with the Gs
All my life I've been an academic reject
Teachers be sayin' my brain has a defect
But I was taught by the O.G.s, told to stay low key
Now everybody in the hood know me
See the world different like if I'm on dope
I'm so tired of livin' off false visions of hope
Tryin' to be as free as can be in this world of imprisonment
May seem wrong to you, but it's the way I'm livin'

Daniel Barron, Grade 8
Jefferson Middle School

Just Because

Just because I'm young
Doesn't mean I'm immature
Don't expect me to fool around
Don't treat me less than who I am

Just because I'm young
Doesn't mean I'm reckless
Don't expect me to make mistakes
Doesn't mean I'm less capable

Just because I'm young
Remember that I have potential
Remember that I can succeed
Just because I'm young — don't hold me back from the world.

Natalie Li, Grade 8
Dorris-Eaton School

Megalomania

M arauding through the world as if it were your own
E lephant, gorilla, and giraffe heads upon your wall
G od is not a thing you praise
A lthough you expect Him to praise you
L osing is not an option
O n top of the world
M ountains fall in your wake
A nswering to no one
N ever would you march
I nto the fire and the flames of war
A nd yet you still call yourself a king

Ethan Sussman, Grade 7
The Mirman School

Conserve Water Today

In Antarctica a penguin balances on the ice.
Thinking, "Less global warming would be nice."
In California, middle schoolers silently wonder,
Is wasting water mankind's greatest blunder?
We may all ponder on this great question
But to solve the problem, we must take action.
We must conserve water to save the Earth.
By taking action we may avoid water dearth.
Stop polluting to save our vast oceans.
To save marine life, reduce toxic emissions.
Each time we waste water we use our limited supply.
If we run out of water, we will eventually die.
All the water in the oceans will soon be gone,
If we humans keep watering our lawns.
There will be no water to sustain any life.
Our lack of water will lead to endless strife.
Strop driving, stop flying, ride a bike instead.
You can save the Earth if you just use your head.
Conserve water, you may need it one day.
Even if you don't, you should save it anyway.

Jonathan Wang, Grade 8
Challenger School – Ardenwood

I Remember…

I remember my Sweet 15
I remember when I practice the dance before my Sweet 15
I remember when the dance teacher came to my house to teach my friends and me to dance for my Sweet 15
I remember the woman fixed/combed my hair before my Sweet 15 party started.
I remember the people that took pictures
I remember Margarita, the designer of the party, dressed me with my Sweet 15 dress.
I remember the fuchsia, pink, and sparkly dress I wore.
I remember my two gentlemen walking beside me.
I remember the scream of the people when I entered/appeared in my Sweet 15 party
I remember the smile of the people
I remember when everyone gave me a hug
I remember when they sang happy b-day
I remember when I danced
I remember how the room was decorated
I remember the candies on the table
I remember how much I laugh, smile
I remember when I drank Cider
I remember how time passed so fast
I remember I cry
I still remember…

Elizabeth Chu, Grade 9
Purple Lotus International Institute

The Painted Boy

The darkness enveloped the boy with the painted face a face adorned with deception and confusion
He ran into the void and the darkness embraced him like a blanket on a cold winter's night
The darkness seemed inviting, even alluring, the temptation to be consumed was strong
Potent enough to overwhelm his senses he continued to run blindly, searching
Searching for an unknown entity housed in the darkness he screeched with intensity into the unknown
His scream was crippled by the darkness the cold hand of despair groped at his heart
As he realized he was alone in the void he was the only one in the darkness
The entity was simply a looking glass a reflection of a bare visage glared at him
From a world of masked actors and false amusement a world that the boy knew all too well
Lived, reveled, and performed in times past but the boy in the darkness was different now
No longer satisfied by theatrical facades he ran through the mirror into the unknown
A place that had yearned for his arrival for so long the boy wiped the crimson paint from his face
He smeared the paint onto the pristine mirror unwilling to return from his sable sojourn
To a world of vapid, listless players he smashed the mirror with pounding fists
And sat on the shards of broken glass eyes, hands, lips staring at him through the fragments
He smiled back, surrendering himself to the darkness

Natalie Kathok, Grade 9
Palisades Charter High School

Me

My hair is like the dark, thick blankets of black pitch night in the day.
My eyes are a deep, never-ending corridor that has a dark black shade of
the darkest of the blackest shade in the entire universe.
My lips are red of the reddest roses out of the garden of reddest roses in the whole world.
My beating heart holds a red ocean of blood that is circulated throughout my body. It is
like fishes being here and there all-a-where.
I live in the library,
And eat all the books and knowledge that is known to mankind.

Christine Nguyen, Grade 8
Citrus Hills Intermediate School

The Illusive Candle

You rise and you grow
gaining knowledge over time
Truth rings like a bell in your head
Your life is like a burning candle.
A spark that may glow to be bright
with your heart; decisions are the light
you feel confident and have dreams
though your fear and loneliness like a dim fire desists
you shone less and nearly vanished
Your passion and faith were around the corner
slowly your personality leaves you
time passes without you knowing
If you listen and open your eyes
you are not alone in every desolate memory
Keep your spirits high and stay luminous
do not hide your silent tears and agony furlough
you will be blown out and lost within shadows
Like a candle you shall flicker against torments
the flame burns with all your heart
your soul enduring cruelty and hardships
Like an endless candle do not let yourself burn out

Angelica Palomares, Grade 9
San Clemente High School

Baseball Dream

Baseball is what I play
I would love to do it every day
I like to hit to be exact
Hitting homeruns is a fact
I like to play defense too
Making errors is a boo
Overall baseball is my favorite sport
The adrenaline and excitement gets you pumped
Baseball is what I play
And I will do it every day.

Ricardo Vargas, Grade 8
McCabe Elementary School

Starlight

The starlit sky makes the dark night bright
I sit on a hill watching the shooting star pass by.
I gave it a thought and decided you knew something.
It bounced in my head, ringing and ringing.

Take me away into the moonlit night.
I'm waiting for you to take me up to the sky.
Please tell me a reason why I lost a friend.
Did I do something in a major offend?

I sit still on the cold, green grass,
wondering if I have another chance.
Oh, starlit sky that makes the dark night bright,
save me from this pain and stay with me tonight.

Jennifer Paek, Grade 8
Robert C Fisler School

The Last Time

There had to be a last time
I made lego forts and had army fights with my GI Joes,
or went from store to store trying to find a Nunchuck.
There had to be a last time
I stayed up all night having my mom
read me Christmas carols on Christmas Eve.
Or a last time watching my brother get stuck
in our tree on Christmas Eve.
There had to be a last time I played catch
with my dad and brother.
Or the last time my mom read me "Rocking Horse Christmas"
by Mary Pope Osborne.
And there had to be a last time I went from
California through Texas to Arkansas
in an RV with my family.
And there had to be a last time I was in Alaska
when my dad ruptured his appendix and we had to stay
an extra week.
I have done so many things
for the very last time.

Jack Dickson, Grade 7
Linfield Christian School

On a Sunny Morning

On a sunny morning in Pearl harbor
Sailors sleeping and sailors working
A strike was on its way to Pearl Harbor
Planes flying by put people on warning

When the first bomb dropped they knew it was war
Japan had sunk five Navy battleships
The planes were flying by with a fierce roar
We could not shoot with the guns on our ships

Wave after wave the planes kept on coming
None of our planes were ready to take off
Two destroyers in dry dock were burning
We could not really defend ourselves off

The attack on Pearl harbor was immense
That attack on Pearl Harbor was intense

Justin Vrooman, Grade 9
Lucerne Valley Jr/Sr High School

Every Father's Nightmare

The news that you never thought you'd hear
Just popped up one evening around midnight
The horrific news pierced your heart
You dreaded to live to know this horrible day
The day that your daughter gives her life away
Fortunately not death but to some unknown man
She calls you to say she's love stricken and engaged
One year later you're sitting at your daughter's wedding day
Only to realize you sat through a wonderful day.

Kyle Von Tour, Grade 8
Long Valley Charter School

Red, White and Blue

Oh, don't you see,
The stars and stripes.
The wavering glory,
Through the day and night.
All of the beauty,
And majesty.
Oh, don't you see,
Oh, don't you see.

Anthony Guizar, Grade 8
McCabe Elementary School

Iraq War

We are still in the Iraq war,
This is like one big chore.
I wish we could stop,
So we could just plop.

We have been fighting too long,
But we have been fighting strong.
We can't quit,
Or Iraq will benefit

It is key to get along,
And sing one great song.
We can't be beat,
Because we are elite.

Let's grow some skin,
So we can win.
We work as one,
And we will not be overrun.

Ryan Mether, Grade 8
Citrus Hills Intermediate School

War in Gaza

Thousands of people are dying
Everywhere the blood is shining
During the war in Gaza

Homes and hospitals are being destroyed
Death the living are trying to avoid
During the war in Gaza

People are losing their relatives
The number of them is massive
During the war in Gaza

Prayers for the living are being said
As each person goes to bed
During the war in Gaza

Hopefully ceasefire will soon dawn
Protests around the globe going on
Against the war in Gaza

Sarah Attia, Grade 8
Sierra Charter School

I Am A Soldier

I wake up every morning getting ready to fight
I go out and see guns pointing at me
I try to fire back but I don't — I Am A Soldier

I try to sleep at night but I can't because I might get killed tomorrow
I try not to think about my family but it's hard
I do not like trying to kill people — I Am A Soldier

I want to come home alive and well
I want to be able to see my kids grow up
I do not want to die soon — I Am A Soldier

I try so hard not to kill people and when I don't I get yelled at
I try to keep myself alive while it is 115 degrees
I want to be a person who cares about anyone — I Am A Soldier

I wake up to a person blowing a trumpet
I am always getting up first and always ready
I don't get to shower every day I shower once a week — I Am A Soldier

I miss my family
I want to see my newest kid
I don't know when that will happen — I Am A Soldier

Jamie Mosman, Grade 8
Twin Peaks Middle School

Shoes

Oh shoes are great they're fun to wear, Tennies running up the stairs.
Sandals while you're at the beach, Give you freedom as you walk the streets.
Now pumps are cool and Heels are hot, But slippers are good for when you're not.

Allison Kearns, Grade 8
Citrus Hills Intermediate School

Missing You One More Time

Tomorrow morning we go our separate ways
Tonight I'm sitting here missing you one more time
Missing you one last time
Holding your hands I wanted to say so many things
How could have I said everything, the time we had with each other
Our promise has broken
I'm sitting here by myself
With an empty room full of our memories
I don't know when I will see you again

Missing you one more time
Missing you one last time
When will you come back to me like the old days

I can't hold your hands anymore
When will you come back
I can't cry on your shoulder, because you're not here
Day by day, you will be erased
But my heart will always love you
Now I realize I had lost you forever.

Kim To, Grade 8
McCabe Elementary School

Love

Love
An everlasting bond within the heart
Yet it has 2 faces
its power is unlimited, the breaker and maker of relationships
As the world crumbles slowly,
Love fulfills desires,
Love is complicated yet simple
You can fall in love easily, yet can't escape it
So when your feeling down and lonely
always know that there will be something there for you
and that is
Love

Vincent Nguyen, Grade 9
La Quinta High School

Love Is Not Smooth

Love does not run smooth for all the lovers.
Love is an unpaved road the keeps on going.
Lovers must complete this to love forever.
It may be sweet to be enjoying.
Hermia found out that her love was away.
Helena's love never did like her at all.
These fair maidens have love with no pathway.
Both are stuck with a big problem near fall.
But, although they suffer, good luck is nice.
Their lovers come back for mischief is gone
All that they have suffered paid its own price.
For now the four lovers are happily done.
   Although the purest of love is hard to get,
   It is obtained by those who seek it.

Nathalie Recendez, Grade 8
John Adams Middle School

Purple

Poems are great, poems are good
You can express yourself as no one else should
But when writing poems don't choose colors
Because some subjects rhyme better than others
For example
Let's take the color purple
What do I say? Nurple? Whirple? Burple?
It just doesn't work in a poem that way
You can't just shape it like a ball of clay
And then there's orange,
No, that's even worse
I think it's time to move to the next verse
Silver —
Shiny, metallic and cool
But if you try to rhyme with it
Be careful, you might sound like a fool
So when writing poems
Don't choose colors
Because some subjects
Rhyme better than others.

Marley Willyoung, Grade 8
John F Kennedy Middle School

WWI

It started on June 28, 1914
The Allied Powers
Against the Central Powers
It was the Great War

Heir to the throne killed
It was in Europe, Africa, and the Middle East
Fifteen million people killed
War to end all wars

Lead to World War II
Central Powers defeated
Ended on November 11, 1918
Treaty signed on June 28, 1919

William Trejo, Grade 9
Lucerne Valley Jr/Sr High School

Ode to Jonas

I watch in awe…how they do it, I don't know!
It's been two hours, and they're still ready to go.
Standing up in my chair, I'm the tired one!
Yet Joe, Kevin, and Nick are at it again.
Playing all night, and the fans are with them.
Oh, the Jonas Brothers…heroes in my eyes.
I don't know why they're the ones some people despise.
They're just normal guys, but one thing is not,
   they call girls beautiful instead of hot.
They're truly good people, with faith strong as a tower.
Their new movie will be a heavenly hour!
Yes, I love them…and I'm NOT ashamed!
Because if you love them, new experiences will be gained.
There's FanFamily, and music galore.
Concerts, movies, books, and more!
Oh, the Jonas Brothers…say it and I'll listen.
But as you're talking, you'll see my eyes glisten.

Nicole Johnson, Grade 7
Linfield Christian School

Making History

There are many days in history
That date back to Adam and Eve
Bubonic plague, bearskin clothes and Britain
Egyptians being obsessed with a kitten.
Crunch, munch, the apple of original sin
The invention of the garbage bin.
Famous people like Marco Polo and Mr. Twain
Diseases like Black Death were really a pain.
Discovering, dying and dividing
Distracted kings and leaders colliding.
Computers, Playstations, XBoxes, and Wiis
What more, for us, could there possibly be
People who made a new discovery
Were the building blocks to our history.

Fiona Cullen, Grade 8
Sacred Heart School

Stop Me

I'm infected it's like a disease
The poison runs through me
My heartbeat, racing so sweetly
What are you thinking
When we're this close

Angels in towers, they're watching,
They're waiting, don't hurt me
Protect me, keep me inside

I hate it when we say goodnight
Alone for the rest of the night
Without you.

Tonight, I am waiting for you
Your soothing voice crooning
Like a dove

I've been trying to send you signs
The doors to you are hard to find
So stop me
Stop me, this time.

Neomi Perera, Grade 8
Madrona Middle School

Hope

Ashes rain down upon the land
And settle on a distant shore

As the life is being burnt away
The Earth weeps

For when this is over,
The land shall be scarred

And the inhabitants shall be gone.
But cry not, my dear Earth,

For the land shall live again.

Serena Harned, Grade 8
Madrona Middle School

The Pain of Losing Someone

When you lose someone
close to you
how it hurts inside

When someone close to you dies
you want to let all your anger out
(would it be a sin?)

When you lose someone close
it is the worst feeling
a person can have

Samuel Gomez, Grade 7
Corpus Christi School

Do I Exist

In my heart, I don't know if I really exist or
I don't.
I'm really confused.
It feels that someone else in your heart is speaking to you
to guide you to believe that when things look tough
you have confidence to confront difficult situations.
Now I really know that I really do exist, and I'm not confused anymore.
I've lost my doubt in my negative thinking in my heart.

Janet Jimenez Tapia, Grade 8
Yolo Middle School

Always Near

WHAM! BAM!
Glass is shattering, it is scattering.
Metal is crushing, and blood is gushing.

I am watching this from my car, that is near, not too far.
Waiting for this scene to end thinking 'Have I lost another friend?'
I know help is sure to hurry, please, please, please do not worry.

Both you and your car are beyond repair, that is really, really unfair!
The man was drunk, now it's a crime, I promise he will do all of his time,
In a few seconds an ambulance will arrive, but you do not look as if you will survive.

There are tears in my eyes, and dark, heavy clouds covering the blue skies.
The paramedics are finally here, with their faces full of fear.
I ask one if you are dying, he says "No;" I can tell he is lying.

It is now two months later, you have become stronger, greater.
I am so glad that you are still here,
And do not forget, I am always near.

Alice Zielinski, Grade 9
La Reina High School

Cassandra

She was the cutest thing that I've ever seen, I was so excited to have a little sister,
To be there for her first word, and to hear her say "dog" in the sweetest way.

If she didn't have her way she would have a fit
Kicking and screaming and fighting without meaning.

To see her smile with her little teeth she was the world's smartest baby
Every time you look back there she was waiting for you like a little lady.

She would say "bye" and blow a kiss of love
I finally felt like someone special on a pedestal up above.

To see her come and go so quickly I didn't think it would hit this much
I think of her so much, I think about her day and night hoping she's all right.

I know she's with a better family now but I wish she's still with me
To love her and to care for her the best big sister that is me.

Misha Shavers, Grade 8
St Joseph's School

Drum Life

Life is easy for others, and hard for some.
But I think of life as a drum.

You can play crazy and break the rules.
But at the end, you'll look like a fool.

You can change the instrument.
But make sure you can play.
Or at the end it will go away.

Make sure you learn to play the drums.
Or at the end, it'll be worth none.

Me, I play the drums with a little kick.
And at the end it turns into music.

Brandon Gamez, Grade 8
McCabe Elementary School

Ode to Shopping

Oh, how shopping is so fun
We don't stop til I say we're done
We go in the stores at the mall
Until we do them all

I spend almost all of my money
And my mom says "Do you think that's enough honey?"
When we come home that day
I have to put all my new clothes away

Samantha Honson, Grade 8
Citrus Hills Intermediate School

Where I Am From

I am from colored television with over a thousand channels
From Direct TV and Dish
I am from jumping on the trampoline
And playing in the sandbox with all the neighbor kids
I am from going to Big Bear every year with my relatives
And being a 100% Dutch girl with blue eyes from
Ancestors, grandparents, and parents
I am from the "3rd grade speech meet champions"
And the "Towheads" because we're blonde
I am from "look both ways before crossing the street"
And "throw yourself on the ground if someone grabs you"
I am from Genesis to Malachi and
Fruit punch with crackers
I am from Temecula, CA, and scrambled eggs
With coffee cake
From the floor under the dinner table, eating
Butter cubes with my cousin
And convincing my mom to go on a river rapid
I am from the laundry room picture boxes
That holds the past, the present, and
The soon-to-be future

Alexa Feddema, Grade 7
Linfield Christian School

Jackie Robinson's Narrative

Baby Jackie Robinson crying
In 1919, a baby born to a Negro family
In Cairo, Georgia
Endured a time with the Spanish flu

Youngest of five
Edgar, Frank,
Mack, Willa Mae,
And himself, Jackie Robinson

At age twenty-eight played baseball on a white man's team
White people hated him, but he let his bat do the talking
Played second baseman
People started to like him and respect him

1947 Rookie of the Year
1972 died from a heart attack

Jamie Fowler, Grade 9
Lucerne Valley Jr/Sr High School

Volleyball

Volleyball is my life
I will try to be the best I can
Try to succeed as much as possible
Practice hard, have fun, but still taking it serious
Volleyball to me is like basketball to Shaq
Volleyball is my dream
If all the hard work pays off maybe I'll get a scholarship
But if I don't I will always love the game of volleyball

Maci Lerno, Grade 8
McCabe Elementary School

Midnight Symphony

Darkness spread over the blue abyss,
accompanied by the lonely quality delivered,
but even so, the night was alive,
the wind singing with its various melodies,
the moon dancing,
rising on its blue platform,
ocean applauding,
rising up and down,
in sync with the wind.
The moon continued rising,
UP
UP
UP
GONE
The tides receded,
giving its one last applause,
the wind came to an abrupt stop,
refusing to sing without the moon or an audience,
yet I was there,
a spectator of the performance,
witnessing midnight.

Natasha Holden, Grade 7
Heritage Oak Private School

Splash!
Running with great speed,
Leaping with great force,
Landing in a world of water.
Nothing on my mind,
Enjoying the coolness,
All over my body!
Now I am running,
Now I am leaping,
Leaping much higher —
I return to my world of water.
Splash!
I'm back!
Reginald Muros, Grade 8
Corpus Christi School

Blind
What's with this heart
As far as I see
It's still hurting

What's with you
Beaten, broken, and
Sadly scarred

Can you not see why
Neglection has come
On you

Can't be sorry for you
Because you were
Blind
Brandon Keller, Grade 8
Holy Family Catholic School

You
Since you said goodbye,
you made me cry.
You took my heart away.
You promised me you'd stay.
Though I knew
we would never last,
it still hurts inside.
Rheanna Ostrea, Grade 7
Corpus Christi School

Spring Days
Spring is when the flowers bloom
Winter is gone, we're out of gloom
All the kids play in the sun
Every day is filled with fun
Wind dances across the sky
Swishing leaves go crossing by
Moon comes up and shines its beams
Children sleep with happy dreams.
Vanessa Osejo, Grade 8
Madrona Middle School

I Miss You
I wanted to say,
you were just here the other day,
or so it seems,
but now you're gone forever,
is that even possible?
You are still here to me,
and so it shall be,
you will never be forgotten.
My heart is broken,
along with many others,
who love you as well.
Mending will take time,
and when you're on my mind,
I get a tear in my eye,
and I just wanted to say goodbye,
and I miss you.
Juliann Coronado, Grade 8
Holy Family Catholic School

Memories
My dear loved ones,
You made me laugh,
I loved visiting you.
You made me happy even in sad times,
I always looked up to you,
You were my second mom and dad.
I ran around for hours in your backyard,
You played with me when I visited.

You loved me I loved you.
But when I heard the news,
I wouldn't believe it.
I cried and said that it wasn't true,
But sadly it was.
You left me for good,
Now the only things I have of you,
Are just pictures and memories.
You were my aunt and uncle,
The memory of you will never leave me.
Chris Jasien, Grade 7
Linfield Christian School

Memories of Christmas
A lovely holiday
People united as one
Celebrating Jesus' birth
The Christmas songs
Sung everywhere.
Looking at Christmas trees
Opening gifts
Sad people smiling
It really brings a big smile to your face.
Everybody has a memory
Of holidays at Christmas.
Natalia Gallegos, Grade 7
St Alphonsus School

Fall/Spring
Fall
cool, windy
jumping, playing, raking
leaves, apples, flowers, butterflies
smelling, walking, watering
beautiful, fragrant
Spring
Mira Wolman, Grade 7
Kadima Heschel West Middle School

Beautiful Butterfly
I used to be a seed deep in the ground
Now I'm a flower bright and beautiful.
I used to be a shy little girl
Now I'm a social butterfly.
I used to be an egg
Now I'm a soaring eagle,
I used to be sugar
Now I'm caramel.
Katherine Ruggles, Grade 8
Citrus Hills Intermediate School

Strobe Light
Flashing, flashing, flashing
Capturing the darkness every second
Letting it free every other.
Flashing, flashing, flashing
Your heart pumping
Your feet thumping
Flashing, flashing, flashing
Chelse Schauwecker, Grade 8
Madrona Middle School

Incomplete
Passion is a gift,
That not all may find.
Passion is
What fills up your time.
Sports. Reading. Writing.
Limits are high.

20, 30, 40 years may pass,
'Til you find
Your passion, alas!

How do you find it?
How will you know?
Will it ever come?
Only He knows.

Passion is truly a gift.
Precious and all.
Without it life would be dull.
Maybe it wouldn't be life at all!
Stephanie Silva, Grade 8
Holy Rosary School

The Theatre

When I'm happy, it's all a show that everyone can see
But no one looks behind the wings, there sits the real me

I sit in my spot, look at my face, tears are in my eyes
They hear happy music play, they're deaf to all my cries

It's the theater, theatre of my life
They see the smile, but not the strife

I take in the faces of the people that look
That think they can read me like an open book

I keep the smiles, hide the pain
Save the burden from sadness' reign

This is it, the theater of me
The play, like a happy one, but is a tragedy

Rasheeda Raheeman, Grade 8
Gaspar De Portola Middle School

Graduation

Graduation is almost here
and most of us are going separate ways.
It is a sad and joyful time,
and I am going to miss
special moments that my classmates and I had.
I wish graduation weren't going to happen yet,
because I'm really going to miss
all the awesome memories.

Lucia Michel, Grade 8
Corpus Christi School

Leaving the Nest

Humans lead a life like birds
Sometimes we travel in herds
Actually like birds of a feather
That flock together
We all start off as little fowls
Or preschoolers ready to learn the vowels
We then head off to summer break
While birds migrate to a cool lake
After the years have gone by
Everyone is ready to fly
Summer has come and gone
And all the learning sessions are back on
Summer comes again
Time to have fun with relatives and a dear friend
Eighth grade is here
Time to leave the nest is near
We prepare to fly our own way
Hoping to meet again one day
We have learned so many things
Now it is time to spread our wings
And leave the nest forever

Julia Rodriguez, Grade 8
St Cyprian School

A Fictional Reality

A fantasy, a dream
My reality never finalizes
What's the chemistry between reality and fiction?
The tale goes as once a friend
Upon a time when anger followed betrayal
A confrontation?
An imitation?
Read on and still the facetious act of a friend
(Live on and tell the story)
I won't see only what I want to see
The truth is only as a whole
Dry lies are dry brush
Burn it on her silver platter
(Bon appétit)
Drown it in her shallow waters
(Announce her defeat)
Call me later and tell me it's karma
A burning falling action
A drowning resolution
Share reality with fiction
Tell this tale with conviction

Victoria Lang, Grade 9
San Marcos High School

Birthday

A birthday means a special day,
Celebrating the birth of a special someone,
Many decorations
Bring the party to life,
Some fun and games,
A great time,
Good food,
And gifts, too,
Nothing says "happy birthday,"
Better than a great big hug from you!

Lucy Diaz, Grade 7
St Alphonsus School

Peter Quince

Your leading and directing says it all
You are like a lion standing up so tall
Your plays produce perfection every time
What if the play fails and is hated by all
If Kings yell boo and queens say "stop this play"
If crowds throw things and get angry
And children throw things so you'll stop
Your reputation may be ruined and scarred
But you shall overcome and fix it all
You'll make amend and all will soon be well
Every single show you do always sells
You shall always make things better forever
And always be the best director ever
For you are peter quince and you always succeed

Tunde Akende, Grade 8
John Adams Middle School

There Is No Eraser
Regrets are in ink
You can't erase them
They never go away
You can cross them out
and try to fix them
but they will always be there
Crossing them out
just makes things messier
There is no eraser
and no way to get rid of them
You try to fill in the blanks
with happiness
but the error remains
it is in the middle of your paper
You can't get rid of it
You can throw the paper away
but the mistake will always exist
McKenzie Canterbury, Grade 8
La Joya Middle School

Passion
Sitting.
Sitting Riding Cantering
Not two but one
Just one
One movement
His mane, my hair
Moving through air.
Air Wind Breeze
Thudding.
Continuous thudding.
Pounding on sand
Breathing.
Slow Heavy Incessant
An incessant beat.
Jumping.
Whooshing Soaring Flying
Flying as one.
Not two but one
Just one
One movement.
Passion.
Lyan Cogan, Grade 8
John F Kennedy Middle School

Seeking Shelter
So soft
Yet
So strong
She stalks along.
Seeking shelter,
Swiftly and silently
Slipping
Between shacks and streams
Hyrum Gentry, Grade 7
Bethany Lutheran School

Fire
The match strikes the box and the phantom comes to life.
Something —
Something all consuming and dangerous has been born.
This tiny flame quickly ignites the fire.
The fire grasps for air with outstretched fingers of flickering light,
Eating away at the wood beneath it,
Constantly being nourished by air and wood.
The heart beating red with fury near the base,
Begging persistently to be fed.
It spurs smoke as a sign of digestion.
But wood stops coming and the air grows cold,
The fire begins to die.
Choking and throwing sparks,
Trying so hard to hold onto life.
But time conquers all,
And you never have enough.
The last remnants left in a pile of warm, aged ash.
A base for the next fire,
To begin its own process once more.
Roxanne Myers, Grade 9
La Reina High School

Summer
Summer is my favorite season it starts with the final rain of spring.
We play and laugh work and rest
We stay at home school is out.

The summer sun has arrived
The rainy days are done. We can now have fun
There are no more clouds up high.

The summer sun brought great weather
We have all the day to play.
We can travel anywhere nothing can stop us.

We all enjoy the summer heat our worries in school are done.
We hang out with our friends
We have our time to play.

Three months of fun is great nothing is in our way.
We saved each day to play
With family, friends, and games.

Summer was great, fall is back, school begins in one day.
We had our fun, timed and spent
But still, fall begins with the final hot day of summer.
Fabian Rodriguez, Grade 8
St Helen Catholic Elementary School

You Say
You say she doesn't like you but she likes you more than I do
You say she is just your friend but inside you want her to be your girlfriend
You always tell me that you love me but you never even hug me
You tell me so many lies but you better stop before you make me cry
Kimberly Flores, Grade 8
Richard Merkin Middle Academy

Gone

All the lives we've lived today,
There different from yesterday.
Like a ripple in a pond.

It floats near,
You see yourself, like in a mirror.
It's a face that's surly fond.

You think of the future traps,
And all of your moments that passed.
Waiting for new bonds.

Cherish your friends and all your family.
Because when they leave you, it'll be insanity,
And that's when they're gone.

Natalie Murillo, Grade 7
Alta Loma Jr High School

Words Hurt

You may not know,
But words hurt,
Just like when you cut yourself,
It hurts,

You think it's fun,
To call people names,
Now look what you've done,
They don't play games,

Words are meaningful,
But you don't know that,
"Oh, you're beautiful,"
They smile just like that,

"I love you,"
That brightens up their smile,
"I hate you,"
Now they're burned up into a pile,

That's how powerful words are,
So don't call people names,
Or else they'll go far,
because they don't like to play your games

Wendy Fong, Grade 8
John Muir Middle School

Do People Really Care?

Do people really care about the world?
They say they do but do they really
They trash it
They burn down our trees
Pollution is a problem but yet they still do it
Do people really care? I think not.

Alycia Kindrex, Grade 8
Richard Merkin Middle Academy

America

Bullets flying
Danger lurking in every corner
Then a silence
This silence is to ask why,
Why do soldiers risk their lives for us?
Why would they sacrifice themselves for us?
Why?
They risk their very lives
Because they care,
They could not bear
To see you get hurt because of war
So instead
They lay down their lives today
So that you may live tomorrow.

Mario Meza, Grade 7
St Alphonsus School

My Hiding Place

A place where I could escape from all my problems
A place no one else knows about
A place where I could escape the world
A place my worries fade away
A place where I could be alone
A place of no more bothering
A place where I could just think
A place where I could be me
A place I could release myself
A place of privacy
A place or relaxation
A place of perfect harmony
My hiding place.

Reginald Tanega, Grade 8
Corpus Christi School

Love and Hurt

I'm confused about you,
And where you are when you're not home.
I wonder what you're doing.
And if you're doing it alone?

I don't know if you meant it
When you say you love me so.
I really hope you do
Why do you treat me so low?

When you kiss me, is it for real?
Do you kiss the other one too?
I hope you don't,
Or I might leave you.

I want to know the truth
You just can't tell me somehow
Are you messing around?
It doesn't matter because it's over now.

Jazzmine Atkins, Grade 8
Madrona Middle School

Teenage Love

My heart felt loved and I thought I was whole, but I got too close and I paid the toll.
Now my heart is broken in two, all because I've trusted you.
I locked it away somewhere deep in a den so that no one else could get in.
My friends say "Girl you've lost your mind. What happened to my friend whose heart was kind?"
No one can see how much it hurts, when you always seem to fall for jerks.
No one will ever see me cry, no one knows how I want to die.
When I was little it was "go away!!!" but now I realize I want to stay.
Isn't it funny how quick we change our minds, one minute you're EVIL and the next you're KIND.
I know this heartache will soon pass but I still wonder how long will it last.
How long can I possibly cry, until my eyes run completely dry?
I know I'll meet someone new, and I'll soon be completely over you.
But as for now I sit and daydream as new boys come in and out like a fast moving stream.
The girls they push and scream and shove, I sit there and say quietly to myself "It's the crazy cycle of teenage love."

Maryann Dodge, Grade 9
West Valley High School

Untitled

I can't wait until I make you mine. If and when that time comes, it'll be the best time of my life. Everyone will call me crazy, and it's true. I'm crazy for you. I love you. I love you. I love you.

I dream of being everywhere with you. I dream of the sun shining down on you and I dream of the wind blowing past us. Heads will turn when we pass by, but you'll never be mine. You'll never be mine. You'll never be mine.

1968. Life wouldn't feel the way it feels now if it weren't for that year. I can't believe you've been around this whole time and I've barely found you. I love you. I love you. I love you.

Now that I've found you, I feel something different. Something completely unexpected. Something beyond my wildest dreams. But now I see my dreams weren't wild at all. You've shown me what a true wild dream is. You are my wildest dream. But you'll never be mine. You'll never be mine. You'll never be mine.

No one will understand truly how much I love you. This love is forbidden. You are a horse that runs wild. You are a wild horse, and we'll run together. I love you. I love you. I love you.

You beautiful 1968 Ford Mustang Fastback. I can't wait to get my hands on you. I'd do anything to see you in front of my eyes. Anything to see your engine. You are the car I dream of. I dream of driving you, but you'll never be mine. You'll never be mine. You'll never be mine.

Sarai Melara, Grade 8
Richard Merkin Middle Academy

Heaven's Isle

There's a place in Heaven, which I have found.
Secluded within a barrier of sound.
Not to be heard by the ears of the weak.
Within does a long labyrinth quarantine
a long narrow path covered in healthy vines of fresh spring.
A long meadow of dying green.
It is an evil lane in siege by demonic aura.
No light to be found, but thin crevices of gray and broken streams of gold.
You have a sensation of anxiety and begin to break down.
You run and never stop.
Colossal emotions of despair and suicide fill your terrified mind.
You become more and more envious of the uncurious and lay to sleep. You didn't wake.
You are still in the path. You give up and go on a wandering soul.
You walk one, and on, and on.

Francisco Abarca, Grade 8
Blessed Sacrament School

Is She Really Gone?

5 minutes gone by,
I think this is all fake.
4 hours gone by,
I still feel the warmth in her frozen hands.
3 days gone by,
I can't believe my eyes.
2 months gone by,
I wonder Is She Really Gone?
1 year later,
I realize she's not gone…
She's still in my heart.

Daisy Jimenez, Grade 7
Jack G Desmond Middle School

Life

Life is unpredictable
So expect the unexpected
One day you have it all
The next, you are on the fall
Life is drama
He said this, she said that
Friendships torn apart
New relationships start
Life is sorrow
The tears that unfortunate events bring
The frown that comes with bad news
All the bad things that make you feel blue
Life is fun
Laugh, and all your troubles are gone
Smile, and there is no sadness
Joke around, and there is no seriousness
Life is life,
So don't waste it
You can love it
You can hate it
It's life

Lynn Racelo, Grade 7
St Victor Elementary School

Love

Wonderful, amazing, and emotion,
This is what I want love to be for me,
Love gives me a great sense of devotion
I'm glad when I think of what it can be
Loving forever loving together
That will be the question I'll be asking,
Overcome with joy light as a feather;
Love is powerful it's everlasting
Feelings of attachment, feelings are strong
I'm looking forward for that special day,
I think of you when I hear my top song,
Don't worry everything will be okay.
It is often said two birds like the dove,
Is a reminder of being in love.

Travis Sovronec, Grade 8
Las Flores Middle School

My Loss

My mom passed away
I never knew it would end this way
My mom said don't take this the wrong way
But I will pass away
And when I do
Don't ever forget
That I will always love you

Flor Pineda, Grade 8
McCabe Elementary School

Anthem of the Abandoned

It's so hard to say that it's finally done
Our passion's burnt out, was it even there?
In my wildest dreams, we'd always be one
But God's willed it not; I'm filled with despair.
I'll cope in some way, please don't be concerned
Somehow I will be all right without you,
But now my heart's shattered, my dreams are burned
It's just not the same without you in view
I hope you're happy, wherever you are
We both know broken hearts can always mend
If you ever need me, I won't be far
But every good thing must come to an end:
   My purpose, my life; now ev'rything's gone
   Forever I'm scarred, but yet I move on.

Melanie Kim, Grade 8
Las Flores Middle School

Home No Home

A home I do not call home
How welcoming it was
How happy I was there
A home I want to call home
How I remember the scent of my room
And the warmth of the red, fluffy pillow

A home I want to touch
How it was a place of laughter and happiness
And a place where I used to smile
A home I can never call home again
How I remember that sad day
When I left it all alone

A home that is forever gone
How much I miss it
How much I want it back
A home I need
How it will never be mine
And never be mine again

A home I cared for
A home I loved
A home I can never call home again

Susan Wang, Grade 7
Chadwick School

Night
Crickets are chirping
A full moon is in the sky
Everything is still.
James Sutton, Grade 7
Santa Rosa Technology Magnet School

Smile a Little Brighter
She rises early,
before the world wakes
sitting alone
in a dark
peaceful place
but the world will wake soon
and all the peace will be gone
yelling, working, causes her to wake up
trying to shake off her tears,
she smiles a little brighter
when a tear should fall,
her friends will hide her
when she's ready,
she smiles again
but at the end of the day,
she can no longer hide herself
or fake that smile
so slowly she falls,
dying within,
all brightness fading,
until it's completely dark
Alisha Ginsberg, Grade 8
La Joya Middle School

Fun/Work
Fun
joy, amusement
playing, laughing, running
games, happy, reading, writing
teachers, homework, school
projects, assignments
Work
Benjamin Lalezari, Grade 7
Kadima Heschel West Middle School

Sports
Sports so fun and action-packed
Running on the clean grass
Catching the ball
Great feeling
When you run it all the way
You hear the fans yelling
All sports are terrific
You feel alive when you play
Whether you play the game
Or watched it
It's still action-packed.
Carlos Zepeda, Grade 7
St Alphonsus School

Reality
Everybody wants to go to heaven,
But no one wants to die
I see little kids just trying to get high,
Thinking one day they're going to fly
Look at this girl trying to get a dime
All she is going to do is just take a dive
Man this kind of world is just a lie
Wasting minutes, wasting life.
Aidee Perez, Grade 8
Richard Merkin Middle Academy

The Japanese Garden
The Koi

Golden yellow koi
Swimming gracefully in pond
Splash, peaceful again

The Plants

Plants stand silently
Raising their leaves to heaven
Swaying in the wind

The Deer Scare

Filling with water
Carved of artistic bamboo
Clank, filling again

The Statues

Carved quite skillfully
Peaceful and nice to look at
Solid, light gray stone
Adam Gates, Grade 7
Monte Vista Christian School

Glittering Sky
A glittering sky
Is filled with happiness
You look at a rainbow
And see forever
The bright sun
Brings you peace
You look at the stars
And see the shape of a bear
When you open your door
You receive flowers and chocolates
You sit in sorrow
And your friend comforts you
A new flower blooms
Your heart opens up
And you sleep the night through
Amber Hernandez, Grade 8
Citrus Hills Intermediate School

Love
Love is like a feather,
Slowly falling down.
When the wind blows
The good times come around.

Love is like a feather,
Slowly falling down.
The tumbles and trials of a relationship
Bring it near the ground.

Love is like a feather,
Slowly falling down.
You think you know what's going on
The rain comes and the love is gone.

Love is like a feather,
Slowly falling down.
There can be rocky days
But, "we won't split our ways"
And then, the feather,
Hits the ground…
Adam Allustiarti, Grade 9
Valley Christian High School

The New Kid
When I first came
I was the new kid
A complete stranger
Surrounded by new faces
I was sad and confused
I missed my old school
But this one was cool
I made some friends
And the sadness came to an end
The teachers were really nice
My friends were also nice
Later on a new kid came
And I wasn't the new kid anymore
Now I don't miss my old school
Bernardo Ng, Grade 8
McCabe Elementary School

Beautiful
The dark sky
People are relaxing
Having coffee
Some people are strolling around
Shining stars in the sky
A green tree
A pretty balcony
A bright light
Shining on the terrace
Shops with lights
Beautiful
Iveth Gonzalez, Grade 8
Daniel Savage Middle School

Music

The important thing about music is:
that the melody is ongoing.
It gives you more energy and happiness
You feel warm and ready for a new day,
the sound of the music makes you feel sad
or feel lonely like you are in the desert alone
and sometimes you feel a smooth, soft wind
is coming to you that is made by you — no one else.
But the most important thing about music
is that the melody is ongoing.

Christopher Doan, Grade 7
St Mary of Assumption School

The Girl for Me

The girl for me is out there, doesn't know it yet
I think her eyes shine as bright as the sun
I think she's as smart as a person's bet
Her smile lights me up then I'm someone
Her body is like looking at heaven,
But in another way in a good way
She's sweet as food from 7 Eleven
She's as funny like clowns amazing days
Her hair is so curly like curly fries
Her personality makes my day
Makes me feel like I have won a grand prize
She's pretty as a rose in the bouquet
The perfect girl for me is soon to be,
But for how much longer we shall see.

Daniel Melgoza, Grade 8
Henry T Gage Middle School

In the Dark

I'm here all alone, alone in the dark
I want you to be here, running away was not so smart
I miss you, I miss us
but most of all
I miss your gentle touch
you don't know how scared I am
'cause there is no sign of light
I'm somewhere up high, somewhere
I did not know I can
I know I'm up high
'cause I could feel the clouds and the sky
and I'm not gonna move from here
When I think about it, my eyes start to tear
too bad I can't see anything
it must be beautiful, I hear birds and bees
But it's pitch black
and light is what this place lacks
I feel unwanted
like I'm being watched and hunted
I wanna be with you
and once again call you my baby, my boo

Akina Afable, Grade 9
Hiram W Johnson High School

Just Because…

Just because I am not you
Don't treat me like dirt
Don't act like I'm not hurt
Don't hate me for who I ma

Just because I am not you
It doesn't mean you can push me aside
It doesn't mean you can be full of pride.
It doesn't mean you can hate me for who I am.

Just because I am not you
It doesn't mean you are so great
It doesn't mean I am jealous

Just because I am not you
Let me be who I am.

Victoria Lim, Grade 8
Dorris-Eaton School

Education

White clouds atop my head,
Fill my worries with no dread
When walking to my place of learning,
My body has an irresistible yearning
When I am there,
Everything seems fair
Instead of a demeaning goodbye,
I hear a pleasant hi
It is from a truly good friend,
Our fun shall never end
When sitting in my chair at school,
I let my wisdom sit down and rule
When my mind comes to play,
My body wishes I could just stay
I feel it's not nice to expel anyone,
But they may have the wrong idea of fun
Sooner or later we all have to leave,
But that still doesn't mean we still can't ACHIEVE

Jonathan Vazquez, Grade 8
Nobel Middle School

Midsummer Night's Dream

A play of Shakespeare, *Midsummer Night's Dream*,
It was not as easy as it had seemed.
A promptbook we had to do as a team,
When we get a bad grade I would go scream.
Memorizing lines is as hard as rock.
We have to try are best to really mock,
As Shakespeare's fairy character boy Puck.
But now we figured were going to pass,
Maybe we can be the best of the class,
Good thing we finished this and very fast.
Our play was like being made out of brass.
We finished, it's now all out, for good this time.

Juan Gonzalez, Grade 8
John Adams Middle School

Colors

Pour the streets with noises
sink the child's happiness
break the bondage of sunny clear skies

You are the fruit of the world
you bring human existence to reality
when the rain stops
you are in the world
to bring joy once again

Daniel Ahn, Grade 8
Robert C Fisler School

Best of Friends

We are the best of friends
We are there for each other till the end
Somehow we just fit together
Like peanut butter and jelly
between two breads
Can't be separated one put together
Like moons and stars
We both shine brightly
Even from afar
Like sisters and brothers
Always helping each other
Like cows and their moos
We just can't be separated into twos
Like pen and paper
One can't work without the other
We can never be
Separated we were
Both meant to be
We are the best of friends
Both you and me
Like honey and its special bee

Yadira Mata, Grade 8
St Helen Catholic Elementary School

You Did Me Wrong

When I talk, you don't listen.
I look extra nice, you don't notice.
I try to make it work, you don't.
You did me wrong.

I open my door, yours stays closed.
You are all talk, and no walk.
You did me wrong.

You think you are too cool.
I reach out, you pull back
I hope you know
You did me wrong.

And now you know
That's why I'm done with you.

Adriana Martinez, Grade 8
Corpus Christi School

Bottom of the Ocean

I'm sorry our feelings became so strong
But I had to leave you
You spent endless nights with me
But I never said goodbye
It was just too hard to speak those words
You keep me warm even in the coldest of nights
Now I'm left alone, wishing you were next to me
I'm sorry I made you search for me
Not telling you where to begin
I wish we can start all over
But nothing would change
Nothing can change
I had to leave you, what other choice did I have?
We live in different worlds
I'll just have to forget you
And search for someone more perfect than you, if there is such a person
I'm sorry I can never be as sincere as you were to me
But what does it matter now?
You're gone, forever and always
Just like something I'll never find again
At the bottom of the ocean

Devyn Galyardt-Carr, Grade 8
Madrona Middle School

Proud

My face is brown among all different races
but black, I strive to become a P.A.
but society looks down on black people who come from the ghetto
I'm not shamed, nor less from where I came from
just because my mom worked two jobs to keep a roof over my head
and food in my mouth,
just because my sorry father left her to manage on her own
just because she tries to give me a better life than the one she had
I say I will be proud to sit here in this classroom and be the only black,
to walk on stage and get my diploma, and see in that crowd
my mother's black face with tears streaming down
clapping because she abandoned her dreams for mine
I will always be proud.

Bridgette Harrison, Grade 8
La Joya Middle School

Chasing a Good Life!!!

Day and night
I struggle through my life
Wondering, are we living in a dream, or is this all a vision
I question myself, is this all being planned?
You know the world's crisis like the bad economy and these pointless wars
Is my mind being poisoned?
Or is it just the way I'm living
Man will I ever grow out of the Ghetto, or stay in this dump all my life,
well the way things are going, man I don't know
You might as well try to chase the good life

Enoc Valdez, Grade 8
Richard Merkin Middle Academy

Christmas

It's the time of season
Everyone's jolly.
The smell of cider in your home
Freshly baked cookies
And their desirable smell
Ready to eat.
Bright red ornaments dangling from the tree.
All the decorations outside your home
Candles glowing at night.
That's when you know
It's truly Christmas.

Lauren Villarreal, Grade 7
St Alphonsus School

Wilted

The sun will rise another day,
But you will not.
The sky will cry down upon the city,
But your tears have all dried.
The flowers will once again bloom in the sun-filled spring,
But your growth has stopped.
You have wilted.
The clouds will once again block out the light
But your moods have been used for good.

You have been tamed,
Your promises have fallen to the ground,
They are withered echoes of the life you left.
You swore to me,
You cared for me,
But you have left me.

I cannot be angry with someone who doesn't exist,
But I am.
Our futures have both been ripped from the quilt of time,
And you have left me without a needle.

Alex Kovary, Grade 8
Rolling Hills Country Day School

The Sea

Go into the sea,
Gently waving through and through.
Weaving to make the blanket of the ocean,
The one who makes it is He.

Dive into the ocean,
Into the waves.
Beautiful and calming motions,
For all, it saves.

See the ocean,
Its troubles layed to rest.
With nothing that worries it,
But still can become a mess.

Gabriel Elliott, Grade 7
Alta Loma Jr High School

Sam the Fisher

There was once a fisher named Sam
who once caught a half fish half ram
this ram fish ran around and around
it was something to see on the ground
it said, "Give you anything I can"

Sam asked for a house
that would never have a mouse
the fish gave it to him
and allowed his every other whim
his final wish was to have a stadium to joust

Rhad White, Grade 7
Monte Vista Christian School

Nick Jonas Is the Perfect Man

I see your face and I start to burn up
Your heart-stopping smile brings blush to my face
If your love was a drop I'd like a whole cup
Thinking of you makes my heart start to race
I hear your voice and my heart wants to melt
I adore your mane of curly black hair
N-i-c-k that's the way love is spelled
A sweet guy like you is something that's rare
I love you more than a certain vampire
It makes me smile when I hear your laughter
When you sing it takes my spirits higher
We will live happily ever after
Nick Jonas I am your number one fan
What else can I say you're the perfect man

Megan Mittleman, Grade 8
Las Flores Middle School

Dungeons

Dungeons are dark and scary.
Dungeons hold dragons.
Dungeons feel cold and flood.
Dungeons punish and torture.

Dungeons create depression.
Dungeons mock education.
Dungeons shouldn't exist in a world of caring.

Dungeons are prisons
Without the cool suits.
Dungeons are math class…ugh.

Dungeons make me cry; they lower my self-esteem.
Dungeons make me angry
When they are supposed to "teach lessons."

When I come out,
I still don't understand what I did wrong.
But I don't care; school's over.

Jonathan Smart-Abbey, Grade 7
Rolling Hills Country Day School

Black and White

First I fumble, then I soar,
As I read the music score.
I feel the keys with my fingertips,
When the melody suddenly dips.
Lightly I press the pedal down.
My finger slips, I frown.
I fix the mistake, continue to play,
And melt into the lovely ballet.
As the music slowly descends,
I think to myself why must this end?
Megan Baker, Grade 9
Tesoro High School

It Doesn't Matter

If you have curly hair
If you have straight hair
If you have white skin
If you have black skin
If you have big eyes
If you have small eyes
If your name's Glen
If your name's Ben
It doesn't matter
Who you are
Just be my friend
I won't be far
Andrew Chval, Grade 8
Robert C Fisler School

Day/Night

Day
bright, noisy
learning, playing, running
working, talking, joy, happy
sleeping, relax, calm
quiet, dark
Night
Nima Natanzi, Grade 7
Kadima Heschel West Middle School

It's Unfair

I tried and tried
and tried again
to put my work
together again.

I cranked it left
I turned it right
I turned it with all my might.

But no matter
how much I tried
I could never
get it just right.
Joaquin Clay, Grade 8
Odyssey Charter School

Speechless

There I was standing there
As chaos broke out
People hurting
Hurting others
Trying to control
The riot
As people were being killed
And me
Standing there not knowing what to do
Or what to say
Stunned
Speechless
This whole incident
Unbelievable
Sean Kincaid, Grade 8
La Joya Middle School

Homework

Oh homework, oh homework
You're as bad as a bee.

You're like my mother,
When she's mad at me.

Oh homework, oh homework
How can this be?

You're like an anchor,
Drowning me in the sea.

Oh homework, oh homework
You're always so bad.

You're just so horrible,
You can't even be sad.
Christian Bitz, Grade 7
Santa Rosa Technology Magnet School

Sunlight

Flying high to the sky
Always putting light in my eyes
Always reminding me it is day
The most beautiful light by the way

Do I ever get tired of it?
Seeing it every day
Oh no! It reminds me of God
Telling me there's a future in my life
Telling me there's no worry

Just believe in the sunlight
Play under the light with a kite
Or anything; just believe
It's God's little messenger. Just see.
David Medina Jr., Grade 8
Madrona Middle School

Holiday Lights

Bright flashing lights
That will never cease
Their happy dancing and endless song
Of joy and love, hope and peace.

The lights are winking
Like eyes in the night
Everyone will cheer
At tomorrow's delight.

All the bright lights
Running around the tree
Circling around, moving about
Filling peoples' hearts with glee.

As everyone waits
For tomorrow to bring
Smiles around, from ear to ear
Then they will cheer and sing.
Adam Wolverton, Grade 8
Madrona Middle School

My Eyes Don't Cry Anymore

There is no such word as tears to me,
because my eyes just can't cry.
There's no such word as sobbing to me,
because my eyes are always dry.
I'll never need a tissue, thank you,
because I just can't do what you do.
I just don't have any soft part
in my heart, to make me start.
Death, sicknesses, and tragedies,
just don't seem to do the trick
I'm not even certain
what the definition of crying is.
It seems so strange for everyone else
to see someone never weep.
But to me it's just an everyday sweep.
There just seems to be no effect on me,
and the result are my eyes —
they won't cry anymore.
Tatiana Martinez Navarro, Grade 7
Temecula Valley Charter School

Football

Football is…
Extremely fun
In the hot, gleaming sun
Talking some trash
Maybe making some cash
Throwing a ball
Catch and then fall
Win or lose
You'll be left with a bruise
Chase Krivashei, Grade 8
Citrus Hills Intermediate School

With You

My love for you is larger than life.
Your eyes are as bright as a lit candle.
I hope you will stay and become my wife.
Your hair is as wavy as a Ruffle.
If we were older I would marry you.
You gave me hope to find love in this world.
If we were on stage I'd kiss you on cue.
Your hair looks wonderful when it is curled.
You are so kind you could become a nun.
I wish I could be with you all day long.
I love you like a mother loves her son.
With you by my side, I cannot go wrong.
For you I would put everything else aside.
If you only knew how I feel inside.

Arturo Pulido, Grade 8
Henry T Gage Middle School

Grim Reaper

Grim Reaper is forever on the chase
The game he plays will never cease to tie
How much, oh dear, I wish to see your face
But no longer can you hear my loud cries

For you have lost the war against darkness
And so, therefore, daylight has left us all
When the Devil came, he left me starkness
Now and forever I will curse your fall

What am I left with but your gray ashes?
And a few teardrops that refuse to leave
No sympathies when the spirit lashes
Does he not see the burdens I must heave?

But as long as I live, it's for us two
Not for the compassion I feel towards you

Ruby He, Grade 8
Carmel Valley Middle School

Manhattan

As I am walking in Manhattan
I feel the snowflakes covering my black raincoat
turning my lukewarm skin wintry
fresh snow on the crowded streets
you can see tourists taking pictures
and lights shimmering from Times Square
The city that never sleeps
people walking around in crowds
having the time of their lives
you can hear different music
blasting from clothing and toy stores
everyone talking loudly
Taxis honking
as if there is no tomorrow

Eilanit Kashani, Grade 8
Emek Hebrew Academy

Rage

Rage ballistically flies
Through the doors
Screaming and yelling.
It is introduced to the wild,
Untamed bear that is
Ignored by his family and friends
A furious child is noticed
Due to his outrageous tantrum
Caused when not able to find
His action figure.
Toys and furniture thrown across the room
The green, bumpy walls are terrified.
Rage storms out of the room
And at last, there is peace.

Alejandra Armenta, Grade 8
St Alphonsus School

Linger

From the moment I saw it through the window
And the moment I rested it upon my shoulder
I knew my fate was music
A life without the strike of a bow would grow colder
A day without the melodies will bring me to a new low

Sonatas make up one breath
And the 1/16 notes put me to the test
But without them I am led to my death

I knew a girl who had a dream
The idea that she wanted to sing
But life started pulling on her seams

She never tried hard enough
And she never overcame the idea
The idea that to do what you love is tough

An octave doesn't just run through your fingers
You practice and it flows from your brain to your bones
And all notes out of tune fall and a magical fate lingers

Bailee Oliva, Grade 8
La Joya Middle School

Hummingbirds

Working day and night
Known as the fast worker
Flapping their wings
To a beat that can never be played
Looking for sweet nectar to feed their young
Their wings cause a blur in the sky
Colors of green, red and white
Not just green, red and white
Dark green, sapphire red, vanilla white
Remarkable colors that flutter through the land
Working day and night

Krista Dale, Grade 8
Madrona Middle School

My Best Friend

My best friend Clarissa
Is truly divine,
I can tell her anything
And I know she won't mind.
From parties to movies
We do everything together
What can I do,
What can I say
My best friend Clarissa
Is never in my way.

Leslie Gonzalez, Grade 8
McCabe Elementary School

Sea of Fire

Sea of fire —
your being is higher
than any object.
But your situation is dire —
you are mired
in your own world.
Seeking freedom
to see the world
and become the sea of fire.

Ryan McClintock, Grade 7
Odyssey Charter School

Mommy

When I need her she's there
When I want her she's there
She has always been there
When I was born she was there
When I cried she was there
When my birthday is here she's there
When I laugh she is always there
When she's there I'm happy
I love her
She is my mother

Andrew Gonsalves, Grade 7
Daniel Savage Middle School

My Life: Music

Music is my life.
Every beat, a new day.
Every song, a new chapter.
Every minute, passion.
Each album, a new beginning.

Every measure, every breath I take.
Every note, one of my friends.
Every pause, breathless anticipation.
Every mistake, a sadness.
Each artist, new inspiration.

Music, I just can't live without it.

Veronica Norio-Tomasino, Grade 8
Corpus Christi School

Swimmy

Swimmy, you were my favorite goldfish
I didn't think of you as a tasty dish
But now you are dead
Because you were too well fed

You were so plump and round
But when I came back, you were dead, that's what I found
When you were flushed down the drain in a circle
I swear my face was sort of purple

I remember because you were so fat
You landed in the toilet water with a splat
When you went down the drain
I knew I shouldn't laugh but my laughter was something I couldn't explain

But now that you are gone
My time with you is now done
I will miss you, you see
Even though you were a fish, you knew how much you meant to me

Joanne Park, Grade 8
Robert C Fisler School

A Purse Knows

A purse knows how to protect your money
A purse knows how to keep things safe
A purse helps you carry your stuff
A purse hangs on your shoulder or just in you hands
A purse does not have to be just a purse, but it is also an accessory
A purse knows how to make you elegant
A purse knows how to make you happy
A purse is the best thing you can have
(For a girl, of course)

Yesenia Mendoza, Grade 7
Yolo Middle School

Kobe Bryant

Kobe Bryant was born in Philadelphia August 23, 1978
His parents named him after the famous beef of Kobe, Japan
Which they saw on a restaurant menu

When Kobe Bryant was six his father left the NBA and moved
His family to Italy to begin playing professional basketball
Kobe's nickname is Black Mamba

Bryant led the Lakers to three consecutive NBA championships
From 2000 to 2002, Bryant became the cornerstone of the Lakers
He lead the NBA in scoring during the "05-06" and "06-07" season

In 2006, Bryan scored a career high 81 points again the Toronto Raptors,
The second highest number of points
Scored in a single game in the NBA history
Second only to Wilt Chamberlain's 100 point
Performed
One of the best — Kobe Bryant

Alber Flores, Grade 9
Lucerne Valley Jr/Sr High School

I Don't Understand

I don't understand, she was my best friend
I can now understand that I will always help her
When she needed me, I was always there
When she was happy, I was too
When she cried I didn't know what to do
I felt really bad
I always had her back
She was so friendly to me
Then one day I felt as if she slapped me
I really feel bad
I didn't understand
She didn't really care about me
She thinks she is the best
Because she has a lot of friends
When I needed her
She was not there
I realize she was not a good friend.

Elisabet Luna, Grade 9
McCabe Elementary School

I Am Jackie Robinson

I am an African American
I hear racist comments
I see segregation everywhere I go
I say "No!" to those who urge on discrimination
I cry for the hope of equality
I am African American

I am Jackie Robinson
I feel brave and courageous whenever I step onto the field
I try to rise above all racism
I dream of unity among all different races
I am Jackie Robinson

Power Lee, Grade 8
Robert C Fisler School

Our World

Day by day,
Night by night,
All we do is stand and fight,
For what we think is right or wrong,
For all we need is a simple song.

One that says we are one,
Whether we're up against the mighty sun,
Or up against the midnight moon,
Peace must come or we end soon.

Take away all the blame,
And what is left is just our shame,
So pray with me to save our souls,
To fill all our empty bowls,
With all the love and kindness we share,
For all the consequences we have to bear.

Mari Valenzuela, Grade 8
McCabe Elementary School

Puck's Misunderstanding

When Oberon gives Puck a special order
Puck is expected to complete that order
Now Oberon sends Puck to charm a man's eyes
Puck sees sleeping a man and confuses him
Puck charms his eyes and then tells Oberon
Oberon then finds out that Puck was confused
But Oberon stayed calm for he knew what to do
He gave Puck the herb once again and explained
Puck was to undo the spell and fix it all
Once again he went back to the man
And fixed the problem for Oberon wouldn't be mad
Oberon was finally very happy that Puck
Fixed the problem and won't cause confusion
 Or problems to people and Oberon

Flor Leon, Grade 8
John Adams Middle School

Missing Something

Have you ever felt out of place,
Like something was gone without a trace?
Just because something is missing from your heart,
Like your whole life was torn apart,
You couldn't believe the horrible sight,
Because you keep on crying every night,
You miss their face, their laugh, and their smile,
And keep thinking 'where do they live and how many miles?'
You can't face the fact that they have moved on,
That they will now and forever will be,
Gone.

Isabel Sanchez, Grade 7
Bill E Young Middle School

My Meadow

As I walked through the trees
A type of magic swirled around me
It was the magic of nature
Guiding me through its silent beauty
I strolled down the path to a beautiful place
Where all is forgotten even time and space
For this place is magical you get lost in its splendor
What had even brought you there
You can never remember
This place is special to all who visit
Once you leave you will most certainly miss it
You must treat this place with caution and care
Because what you see may not always be there
I looked down the path past the sycamore tree
And there it was this place so precious to me
I walked into the sunlight I was finally home
To this place that I would never loan
To anyone or anything
For it is my meadow
So special to me

Nicole Warmerdam, Grade 9
Mount Whitney High School

The Lone Girl

She stares at me, her eyes drowning in hunger. I give her all I have, a package of crackers with a bitter apple.
Her face lights up, and her swollen hands brush against mine. I watch as she savors every morsel
Walking down the barren path, I am determined to come back, her plea of help replaying in my head.
I realize how lucky I am, a roof over my head, food always in reach.
She is a mere 10 years old, calluses on her feet from making the daily trek for water.
Her body burnt to a crisp from toiling in the fields under the scorching sun, bones jutting out of her emaciated body.
When I come back a month later, she still remembers me. This time, I search her face for hunger.
My search turns up fruitless. Something is different, something my naïve mind cannot grasp.
Then, as if something has struck me, I know her dark eyes no longer have hunger
NOT because she has been fed, but because of sorrow. Her parents are dead.
She leads me to her hut inside, I discover she has six brothers and sisters.
At 10, she is the second oldest and the weight of the world rests on her shoulders.
I wake up, startled and I know it was but a dream but her searching gaze is etched in my memory.
I know I am now unable to sit and watch from the sidelines, not when thousands starve every day.
I must take action, not tomorrow but today for ones like the girl in my dream are still suffering a horrendous fate.

Amanda Gao, Grade 8
Carmel Valley Middle School

That One Special Song

Bad days occur.
Sometimes really bad days occur.
I have had days when I failed three tests.
I have had days also when I got detentions.
Adults have days when they get fired from their jobs.
They also have days when they slip and fall into a puddle.
Splash!
Is there hope?
I know one way to find hope.
When I hop into the car to ride home, I turn on my favorite song.
It's simple.
Listen to the meaning and sing along.
Even if it's just heavy metal or a punk rock
Just listen.
For those two to three minutes,
Then I'll smile.
I will feel relaxed and cheerful.
I may even get my required eight hours of sleep that night.
When the next day arrives
My parent might get his job back, my detentions canceled, and my test's grade tossed out.
Now that would be a sweet song.

Jack Mills, Grade 7
Rolling Hills Country Day School

Heartbroken

The worst thing about tonight is you are fighting, could it be that you have been this way before? I hope you both know that I am trying, I just can't see who's gonna win this war. So I'll hold my breath, till you both stop and God knows when, but I just know this is going to replay over and over again. This is not what I needed, and I promised myself I'd never fall apart, I know that I am stronger and I may have failed, but I don't think I can go back to start. You both wake me up, in the middle of the night, by hearing screaming and shouting, I know there's gotta be a fight. I am dying inside, I know it's true, I can feel it in my heart, how about you? The best thing about tonight is that I am in a deep sleep, I don't have to listen to you guys bag on each other, because you both make me weak. So listen to me, I am not a prize token, I just want you two to know, that I am heartbroken!

Lauren Renteria, Grade 7
Citrus Hills Intermediate School

When Love Returns
The day was long, but the night was longer,
My dark eyes are sore from the tears which fell,
My stomach aches; I am weak from hunger,
And yet I have still a story to tell:
The day you met me, you did not falter;
You saw my face and fell deeply in love,
One year later we were at the altar:
Together we set free the pure white doves.
One decade passed, the two of us young still,
Younger than us were three darling children,
That go by the names of Sam, Mark, and Will.
They were my past; the present I am in:
Together we'll live, we'll laugh, and we'll learn,
Someday, that one day, when my love returns.

Miranda Tate, Grade 8
Las Flores Middle School

A Thousand Words
one letter
it doesn't do much
just sits there and bellows its sound
unaccompanied and all alone
it does its small job and then moves on

one word
tells you some more
gives you an idea and lets your mind soar
but still not enough to tell you a story
to give information about its glory

one picture
now that's what we need
it tells you a story and won't mislead
description, and detail, and color, and life
it's all included in this sight
it's a universal language
a picture says a thousand words

Karishma Parikh, Grade 8
Robert C Fisler School

Ode to Friendship
True friends don't care what you wear or do,
All they care about is being with you.
We hang out at the movies or even the park,
At sleepovers we talk late into the dark.

True friends keep secrets all day and all night,
We laugh and sing and our smiles are bright.
We care for and love each other very much,
Knowing that has a special magic touch.

True friends will always be there in the end,
That's why I have many special best friends.

Lauren Williams, Grade 8
Citrus Hills Intermediate School

Fallin'
I see my life flash before my eyes.
Every moment, clear and pristine.
My first word, first kiss, first love.
My last word, last kiss, last love.
All my firsts and lasts.
His face in every single memory.
His smile happy and loving.
His eyes soft and gentle.
His laugh beautiful and full of joy.
His arms always wrapped around me.
Those arms disappear.
I am falling into a deep and dark hole.
A light breaks through the darkness.
His hands reach out for me.
I grasp them and he pulls me out.
Once again he has saved me from the darkness
And has brought love into my life.

Leticia Monzon, Grade 9
San Diego High School of International Studies

My Weakness for You
You made me, molded me, and tore me down
Ripped out my heart and carried it around.
Yet you didn't even see,
Didn't ever know
For it was the single part of me,
That I refused to show:

My weakness for you.

Merilyn Stuck, Grade 9
Mission Bay High School

Virtues
Virtues…Love, Patience, Passion,
All but war and hate.
To every man his own,
And to every child their fate.

Love, by any other name
Would be just as deep.
It comes for one sole reason,
It spreads throughout the heart,
Like an endless, burning season,
It only has to start.

Patience is calm, courteous, and kind.
It works with love while intertwined,
And takes any form it can find.

Passion, my passion, is all around me.
This sensation never ends,
For at the end of the flight,
I've seen the light.
To know that my passion is with my friends.

Brian Wheeler, Grade 8
Holy Rosary School

Who Are We?

You don't know me!
Yet you think you do.
You read this
So that you can find you.

I don't know you!
The one I write towards
To get a point across
So that you can move forward.

I don't know me!
Do you know you?
I found you and you found me.
What are we going to do?

Lane Simmons, Grade 9
University Preparatory School

Bittersweet Memories

Calm, gentle wind
Drift through these trees,
And bring a sweet new desire;
For those who weep,
A secret they hold,
It fills their hearts with fire.

To the harsh grandeur
That houses our dreams
And keeps us moving ahead;
To the blatant blithe
That holds us inside,
While the world around fills with dread.

The serene anguish
Of each passing day
It's enough to bind us within;
A bittersweet memory
That strives to preside,
Is merely guilt not forgotten.

Chloe Folena, Grade 8
Palm Desert Charter Middle School

Love

Love. It's like a nightmare
that's not worth staying up for.
And when you do, everyone just ends up
dying…alone.
But once…only in a lifetime,
like a candle in the darkness,
true love is found.
and all searching is ceased.
and for the first time ever,
you can honestly say
that you are…
happy.

Savannah Inga, Grade 7
Citrus Hills Intermediate School

What Is a Best Friend?

A best friend is someone who doesn't leave,
Someone who makes you feel special even when you've done nothing special at all,
A best friend is someone who tells you everything,
A best friend is someone who will support you through thick and thin,
A best friend is someone more like a sister or a brother than anything else,
But most of all a best friend is someone who is going to be there for you always.

Madaline Helmsin, Grade 7
Holy Family Catholic School

The Evil That Keeps Us Apart

I did everything I could for you
I gave you my life
And your ignorance was like a crown of thorns upon me
Humiliation that proudly sat atop my head
An insult almost as obvious as my love for you
Yet, I was still nothing
Nothing but a simple object on which to set your
Crown of thorns
And then, I was gone
It was impossible to get to me, for there was something that kept blocking you
Something bigger than you and me
Something that is almost impossible to overcome
It has taken over so many of us
Only the truly righteous can prevent it
But all you have to do is try
Try for me, and for all who can't surpass this evil
This true evil that is humanity

Adrienne Hatter, Grade 9
University Preparatory School

Hope and Despair

The Emancipation Proclamation has passed, but we aren't truly free.
Why can't a white man see a black man's integrity?
"We are not makers of history, we are made by history."
O' Lord, I greatly fear,
Why were these six kids murdered here?
"Mommy why can't Martin stay?"
"He's black, honey. He needs to go away."
"We are not makers of history, we are made by history."
One woman bravely stayed in her seat,
Knowing that she may be beat.
One man, Jackie Robinson was his name,
Went out and played a white man's game.
In Washington, 250,000 people marched for freedom from segregation.
Martin Luther King Jr. was there; it impacted the nation.
This country has been through thick and thin,
Why is being black such a terrible sin?
For true freedom, we must all take a part,
We must all take a change of heart.
"Let Freedom ring!" the crowd is roaring.
"We are not makers of history, we are made by history."

Karen Angeles, Grade 9
Lucerne Valley Jr/Sr High School

Ode to My Best Friend

You cheer me up when I'm sad
you always make sure I'm glad
you will always be my best friend

I'd rather be with you
than anyone, anywhere, any time
you will always be my best friend

You understand me when others don't
you listen to me when others won't
you will always be my best friend

We go together like peanut butter and jelly
we would never work if we were apart
you will always be my best friend

No matter what happens
you will always be my best friend
nothing can tear us apart
you will always be my best friend

Mommy…
you will always be my best friend

Brooke Battle, Grade 8
La Joya Middle School

A Day to Remember

Rain falls quietly to the ground.
I love to run, jump, and play around.
To sit inside and peer back out,
And dream I am in an open field
On a warm sunny day.
The rain hits the window and brings me back.
I can hear the rain trickling on the roof,
And imagine how it feels when it hits my skin,
Slippery and wet like a dolphin's fin.
The rain still running from the clouds
looks like mini rivers on the ground.
I feel elated to know the sun will come again.

Hailey Sweeley, Grade 9
Fountain Valley High School

I Touched the Sun Today

I touched it
I touched the sun today
I felt it
I held it tight
I cupped it in my hand and felt its glory
It didn't burn me
It was surprisingly warm
It shook my hand
And caressed my heart
I touched the sun today and when I was done
I felt warm

Breanna Tennell, Grade 9
Alta Loma High School

Math Class

In math class,
teacher tells the students how to do
addition, subtraction, multiplication, and division.
One plus one is two, which is addition.
Four minus two is two, which is subtraction.
Three times five is fifteen, which is multiplication.
Sixteen divided by four is four, which is division.

After Math class,
students learned how to use
addition, subtraction, multiplication, and division.
Add the cheer to others, which is addition.
Subtract the anger about others, which is subtraction.
Multiply the joy with others, which is multiplication.
Divide the sadness with others, which is division.

Jennifer Kim, Grade 8
Robert C Fisler School

A Small Boy in a Big World

I am a small boy in a big world
I hear them snicker at me when I pass by
I see them laugh at me when I fall
I say nothing, afraid they may hurt me some more
I cry when nobody's around
I am hopeless
I am someone who is easily hurt
I feel pain at each insulting word
I try my best to not cry, but the tears just fall
I dream of a better place where people won't hurt me
I am a small boy in a big world

Brian Parungao, Grade 8
Robert C Fisler School

Washington D.C.

Washington D.C.
Is such an exciting place to be
With so many places to explore
There's history galore!

When we get there
I hope I don't stare
It will be so interesting
I won't want to miss a thing

There's the museums and ceremonies,
The White House and delicious strawberries
Maybe we'll see President Obama
He might even take a picture with me and my mama

Before you know it, we'll be
Leaving D.C.,
And all that history
Why we have to leave is such a mystery

Samantha Pereira, Grade 8
St Victor Elementary School

Just Another Problem

Drugs have trapped me
Drugs have made me feel weak
Drugs have degraded me to nothing

Although, I have not done them
They undermined my life
Although, I have not done them
They are hurting me constantly

I cannot escape this problem
I cannot escape this pain

Me, you tried to protect
But I got the worst effect

Ashley Cooper, Grade 9
Oakdale Charter High School

Teenagers

Teenagers are —
Buying blouses and shirts
Cute shorts and skirts
Giggling and flirting
Recovering from hurting
Surfing and shopping
And the popcorn we're popping
School is a drag
With all the teachers who nag.
But all my friends make it worthwhile
With their permanent smiles

Kayla Clark, Grade 8
Citrus Hills Intermediate School

Night Is a Hunter

Night is the hunter
Who needs no light.
His shelter
Is everywhere.
The tool for his hunting
Is nothing.
But
The dark shadows.
He is watching,
Waiting
To strike at anything.
His allies
Are the nocturnal creatures
Of the night.
The night
Will never show emotions.
Night
Is the king
Of shadows.
He will be known as
The hunter of the dark.

Chris Larson, Grade 8
Bethany Lutheran School

Indescribable

The grass oh so still,
The flowers standing perfectly erect,
I watch and wonder how nature could be oh so beautiful.
The sun, barely on the horizon,
Seems to greet the Earth with its breath from God.
The dewdrops from the morning atmosphere
Slowly drip off each leaf as though they're crying
And ever so slowly land on the Earth's cold surface.

I listen as the wind blows through my hair,
As though it is telling me something.
I start to leave then realize that it's telling me to stay and enjoy God's beauty
I stay and take in every ounce of beauty around me
Every ounce of beauty that is indescribable.

Nicholas Leapley, Grade 7
Holy Family Catholic School

Forgotten Doll

On a cold Christmas night many years ago a doll was given to a girl,
"I'll never forget this" said she as she embraces the doll with great force,
But through the years, fewer and fewer time is spent with the doll,
Until soon enough it is forgotten without a single memory left from the girl.

Now the doll just lays on the top unnoticed shelf collecting dust,
Going through year after year watching its owner playing with some other game or toy,
But then the doll's owner comes and collects toys for an unknown event,
The doll is picked up and put into a large cube made of a brown papery substance!

The brown cube is carried by the owner into the front of the house,
The doll was then taken out of the box, embraced for the final time,
Then was traded with another person for a green rectangular paper.
The doll is now being carried away to another home.

Leon Sengchanthavong, Grade 8
Robert C Fisler School

Inspiration Baseball Player

On January 31, 1919 a great legend was born.
As he grew older he became wiser.
He never let anyone interfere with his goals.
In college he made varsity level at UCLA in all sports as freshman.

Battling all odds Jackie was awarded National League MVP.
His first debut to the Brooklyn Dodgers was April 15, 1947.
When Jackie played there was a lot of racial tension.
Some people were all for Jackie being the first African American to play in MLB.

Although Jackie was skilled at all sports, baseball was his preferred sport.
Jackie played 2nd base and batted with his right.
Jackie Robinson's last appearance was October 10, 1956.
He was also awarded National League Rookie of the year.

He was a great baseball player.
Jackie Robinson was not only a great baseball player but was also
Inspiring!

Alicia Albillar, Grade 9
Lucerne Valley Jr/Sr High School

Freedom

Freedom is one of the most precious gifts a person can have.
Freedom allows us to do what we want to do.
Everyone who has freedom treasures it.
Freedom can be gained or lost.
Freedom can be lost as simply as ABC.
Freedom can be gained,
But not so easily.
It has to be fought for.
Our forefathers fought very hard just for us.
That is the reason why we are not slaves.
Let us not forget the price our forefathers paid
For our freedom.
We should not take this for granted.
Let us forever treasure our freedom.

Shreshth Kumar, Grade 7
Rolling Hills Country Day School

My Dress

You may believe I'm different
When you see my dress
You may think I'm not participating in society
And staying home, isolating myself
You may believe I'm embarrassed covering
Only showing my face and hands
You may think I'm ashamed
Dressing up modestly to represent Islam

    I feel every step I take
    Is only for God's sake
    I'm covered and I'm proud
    Who I really am, I want to shout out loud
    My dress code no, doesn't stop me
    I play sports and participate in activities
    The stares of others are my test
    But I believe my dress code is the best!
    I don't have doubts
    About the way I'm dressed

Munazzil Hussein, Grade 8
Islamic School of San Diego

The Happiest Place on Earth

A sudden rush of happiness comes,
Seeing rides and Disney characters.
While the food calls to me,
To my mom I beg,
For a seven dollar turkey leg.
I run to the lines of the rides,
Entering in, hearing only echoing screams,
Throw my hands in the air, for a thrill of a lifetime.
It's time to go now,
But I need a memory.
Into the store I flee to buy souvenirs,
Of the Mickey Mouse musketeers.

Amanda Nguyen, Grade 9
Fountain Valley High School

My Mother

My mother has been with me through everything
From my first word to my first teething ring!!
I have a special place for her in my heart
Always smiling and very smart.
I'll look to her for advice
Her advice to me is like gold
Precious and bold
No matter how much I can be a bother
I love my mother
Unlike any other!

Vanessa Ramirez, Grade 8
McCabe Elementary School

Thanks for the Laugh

I thank comedy.
For pulling out giggles within my belly.
For lighting the day and making it sunny.

Thank you for making me laugh.
You are like the a shooting star.
Coming unexpectedly, leaving fast, but
Filling me with joy and long lasting wonder.

You brighten my day
I look forward for you to make me smile.
Just stay. Stay and let me laugh a while
Before your bit is gone
Thank you for all you have given me.
Thank you comedy.

Isabelle Yee, Grade 8
Robert C Fisler School

A Day at the Beach

On a day at the beach, I run and
Watch the waves crash in clanging silence.
The lustrous, golden, enchanted sun
Dazzles through the melancholy air.
The clouds drift into the dusky day,
Carried by the silver whistling wind.
"BURR!" what a cold sway
As the sun silently fades dimly into the night.
The bright, white moon burns brilliantly beyond the sea.
Its captive scent lures the legacy of darkness
While palm trees lean swiftly with glee
Into the curious, lonely night.
The contagious darkness spreads throughout the earth
Welcoming its light soothing breeze,
Warming the vacancy like a hearth,
Yet steadily occupying the velvet dusk.
The beach uses magic
To help the world each day.
Without it — would be tragic
But to know that it's there
Brings peace and joy my way

Andrew Taira, Grade 7
Rolling Hills Country Day School

Too Late

Please go away
I don't want you here

Please go away
I don't want you near

Please go away
You are just a burden

Oops!
This is not right

Don't go away
I did not mean it

Don't go away
I am so sorry

Don't go away
I guess it's too late.
Christina Yoo, Grade 8
Robert C Fisler School

Love

Love flies, love floats,
On rivers, in boats
Or comes from above
On the wings of a dove

From family and friends
Love never ends
It comes and stays
Though with yeas and nays

A bouquet of flowers
A sweet box of chocolates
A peck on the cheek
Yes, something so meek

And alas there it is
And always remember
Love does not come
And then leave in December
Darien Caine, Grade 8
Hillwood Academic Day School

Two Sides of the Same Coin

Peace
Untroubled, content
Remaining, easing, becalming
A motionless river; a senseless war
Altering, distorting, razing
Anomalous, variant
Conflict
Cyril David Millendez, Grade 8
St Cyprian School

The Sunset

Red, Orange, Yellow,
Beautiful bright ball of fire,
Sinks into the sea

Lonely beach sunset,
Waves crashing along the shore
Sand meets the water

Gulls soar endlessly
The sky becomes a deep red
All is now shadowed
Evan Rickel, Grade 7
Monte Vista Christian School

Change

Change is like weather,
Fickle yet fair.
Change is a challenge,
To be faced with courage.
But what exactly is this condition,
The one we call change?
Change is a risk,
Change is a chance,
To step out of your comfort,
To leave your past,
Thrust your mind,
Push your body,
Shove your soul,
Into something new.
Often for the better,
Sometimes for the worse,
Change is what keeps us going.
Change is the spice,
Which adds flavor,
Adds color,
To life.
Sofia Dhanani, Grade 8
Gretchen Whitney High School

New Years

A night full of emotions
Giving loved ones hugs and kisses
Full of smiles and tears
Missing loved ones
Who have passed away.
Forgiving and forgetting
Starting the year off new
Thankful you made it
Through another year
At the same time rueful
Life is flying by so fast
Just enjoy life
Enjoy every second of it.
Viviana Marquez, Grade 7
St Alphonsus School

Legos!

Finally, it's done!
My perfect creation,
the perfect little world that I control!
It's mine, all mine!
The Legos are all mine,
what should I do with them?
Should I build them up?
Break them down?
So many possibilities with Legos.
I can create whatever I please.
Whatever I feel like making
I will create!
They are all mine!
Darn…
Mom just said I had to share.
Andrew Russell, Grade 7
Linfield Christian School

Untitled

close your eyes
listen to the song
in the air
the song your
heart is beating
the rhythm is the same
as mine
please don't stop
listening to
what only you and I can hear
because it's the only thing
left of you that we share
and once you stop
you can't listen again
and if you stop
then I will
just so I can be with you
Allison Nguyen, Grade 8
La Joya Middle School

My Mom

To understand her beauty
I can't imagine
Life without her
Is empty; and useless

She gives me hugs
When the time is right
She understands my pain
And listens to every step
Or path I take

Searching for the right word
To say to you; I love you
Jenny Song, Grade 8
McCabe Elementary School

Rhapsody

A rain rhapsody throws a canopied veil over the world,
Heaving its burden to the ground,
In a black and white silence.

She walks along the railroad,
Grimacing at the etchings of her stained past.
Tearing at the map of her lost soul,
A phantom of yesterday.

The tears of the sky enveloping her,
Her head is held high,
While her closed eyes plead.

The water seeps through her thin cotton clothing,
Rippling through her glistening skin,
As it purges faceless memories in f minor.

Rain begins to blow away the dust,
Singing a serenade to the girl jailed in her woven cocoon,
Entreating her tremulous heart to wake up,
To hold its hand — an escapade,
A metamorphosis,
One, two, babysteps.

Sharon Lo, Grade 9
Henry M Gunn High School

Weather

You are the tornado of my life.
You sweep me off my feet
and destroy bridges in your way,
leaving behind debris, yourself, family.
But sometimes your annihilation pushes me away.
I wonder why without you
I wanna cry.

Gionny Singleton, Grade 7
St Timothy School

My 10th Birthday

It was a day unlike any other,
I was the star of a party, thanks to my mother.
By the end of the day, I would be ten,
I couldn't wait for the fun to begin,
My stomach butterflies were flying about,
I was laughing all day and gave a happy shout.
The excitement would last all day and through the night,
While colorful decorations were gleaming so bright.
Streamers were taped and swayed in the air,
The napkins and plates were stacked as a pair.
Balloons danced on the ceiling and the stereo sang a beat,
The cake's shiny icing looked tasty and sweet.
I laughed with my cousins and played with my friends,
The birthday excitement would soon be gone,
I wished the day never end,
And wished my next birthday would be just as fun.

Henry Nguyen, Grade 9
Fountain Valley High School

My Lost Love

For months and months I've been lonely.
I prayed to God night after night.
One day I woke up and felt great, amazingly.
I had found my princess, such a beautiful sight.

Days went on, I'm in love.
Unfortunately the tables turned.
She was so perfect, as beautiful as a soaring dove.
She then hurt me horribly, like I got burned!

Once again I am praying.
Calling to God over and over.
Waiting for another sign, oh He is so giving.
Searching and waiting for my lost lover.

Daniel M. Moreno Jr., Grade 8
Madrona Middle School

On the Shore

The red dawn breaks and the great sun rises,
Howling winds whip the sand of the bare shore,
The crashing of the waves mesmerizes;
I stand there alone, sinking to the floor,
It feels so long ago that you were here,
Smiling at me without a single care,
Now everything has become what I fear:
You departed and left me in despair,
They sent you out on the eternal sea,
To brave death, pain, and the dark wounds of hate
Those devils trying to take you from me,
Though I know you won't come back I still wait,
Without you my spirit is in pieces,
So I will stand here until time ceases.

Naseem Fazeli, Grade 8
Las Flores Middle School

Rusty Old Love

Wind thrust rain rusting dirty windows
Termites are crawling throughout the wood chipped pane
But what is inside or outside does not matter so don't be vain
Six little kids and a single mother inside here
Nice and loving as she tries to steer
These little younglings into a world of cheer
Even though they must not live in luxury
Come on inside come you must hurry
Brother and sister holding hands tight
Roaming the house, there is no fight
Wearing the same outfit day after day
This family's love does not decay
Tired of working an 18 hour job
She comes home to a door with a broken knob
She doesn't care as long as she tries
When her kids run up to give her a hug
She makes sure that she doesn't cry

Cierra Voelkl, Grade 7
Columbus Tustin School

Late Night

Late night hard to sleep
Bored out of your mind
Just trying to kill time
Until the next day
Trying to stay up in school
But it is really hard to do
After a late night
Juan Carlos Romaguera, Grade 8
Richard Merkin Middle Academy

One More Prayer

Sitting in the pews
Behind me,
The entire church,
Filled.
My grandma,
No longer
Here.
Remembering
Her smile
Her laugh
Her love
Stay strong,
Suck it up,
I try to swallow
This supersize lump
In my throat.
Today,
Will not be the end,
Yet just the start,
Of our lives
Without her.
Nicole Schouten, Grade 8
La Joya Middle School

Acquaintance

When I cry
He blames himself.
When I laugh
He smiles.

When I'm bored
He knows just
What to do.

When I'm ready
To open up to him
He's ready to listen
To me.

We know each other
Too well
To see this friendship fail.
He's my acquaintance.
Lindsey Murillo, Grade 7
Holy Family Catholic School

Apple Tree

Day by day apples are falling,
Falling from our tall and large hazel-colored tree.
I watch them closely and eagerly, hoping it will happen to me.

Day by day apples are falling.
I haven't had my chance to fall yet.
Red apples, green apples, even yellow apples, but for some reason not me.

Day by day apples are falling,
Hitting the sharp, tall, green grass.
I wait for my turn to fall, while the others leave me.

Day by day apples are falling,
I grow more impatient each day.
Still watching other apples fall from our tree, I wish the time had come for me.

Day by day apples are falling,
Separating from their long branches and green leaves.
They go one by one, two by two, and three by three, the groups not including me.

Day by day apples are falling.
It seems as though I am the only apple left.
Why hasn't my turn come yet? Someone, please answer me.
Kirsten Biagtan, Grade 8
St Victor Elementary School

Sunshine

How you creep from the east and meet my eyes as they first open,
How as an infant I let your warm arms tickle my smooth conscience,
How you seem foreign and yet give me a dose of remembrance of my mother's womb,
How whisper in my ear, "Stay Gold."

How I jump out of bed with a bird's nest on my head,
How I feel the afternoon will never grow old,
How you create a companion by forming my loyal shadow,
How you follow me until dinnertime, encouraging me, "Stay Gold."

How you have ripened the fruit of my dreams similar to that of Eden,
How that fruit protects the seeds of my innocence,
How you banish all things evil from my paradise of youth,
How as I sit under your warmth considering my future, you remind me, "Stay Gold."

How your rays dry up my salty tears as I see my childhood slip between my fingertips,
How you bring this warm mantle over me as our world becomes colder and colder,
How in a time of uncertainty you come to meet us across the horizon so consistently,
How you never cease to brighten this dark world, urging me, "Stay Gold."

How you are suddenly sinking under the hills of the west
How as I am older I see the value of gold not for profit but for its purity
How the nostalgia of younger times seems close enough to taste
How I wish I had stayed gold.
Stephany Yong, Grade 9
Walnut High School

Water Pollution

When people throw trash in the lake,
The fish and creatures get small.
When a ship spills on the ocean by mistake,
People start to call.

Different kinds of fish and creatures cannot breathe,
Near the ocean you can find poor dead fish.
The startled people are starting to seethe,
People are trying to find trash to squash.

They are making a rule to stop the trash.
Now the water is becoming clean.
The happy fish can splash,
Which people have never seen.

Now the water sparkles like a star,
And the children smile at how beautiful the fish are.

Esther Woo, Grade 8
Robert C Fisler School

Bright as Jewels

Nine o'clock at night if you try to see the stars
You get a sky all so bright with the city's lights

Ten o'clock at night if you try to see the stars
You can barley make out mars

Eleven o'clock at night if you try to see the stars
You will witness a land far off bright as jewels and zooming cars

Twelve o'clock in the morning if you try to see the stars
You are too tired and fall asleep and dream about the stars

Sometime sometimes
They should turn off those streetlights of ours

Kayla Drexel, Grade 7
Sutter Middle School

Love Is Complicated

Love is something beautiful and breathless
However love can be complicated
I read *A Midsummer Night's Dream* and felt helpless
I realized love can't be prevented
Demetrius hated Helena
However she loved him with all her heart
So she wouldn't give up with that fella
She wanted him like if he was a tart
Lysander and Hermia loved each other
Their true love was as strong as steel
They had complications with some other
They didn't know if their hearts would heal
But their love had to be well accepted
And yes love is truly complicated

Carolina Luis, Grade 8
John Adams Middle School

What Only Our Touch Can Feel

What makes the trees move?
What makes the clouds move?
What do we always feel that we never see?
It is what so many people call the wind,
But how can we call something that we cannot see
Or something that we cannot taste?
Of all the senses that we have, we can only feel it,
Blowing against your face,
As it goes around the world.
It sees everything,
Never dying, yet always living on,
Always to see the world in constant motion,
And the wind always with it.

Karl Ames, Grade 9
St Michael's Preparatory School

Roller Coaster on the River

Roller coaster on the river,
Like a snake we slide and slither;
Riding over turbulent waves,
Steering clear of sunken caves.

Nervous laughter, bodies shiver,
Roller coaster on the river;
Gripping paddle and gritting teeth,
Keeping watch for rocks beneath.

The shock of spray on our bare skin,
Our guide shouts "HARD LEFT! ALL HANDS IN!"
Roller coaster on the river,
Working hard we will not wither.

Rocks rush by and water crashes,
Screams erupt from all the splashes;
White water thrills will deliver,
Roller coaster on the river.

Max Worthington, Grade 7
Shorecliffs Middle School

Heinous Fetter

H ungry for destruction, no
E xceptions
I leech your life away
N othing can stop me
O mnivorous, I devour both love and sadness
U surping your happiness, I
S erve only myself

F ound, chained to a wall
E verlasting bonds that
T ake away heart and soul
T rapped in this prison of mine
E roding my ability to love
R usting my mind away

Shayne Bennington, Grade 7
The Mirman School

Life

Life is a roller coaster.
It has its ups and downs,
But you always get through it.
Life is like a river.
Sometimes you don't know which way to turn.
Life has its own mistakes but that's what makes your own life stronger.
Sometimes you don't know what other people go through.
Everyone has their own opinions, theories, questions,
And if you don't go through life with any of them than you're not living life right.
People should worry about how THEIR OWN life goes.
Not about others.
You sit there as the clock goes by ticking away and you do nothing. Just sitting a waste of air.
But when you do get up and do something about your life,
You get that feeling where you have something that's rightfully yours.
Your OWN life. Precious, beautiful, fun.
You finally got up and did something with your life.
Life is too precious for it to be taken advantage of.
Life has to choose which way to go on that river.
It always gets through those high ups and downs on that roller coaster.
Even those boulders on that road.
Life is something only a real person could handle.

Kimberly Baldarrago, Grade 7
Rancho Pico Jr High School

In Memory of My Brother

On late nights such as these
the wind breathes secrets of this life's ingratitude
thinly unveiling the mysterious face of heaven, and
my brother stares down at me from above
and tears fall from my eyes, idle tears
remembering the days that are no more
how he left her...the treasure of his heart behind
separating hands and future from her, leaving a young breasting mother ashore.
how he failed to cry amidst the wild epilepsy of tears from a loving family
and with quarantined thoughts behind those burnished eyes
told us that he would return and everything would be all right.
how he waved farewell...
acknowledging the weight of the many on his shoulders
and prepared himself with his brothers over the ocean.
he fought to terminate hateful iniquity
blood splashing daily from street fights, parched miles and fatigued days of blinding sand
fire cremating his eyes, simply growing numb.
yet, he fell, bullet in chest
twenty four year fingers faltering
a tear rolling down that flushed cheek
silently crying not for himself, but for us.

William Liu, Grade 9
Oliver Wendell Holmes Jr High School

Lonely Tear Drops

Day by day I wake up and I end up sleeping. Seconds by minutes, minutes by hours, hours by days, days by weeks, weeks by months, months by years, years by decades, decades by centuries, centuries by millenniums. Lonely tear drops sigh from my eyes to my chin. Tears of joy, sadness, happiness, and loneliness splash down to the concrete ground. They keep coming down and down...lonely tear drops.

Murtaza Amirzada, Grade 8
Thornton Jr High School

High Merit Poems – Grades 7, 8 and 9

My Pencil Haunts Me

My Pencil haunts me
it's always there
waiting at the top of the stair
It draws doodles on the walls
and pictures on the floor
scribbles just behind each window and door
My Pencil is nocturnal
It gets sharpened each night
It doodles and draws 'till I turn on the light
It doesn't draw straight
like most pencils should
but I don't think it would if it could
It pokes me some time
It writes on my ear
He has lots of good ideas for me to hear
My Pencil annoys me
when I switch to a pen
He doesn't like formulas or FEN
It constantly haunts me
from the top of the stair
never just sits — It's always writing there.

Patrick Marinelli, Grade 8
La Joya Middle School

The Reality of Reality

I wonder, gazing out into the chilled wind,
if every action, every moment of the day,
stiffening of the muscles, gaze of the eyes,
is already planned.
Like the video games my brother plays in his room.
For I wonder how real this life is that I live.
I think back, to times of the past,
where I wish I had done something differently,
where I should have lived more fully; more freely.
Strained by the bounds of life,
by the cords holding the world together,
and the expectations of my actions,
I am restrained;
unable to live more fully; more freely.
I wonder, gazing out into the chilled wind,
If I were to cut these bounds and break these chains,
would anything change?
Or am I merely trapped inside a video game,
with no hope of separating from my future self,
whom I expect, will be tied down just as I am now.

Jennie Christensen, Grade 9
Castilleja School

Read

Read
Slowly, carefully, proudly
Book opens. Knowledge flows. Words scatter.
Interesting, fascinating, nice
Dream

Tristan Bala, Grade 7
St Cyprian School

The Red, White, and Blue

The colors of America are red, white, and blue
The colors that represent me and you
If you look at the colors you won't see
What those colors mean to me
Red is for all the men that die
Leaving their families left to cry
White is the flag our enemies wave
Because they surrender to the U.S.A.
Blue is sky where the eagles soar
So we have freedom from shore to shore
So when you fall asleep at night
Thank them all for willing to fight.

Jason Patterson, Grade 7
Monte Vista Christian School

The Unique Thing About a Book

All books have one scent
They all share a look
But each book has one thing
That the others cannot hook

Each book has a story
That with everyone they share
Each is the vessel of a plot
That can be carried anywhere

A book is unique in that single way
It can share its story with everyone
Each and every day it can bring someone joy
Or it can bring sorrow or lots and lots of fun!

KC Brunson, Grade 8
Lindero Canyon Middle School

Breathe

Breathing heavily,
I lay in my bed.
My head is spinning,
from the crazy thoughts in my head;

A million needles,
devour my mind.
Needles infused with confusion,
an answer I struggle to find.

These thoughts I slowly try to unravel,
my body calmly gives out.
I always hit the gravel.
I always seem to have doubts.

My eyelids gradually closing,
my mind shuts down.
Finally, I fall asleep.
Until tomorrow, my thoughts I'm disposing.

Lora Neshovska, Grade 8
Roosevelt Middle School

Judgment

Who are you to judge someone?
Meeting face to face,
Giving a little stare to one another,
Piercing eyes that frighten all,
A deep frown that blackens day,
But underneath,
A soft warm heart,
With innocence to spare,
Don't you see?
You've misjudged,
Someone kind,
For another,
So change your mind and reconsider.

Tu Pham, Grade 7
Sarah McGarvin Intermediate School

Her Story
(Mrs. Logan)

Just like a flower
you stood tall
Standing high
above us all

for long
you stood strong
Just to watch us all
move along…

Through your battles…
and your fights
we watched you through
the days and nights
we all saw, but didn't want to believe
how you got closer and closer
to being ready to leave…

we all knew of the day
and how it was coming our way…
now we understand
just how safe you are in God's hands.
We think of you every day
and you will never fade away…

Danielle Snook, Grade 7
Citrus Hills Intermediate School

Lord of the Flies*

Friendship may turn to power,
Like a sun over the rainbow,
Everyone wants to be the leader,
Not the follower,
The friendship flows,
Like a river,
Until someone gets hurt.

Ronnel Azizollahi, Grade 7
Kadima Heschel West Middle School
*Inspired by "Lord of the Flies"

I Am Redeemed

O God, You are so wonderful, none can compare
To Your glory and magnificent art
When I see Your creation, I am in awe
Of your amazing works, I love You Lord.
Why have You created me?
I am a sinner, and You set me free.
Your blood was shed so that I can abide with You, why Lord?
I do not deserve Your grace, me a sinner,
Why do You do this for me Lord?
I am just a worthless, little tiny piece of sand.
Yet You hold me in Your mighty powerful hand.
I am astonished by what You have to offer
You are a creature I could never imagine, even in my wildest dreams,
To have someone accept that they were going to die a painful and dreaded death,
So that I could have the eternal and everlasting breath.
You are the rock of my life, You support my every need.
You lift me up when I am down, and You hold my hand through every step.
You are the Shepherd, and I am the lamb,
You watch me when I stumble, and are there to put me back up again.
I praise You Lord, for all You do for me
Praise be to God in the highest place!

Peter Watkins, Grade 8
Chino Valley Christian School

Our Soldiers in Iraq

Although we are safe inside our nation,
Our fellow soldiers are in a far different situation.
Instead they are fighting far away from their families.
They must seek cover in caves and crannies.

They are fighting for a major cause other than oil.
However, we still want them here, on American soil.
While they are saving innocent lives,
They are drifting away from their children and wives.

Their families are alone and brokenhearted.
We wish that the war had never started.
We all hope and pray,
That our fellow soldiers will be okay.

The soldiers that return will not be forgotten.
Although their hearts are brave, their memories are rotten.
Their nightmares may haunt them the rest of their lives,
But it doesn't matter as long as they can sit and enjoy the blue skies.

Nathan Ramos, Grade 8
Citrus Hills Intermediate School

Heroes

Heroes are persons who are there to help when needed
Who are your heroes?
My heroes are my parents because they are always there for me when I need them
My parents are heroes because they protect me from harm
My parents are heroes because they often sacrifice for me without complaining
My parents are heroes because they always want what's best for me

Kim Cheng, Grade 8
Jefferson Middle School

Winter, Snow, Then Spring

I watched it as it fell,
Covering the solid ground
With a smooth blanket
Which hid the old landscape.

The green is fading, fading is green
Like a ninja in the night.
The orange, yellow, and brown
Say their slow, sad sayonaras.

It completely envelopes the horizon.
The snow shows no expression, nothing to express.
Then with a blink of an eye,
The snow sobs.

I watch it as it melts
Showing the solid ground again.
The snow's blanket fades
As busy spring begins to buzz.
I realize I live
In all seasons of the year

Matt Sinsioco, Grade 7
Rolling Hills Country Day School

Love by Numbers

Five soldiers stand on a hill
Four birds fly in the air
Three people are broken
Two hearts in despair
Four fish fly freely, in the very still water.
While she's thinking of him,
He's fighting for her.
Three lions fly proudly, across the arid land.
While he's fighting for all,
She's his biggest fan.
Two hearts separated, across a raging sea.
While they're not together,
Love is plain to see.
One more time to say, across the two hearts
Three words, "I love you."
Not to end, but to start.
One man's legacy
Is flying high, not dead.
So why does one heart,
Have so many tears to shed?

Arthur Guitarte, Grade 8
Holy Family Catholic School

God's Gifts in My Life

God's gifts in my life are my family and friends.
I am lucky to have these gifts that God sends.
When they hug and comfort me you can see.
They are all wonderful people and will always love me.

Andrea Aguilar, Grade 7
St Mary of Assumption School

Your Love Is Like a Drug

Your love is like a drug,
the longer you continue to ignore what we have,
the more I want to be with you.
I've never wanted to love until I met you,
you are the one who I will always want,
even if you don't feel that way,
I wouldn't cause you any pain,
I will love you like no other and I hope you want the same.

Nanette Liberatori, Grade 8
Blessed Sacrament School

Moonlight

Moonlight reaches all of us as night,
you must be crazy if you don't think it's a pretty sight.
The light of the moon is so beautiful,
it makes your night happy and fruitful.

Imagine being on an airplane at night,
right in the midst of moonlight.
I have experienced this sight,
and on my tongue I almost bite.

The moon keeps me staring,
almost glaring.
I would love to go to the moon and be daring,
but somehow I think it would be too scaring.

Moonlight is so elegant,
while I was walking and staring I almost fell again.
The sun is down and flaring,
while the moon is up, and every night, I am still staring.

Amanda Bradford, Grade 8
Madrona Middle School

The Light in the Sky

The light up in the sky
Making the world a better place and
The world will be nothing without it

It hugs you and keeps you warm
But without it,
This place will be freezing.

It is in the sky smiling softly at people
But without it,
People will be grumpy and in a bad mood.

It is in the sky making the world a brighter place
But without it,
The world will be a cold dark place.

The light is up in the sky
And will be forever
Making the world a better place.

Ryota Yamaoka, Grade 8
Madrona Middle School

I Used to Be…Now I Am
I used to be a water puddle,
Now I am a big white snowman.
I used to be a caterpillar,
Now I am a beautiful butterfly.
I used to be a purple grape,
Now I am a shriveled raisin.
I used to be a little plant,
Now I am a big beautiful tree.
Brianna Garcia, Grade 8
Citrus Hills Intermediate School

Yellow Joys
Yellow flowers
Shine like the sun
So everyone can see their beauty
So everyone can see their sorrow
Water scarce, times are hard
To see their everlasting beauty
Yellow flowers
Like sadness and happiness
Bring unique honor
Bring common hope
To see their everlasting beauty
Yellow joys.
Stephanie Escobar, Grade 8
Daniel Savage Middle School

America
I wish
All these wars would stop.
I dream.
And hear the gunshots
When the bullets touch
The ground,
I really care for the people
That have died and
Gave up their lives by accident,
But I am sure
That they had a lot of pride
And free justice.
Jennifer Hurtado, Grade 7
St Alphonsus School

Leonardo
You are Leonardo,
grüss Gott,
the only painter anymore.
You make tourists travel
to see your magnificent Mona Lisa
the once noble woman of your town.
People stare at your angels
and fill their hearts with God.
You are the reason I want to draw —
Ciao, great Leonardo!
Chasen Brehm, Grade 7
St Timothy School

Homework
Homework piled right up to the sky,
Over a million gazillion miles high.
Twenty hours a day,
I will finish, no way,
I have written so much there is nothing else to say.

A sixty page analytic mystery,
Three billion years of U.S. history,
Five hundred problems of math so hard,
Astrophysics learned by the yard,
A thousand words of prose and verse,
It makes me feel so very terse.
My brain implodes with so much grammar,
It feels as though it has been struck by a fifty-pound hammer.
So many projects, none are done,
When is it I get to have some fun?

Oh me, Oh my I ask myself why, if I would rather a million times die,
What is the point to even try?

When I am done I will be old and tired, my body spent, my brain wired.
I have learned it all, I can be part of the team,
I can work at McDonald's, and fulfill my dream.
Meagan Easton, Grade 8
Lindero Canyon Middle School

My World
My world is untold and yet it holds
Everything bright and everything bold nothing bought but everything sold

Nothing here really makes sense like a dollar is a million pence
And a hundred quarters is just five cents everything else is broken and bent

In my world you see everybody lives in glee
Where the rich are poor and the leprechauns soar

In my world it's a bit strange but the strange goes out in different range
In this range you see the giraffes sliding eventually falling together and then colliding

In this world the penguins fly and whales fall from the sky
The lobsters fight with steel knives and into the waters In which the chickens dive

People dance on their heads we take showers on our beds
This world is where books read themselves and people shave when they turn twelve
Where pineapples dance into the night and monsters give themselves the fright

Where the bogeyman really does dance and where armadillos lance
In my world the frogs wear weasel skins and the flowers fight with pointy pins

People who don't write poems like this are lazy
But you could say that I am just as crazy
Quincy Y. Lim, Grade 8
Robert C Fisler School

Happiness

Happiness is yellow and orange
It tastes like sweet candy.
It sounds like chirping birds in the morning
And smells like fresh buttered popcorn.
It looks like smiles everywhere.
It makes you feel like you are glad, cheerful, and excited.

Tatiana Velasco, Grade 7
St Mary of Assumption School

The Resurrection of SpongeBob

Mourns are heard from the bottom of the ocean,
Sad cries from children,
The barking from worms,
The meows from snails,

Everybody missed the smell of the grease from Krabby Patties,
They missed the annoying laughter of the Sponge,
They missed the masterpiece bubbles blown into their houses,
And also that pineapple next door,
Although these conditions were just temporary,

In just a few days,
Upbeat music was playing,
Happy fish danced happily,
And new flowers bloomed every day,

Suddenly SpongeBob's voice was heard by Bikini Bottom,
They thought it was just hallucination,
They thought they were going mad!

Janette Kim, Grade 8
Robert C Fisler School

Daughter of the Sea

Disney was wrong; she didn't live; she died,
Her life was snuffed like an innocent candle,
All for the man she loved,
But he loved another.
Her sisters told her to kill this monster,
One so vile and evil it could take the place of the devil.
That would stop the torment of love.
But when she was about to extinguish his life,
She stopped and looked at his handsome face and said,
"No."
She tossed the knife in the water and threw herself underneath.
It was straight through her heart.
Her selfish sisters did something no one expected.
They lined like soldier about to go to war, and
They died,
All the daughters of the sea.
The man remembered her vaguely,
But he only saw her beauty.
Her name he never knew.
Her name was Ariel,
Daughter of the sea.

Tori Lowell, Grade 7
Rolling Hills Country Day School

A Desert Miracle

I walk into a desert, finding my way home
Not knowing any dangers will harm me
I trot into the heart of this desert
Becoming weaker and weaker
Thirst is mocking me
As I crawl to shade slowly, hoping to find water
I find nothing but shade
I slowly drift away.
I see a light heading towards my face
I know this is the end for me
But the light goes away
And I hear a voice
I cannot see this being
But I feel his goodness upon me
I slip into a sleep
And wake near my home
To this day I wonder
If an angel or human saved me

Anthony Nguyen, Grade 7
Holy Family Catholic School

A Miracle

The lucky parents
Said she was a miracle.
Her golden hair
And crystal eyes, brought joy to their hearts.
The starving, homeless person
Thought the food was a miracle.
Its sweet, delicious smell,
And how it went crunch when he bit it made him feel satisfied.
The bored, unhappy toddler
Saw the swing as a miracle.
Its shiny, inviting seat
And strong yellow ropes delighted him.
The poor girl with no friends
Thought the book was a miracle.
Its billions of interesting words
And sturdy cover kept her occupied.
The single, eager lady
Said he was a miracle.
His fun, upbeat attitude
And perfect smile, were the exact match for her.
A miracle can be seen from many different perspectives.

Jessi Johnson, Grade 7
Rolling Hills Country Day School

Lost Beauty

Lost souls of the past
Twisting, meandering, winding through your memories
They lead you to confusion
Stop; run away
Unexpected happy things fill your mind
Beauty is found again

Katie Weber, Grade 9
La Costa Canyon High School

The Moon
The moon the moon
So round and bright
You give us light

The moon is so fun
While we feast and run
You cheer me up when I am down

The moon goes bye
The next day comes
We wake up to see the morning sun
Benjamin Parra, Grade 7
Santa Rosa Technology Magnet School

A Beginning and End
I stand waiting
beside her
holding her hand
hoping
praying
the doctor comes in
to deliver the dreadful news
"There is nothing we can do"
the last thing she says to me is
"I love you"
then she closes her eyes
peace comes to her face

The nurse walks in
hands me
the last thing I have
She blinks at me
in her little pink blanket
I hold her tight
It is the last thing I have to cherish
Kelli Mayhew, Grade 8
La Joya Middle School

True Friends
True friends are like diamonds
precious and rare
Fake friends are like leaves
found everywhere
You would have to look around
to see what's right
even if it would take all night
A true friend knows how our friendship
became so deep
They never tell the secrets
that we keep
Our friendship will always be
because my true friend
will always be there for me
Kimberly Perez, Grade 8
McCabe Elementary School

Bubble
I wish I wasn't in a bubble
Just to escape and be free.
If I wasn't in this bubble
My life would be full of glee.

It's crazy and sad.
It's annoying me…bad.
Maybe I will go mad,
Being in this bubble.

I hate it. It's dumb.
It's like a baby
Sucking its thumb.

Life isn't perfect.
Nothing is worth it.
I just don't want to be
Trapped in this bubble.
Zabreena Sauceda, Grade 8
McCabe Elementary School

The Dancing Dawn
As the dawn danced across the sky
as the birds chirped their
morning song a bright
new sun came to
bring us a
fresh
new
day
!
Alex Lee, Grade 7
Bethany Lutheran School

Why, Daddy?
Since you divorced Mommy,
You've hurt me
Why, Daddy?
Why do you hurt me so?
Do you even care?
Please don't hurt me anymore
Do you know how I feel?
I bet you don't, 'cause you
Probably don't even care
Why, Daddy?
Why do you hurt me so?
You've made me cry,
You've made me hurt,
Don't you love me?
I beg of you,
Please don't hurt me anymore
Why, Daddy?
Why do you hurt me so?
Monica Lazo, Grade 7
Corpus Christi School

Summer Vacation
It was the end of school
And the beginning of summer vacation
No more pants and jackets
No more long sleeved shirts

Now, shorts and flip-flops
And bathing suits;
Swimming pools and beaches
No more rain. No more umbrellas

No more waking up early
(At least for some of us)
Get ready for summer vacation
It's coming fast and loud!
Summer — the Bomb!
Sabrina Ontiveros, Grade 7
Packinghouse Christian Academy

The Grey Soccer Ball
So much depends
Upon

A grey soccer
Ball

Feet touching it
Slowly

Just real pure
Magic
Jorge Giron, Grade 7
Santa Rosa Technology Magnet School

Enigma?
I feel pulled apart
like two different people
one is a loner
one is quite social

As a social I feel connected
like I have a lot of friends
together what we accomplished
would be praiseworthy without end

But as a loner I feel strong
like I need no one else
I could do much more
with no one else's help

But which one of these is me
will I be social
or alone
maybe who I am is the best of both
Mason Lingberg, Grade 8
La Joya Middle School

Love

Why is love so difficult in this world?
Love is usually hard to understand
And can ruin your life and leave it twirled
And it will take years for your heart to mend
It's like trying to save each animal
Or rather saving every human life
And we should all at least try, and we shall
Love is why people sometimes get a wife
But love can sometimes be magnificent
It can be a wonderful thing in life
Love will not be or cannot be rent
It's the sharpest decision as a knife
Love is terrific and is marvelous
Extraordinary and is wondrous

Alexis Maldonado, Grade 8
John Adams Middle School

Warmth

I stared into his eyes
and as the sky opened up,
I thought I could feel the sun's warmth,
but for a reason that I cannot understand,
my body felt cold
and my heart warm.
With a new feeling inside of me,
I am finally close enough to touch his cheek
and as I do so,
his crystal blue eyes catch the sun's rays,
and he's gone.
The warmth is quickly drained from my body
and I am left with a sunny sky,
but can still feel no warmth.

Katrina Cazel, Grade 7
Holy Family Catholic School

The Amusement Park

Rides going 'round and 'round
Benches for people to hang around

A sizzling sun beating down on my back
A whoosh of air hits my face like a surprise attack

The aroma of burgers being cooked on the grill fills the air
Buttery popcorn is what I smell in my hair.

Icy, cold lemonade is what I like
Eating some nachos as if I came from a hunger strike

High pitched screams, I cannot stand
Children filled with happiness like a good old band

All this is nice, but I cannot last
I think I need to lie on the comfy green grass.

Brittany Squarcia, Grade 9
Homestead High School

Being Someone You Aren't

Have you ever been someone you aren't?
Have you ever dressed like how other people dressed
But you know this isn't me inside,
Have you ever took a chance to think about it,
But you know people would make fun of you.

Don't you want to be yourself?
Act like yourself,
Dress like yourself,
Have you ever thought about it?

Don't you just want freedom?
Freedom to do whatever you want
But you know if you try people would make fun of you,
You think it's too hard.

Just try it and see what happens,
Just be yourself.

Hannah Michalak, Grade 8
Santa Rosa Technology Magnet School

Keep Moving Forward

Around here, however,
we don't look backwards for very long.

We keep moving forward,
opening up new doors and doing new things
because we're curious…
and curiosity keeps leading us down new paths.

Daniel Villa, Grade 8
La Joya Middle School

A Life Worth Living

There is no price you can pay,
I will always live my life, my very own way,
You can't stop me, I am determined,
There's no way, I will end up losing.
You may have some doubts, everyone always does;
You may try to put me down, I will only rise above.
Don't try to hurt me, you will always fail;
Don't try to burn me, you will only bail.
I may sin, so everybody does,
I may hurt a loved one, but it's for a good cause.
You may see me as a demand, a fright, a scare,
Or even as a ferocious bear;
But I only hurt you out of love.
A family can keep you afloat,
Sometimes they can sink your boat.
No matter how mad,
No matter how bad;
No matter how sad,
I will always be glad.
For I have a family and life is worth living,
For I have a helping hand, and I'm glad that I am living.

Anthony Colvard, Grade 8
Holy Family Catholic School

Friends

Friends are wonderful,
and are especially beautiful.
Friends are very caring,
but not overbearing.
Friends help you when you fall,
by taking you to the mall.
Friends are very forgiving,
and are also very giving.
Friends are there forever,
and will be there whenever.

Celine Garcia, Grade 7
Monte Vista Christian School

Complete

You made me complete.
You fill my heart with
warmth,
My heart bounces twice
when I'm with you.
I laugh,
smile,
because of you.
Once I was sad,
lonely,
and cold,
but now you're here —
you're sweet fire
in my heart,
And now my heart is warm,
because you are here…
with me

Vivian Yu, Grade 8
Corpus Christi School

As We Appear

You can't just look at someone
And assume that what you see
Is everything about them,
There's so much more they could be.

Just because they look happy
Doesn't mean they're not sad;
Just because they're always smiling
Doesn't mean they're never mad.

People don't always show it
They're not always as they appear.
Just because they act brave
Doesn't mean they're not full of fear.

Some of us are just good at hiding,
We're good at pretending we're fine.
We know how to act like we're okay,
We know to walk that fine line.

Megan Archer, Grade 8
Carden School of Sacramento

Incredible Me

I can do whatever I want because people will follow in my footsteps.
I'm so cool I can tell the arctic where to go.
The sun is my eyes and the moon is my smile.
Even the gods bow down to me.
I'm so smart the president comes to me for advice.
When I get serious all the world's problems disappear.
When I die the planet will go into a deep depression.

Isaiah Barth, Grade 7
Odyssey Charter School

The Fate of Humanity

Inscribed somewhere on a grain of rice is the fate of humanity
Chiseled on the underside in golden letters
That the intentions of man outweighed the decisions of mankind.
One righteous deed weighed against one trillion disasters
Saved humanity from questioning itself
From asking why it was so intelligent, so resilient, so noble
That to prove itself, to prove humanity was fearless,
Humanity challenged humanity. Human beings opposed being humans.
Breathing. Feeling. Thinking. Being.
A crescendo of contests waged against itself, humanity
Tore itself apart and flung the dismembered parts to the four corners
To the four seasons, to the five senses, to the seven wonders, to the one man
Who did not think of himself as one man
But as one part of the greater community of mankind.
And as he began to rebuild the community with nothing but his belief
That humanity cannot exist without humans, that mankind cannot exist without men
So the great grain of rice decided in golden letters,
Humanely,
That one righteous deed might save humanity from a trillion disasters
As long as man remembers that he represents not himself but all of mankind.

Alex Mabanta, Grade 9
The Harker School - Upper Campus

The Whole Display

Tears come down upon me, they drown me away
I'm full with misery, from the whole display
I remember coming home, seeing my grandpa with a smile on his face
Outshining the bright sun, with all his happiness, full of energy
And ready for the next day, the next day wasn't a good day
I came home and I saw my mom, she was on the floor crying
I was only five years old, asking what's wrong, nobody answers
I look for my grandpa, he isn't home
The next day I am at a dark place, everybody is wearing black
I see my grandpa in a coffin in place
With only black clothes
His face pale white as snow
His eyes are closed
I can't see his emerald green eyes no more
He doesn't move
He doesn't breathe
He doesn't do anything
Tears come down upon me, and they drown me away
I'm still full with misery, from the whole display

Melissa Simo, Grade 8
McCabe Elementary School

NASCAR

I pull out of the pit stop
Just three laps to go
Ahead by 1/4 lap
Excitement is around the corner
My crew already celebrating
As well as I
It seems our victory is locked in
I'm smiling, laughing,
While speeding down the straight away at 180
I smell burning
I look around
I feel a thump as my tire flies off
As my car begins to skid,
I have no control over its actions
I hit the wall with a thud
And begin flipping
I'm engorged in flames
Everything goes black

Jesse King, Grade 8
Carmel Valley Middle School

I Love You

I'm writing this just to say thank you for each and every day
You're everything I've been looking for
I was knocking and you opened the door
You make me smile
You make me laugh
You make me feel we're all intact
It feels so right when I'm with you
And I hope you feel the same way too
I'm bottled up with all these words I don't know how to say
But they sum up to saying
You're wonderful in every single way
So once again I'm saying thanks for everything you do
But some other words I want to say are
I love you

Shannon Jose, Grade 7
Holy Family Catholic School

Chocolate Cake

Just like my best friend,
Chocolate cake never betrays me,
Whenever I am hungry and feeling' gloomy
It is sweet as my baby cousin
It is soft as a pillow

Chocolate cake, makes me happy all the time
Chocolate cake, leads me to my childhood
The smell of chocolate cake reminds me of
My forgotten memories
Playing with Julie, my best friend
Running under the rain, with my best friend Julie
Catching the kites, with my her
Chocolate cake brings me a lot of sweet things!

Yuri Park, Grade 8
Robert C Fisler School

My Special Place

My special place is warm and safe
Secret as well, except to Miguel

It is in my old tree, back up the meadow
Perched on a hill, like a grand old widow

My old pepper tree that bends and creaks
More than fifty feet high, when I first lift my feet

The higher I go, the stronger the breeze
Until I reach the top, then I'll tuck in my knees

I'll lean back my head and admire the view
I'll sway with the breeze, and I'll never let go

It will stay with my heart even when I leave
That special place, that is my old tree

Taylor Steele, Grade 7
Linfield Christian School

September 11th

It was the worst day in history so far
On September 11th two planes did fall
Planes hit the Twin Towers with a crash
There was nothing left, for they were smashed

Many of lives were taken that day
Firefighters, police, and more I do say
The taste of smoke and fear was in all the air
And ashes is all that most people would wear

Sirens, screams, and cries were the only sounds
For the Twin Towers had a fiery crown
Very few were able to get out
This horribly day left the country in doubt

After burning in big, red, treacherous flames
The towers tumbled, leaving all their remains
A day in New York ended in fear
Let us all never forget what happened here

Kelsey McNeeley, Grade 9
Lucerne Valley Jr/Sr High School

Marshmallows

On the outside, you look like clouds floating in the sky.
You feel like fluffy pillows.
When I roast you, you turn a crispy brown color.
When I slice you, you sound like a sponge.
Inside you look like mushy white chocolate.
You smell like a very good aroma.
You taste like a sugary explosion.
Tell me, marshmallow, how is it possible for you to taste
So good?

Stephanie Cuamani, Grade 7
Yolo Middle School

Battle Zone

I look out the window and what do I see, a hundred, a thousand, a million and three.
They fall in no rhythm or in a beat, just pitter patter like a pair of small feet,
And just when it seems to stop, the gunshots continue to drop.
All night the fighting continues, I'm in a battle zone,
I think our tanker's been hit! I see the flash of a cannon being lit,
And then I hear a boom, its roar is heard throughout my room.
The morning has finally arrived, and instead of staying inside,
I find myself preparing for what might be outside.
With one last breath of dry air, I take a step and find my home stranded in the middle of nowhere,
We are cut off from the town we know, with neighbors in camouflage and supplies in tow.
I notice the battle has left many scars on our streets, but it does not show one ounce of defeat,
Just as I leap over bodies of water, the war sounds as it begins again.
Everyone quickly runs back to their forts. "It's only rain!" my brother snorts.

Julia Farfan, Grade 8
Lindero Canyon Middle School

The Golden Eagle

So defined a character, so sharp a mind,
it outlasts all other creatures in the planet,
a godlike statue as it stands, gazing, on a tall wooden fence post.

It is ready to fly;
broad wings stretch into the blue evening sky, the stars a bright twinkling as the warrior launches midair,
the wind a friend, guiding it so, this way and that.

The purple mountains stretch tall behind,
the sea of grass, a prairie, extending as far as the eye can see below;
after the slightest disturbance of a quick flap of its wings,
the bird quietly soars higher and farther towards the glowing horizon as the sun slowly sets.

Josephine Wong, Grade 7
Jefferson Middle School

Through the Eyes of a Sister

Your brother was just born, you're ecstatic to be a sister
Feed him, clean him, and play with him later he will remember
He just turned 2, trying to speak, and explore the world
Show him how to use the toilet. Teach him new words run with him wherever he goes.
Now he is 4: able to jump, spin and run around the house.
Stay with him when he gets nightmares,
Teach him the ABCs and the 123s maybe even watch some *Blue's Clues*
He just turned 6: time to ride the bike, go to school, and learn new things.
Help him with his homework, read to him,
Go to the park and play on the swings, ride your bikes, or pass the ball
8 years old, he's growing up celebrate at Chuck E Cheese, his favorite
Give him your tokens just because you love him
Play with his new game even if you have to be the bad guy
Here comes the big 1-0 he's been playing video games all day long begging you to play,
You lose on purpose just to make him smile.
He's starting to read the big books like Harry Potter you're sure he is ready
Finally he is in his teenage years he doesn't talk to you,
You go to his room offer to play he slams the door in your face,
Yells at you to mind your own business, you wonder, what happened? He grew up that's all.
But you know he will always remember his childhood
And you right by his side day and night, no matter what

Lillian Arjona, Grade 9
Calvin Christian School

The Valley of Death

There is a valley full of evil called the Valley of Death
Where nothing lives or grows
Except the tree of life that none shall touch
Protected by death itself
The land around the valley is full of life,
Beautiful trees and plants fill the landscape
And the tree of knowledge that makes you mortal
No longer exists because of humans
And now humans are the tree of knowledge
The Valley of Death is filled with sorrow,
Hate, and rage no mortal shall enter
The Valley of Death

James Sas, Grade 8
Long Valley Charter School

The Assignment

This assignment is hard for me to do
I have to write a poem. About what? I have no clue
I tried to write about my skateboard,
I tried to write about my video game,
I even thought about basketball,
But they all sounded so lame.
I feel so frustrated,
Trying to make things rhyme,
I wanna hurry up and finish.
This is a waste of my time.
I dread this assignment,
But this rhyme is what I made.
If I get pretty lucky,
I just might make the grade.

Cesar Ahumada, Grade 8
McCabe Elementary School

Ode to Flying

Flying high above the clouds,
Soaring free of all troubles.
You will soon have a different view of life
Poking holes in the great white monsters,
Your mind…ERASED.

As you reach for the stars,
Your dreams have come true
You now see the world through a different eye.
When rain starts,
You know you have to come home,

Back to reality, you must come.

As you approach the port,
You will always have great memories,
Of those great white monstrous clouds
With holes through the center of them,
As you land, reality has come back in your life.

Cameron O'Brien, Grade 7
Santa Rosa Technology Magnet School

Change

Time has come for a change we all know
things could never stay the same.
Years ago MLK said things would get better for us.
And sure enough 2009 is the year for us.
On January 21, 2009 was the day a
black president went into the White House

Yes, he is black and common sense is
something he does not lack.
Let's all give him a pat on the back

Time changes, but right from wrong stays the same.
When you hold on to your faith lean
and depend on God.
You will have love without hate.

So let us work together and walk in the light
with all wisdom and might, all honor,
a blessing with angels above and
thank God for our love.
This change is not a single step,
but a life lived with Christ
and a cry for help.

Sallie Green, Grade 8
Jefferson Middle School

Lighthouse

As I steer my ship and look up at the sky,
I see the lighthouse's blinking eye
I watch the beam, ever so bright,
As it wanders through the pitch-black night

I follow the light, always on the roam,
As it guides me through the water's foam
The lighthouse pilots me through the midnight breeze,
Its radiant light saying, "Come home please."

Alec Brubaker, Grade 8
Madrona Middle School

I Don't Understand

I don't understand
Why being different gives you a name
Why we can't be proud with who we are
Why we are pressured into acting the same

But most of all
Why people choose to be someone they are not
Why we shouldn't try new things
Why everyone thinks being perfect can be taught

What I understand most is
Why I don't listen to negative liars
Why I take pride in who I am, not what others want me to be
Why people push others down, to bring themselves higher

Tara Hayes, Grade 8
Dorris-Eaton School

Christmas

A time with your family
Spreading joy to other people
Children excited opening gifts
Then building snowmen
Kids filled with joy
The most important part is
Spending time with family.

Kassandra Murillo, Grade 7
St Alphonsus School

Winter

Winter is very cold,
but can be very bold.
The snow falls,
like little fluffy balls.
Animals are out,
they're moving all about.
Foxes spot a mouse,
then they leap and pounce.
The wind is changing,
from soft to raging.
A blizzard is near,
the animals are full of fear.
They run and scatter,
and everyone will matter.
They're in their different homes,
with a chill in their bones.
The blizzard goes by,
then you can see the sky.
They leave their den,
and start over again.

Kara Oberheim, Grade 8
Chico Jr High School

Move

Move, I need
to get to class
no more talk
I must go fast

Move, hurry up
no longer can I wait
don't you see
you'll make me late

Move, or I will
swing my fists
and then another
class I'll miss

DING! DING! DING!
Look what you did
you made me late
you stupid kid!

Caleb Ashurst, Grade 8
McCabe Elementary School

The Reasons I Love You

Baby you have me attracted to you, like a bee is to honey.
I always have you in my mind, I love you like a squirrel loves nuts.
My heart is always in your debt, another reason to be by your side.
I love so much that on a bad day, you brighten my day with your personality.
You always drift me away like the wind.
When I see you my feelings get deeper and deeper.
When you leave I miss you, miss you like if there is no tomorrow.
I'm like a puzzle that can't be solved, but you are my missing piece.
You are my nature and paradise, like animals need the forest.
This is why I love you with my life.

Edgar A. Arambula, Grade 8
Henry T Gage Middle School

Challenging the Mountain

I'm on top of a mountain.
My feet are strapped to my board, and
I'm ready for a ride.
I begin slowly,
But gain speed, maybe a little too much speed.
I panic and am a wobbly fledging.
I fall to the soft snow sitting at my feet.
Again I challenge the mountain,
And gain too much speed.
Thud! I greet the ground once again.
Time passes.
I lose track of how many times I have said hello to the cold, unwelcoming snow.
I ponder on whether I should stop and admit defeat,
But I cannot let the mountain win.
I get up and renew my quest.
For a change I come to a halt, and smile to myself.
I keep on smiling and stopping successfully until I reach the mountain's foot;
The mountain has lost, and I have finally won.

Mallory Thompson, Grade 8
Rolling Hills Country Day School

Questionable

Stunning
One word to describe the beauty
But what does he think of you?
He takes your breath away every time you hear him say your name
You feel an unbelievable attraction
A spark
Something clicks
But does he feel the same?
Waiting and waiting
Searching for the answer
Yet you come up short
What's next?
You can't wait forever
It's not worth the heart ache
Not again.

Sierra Howard, Grade 8
Natomas Charter School

My Love

On the power shores all I see is she
For all my sight is vast as the great ocean
My heart, large as sight, has one scene, the sea.
Love is a sea, a soothing blue lotion

For you are waiting across the black hole
Each time I sail the wind of courage fail.
Like my path I have a hole in my soul
All I wish is to end my pain, prevail.

No! I won't have it. Once more I will try.
Your gold hair reveals all seas of seven.
No more, shall I sly like a hired spy
And if I fail we greet in heaven.

I aimed my arrow when stood out of seat
My heart won and braved the sea of ten feet.

Darian Ghadiri, Grade 8
Carmel Valley Middle School

Skaters

Skating is half my life
I love the texture and the feel of it
It's faster and less tiring than running
Skaters is the new life in my neighborhood

The wheels are perfectly round
The only flaw of it is the pebbles in the ground
Once hitting a pebble…CRASH!!!
But who cares because skating is fun

I love when the air hits my face
Passing through obstacles is a challenge
But hey challenges could be fun
Skating is half my life and it always will be.

Juan Venegas, Grade 8
McCabe Elementary School

Winter Sting

The leaves have fallen and winter is here,
The snow is falling and the days are white,
But it's cold and it's dark all through the night,
The bold sting of winter has spread here and there,
So a strong word of warning is to take care,
For it seems as though a blizzard's in sight,
And the stars are the only things shinning bright,
As shadows fall on the old man in his chair.

The light protected him all through the spring,
But faint it grew when summer turned to fall,
When birds of spring no longer cheer nor sing,
And all that was beautiful and tall,
Turned pale and naked by the winter sting,
That's what quieted the old man's call.

Arash Abiri, Grade 8
South Lake Middle School

First Love

Did I see you under a sparkling light?
My heart is beating faster than ever.
I'm in love with you just at the first sight.
I asked you if we could be together.

You said that you didn't want anyone.
At those words my heart had just skipped a beat.
Looking at you I thought you were the one.
Despite your words we had to again meet.

I ran after you like lovers would do.
Again I asked you and you had said no
I stood there thinking only if I knew.
First heart break and I just went with the flow.

Still though my heart had not been quickly fixed
Until I met Sally and we just mixed.

Rithika Verma, Grade 8
Carmel Valley Middle School

The Understanding Rainbow

Purple the color of the bruises on my wrists.
Blue the color of the eyes looking down on me with annoyance.
Green the color of envy, festering in my mind.
Yellow the color of the sun, bright, and happy above me.
Orange the color of the dusty sand I lie on.
Red the color of my flushed cheeks,
As I stay waiting, just waiting.

Olivia Ryley, Grade 8
Curden School of Sacramento

Remembering You

Whenever I go to your daughter's house
I see your home
I used to hate going there
It smelled like old people
But now I miss it

I remember walking in the front
Listening to the loud canaries chirp their songs
Walking to your bed and staying there for hours
I remember your TV and the channels I never liked

But I guess I never realized how much I loved you —
Until you were gone
I was quite young when you died
But at least I knew you

You made it to see your 88th birthday
But then the Lord asked you to come home
We'll always remember each other
And I will one day come to visit you, too
I love you, Great-Grandma

Kylie Canales, Grade 7
Linfield Christian School

Sisters

Happily we sat and played
Smelling the cookies Mom made.

Tumbling down the great hill
Back then was our kind of thrill.

We helped each other move on
Thinking not of what has gone.

Hand in hand we walk on through
Under the vast sky of blue.

Jennifer Alexanians, Grade 9
La Quinta High School

What We Cannot Face

Our world…
Are we doing our best?
Are we doing everything we can?
To help every crisis?
In our world right now?
This Earth is so…
Amazing, bizarre, diverse,
Compelling, extravagant, lush
That we cannot afford
To lose it all
Because of our mistakes.
It's happening.
It's coming.
No one can bear to face it.
But it's our sad truth.

Kathleen Kelejian, Grade 8
American Canyon Middle School

Strawberries*

I took your strawberries
To make a smoothie blend
I didn't want to make you mad
So I didn't say a word

My eyes were hypnotized
By the strawberries
So red, sweet, and cold
I took the strawberries to
Check if it was good and took
A bite
When no one was there
My taste buds were
Going crazy
I just had to take them

Please forgive me
For telling you now
But I just love fruits

Lydia Lee, Grade 8
Madrona Middle School
*Inspired by William Carlos Williams

Our World

Teasing rain, tempting snow,
Oceans miles long, valleys low.
Squawking bird, grazing sheep,
Grassy plains, where the buffalo reap.
Gentle flowers, polar bears,
Beautiful sights, far and near.
Buildings scraping the humble blue sky,
But the mountains beat them because they reach so high.
Beautiful sights for us to see,
But will they always last? Will they always be?
Why do we choose to destroy our world so good?
Why don't we choose to save it like we should?
Not recycling and then there's pollution,
This is the best time to find a solution.
Of course when we do it, we can do it with joy
Us helping the Earth now can make it better for future girls and boys.
So lend a hand and make each life better,
Let us live in peace, love and harmony forever.

Arianna Clarke-Ball, Grade 8
Blessed Sacrament School

Candyland

Candy here, candy there sweet and juicy everywhere
A land filled of taste and smell makes my lips water and melt
Chocolate drizzling down a hill makes my tummy fill with thrill
Clouds of pink, clouds of blue made of cotton candy goo
Cups of red, cups of white, made of candies sweetest delights
When I leave, the gummy bears cry, while a juicy tear drops down their eye
Never want to say goodbye when flying home in the gumdrop sky.
It's a land for me, it's a land for you, it's a land for anyone who has a sweet tooth
I want to go again but this time I'd like a friend
So come with me to the land of glee it's candy's biggest mystery!

Shannon Grover, Grade 7
Holy Family Catholic School

A Cream Tea

Outside our Dorset cottage at 4 o'clock pm,
The whole family gathers in the garden for tea.
Mum lays the table with all of the treats.
Oh my, oh my! — what a delicious feast!
Teeny, tiny sandwiches cut into perfect squares
With slices of green cucumber nestled between the soft, brown, bread.
Near them lie the sausage rolls, like podgy little babies
Wrapped in blankets of light and flaky pastry.
A tall, majestic teapot stands proudly in the center,
On either side of it are its friends — the milk and the sugar.
It's blissful to sit among the roses; whiter than a full moon,
And simply bask in the rays of the sun, while listening to the birds chirp.
Now, for the culmination of the day, the highlight of the meal.
There they are, on a platter of brilliant blue — the scones.
Buttery and crumbly, melting in your mouth.
Spread with a thick layer of homemade strawberry jam
And topped with a dollop of fresh, sweet clotted cream.
Each and every bite is a taste of Heaven!

Sophie Glander, Grade 9
La Reina High School

Stargazing

I take the metal ladder to the roof —
the stranger way to view the sky; perhaps you may be right.

You laugh as careful step by step we take,
stumbling up the road to the moon.

We lie back on wet shingles,
splinters like blunt daggers digging into our backs.

The city is no place for astronomers like us,
no place for sympathy or poets. But here we lie,
rubbing our hands together,
talking in whispers,
hair mingled, and
tangible gazes looking up at the sky.

Constance Chan, Grade 9
South Bay Faith Academy

True Love

When you dream tonight
Would you mind if I stopped by
To hitch a ride on your cloud
And get lost in your eyes

The sun sets, beaches drown,
No matter what I'll wait for that sound,

The moon shines, the oceans sway,
I want to hear your voice so our hearts can play,

The stars dazzle, darkness envelopes the sky,
Yet somehow your light always illuminates the night,

Light that follows wherever I may go,
You're the stars all around me falling like flakes of snow,

So come with me
I'll keep you safe
From the tempest and the storm
And never again will you shiver
Because I'll always keep you warm

Luis Tobar, Grade 8
Richard Merkin Middle Academy

Radiant Sunlight

Pillars of light shine down from the sky —
warm rays reach down and embrace the Earth,
like hands of creation that sprouts life from the ground.

Sleeping plants awaken and feed upon this light —
it is the food for the flowering grass, and towering trees.
Without this light, they can no longer live
for they will wither and die.

Brian Kao, Grade 8
Madrona Middle School

Beautiful Girl

You make my life sweet like bees with honey.
You're as a dream makes me happy and good.
You're like jewelry worth lots of money.
When I see you I'm in a good mood.
Some shiny eyes they compare to the sun.
Bright smile it looks like a shiny star.
Every time I'm around you I have fun.
So special like when you get your new car.
You're like a perfume you smell so sweet.
You're as beautiful as a bloomed rose.
You're gorgeous you swept me off my feet.
You take my heart away when you're close.
Smile so beautiful it makes my day.
You're so beautiful you could be an art display.

Sebastian Peliz, Grade 8
Henry T Gage Middle School

Betrayed

I should have known you would leave me
At my time of need
Like the bad friend that you are

Now I'm here
All alone in the rain
Sitting on a worn out wood bench
Softly swaying my bare foot
Back and forth back and forth
Throwing rocks into small puddles
Thinking of how you could just
Betray me after all we've been through
I remember so clearly those words you said to me
That night in camp
Like a song replaying in my head about ten times
As I laid there on the black blanket we shared
Pouring my heart out to you

I would have never imagined
That this day would come

At least the rain is here
To disguise my tears

Sarah Shapov, Grade 8
Emek Hebrew Academy

Love of Books

You're full of love and imagination
I must keep reading because you're a sensation
The authors write you with so much dedication
And you're always filled with lots of temptation
Sometimes you are full of frustration
But I can't get over my fascination
Every now and then I have some hesitation
I do not want to miss the ending's celebration
You are so good that I always feel heaps of admiration

Marissa Verdi, Grade 8
Citrus Hills Intermediate School

The Broken Window
The window all shattered
Broken all over the floor
It was an air ball
Surely it didn't go next door

The wind was making
The baseball mad
It broke your poor window
And that made me really sad

I was just trying to have fun
Although I was rude
I'm just trying to say
That I'm sorry dude

Please forgive me
I won't do it again
Don't send me to jail
I'll be your best friend
Lily Kim, Grade 8
Madrona Middle School

Poetry Is…
Rhyme to the beat of its own drum;
A budding flower of emotions;
A soaring plane of thoughts;
An undiscovered meaning to life itself;
My view of the world written on paper;
The things that go through my head?
And out through my fingers in ink.
Analise Gore, Grade 8
Madrona Middle School

Summer
Summer is fun
Although it goes by fast
Summer is a great time
Act like it's your last

It's the greatest season
The best time of the year
We all can't wait for summer
It feels far yet still so near

The leaves are green
The sky is blue
Summer is so much fun
We have lots to do

This may be your last time
To have so much fun
Summer o summer
I wish it is never done
Jesse Hoffmann, Grade 7
Santa Rosa Technology Magnet School

What Is Music?
What is music?
Is it the splash of water,
Over smooth stone?
Is it the bass of the beat,
That you feel vibrating your bones?
Is it the melodies of birds,
Going about their day?
Is it the sound of a animal's happiness,
As it prances and plays?
Is it the love a couple,
Who are tuned in harmony?
Is it the hum of a machine,
working tirelessly?
Is it the beat of a drum,
That makes you dance on your feet?
Is it the joy of a person,
Who greets a friend as they meet?
What is music?
It is the harmony of the world,
In all its forms.
It is this and much, much more.
Zechariah Deckert, Grade 9
University Preparatory School

Reality
People are cruel,
People are kind,
Some people are deaf,
And some people are blind.

It was a sad day,
When I came to find;
That people don't really care,
About the deaf or the blind.

If only the world,
Could care a bit more
About everyone;
Not only the rich,
But also the poor.

The fact of the matter
Is very easy to see:
All these other people
are just like you,
and also like me.
James Hahn, Grade 8
Packinghouse Christian Academy

The Leaves
Falling to the ground,
I watch a leaf settle down
In a bed of brown
Randy Richardson, Grade 7
Santa Rosa Technology Magnet School

The Hobo Man
Tink, tink, tink went the can
Boom, boom, boom went
When he banged the trash can
There he is sad and blue
Thinking on what to do
Loving man was he
But his wife left him and let him be
Tink, tink, tink went the can
O what a sad hobo man
Matthew Baciu, Grade 8
Robert C Fisler School

McCabe
I've gone to McCabe awhile.
Ever since I was a child.

I have good memories at this school.
Probably because it was really cool.

Next year I will go to high school.
Where I will probably feel like a fool.

I don't want to leave this place.
But I guess this, I will have to face.

I have to go on with my life.
To go live the high school life.

I'm sure when I leave I'll feel regret.
This school I surely won't forget!
David Romero, Grade 8
McCabe Elementary School

Haunted Memories
I scream, my mouth open
But no sound is made
The echo of my memories
Haunting my mind into insanity

No one but me is here
Yet I wonder if that's true
Am I really here or am I
Not really here?

Am I just a figment of memory?
Am I just not there?
Or am I really here?
Am I here and no one else?

I scream, my mouth open
But no sound is made
I don't know anything
I only have fragmented parts
Tessa Lounsbury, Grade 7
The Classical Academy

Surfing

Surfing is…
Hanging out with your old man
When you can catch a nice tan
Enjoying the ocean under the sun
Catching waves that are fun
Relaxing as you wait for a wave
When the perfect wave comes being brave
Just the right way to end the day
When all your stress goes away

Mason Klerks, Grade 8
Citrus Hills Intermediate School

Keep on Living

I thought there was so much more time to spare
But what has happened is too much to bear
I watched and waited and now I feel so numb
But as the candle runs low winter has come

His life was taken but not without a fight
I swear he did everything right
He was so close and dear
His sudden death was my only fear

It was the coldest winter today
But autumn has just come this way
Together we all mourn
Even though he will never be reborn

The reality is oh so dreary
It is all right to be teary
You may have reached an all time low
But understand you're the one in the show

Charlie Frishberg, Grade 8
Carmel Valley Middle School

Spring

What is this form of change I see,
Which turns the leaves of trees green?
What is it that melts the ice on top of the lake?
A force that makes the body quake.

What is it that wakes the animals from their sleep?
For it makes these creatures creep.
It's a force that gives new birth
To everybody on Earth.

During this time, the new bird sings a new song,
However, I look far beyond
The meaning of this song.

It may be new to you,
But not to me.
This song it sings,
Is that of the upcoming spring!

Christopher Denson, Grade 8
Holy Family Catholic School

Clouds

They're fluffy and puffy,
They're swirly and curly.
You can also make shapes with them.
You can fall into them in a dream,
And it's always fun to make words out of them.
But most of all,
They are always fun to look at.

Eddie Cooper, Grade 8
Holy Family Catholic School

Friends and Family

Friends and family are the most precious things
it's what keeps people going
there to support you
in any way possible
always and forever

They'll be there for you
in the day or night
anytime you want
just give them a call

They'll be there when you need
support, faith, hope, love
anything at all
so my friends and family thank you all

Stephanie Perez, Grade 8
Huron Middle School

Moonlight, Starlight

The dark sky covers the world;
Like a bottomless pit, it is endless
Darker than ever the abyss,
but defying the night is the light of the moon.
It rebels against the darkness,
hanging like a spider from its thread above the Earth,
shining like a light bulb, bright like the sun.

It's proud like a lion, high like an eagle.
The light around it is its mane,
the light around it is its wings.
Many look up to it at night —
and the moon seems to look back down
like a watchman of the world below,
this radiant, glowing diamond of the night.

Joining the moon is the stars.
They seem to dance as they twinkle.
And when they shoot across the sky, on occasion,
never has the Earth seen such a show.
But the coming dawn approaches, vanquishing the night.
Yet, they will always be up there,
looking down from the heavens above.

Hannah Barke, Grade 8
Madrona Middle School

Ode to Tacos!

Mmm! So good!
Your crunchy shell.
Tomatoes, cheese, chicken, lettuce,
Salsa, guacamole, olives, and sour cream
Fresh and delicious —
You never fail
Your goodness will last forever
And ever and ever
You have been around for oh so long
I've never found someone
Who has hated you
Juice dripping, flavors flaming
The ingredients of a well-made taco
I take a bite…
The perfect taco!

Kylie Johnson, Grade 7
Linfield Christian School

Writing Is My Life

Writing is
Traveling to new worlds
Writing is imagination
Creativity
And passion…
Writing is about emotions
Being expressed,
Truth and dedication…
Writing is
My life

Delilah Useda, Grade 8
Corpus Christi School

Fate

Stranded in the darkness
My light has faded away
No longer part of this world
beyond my reach
To what fate shall
I be doomed to live?
I fear the nothingness that awaits me
My life was of no avail
I tried my best
to overcome the obstacles that
challenged me in my life
only to face the force
that would gain dominance
over me in the end
I linger on in darkness
Unable to dream
Unable to escape
Unable to hope
I live now
In the fate that we must all face
someday

Paolo Joson, Grade 8
Robert C Fisler School

How Could You Leave Me Now

I knew it was coming I just didn't know when
As my heart was pounding I was crying to the end
You said you would stay forever but that was all a lie
I knew you were leaving, however I just didn't think you would die.

How could you leave me now I wanted to stay with you
You're gone from head to toe and you're making me feel so blue
You were my grandpa and my best friend I'm gonna miss you until the end.

My heart is filled with sadness and all these memories in my head
My feelings turn into madness and still some words unsaid
No one knows how I feel I don't say much about it
It's still a big deal I really don't understand it.

Kelly Cifu, Grade 8
St Francis de Sales School

Love Life and Live Large

Please miss take charge.
Love life and live large.
Remain proud and chase your dream
Be loud but never scream.
Say what you know and never flee from life's rat race
Don't forget who you are and sail at your own pace
When life gets to be more than a notion just relax
And take notice of the trees, the bees, and the birds.
Truly admire the beauty of this day that you can't put into words.
Please miss take charge
Love life and live large.
Pay no attention to what they say
And always try to seize the day.

Morgan Mayfield, Grade 8
Madrona Middle School

If You Were Here

It's so amazing how time has flown by so fast,
I will always remember that night you passed,
I wasn't there to say my final goodbye,
And just the thought of that makes me want to cry,
I will always cherish the memories we had,
And you not being here with me to make more makes me sad,
Holiday get-togethers aren't the same,
Because without you there, they seem so plain,
If you were still here I know you'd be proud of me,
And the thought of that makes me happy,
There aren't any words that could explain how much I miss you,
But I know you're in a better place now,
And wouldn't want me to go on in sorrow,
I really wish you didn't have to part,
You may not physically be here with me,
But always and forever you'll be in my heart.

Mariah Hacegaba, Grade 8
McCabe Elementary School

Faith

A companion
That never abandons you
Splendid, mysterious feeling
Guiding and advising
Through arduous times
That seem to arrest you in a prison
With no visible escape;
It is that distant star
Gazing at you from afar
Helps one overcome any barrier;
When I ponder about faith,
I smell a subtle,
But comforting scent of roses
Mingled with honey
Transforming my problems into vapor;
Blue resembles the faith
That inhabits your soul
Never say, "I quit"
Instead, keep it alive
For its splendor increases
When malice, hate, and envy attempt to obliterate it.

Jorge Luevano, Grade 8
St Alphonsus School

My Parents

Don't know what I would do without you
Where would I be without you two?
You are the center of my life
Without you, it would cause me strife

You provide me with a great home and food
When I talk with you, I'm in a good mood
You care for me like I'm the best child
Even though sometimes I'm mean and wild

When you're old and alone and gray
I promise you'll see me every day
I'll support you like you did for me
I'll give you the best treatment (oh, you'll see)

Even if we get in a fight
I'll always love you with all my might

Vanessa Liu, Grade 8
Citrus Hills Intermediate School

I Am

I am a wave crashing against the ocean rocks.
I am a cloud in the endless, beautiful, blue sky.
I am the color to a magical painting in the hall.
I am the beat to the song that plays over and over.
I am the reflection you see when you look in the water.
I am the brightest star in the night sky.
I am the rainbow of colors from the morning sunrise.

Dalice Stogden, Grade 7
St. Mary of the Assumption School

Eyes

It seems that they have seen too much,
But never heard one sound, nor felt one touch.
It looks as if they are unbiased, yet looks can be deceiving,
For eyes aren't thinking, they are simply believing.
Believing in evil or good,
Much that we see is misunderstood.
What we see, what we choose to see,
But the truth is, our eyes aren't free.
They are trapped by our thoughts, our mind,
They trap the truth that we finally find.
The truth that is hidden behind a number of lies,
That appear to be good, but are bombs in disguise.
They are waiting to explode, to tear us to shreds,
To take our souls, to fill our lives with dread.
But if our eyes can break through this wall of deception,
Then there is room in our lives for a little correction.

Tressa Mikel, Grade 8
Chino Valley Christian School

Metamorphosis

I used to be wheat on a farm,
Now I'm a taquito with guacamole and cheese.
I used to be a little seed,
Now I am a peanut-caramel apple.
I used to be water,
Now I'm ice-cold lemonade.
I used to be a corn chip,
Now I am a plate of supreme nachos.
I used to be food on a plate,
Now I am food in a stomach.

Jordan Evans, Grade 8
Citrus Hills Intermediate School

Metal

Rage and fire, engulf the stage.
Metal madness, it's on the loose.
Pulses race, across the floor.
As maniacs push, their fists bite.
For nothing more can survive this night.

Air burning, club caught on fire.
The audience deaf, they yearn for more.
Stage explodes, the band pays due.
They return to finish it off.
Crowds rejoice, the flame is back.
Jump in the pit, ready to attack
The master of puppets, it's pulling your strings.
The shockwave silences, many who fear
The power of metal, too great for some to be near.

Metal lives on.
It is now complete.
Its job is done.
And now no more damage can be done.

Dustin Chhum, Grade 9
Fountain Valley High School

A Wave

We passed our neighbors. My dad and I. In the car. He waved. I didn't. Because I was ashamed. And embarrassed.
I asked him
Why?
Why did you wave? Why did you greet them? They didn't say hi to you.
They didn't even wave back. So why bother?
Then my dad got angry.
Son, what's wrong with you! So what if they didn't wave first or if they didn't wave back?
If you look at a mirror, what do you see? You see yourself. Waiting. Watching.
Waiting and watching for the first movement. From you. Your first movement. You frown, the mirror frowns.
But if you smile, the mirror smiles back. If you say hello, the mirror says hello.
If you laugh, the mirror laughs. If you praise the mirror, the mirror praises you.
Son, the world is just one big mirror.
People are just mirrors.
You'll never know if they're going to wave back unless you wave first.
Son, you have to wave first.
Or else no one's going to wave back.
Wave first, and the whole world waves back.
The whole world.
Imagine.
The whole world.

Min-Woo Park, Grade 9
Palos Verdes Peninsula High School

Poetry on Your Mind

Let your mind go like a rapid stream, twisting, flipping and jumping.
Let the words, as colorful as a rainbow, run through your mind.
Let your pencil build up with ideas then erupt onto your paper.
Let your imagination run wild like twelve horses running away from one hundred snakes.
Poetry has her own mind, dancing through yours.
Poetry is something you keep. Even if you're not thinking.

Brooke Rocha, Grade 7
Yolo Middle School

American Dream

I can wish for riches, I can dream of gold.
But after that I'll only want more.
I can wish for all of my wishes and dreams to come true,
But none of that is likely to happen — no matter how much wishing and dreaming I do.
I can want peace and equality, I can need a job.
I can want a family, as well.
Even after all that wanting and needing I know I still have to work hard.
You may call me a dreamer, but!
If we don't want, if we don't dream,
If we don't wish, if we don't need,
How will we know? How will we know what to work toward?
Even though my wish list will always be full, there will always be one less thing to wish for.
This is because those before me had the same wish as well so this is what they got;
The wish, the desire for,
A beautiful place, an equal land,
An America!
And now I understand,
I must keep high hopes, I must work hard.
But no doubt it'll be worth it,
Because I'm a true American as you can see and I have a true American Dream!

Jugleen Sandhu, Grade 8
Union Middle School

Dance Is…
Showing your moves
Getting in the groove
Step it up
Feel the beat
Show what you can do
Flip, flop, turn, hop
Music is so mesmerizing, you just can't stop
No worries,
Feeling free
Come dance with me

Ashtyn Feragen, Grade 8
Citrus Hills Intermediate School

I Am Me
I am me
I am a tiger that's hunting to find someone in this world
I am a butterfly gentle and quiet as I can be
A leaf that flows in the breeze
The wind that blows all your troubles away
I'm a soldier for Mother Nature protecting the planet
And everybody in it
I'm a little dawn confused where to go barely coming in
The world trying to find a friend
The spirit in the forest protecting it from predators
I'm the ocean flow being gentle as I can be
I'm a prisoner of the demon's dungeon
Trying to find a friend in this world in this one life
Can't find no one to trust no one to love
I'm a provider for others but not for me
This is me the only me
I'm myself

Vanessa Gonzales, Grade 8
Buchser Middle School

Impossible
The video game legged cat,
swims to the shopping bag mountains.

And as the clock cupcakes get their
twelve o'clock frosting withered away
by the vanilla flavored wind.

Bull shaped popcorn skips into a
plane full of telephones and watermelons.

Only to crash the plane into a
shopping bag mountain, sparks flying everywhere.

The video game legged cat catches
on water and melts.
The vanilla flavored wind
borrows five dollars from my blouse
and gets stronger
as a dog tastes its intestines.

Sennuwy Johnson, Grade 7
Odyssey Charter School

Iraq War Memorial
You men are all so brave,
it's sad to see your name on a grave.
You fought day and night in Iraq,
and fired bullets the size of a tic-tac.

You are out there without taking a bath,
while we are over here working on math.
Some of you lived and some of you died,
and we figured out and cried.

I wish there were no more war,
and be safe in my home with no door.
I wish the president will shout "no more!"
and everyone's weapons will fall to the floor.

So I build this in memory of you,
because you keep our flag red, white, and blue.
I hope people honor this monument,
And it stands for years without having a dent.

Arthur Gonzalez, Grade 8
Citrus Hills Intermediate School

Ode to Mom
Oh mom, why do you clean for us
When you could make us do it for you
You should never clean after us
We can clean after ourselves
You shouldn't clean after us
We want to help you but you don't want help
We love you enough to clean after ourselves
We mess up and there you are cleaning the mess
We sometimes want to help you
When you work hard it makes us feel bad
Please let us help
You don't have to do it all by yourself
We love you so let us help
Please let us help…
Love your children
Brandon, Yuri, Kimberly, and Julio
Love you too much mom

Brandon Pineda, Grade 7
Santa Rosa Technology Magnet School

I Know
I know basketball
Players running, smart and cunning
Dripping sweat with people you haven't met.
I know basketball
"Ay ref that's a foul"
"No need to growl"
I know basketball
Players dribbling, fans nibbling,
Coaches yelling, food stands selling.

Salman Nazaar, Grade 8
Citrus Hills Intermediate School

Sports

Sports: dedicated to a profession
Sports: you love with passion
Basketball, baseball, football
I love them all
Sports: the love of the game
Sports: hoping for fortune and fame
Basketball, baseball, football
I love them all
Xavier Wells, Grade 8
Long Valley Charter School

Cheat

He promised to love me
And never stop,
But when I found out he cheated
My heart had dropped.

I thought of all the times
We kissed and all the
Other things I missed
He broke my heart in two.

Something he said
He would never do.
I asked myself
Why he cheated…why?

Then I told myself
To stay strong
And move on.
Lauren Andrade, Grade 8
McCabe Elementary School

Winter's Angel

Oh Mei Song. Your alabaster hair,
White as winter's air.
Mei Song. Eyes of cool blue ice.
So calm yet so precise.
Ms. Mei Song. Skin of porcelain.
As soft as smooth linen.
Yet the chilled season,
Has taken you so sudden.
Yes the beautiful Mei Song.
Now long long gone.
How the winter is harsh and cruel.
Yet frail and forever a jewel.
Almost like…Mei Song.
Now as I look upon the snowflakes,
My heart tries not to break.
For it is Mei Song.
This is where she belongs.
In twirled in the cold of ice and snow.
She will stay with wings on her back.
And an ice crystal halo.
Nicole De La Torre, Grade 7
Frank M Wright Middle School

Abraham Lincoln

The wonderful 16th president, Abraham Lincoln, born February 12, 1809
An inspirational president: Abraham Lincoln
A respected man whose nationality was American
Had a faithful spouse, Mary Todd Lincoln, and was a proud parent

Member of the U.S. House of Representatives from Illinois
Against expansion of slavery
Lincoln won the magnificent Republican Party nomination

He had great days and the worst
As his life took its course
He was assassinated and was the first
At 57 to go out with force

The president of the U.S. is really dead —
But maybe not in your head
He went down in history; at least he got to feel what it's like to be
A significant person in our nation: Abraham Lincoln
Kasie Sorey, Grade 9
Lucerne Valley Jr/Sr High School

My House

My house.
I smell the food my mom is preparing.
I see my cat playing with a string on the floor.
I hear my favorite show on the TV.
I touch the remote to change the channel.
I taste the cold and refreshing orange soda as it goes down my throat.
My house is where my five senses come to life and become me.
Max Brogley, Grade 7
St Cyprian School

isolated

i feel so trapped inside
just like a bird who cannot fly,
i wish i could be me
i only dreamed of being free.
i have to hide my face
behind this mocking mask,
not really showing the world who i truly am
always alone in this haunting four-wall cellar.
at times i feel so sad
as if i had lost a loved one,
other times i feel so happy
like i succeeded something on my own.
always standing out
from the rest of the crowd,
being teased and called names
being misjudged and misunderstood.
when i was safe i'd cry
my cries would dance around hysterically and laugh at me,
eventually the real me was suppressed behind this mocking mask
i am no longer me, i am no longer free.
i am isolated from myself, and from the rest of the crowd.
Richard Suwa, Grade 8
Madrona Middle School

Love

Love is pain,
but it is also everlasting joy.
With it, there is no shame,
it is in every girl and boy.
Our hearts shade our true feelings,
we must keep faith,
and keep believing.
Love is blind,
for you are not aware where you are going,
or what you are bound to find.
If you pursue love and persevere,
your loved one will grow ever near.
Love will last if you are kind,
but not unless you set differences aside.
Love is forever if you are smart,
lovers promise, "till death do us part."
Love is the angels' song,
that remains ever long.
Do not let love fool you,
whether it fills you with anger, sorrow or glee.
Love is never free.

Vence Quirante, Grade 7
Holy Family Catholic School

Locked Up

When I'm alone I am myself
But with people I am someone else
I don't know why that I am so shy
But with my friends I'm kind of myself
I don't know why I feel locked up inside,
Like myself can't get through
But somehow the other person managed to.

Myranda Macias, Grade 8
McCabe Elementary School

What Is Life?

Life is in all of us.
Life is feeling, breathing, and living,
From the smallest baby to the oldest man.

Life is in all of us.
Life is love, hope, and loneliness,
From times of despair, to times of regret.
Life is like a wave strong, and fragile,
Like a baby's heart.

Life is in all of us.
Life has its ups, downs, twists, and turns.
Life is an inexplicable miracle,
A joy that warms one's heart.
Most importantly
Life is all of us.

Mayra Villa, Grade 7
Blessed Sacrament School

Winter Winds

Snowflakes dancing as they fall,
Wind is blowing like a call.
Nothing growing, nothing there,
An animal hides in its lair.

Kids playing in the snow,
On their sleds, down they go.
Winter winds are unkind,
Soon spring approaches from behind.

Leaves re-grow and snow melts away,
Progress speeds every day.
Pretty soon, here you have it,
Flowers blossom bit-by-bit.

As the last hints of winter are no longer present,
The weather begins to feel quite pleasant.
Winter frost bite is a thing of the past,
Wow, you realize winter came quite fast.

Now the birds and bees are about,
Frolicking in the park, you give a shout.
For no longer you don your hats and mittens,
And the sun suddenly begins to brighten.

Cassie Kocalis, Grade 8
Madrona Middle School

The Deepest Depth

My wildest dreams come from my imagination
Which guides me through this road called life
My mind creates my determination
To hustle, succeed, and fight
My eyes create my vision
To guide, coordinate, and seek
My mouth creates my gentle voice
To eat, laugh, and speak
My ears create my hearing
To obey, learn, and hear
My hands create my sensitive touch
To hold, feel, and grab
My legs create my mobility
To walk, run, and dance
My self-expression as a human is
The gateway key to life
But only if I had soft wings
To float, soar, and fly…

Johnny Vasquez, Grade 8
La Joya Middle School

Summer

Summer time is full of fun
School ends and summer begins
It gets hot outside so you can take a swim.
Vacations and 4th of July are great memories.

Chase Lockwood, Grade 7
Packinghouse Christian Academy

Gentle Goodbye

Oh sweet, sweet sun, rise
As I fall with such great demise.

I do not want to hurt you so,
But I really really have to go.

My dear, you're so very sweet,
Someday again I'd hope to meet.

My dear, be strong, do not cry,
It is but only a gentle goodbye.

Kellie Carlson, Grade 7
Citrus Hills Intermediate School

Bare Are the Trees of Winter

Bare are the trees of winter
'Tis night of winter day
It sends my heart a flutter
Which I gladly set away

The wind bellows with no allay
But the skin feels not a scar
Though the turmoil had its harsh way
It's presence is never afar

Hark! The wind thrashes in its tempest
But near time it will calm
And again return to the forest
Serene, shy, chary, and qualm

The gale carries its seeds in bliss
How rapid the seeds enliven
It brings the seeds from the abyss
And into the mouths of heaven

Bare are the trees of winter
'Tis night of winter day
Bearing the marks of friendship
Please, do not go away!

Jeffrey Wang, Grade 8
Chino Valley Christian School

Taking It the Hard Way

Taking the vigorous road
Is like a sour patch
At first it is so hard and sour
But then it starts to dissolve into its
Sweeter state.
The goodness of what I learned
The knowledge much I've gained
Now I have so many
Accomplishments in my brain
I have finally reached
The sweeter side of life.

Regina Park, Grade 8
Robert C Fisler School

My Green-eyed Tiger

My cat Rose is a rag doll, covered in fluff with a long furry tail.
His purr is soothing like music.
He talks to me like he always knows what I'm saying.
Rose and I play mouse and string games, and spend lots of time together.
I love him, and he is my pal.

One day, my stuffed tiger began to limp.
The vet said he had cancer.
My heart was broken.
Would I lose my best buddy?
Would he survive?

The doctor took him as I held in the tears.
My hand trembled as she took the cage.
He looked out at me with big watery green eyes.
I said my last goodbye and cried.
What would life be without him?

The doctor took his leg, but not his soul.
He got better, and everyone rejoiced and smiled.
Though he has only three legs, he still has a tiger's heart.
He races up the stairs in front of me, and perches on the back of the couch.
One night he chased a raccoon out of his yard.
I will always love him, he is my pal.

Megan Hillendahl, Grade 8
Bethany Lutheran School

My Friend's Smile

I remember when my friend would smile at me every day
She would run to me yelling my name with a long curved line replacing her mouth
I remember when she would daily tell me her dreams
She would explain it in a way that would always make me confused
I remember that night when we went out together to the by
The wind was breezy
The water was wavy
The leaves were applauding
The moon was shimmering together with some clouds
And she was smiling at me
But just at that moment
That moment that I never forgot
That moment that I hated my whole life
That moment when I spoke the three words
That three words that ruined my life
The three words
I love you
Those three words that slipped out of my mouth
Those three words that took her smile away
And sliced the only string of friendship that I had in half

I never saw that smile again

Ernesto Ng, Grade 7
Purple Lotus International Institute

Halloween

What an orange holiday.
Myths and legends on a foggy night
Are scary and rare
Little children running to a haunted house,
Adults tossing candy out
To all the excited kids on the block
All the trick-or-treaters
Hunting for candy in the busy city
Candy wrappers scattered on the streets,
Waiting hours to be picked up
Everyone is putting a candle in a pumpkin.

Daniel Caracoza, Grade 7
St Alphonsus School

When You Learn

When you learn that Death is waiting around every corner
Waiting to embrace life with his bony fingers;
When you learn that Love is the only thing
That hurts and heals at the same time;
When you learn that Life is unfair
And that it'll trip you up every chance it gets;
When you learn that sometimes friends aren't friends
And that it's wise to keep your enemies close;
When you learn that sometimes you have to hurt loved ones
Just for them to become better people;
When you learn that you can't save everyone
And that Life forces Change whether you like it or not;
When you learn that Faith takes you a long way in life
And that Trust joins it hand in hand;
When you learn that you have to pick yourself up
Especially when you've fallen from a great height
When you learn that you need your family and friends
And you learn that you need God to be in control;
When you, like me, learn that you're still learning
Then you, my dear brother, are on your way to growing up.

Samantha Chong, Grade 9
Valley Christian High School

Memory

I remember you were so beautiful and kind
You always made me feel special, having fun
Not caring what would happen tomorrow
As long as we had fun today
You made me happy, always knowing what to say
You were so happy and full of life
You were the one thing that made me happy
But unfortunately all good things must come to an end
And when you were in the hospital we would visit
But it seemed no one was home, you were tired
I could tell that fire that you had had been put out
So when the time came for you to let go
I felt relieved that you didn't have to struggle anymore
And I knew you were at peace with the Lord.
I will miss you now and forever, Nana.

Nathan Lamonte, Grade 7
Linfield Christian School

Continuous Pain

Continuous pain never stops
Never decreases but increases
Never to feel the warmth you once felt
The warmth of a bed
The feeling of a pillow snug under your head
But now you feel
The pain that is real
The continuous pain goes on and on
Until the one you once knew as yourself is gone
Your body, indulged in pain
Your mind, dark
Your soul, bitter
Oh only if you knew the feeling
The feeling that I have had
Then you would understand
The feeling of continuous pain

Michael Tait, Grade 8
Santa Rosa Technology Magnet School

Observation of a Masterpiece

I think it's beautiful
Because of how the river flows
Because of how the tree grows
Because of how the plains roam
The house is old and bright
The people there are full of life
What holds the bridge is the brick foundation
Creaky wood planks help to come across
Clouds as fluffy and bright as ever
The sky fades into the darkest blue
On the side of the river the fishermen fish
A dark shady lady crosses the river
She uses her trusty umbrella to block the sun
Another dark figure
But I question if it's a man or woman
Trotting his horse attached to a carriage
The river calm so steady
How the artist makes magic
Better he makes it out of nothing
Just a white canvas
It is a masterpiece

Gabriela Bolin, Grade 8
Daniel Savage Middle School

Elaina

My lips are like the juice of a fruit
My eyes are like the bloom of a flower
My hands are soft as a baby's bottom
My loving heart holds personality
That is joyful as a sunny day
I live in my own world that suits my personality
And I eat the success that comes to me.

Elaina Chapman, Grade 8
Citrus Hills Intermediate School

Ode to Baseball Games

I love the smell
of freshly cut grass
walking into a stadium
I love the taste
of hot roasted peanuts
watching my favorite team
play their rivals
The loud echo of
the crack of the bat
after my favorite player
takes one deep
I love going to
baseball games

Jonathan Mederos, Grade 8
La Joya Middle School

Old Bike

I have an old bike,
don't use it anymore
compared to my new one it is a bore

It's pretty rusty and dirty
but underneath that dirt and mold,
it is some real gold

Wow I had lots of fun with that bike
it was really sturdy and never failed

I think I'm going to clean it up
I hope it rides the same, probably won't.

Mohammed Hamdy, Grade 8
McCabe Elementary School

Nature's Time

The bark of a dog,
The meow of a cat.
The roll of a log,
The chipmunk's quick chat.

The rustling of leaves,
The spray of the seas.
The new morning eves
With the buzzing of bees.

The blue jay's smooth tweet,
The apple tree's bud.
The deer's eyes so sweet,
A tiny white dove.

The coyote's loud howl,
The moon shining bright.
The hoot of an owl,
It's now nature's night.

Kaelen Jones, Grade 7
Chino Valley Christian School

Wonder

In an elevator
In a car
At school

In the house
On the train
Or with you

My dreams are flowing
Like a river into
The ocean

As they linger in the
Atmosphere and will
Never disappear

Jasmine Mueller, Grade 8
Jefferson Middle School

Skateboarding

Skateboarding
A way of life
The people you'll meet
The tricks you'll do
The places you will go
Are yet to be discovered
The reputations hurt
You create your name
Along with your fame
The lifestyle is hard
Pain is always near
The falling
The fun
The reward is great
Like nothing else
My dream is to rise to the top
The key is to stay true
Let skateboarding become you
A way of life

Brad Power, Grade 8
Coronado Middle School

Imagination

I n your mind
M agical
A nything you dream of
G reat
I ncredible
N o limits
A visual dream
T ruly yours
I nfinite possibilities
O ne of a kind
N ot controllable

Marie Aguinaldo, Grade 7
St Mary of Assumption School

The Simpsons

Oh, TV you hang on the wall
Without a complaint at all.
You make the room brighten up
On dark stormy days
As I watch the Simpsons
Live out their days.
You tell me what's hip,
But you also tell me what's
Going on around the globe.
You can use rabbit ears or
Satellite
To get your channels
From high to low.

Cynthia Ruiz, Grade 8
Citrus Hills Intermediate School

Reflection

look upon thee
into thy eyes
see what I've seen
what I wish I didn't see
what I wish I could forget
look upon thee
at thy hands
dirty as they are
yet strong soldiers
look upon thee
at thy back
with burdening scars of lashes
look upon thee
into thy heart
thy soul
thy mind
look upon thee
find me

Madison Tegen, Grade 7
Black Mountain Middle School

Is Revenge Always So Sweet?

You go into it thinking one thing,
you expect to feel so great
But the sounds you hear,
may not always suffice

Revenge is a tricky business,
you don't always like how you feel
You've thought about it for awhile,
but how you feel just isn't nice

Some people feel great in the end,
others just aren't the same
Some are filled with happiness,
others with pure shame

Hailee Stanton, Grade 8
La Joya Middle School

Sailing into Spring
Spring is coming about…
With flowers and trees
Coming to life…
With the birds and the bees sailing around…

The fresh fragrances of spring…
The warm breeze splashing against your skin…
The lively scenes of active play…
On course for adventure and holiday!

Truly, spring is coming about!

Claudia Alvarenga, Grade 8
Corpus Christi School

Goodbye for I Won't See You Until It's Time
I've said hello
I've said goodbye

I'd tell you I'll see you tomorrow
But then it would be a lie

There is something wrong
God thought you shouldn't live for long

So now you are up above
And looking down on us like a dove

Better yet an angel

Andrew Quezada, Grade 8
McCabe Elementary School

Our Almighty Protector
God is ruler of all things
He reaches out His hands,
And gives us what we don't deserve.
God has all the power in the world,
And He still cares for us,
Even though we are very small in comparison.
He shows us the right way down our path,
The path He has known for us to be,
How we will live and where we'll end up,
He already knows.
God of gods, He rules above,
Not one enemy can prevail.
Through everything God is good
And He leads us to victory.
Through the hardest times of our lives
When we think no one understands,
God's mighty hand will come down,
And bless each disturbed soul
So that we can live for eternity
With the God that made everything.

Erin McLean, Grade 7
Chino Valley Christian School

Ode to Vans
Ahhhh, Vans the shoes,
How I love my white-soled purple Vans.
They always put my outfit together.
Every time I go to the shoe store,
I squeal with joy for the squeaky-clean shoes.
I never know which color I'm going to get,
There are blue and green, yellow and red,
Turquoise, baby blue, even multicolored!
Sometimes there are suede Vans up on the wall,
Looking as beautiful as can be.
They call to me from the rack,
"Buy me, Buy me, please?"
I see my fellow Vans lovers
Walking down the street,
In their simple but gorgeous shoes.
I call to them "Hey" or "What's up?" when I see them.
I think everyone should own a pair,
Of the comfortable Vans shoes!

Elizabeth Kunde, Grade 7
Linfield Christian School

Musical Memories
Orchestra is a calm world with friends
Memories of middle school practicing a note
Long hours playing what a musician wrote
The air has scents of rosin and polished wood
Bows dancing on strings, sounding so good
Strings lightly touching smooth horse hair
Makes everything sound so fair
Performance of classical music centering violins and cellos
All eyes were on the magnificent fellows
The song will soon be over
As the curtains will cover
Music will never be put to an end

Angeline Nguyen, Grade 9
Fountain Valley High School

Sorrow
A beautiful, one of a kind, blue lady who has
two beautiful blue eyes,

who cries out sadness in every tear drop, who
has a death wish in her mind,

her skin is her favorite color; she hopes for a
date full of happiness,

she is so sad she can't even eat anything but
sadness and stress,

her best friend named fear died of unhappiness and stress,
and that is what she thinks is going to

happen to her.

Bria Marie Scott, Grade 8
Odyssey Charter School

About My Pets

My bird Chico
Plays with his toys
At noon every day
At my house in his cage
He is bored.

My eel
Hiding in his cave
All day and all night except when feeding
In his fish tank
For protection.

My dead fish
Floating upside-down
Until he decays
Down my flushed toilet
My eel bit him.

Kai Paresa, Grade 7
Monte Vista Christian School

Wrong, Wrong, Wrong!

Everything went wrong,
From English to math.
I felt very depressed.
I got lost in my path.

Nothing was working,
Nothing at all.
I didn't know what to do.
My problems grew tall.

I finally gathered courage,
To do what I must do.
Working hard and smart,
I found a way through.

Life goes on,
And my troubles have passed.
I am calm and peaceful.
I am sure that will last.

Apoorva Dornadula, Grade 8
Hopkins Jr High School

Summer Storm

A stormy day
The clouds are mad
Booming every minute
Keeping back the sun today
The world seems very gloomy

Bolts of light flashing down
Coming closer every time
Raindrops fall one by one
I can tell this won't be fun

Cooper Wilkerson, Grade 8
Madrona Middle School

And Now It's Gone

It started with the words, "I have a tumor…"
When I heard this, I knew it was no rumor.
At this point, a frown fell upon my face,
And I felt as though I had lost the ultimate race.
There was definitely no happiness or cheer,
But in my heart crept a wave of fear.
I kept my faith and my persistence,
From her side I was never a long distance.
When I got this call, I was not alone
For I got the greatest news from a call on my phone.
It was about two or three hours from dawn,
When I got the news, "The tumor was there! And now it's gone!"

Chase Lombard, Grade 8
Chino Valley Christian School

Nature

Our lives and our world are filled with nature
From mountainous peaks over shady, foggy valleys
To the windy meadows, basking in the sun's warm rays
To the deep cave pond, where the dripping of water is only heard

Nature is all around us, surrounding us with exultant beauty
And feeling ever so extricate in this open world.
Nature is everything in this world and how each
Individual views it as, whether it is unpleasant or admirable

From lush trees that are ever so verdant
To the plateaus and mesas that seem so vacant
From the dank bayou, so stick and somber
To the snow on the hill that won't last much longer

From the open plains, with fresh bloom and bouquet
To the lawn where elders play croquet
From the delicate, innocent flower as small as can be
Nature is everything, everything you see.

Chris Bugarin, Grade 8
St Victor Elementary School

Next Door Savior

Someone came knocking, knocking at my door.
I opened to find him.
He invited himself in, and I am surprised to see I let this stranger in.
He knew I had troubles, and he came to help.
He listened to my troubles, and my ordinary needs.
I am startled to see I did not find him slumbering.
To every little trouble he had a resolution.
To every little need he solved it with an explanation.
I was on the brink of darkness, despair, to never come back,
But he fished me out and brought me back.
When I plummeted down the wrong way he took my hand and guided me back.
When I stumbled or strayed he had carried me on.
When I went astray like a shepherd he had guided me back.
This man was a neighborhood friendly, my next door savior.
But, it really was Jesus Christ my Redeemer.

Joseph Lee, Grade 7
Chaminade College Prep Middle School

Sundays Wash

Sunday is the day she bathes
And so I wish my dog behaves
The time it takes to get her done
Is worth it all because she'll shine like the light from the sun
When I wash her with shampoo
My brother prays she would not poo
Then she jumps out of the tub
And squirms like a cold baby cub
I click on the black blow dyer
And the water on her fur slowly dances away
Now Ellie is done with her bath
My reward is a kiss and a half

Melissa Le, Grade 9
Fountain Valley High School

Friends

Friends are mostly people you know and trust.
Friends are so sweet they could be candy.
Friends are there for you and will never fuss.
They hang with you like cloth and are handy.
Friends are cool because you can go out with them.
They are also cool as some ice.
Friends can call you at 8 o'clock p.m.
Friends are like psychologists with no price.
You can talk to friends about everything.
True friends do not tell secrets to others.
True friends can also tell you anything.
Good friends can also count on one another.
Friends give you all the company you need.
Friends can also keep you from smoking weed.

Priscilla Toro, Grade 8
Henry T Gage Middle School

Life Is…

Life is a ship, sailing on the ocean
and you are the captain,
leading every command
and your ship is caught up in a storm
but you steer your way right out of it,
unharmed and heading wherever the waters take you

Life is a book, filled with pages
and you are the author,
creating infinite tales
but you don't like this story,
so you change it, rearrange it
every day is a new chapter, waiting for you to write it

Life is a mystery, full of suspense and adventure
and you are the detective,
searching for clues
but life is a case nobody can crack
so instead of trying to solve it,
just live it, and you might find a greater clue along the way

Kimberly Tran, Grade 8
Thornton Jr High School

Taxes Aren't Bad

Taxes are high you say
Hundreds of dollars a day
The money you see go
The government seems to be our foe

Well, it goes to a good cause
It helps to enforce laws
You get to drive your cars on paved roads
Helps enforce our penal codes

Your children get well educated
The fire department is very dedicated
Taxes aren't bad
In face they're rad!

Jimmy Dempsey, Grade 8
Carmel Valley Middle School

School

School may be cool
School might be for a fool
School school what to do
School is a place to learn and experience new things
School shows you how to succeed in life
School is only 13 years plus college
School is a place to make friends
School is a fun place to be
School is the only place to be on Monday thru Friday

Jason Cardenas, Grade 8
McCabe Elementary School

my life is like a river

sometimes
i fall into the rapids and
i have no control of where i am going or
what is happening.
the weight of the world is on my shoulders
the waters slam me against hidden boulders and
my head is dunked underneath the current.
i cannot breathe. i scream.
the water fills my lungs.
the stress suffocates me.

other times
the current is calm.
i can control where i am heading and
nothing slams me about.
relaxation flows around and over me.
i gently float on down
without worry.
i am cool. i laugh.
the water washes away my worry.
the stress has left.

Amber Suto, Grade 8
Robert C Fisler School

Girl

The duration of my days are spent under the excruciatingly bright lights of a man-made microscope
Unlike the twinkling stars seen crystal clearly through a gateway to heaven AKA the telescope

People say I am exceptionally gorgeous, and effortlessly beautiful
Yet what I see in myself is so short of ever achieving anything meaningful

I am surrounded by a startling sea of perfectly starved size two's
Size two are you kidding me? My fat feet would never fit into those skinny shoes

I am not affected in the slightest way by overpriced pressure from my exceedingly infantile peers
My own piercingly painfully perfect criticism of my most minuscule deformities
Evokes more than my fair share of pointless and wasted tears

I was always told to never give up to keep valiantly trying
But with trying comes failing
Failing flat on my "gorgeous" blue-eyed face
What if I fail when I am going my fastest of pace?

At the moment love is an abstract intangible fantasy
I have to vividly wonder is there really anyone out there who would truly undoubtedly want me?

To many growing older, further away from your prime, is an overbearing tragedy
Not being bold enough to take the simple risks I need to take to grasp my innermost desires is and would be my tragedy
What's yours?

Riley Driscoll, Grade 8
Carmel Valley Middle School

She Is

I have a strong feeling, an uncontrollable urge
It can't be contained or cloaked
The simple idea torments my mind
Leaving an incessant thought that can't be diverted or appeased
Do you know what this is?
It's the thought that keeps me from sleeping
One who I will not cede for. Now do you know?
It's a girl

There are many great reasons why she can't escape my mind
Some of the reasons are because she is delicate, intelligent, and kind
She is like a star who shines for all to see
She is like a lotus, a true miracle of nature
She is like a rose, her moods change the colors, but still remaining adorable
She is transcendent, an angel in disguise
She is one of my blessings, her voice is my favorite soundtrack

Finding one like her would be, like finding a needle in a world covered with haystacks
Like finding your place when all you see is darkness, like escaping a bottomless hole,
Many lambaste me for this, giving me ignominy, with criticism and strife
But the thought of her diverts my attention from the attrition and discord
There would be no shortcuts I'd take to her, because there are no shortcuts to a place worth going to
She is everything I want because she is everything I'm not

Christian Casuga, Grade 8
St Victor Elementary School

Moving School

Its a new day and I'm going to a new school
Everything is new to me.
Everyone is curious about me,
And I'm embarrassed each time they stare at me.
First day is hardest,
New teacher, new friend, new house.
Everything is new to me
I remember about my old friend, house, and teachers
One day he gave me a hand and was friends with me.

James Cho, Grade 8
Robert C Fisler School

Music

Music is what I use to get by
Lets me sleep well every night
Helps me better myself to become a new person
In my body all day long
Helps me to focus
This is my high
Makes me feel so good
This is what I need
This is what I love
This is what makes me tough
What soothes me and makes me rough
Music is my everything

Jorge Gamboa, Grade 8
Richard Merkin Middle Academy

How He Left Us

There was dark shadows over our heads,
It looked like it was going to rain.
I felt lonely and left out.
I thought that the world was going to end.
Everything that I saw was turning black.
Everyone was wearing black.
Everyone was crying their hearts out.
I couldn't see him.
I couldn't see him.

All the time, I could picture him how he looked like.
All the time, I could picture him what his personality was like.
All the time, I could picture him in life.
All I could do is picture him.
Nothing else.
I couldn't see him.
I couldn't see him.

Yes, he just went to heaven like that.
Didn't get to see him.
Didn't get to talk to him.
Couldn't believe he just left our family like that.
My grandfather, my grandfather, my grandfather...

Juliana Lee, Grade 8
Robert C Fisler School

The Mighty Mouse Named Paul Revere

Paul Revere the mouse rode on a very fast cat
The cat was always prepared to leave and never sat
It was ready to go far and near
With his friend Paul Revere.
Paul Revere the mouse
Was fleeing from his house
He wanted to share his voice
With his newfound choice.
Cheese is one thing he was fighting for
He did not want one type but more
Paul Revere also wanted to be free
And never again have to flee.
Concord was where Paul was heading
But the British bull dogs saw him, that he was dreading
As you may not know there was not one but another two
Who were fighting for freedom too
Sadly two of the mice were captured at last
But the third one was very fast.
Now the mice knew how to defend
Mice no longer had something to fear
The ride to freedom was very near!

Cynthia Echeverria, Grade 8
Palm Desert Charter Middle School

My Heart My Soul

My soul is hungry for friendship
My heart aches for forgiveness
I can't seem to make things long
Every day, every year where we change in time
The absolute gives me ease to my soul
Afternoon blaze, morning heat, night times — daze
Make it cruel it doesn't feel good
Heart why do you do so?
The art and spirit of *a* soul is not very pleasant
Lovely person, beautiful spirit
My soul my heart is just
Broken up, shriveled up dusty old pieces
Blow away my heart my soul

Ismael Noel Ramirez, Grade 8
McCabe Elementary School

Love Is True

You are the love of my life,
But you are not considered my wife,
My knees go weak when I see you walk,
My throat goes dry when I hear you talk,
Your eyes are like a perfect chocolate bar,
They're so sweet and you're beautiful the way you are,
You are the only girl I wouldn't let go by,
Because you are the apple of my eye,
You are the most beautiful girl ever,
If I had to stay away I'd say never,
This is too good to be true,
I know what love is because of you.

Cody Den Beste, Grade 8
Madrona Middle School

Nothing But Change

I've watched you change
In the meadow of burning grass
Your eyes hunger for compassion
Staring into the green blue lights,

You feel so alive
Dancing in the modest burning meadow
Eyes savage with lies
Lights screaming in the night sky,

It's like you don't have wings
Singing in the fire that surrounds you
Eyes composed of overjoyed fear
Windows tinted with green lights,

You gave all love
You bring your knees to the earth
Your eyes break down reality
I've watched you change.

Kyle Bumacod, Grade 8
Madrona Middle School

Battle in the Night

Boom boom, goes the drums.
Bang bang, goes the guns.
When the sun comes up,
The hero's day is done.

Boom boom, goes his heart.
Bang bang, goes his soul.
When victory is in sight,
He finally is whole.

Boom boom, goes the friend.
Bang bang, then he falls.
At the blow of the trumpet,
He will answer God's call.

Boom boom, goes the drums.
Bang bang, goes the guns.
When the sun comes up,
The victory is won.

Madeline Block, Grade 8
La Reina High School

Priceless

You are very special to me
I rarely tell you so
Because you mean so much
More than words can ever show
I love you with all my heart
Whether you realize it or not
You are the reason I'm happy
The love you show me is priceless

Sergio Vargas, Grade 8
Richard Merkin Middle Academy

Riding

When I start my dirtbike my heart starts racing
My mind starts pacing when I pull in the clutch
I feel adrenaline rush through my veins
As my left shifts up and I feel the bike jump. I'm hooked and can't get away,
As I turn the throttle and slowly release the clutch
My bike starts accelerating as I let go of the clutch and shift up
I feel free and in control when the terrain gets rougher
My mind starts asking my questions both dangerous and safe
Some I answer and regret but some I don't
When she stops and the motor comes to a final purr
I get off ready and already waiting
For the next day.

Austin Ball, Grade 8
McCabe Elementary School

Love Is

People who don't know what love is are those who don't love
and those who don't love have no one to love
Love is a feeling that fills you up inside
Love is joy and happiness
Love is an excuse for dying, a reason to live
Love is pain when it leaves, but heals you when you're hurt
Love makes the world spin around and I wanted to give you some of mine

Demi Ayala, Grade 7
Chaparral Middle School

The Heart Touching World War I

World War I was also called the Great War.
Over 71 million military personnel were mobilized.
Over 15 million people were demolished in the war.
June 28, 1914, was the assassination of Archduke Franz Ferdinand.

The war began as a clash between the coalitions of European countries.
World War I involved many countries of Europe.
World War I Eventually lead in to World War II in 1939,
The League of Nations was formed in the hope of preventing another conflict.

By the end of the war there were 4 major imperial powers.
Russia had been militarily and politically defeated.
The revolutionized Soviet Union emerged from the Russia Empire.
The map of central Europe was completely redrawn.

When everyone was shooting, it was deafening.
People were running and rolling around for their lives.
Some people were in deep trenches to hide.
Everyone's heart and faith were crumbling.

Yet after all of this pain and demolition,
Most people do not realize and remember
What they went through for every man's freedom.

Bryce Beavers, Grade 9
Lucerne Valley Jr/Sr High School

Life All Around Us

When you look around you,
What do you see?
I see live trees, live flowers, live growing
Grass, live bees, live butterflies, live birds,
That means God gifted us with life.

Blossom Castaneda, Grade 7
Our Lady of the Rosary School

The Unknown Presence

The brightness of the sun cannot cease to exist,
because I live in the darkness of the night,
I do come out in day,
because I live in the shadows.
You cannot see me,
you cannot hear me,
and you don't know I'm here.

You can't see me because I'm in the dark,
But I can see you because you're in the light,
and to my sadness that is how it must be.
Me never to see the light,
and you never to see the beauty of stars at night.

Even with the stars there is not light at night,
and even when the clouds go over the sun,
there is never darkness.

Vanessa Caldera, Grade 8
McCabe Elementary School

Life's Stress

Stress is like a seed,
So very innocent and small,
But it begins to grow and leads
Into something quite serious and tall.

Stress can cause both help and harm,
It can motivate you to try your very best,
Or the pressure can be a great alarm,
The tension can also add a little zest.

Stress is like an open sore,
When it disappears you feel relief,
But once again, it's opened like a door,
And the pain comes out from its sheath.

Stress cannot be avoided in full,
And you must learn to understand
That life without it might be very dull,
And nobody would care about our land.

Stress is like an ancient law,
It keeps the world in order and peace.
Without stress there would be many flaws,
Nothing would get done, and work would cease.

Dylan Flanders, Grade 8
Lindero Canyon Middle School

I Will Still Love You

Why when I text him, he doesn't respond?
And when I try to talk to him, he turns the other way?
I smile at him, he ignores me
Every chance I get, I try to hang out with him
But he acts like I am not there
Does he even know I exist?
No matter what, I will still love him…but will I regret this?
I guess I will just let fate intervene.

Ashley Schafer, Grade 8
Holy Family Catholic School

Remember

Remember the time we lied to stay in each other's arms

Remember

Remember how it felt to be loved
how the touch of my lips made you freeze
Thinking about how all we would do is dance
and make it seem like nobody else was around

Remember

I remember the time we wouldn't let go of each other
just because we were afraid to be alone

Remember

Remember every song we sang was like a touch of energy
rushing through our veins hoping the song will never stop

Remember

Tahirah Hill, Grade 9
Golden Valley High School

My Crayon Box

Upon a desk
Lay a box with crayons held within
Handfuls of color
I carefully take out and place on the desk
All so different,
But then so alike
Although different colors and wrappers,
They all start out the same
As I sit and observe,
I come to realize,
"Life's a box of crayons.
We are the crayons
All sorts of colors and sizes,
But we're all made of wax,
Everyone is equal
No matter what they say."

Jessica D. Campos, Grade 8
St Cyprian School

Emotions

Love is the greatest feeling,
Love is like a play,
Love is what I feel for you,
Each and every day,
Love is like a smile,
Love is like a song,

Love is a great emotion,
Keep us going strong,
Loving you with all my heart,
My body and my soul,
Keeps me staying strong.

I love, the way I love,
A wild love, I can't control,
I love with all my heart,
And my entire soul,
Right from the start.

Wendy Vallecillo, Grade 7
Blessed Sacrament School

Singular

I am a single grain of sand
on the beach.
I am a single drop of water
in the rain.
I am a single star
in the night sky.
But I still shine.

Jomari Geronimo, Grade 8
Corpus Christi School

Obsessive Follower

Every little thing I do you see.
What do you want from me?
A conversation with another
you are right between.
The sound of my voice rings
in your ears.
The seed of love you planted
in my heart
has now drowned in
the black water you
poured out onto me.
I can't breathe,
I can't move,
you watch as a hungry hawk
ready to devour me, it seems.
I can't take it much longer.
Leave me and don't look back,
you only wanted me
for your plots and your needs.
Walk away and don't pretend to miss me
because I know you're no good for me.

Michelle Reynoso, Grade 8
Our Lady of the Rosary School

My Dad's Race

The stands are full of yelling people
I stand in the truck bed and turn to take in the moment
The engines start up and they are rumbling
And the crowd becomes quiet
And now they are all just mumbling
The time has come when the cars get very loud
That I have to cover my ears
And so does half the crowd
The tree changes colors going from five yellow lights to one green
Then the cars take off roaring like angry lions down the track
The nerves dance through my body because in one car sits my dad
And all I can do is hope that nothing will ever go bad

Ashlyn Sacchette, Grade 9
Fountain Valley High School

Bessie Coleman

They would have never thought
I was excellent at school
I was accepted in many big places
Where people went and their minds went crazy

My dad never liked where we lived
He was tired, days passed, he was gone
I had to come out of my box and work
I was young; many people believed in me

But what did they believe in?
I couldn't believe it, it was amazing —
I knew I would not live long enough
To fulfill my dreams. I had to do something, but what?

While I was excellent in life and in school
I was confident about myself
My dreams came alive; I was free
I had become the first African American woman to become a pilot
Bessie Coleman

Stephanie Figueroa, Grade 9
Lucerne Valley Jr/Sr High School

New Life

I start out life as a fuzzy, many legged, blob of nothingness
I feel trapped in this body that doesn't belong to me
All the other creatures are beautiful
Vivid colors, magnificent designs, eccentric shapes
But here I am a plain brown caterpillar stuck in the trees, going unnoticed

But a time will come when I am just as lovely as the rest
Soaring up and above those vast trunks I once despised
I will finally be noticed and I will no longer be a plain brown caterpillar
Everyone will envy me!

I don't worry about the time in between the change
I don't worry about the pain I will have to endure
I want a new life

Michele Ost, Grade 8
Longfellow Spanish Immersion Magnet School

War and Peace

War
Cold, sorrowful
Fighting, striking, clashing
Battle, disagreement — agreement, freedom
Helping, uniting, balancing
Harmony, serenity
Peace

Jahmil Fista, Grade 7
St Mary of Assumption School

The Long Dark Cloudy and Sunny Journey

My life is the rain
Sometimes gentle and soft
Or hard and tiresome
The thunder to express emotions
The pitter patter of the drops
Is the sound of every step I take
My life is the rain
It brings peace and love
Sometimes stress or relief
The storm that will cleanse me
Or the one that will change me
The hardest drops
Resemble the struggles I face
The light drizzle is the peace among us
The fog is the long journey one takes in life
My life is the rain

Jake Ortiz, Grade 8
La Joya Middle School

My Love

My love is deep,
deep enough to know,
that I love her,
and that will never change.
My love to her is a mystery,
it will go down in history.
My heart is pure, she is my cure.
My heart keeps on beating,
I can't help the feeling,
but to ask, will you be mine?
I want to say…
that I love you.
My heart is true,
you are the one for me.
To protect, is to reject,
of the one you love and care about.
It's just not fair.
My final last words,
My final last breath,
is to say "My love, my heart is only for her
is true to say I LOVE YOU."

Alex Ortiz, Grade 8
St Helen Catholic Elementary School

Madison the Thief

I remember a day, a day I can't forget.
On that day I met a girl that would blow me off my feet.
She took my heart like a thief.
It all started when she said my name.
It was a perfect voice.
Just as perfect as her.
We walking until the middle of the night.
And when she walks,
She is as swift as a butterfly.
But looks of a cobra.
I don't know what I'll do without her.
She is my best friend.
My best friend.

Alex Loya, Grade 8
McCabe Elementary School

Shopping

Shopping here, shopping there
It's fun to buy things everywhere.
Shoes and bags and earrings too,
Shopping with me and shopping with you.
Nordstrom's, Macy's, Aeropostale and more,
Shopping, shopping, in all kinds of stores.
Saturday, Sunday, any day of the week
Shopping is fun, shopping is sweet.
Sales and clearance racks loaded with treasures
Clothing for less is how I measure.
Trying on items of all kinds of fashions,
Conservative, hip or styles with passion.
Malls filled with people, bumping into each other
Fighting for products, they want no other.
Shopping all day is part of the fun
Feet oh so tired when it is all done.
Your arms will be full
With the bags of your jewels.
The cash will be spent and the cards will be bare
No matter the cost, I really don't care!

Ireland Webb, Grade 7
Holy Family Catholic School

Falling Twilight

Twilight falls across the land
And covers the city like a giant hand
All the sunlight quickly dies
And stars come out and burn up the skies
As the night gets black, the moon shines brighter
Night goes by and the sky gets lighter

Sunlight dances down on the earth
A shiny new day is now at birth
The places are brightest in the afternoon
But the sun will fall very soon
And twilight will fall across the land
And cover the city like a giant hand…

Bryce Tadokoro, Grade 8
Madrona Middle School

The Plane Is a Bird
The plane is a bird
Flying over the city
His wings spread wide
Soaring through the clouds

Its feet scrape the sky
Majestically soaring through the air
Lifting its head with pride
Flying up to reach the highest of dreams
Asem Alahmad, Grade 7
Islamic School of San Diego

Emotional Break Up
Why would you
Emotionally
Hurt me
Slowly bringing
Down the best of me
Quickly deny me
I was
Devotionally
Loving thee
But chaotically
You loudly yell at me
We were so lovely
But you evilly betrayed me
So you gently end it
Departing quietly
With no regrets
You just left me very lonely.
Justin Ng, Grade 8
Presidio Middle School

A Treacherous Beauty
A vast and amazing territory,
The Klondike as it's known.
Filled with great raw beauty,
Also as Yukon know

Home of amazing animals,
Of every shape and size.
They populate the frozen land,
And see with silent eyes.

So beautiful, so deadly,
Overshadowed by mists of cold.
Full of mystical stories,
Many still untold.

The mystical stories the dogs know,
Their truth can only be told.
As by a ragged traveler,
Who speak what only the dogs know.
Tirzah Nuno, Grade 8
Walter F Dexter Middle School

Expect
Many things change,
As life goes on,
Every day's different,
From dusk to dawn.

Babies born,
Teens grow up,
Be positive,
Ask how full is the cup.

People fight,
soon befriend,
Families are there,
Until the end.

Expect the unexpected,
For you don't know what's to come,
Be prepared for anything,
Life is full of tricks and fun!
McKenzie Hicks, Grade 8
La Joya Middle School

Veterans
Veterans should always be honored
Having trained really hard at camp
Honoring their flag of freedom
They faced many battles in their years
Fighting for our freedom
We will always respect them
Praying for their safety and lives
Veterans fought for us
To be a free country.
Jose Medina, Grade 7
St Alphonsus School

Sword
A sword knows war
It knows when to strike
On the flesh of an enemy.
It knows when to block
An incoming attack
From the rival.
It is the one thing
That can keep
You alive in war.
It is like a part of you
It will go with you
Till you fall at last
On top of the hill
The sword may have broken
But it has been returned
To go and serve a new master.
It will go back to war.
Xavier Cuevas, Grade 7
Yolo Middle School

Summer Breeze
Summer is coming near
Birds are chirping clear
The sun comes out bright,
And the days are hot.

I get out my tools
For the pool and beach
No more jackets for now,
Just shorts and flip-flops.

Sitting by the lake
I enjoy a quiet breeze
The wind on my face,
It makes me feel free.
Nina Scoubart, Grade 7
Packinghouse Christian Academy

Myself
My head is like an idea,
That's ready to do
Anything
My eyes are like a compass,
Pointing me in the direction
I want to go.
My hands are the building blocks of life,
For me and
Anyone else in need
My gentle heart holds adventure,
That is raging on as
A wild stampede
I live in a crazy world,
And eat anger and
Emotions
Kenny Rivers, Grade 8
Citrus Hills Intermediate School

Calm
The waves rush,
the birds sing,
the wind blows,
it is calm.
The sun is as bright
as God's holy light,
tourists rest,
no music,
that's how calm it is.
The day ends,
the moon comes out,
coyotes howl,
crickets chirp,
no destructive sound,
not at all,
not at all.
Caleb Liashenko, Grade 7
Bethany Lutheran School

Can't Believe It

My love for her is everlasting.
The way she looks
The way she walks
The way she talks
Her eyes
Her face
Her smile
Her hugs
Her voice
Her love
She is unique.
There is no one like her.
She makes me feel as if I'm in love.
She makes me feel as if I'm with an angel.
She makes me feel as if I'm cared for.
She makes me feel as if she's always going to be there.
She always makes me happy.
She is my everything
I can't believe she is still with me…
I Just Can't Believe It…

Sir Lorenz Cruz, Grade 8
Corpus Christi School

Freedom Soars

Through the night air the eagle shall fly,
To feel the light breeze of the freedom that soon shall die
And on the final flight the eagle shall soar
Taking one last look at the freedom, until it is no more

Ryan Perez, Grade 9
University Preparatory School

A Mark on History

On April 4, 1969, someone died
This person left a mark in history
He had so much pride
He has such an amazing story

His name was Martin Luther King
He was against segregation
He would say, "I have a dream"
He would preach to his congregation

He was born January 15, 1929
The youngest winner of The Nobel Peace Prize
He accomplished so much in his time
He won more than one prize

He was assassinated in Memphis, Tennessee
He was shot right in the heart
It was such a terrible sight to see
He wasn't afraid of dying from the start

His dream came true: racial lines were erased
He made an impact on the whole human race

Janeth Quijada, Grade 9
Lucerne Valley Jr/Sr High School

The Clown

In the castle where the king parties
There is a clown who makes no one laugh
Nobody watches
Not even a smile
She is a nobody said the king
People despise her
She is not funny
In this dark room with no windows
No lights
She is not funny
She is lonely, friendless
So many people with hats
She is despised
There is a clown that makes no one smile or laugh

Major Bielke, Grade 7
Daniel Savage Middle School

Currents of Life

A wave goes on and crashes to the ground.
On the sand there crashes lots of seaweed.
As they peak with perfection they are round,
And I see the ocean a soft blue-green.
Oh! The waves have order and they make sense.
Unlike I without any house or job.
Its cycle so perfect and so condensed
Oh! How it makes me feel like such a slob.
Although I wish my life was so simple,
I accept my life is not like nature.
So 'course in my smile there are no dimples,
For I am only a humble creature.
    As long as I can ride my board on you,
    I'll be content and need nothin' more to do.

Alexander Powell, Grade 8
Carmel Valley Middle School

Best Buddies

When the teacher moved you next to me,
    you barely said anything.

I thought you hated me,
    because you didn't even smile.

Days passed, and you finally talked to me!

Now you make me laugh all the time.
    You turned my frown upside down.

We always talk about our problems,
    and you're the only one who understands.

Even though you don't sit next to me anymore,
    you're still my best buddy!

Erika Olazo, Grade 7
Corpus Christi School

A Dream of Laziness

I woke up at early morning,
I washed my face,
I brushed my teeth,
I changed my cloth,
I packed my bag,
And walked to the school.

I woke up…
Now I have to start all over again.

Jae Kim, Grade 8
Robert C Fisler School

I Am Lucky

I am lucky
To have a family who loves me
Who understands and cares
And wants me to live under safety

I am lucky
To have wonderful friends
Who brighten up my day
And act like angels sent from heaven

I am lucky
To have teachers/coaches ever so great
Who don't just teach
But help me learn from my mistakes

I am lucky
To have a roof over my head
To have food, entertainment
And to go to sleep on a bed

It may not be just luck
Maybe it's fate
But I know I'm lucky
To have a life this great

Mikayla Tan, Grade 7
St Victor Elementary School

He Is Great

He is great
Beyond great
He stays hidden
I'm not kiddin
But he's there
Not here or there
And he's watching
Protecting and guarding
Separating good from evil
With all the people
So…he stays hidden
But hear me in
The world is no coincidence

Adam El Newihi, Grade 9
McCabe Elementary School

The One I Admire

I admire him because he is one of a kind.
He's smart, kind, has a loving heart, and is athletic.
He is always there for me through the good times and the bad.
He is the kind of person that understands me.
He is the person that never gives up and tells me to try different things.
He is the one who tells me to never give up and to never say, "I can't."
He is the person that made me who I am.
He is my cousin.

Aimee Garcia, Grade 8
McCabe Elementary School

Neil Armstrong

On August 5th an important man was born
He has become one of the most famous Americans
Over his life he became a nation hero
He even ended the Cold War between Russia and America

Armstrong became known for his space travels
He broke new ground for the human race
After one specific event he became globally known
Neil Armstrong was the first American man on the moon

Armstrong joined NASA as a typical astronaut
Not too long after, he became the Apollo II commander
July 20, 1969, the world watched as Armstrong took his place on the moon
"One step for man, one giant leap for mankind"

Tori Bartholomew, Grade 9
Lucerne Valley Jr/Sr High School

Metallic Despair

I'm at a constant battle with my tears.
Holding them back has become too hard of a challenge
Uncontrollably streaming down my tender cheeks
For just one! One!
Hit my blouse with a harsh cold
Unlike even the most violent winter night.
These chapped —
    quivering —
Lips
    have a bitter taste of
Metallic Despair

And all the while
The
Darkness
Seems
Darker

For this river of tears my umber eyes have collected and tormented me with
Has drowned me with sadness and utter uncertainty.

Dani Monk, Grade 8
Carmel Valley Middle School

Something to God

It's a Sunday night on the beach
Look at the stars what do they teach
Of gladiators or heroes
Or that no one is a zero

I look at the sky what can there be
A man or an alien with heads in threes
Maybe there is a star about to be born
Maybe a horse with a horn

I look at the moon from this beautiful Earth
You can truly see what we are all worth
How God spent this time to create this land
With maybe a snap or clap of his hands

I look at the stars on a clear night
They shine and twinkle oh so bright
I wonder are we all just spinning on this bright ball
Cause sometimes we feel like we're nothing at all

But I know we are something to God
Some may think it's strange or odd
I feel his love is all around me
As I look into the night sea

Brigid Wheeler, Grade 8
Holy Family Catholic School

Every Time with Each Other

Every time we meet each other
I don't know what to say
You leave me breathless
Every step of the way

Every time we say to each other,
"I Love You,"
It makes me want to be with you more than ever
Because we both know our love is true

Every time we meet, we encourage each other
Our relationship will last forever
Nobody could ever replace you
That's why I so love you

Every time we hug each other
It makes me have the feeling inside
I just don't want to leave you
Because you're my one and only

Every time we think about each other
It just makes our love grow stronger
No matter what I do,
I sure don't want to lose you.

Justin Lucas, Grade 7
Corpus Christi School

Alone

Alone is…
When life gets lonely without friends I feel alone
Alone is…
When my friends don't accept me I feel alone
Alone is…
When my mom gets mad at me I feel alone
Alone is…
When I travel or go away from my house I feel alone
Alone is…
When I feel sad I feel alone

Moody Tobellah, Grade 8
Citrus Hills Intermediate School

Paths and Death

I have 2 paths but both seem like blood baths.
My mind is deciding but my choices are fighting
Is my future good I do not know
Is my life about to end I do not know
Is my death behind me or is it going to let me be
The 2 paths are hard and I cannot play my card
I have the middle path but it has good and bad
Even though it makes me feel like I need my dad
Can I control my life and destiny the answer is no
But I know I can live it and face it.
In real life I know I'm facing death
But I'm trying my hardest not to give up my last breath…?!

Leandro Ramirez, Grade 8
Richard Merkin Middle Academy

The Boy with No Name

I met a boy, full of shame
Running through the midday sun
I asked him for his name
He said that he had none

He has no place to live, not a single place to stay
He was born on the streets, oh no one knows where
I found him on the road one day
It gave me quite a scare

He seemed like an odd young boy
But he sure was full of fun
He showed me a day full of joy
One that was second to none

No one has heard of this child
Or at least they will not tell
There are a few stories that are totally wild
Stories of his mysterious spell

At the end of the day, he said he had to run
As if he had a soul to mend
Then he was gone, he took the fun
Gone as fast as the wind

Mason Jones, Grade 8
Madrona Middle School

The Midnight Water

The midnight water is clear.
It reflects itself; it shows us, that we are afraid of nothing
Nothing that we can't see in the obvious light.

As the moon is shining and we peer over the edge, we see the reflection of us.
I ask myself why we are so afraid.
I hear a voice inside me tell me that is the way we see it.

At the midnight water we are afraid of the ghostly figures around us.
Shadows, sounds, and voices inside your head sneak up on you, and you are afraid.
There are eerie sounds of an owl hooting at midnight and the rats scurrying by.

At the midnight water we see that we can conquer these fears by remembering that
This is nothing that we can't see in the obvious light.
Now we know that those ghostly figures, shadows, and sounds are just a piece of our imagination.
We see that there is nothing to be afraid of and that the owl hooting is now a distant animal, a distant voice.

Jessica Akiyama, Grade 7
Heritage Oak Private Education

It's Magic

Tears steam down my face as I run across the deserted beach.
Memories of pain and heartache run through my body and soul.
My heart, cracking little by little with each ungraceful step I take. I stop…out of breath…heaving with exhaustion and agony. I drop down to my knees crying every inch of salty water left from my moist, red eyes. I lay, letting the sand cool my aching feet. I wiggle each toe exposing it to the tiny grains of sand. The beaming sun providing warmth to every excessible revealing area of skin. The roar of the tide hitting the rocks soothed my scattered, distraught mind. The refreshing smell of the salty sea lingered around me. Then a miracle. The cool ocean breeze flowed through my hair wisping it away from my wet, flushed face. It went past my body, sending chills and tingles down my spine. It wrapped itself around me, giving me the warmth and comfort I had been longing for. It was not who I wished endlessly for, but it made the tears end and for a slight moment the sadness that had overwhelmed every inch of my body disappeared. The beautiful wind is the many wonders of life. It cannot be seen but the magic of its presence can be felt wherever it appears.

Sally Duong, Grade 9
Santiago High School

As the Green Grass Grows

A frozen hush is the sound of winter.
Plants dead with a carcass to prove.
Snow, the blanket of limitless color gleams as treasure itself.
While animals receive refuge in their struggle for warmth,
The green grass grows.
Winter melts with a sensation of life and iridescence.
Spring surges with the color of a billion stars.
Dew-drenched dawn awaits early birds and gives a brilliant gleam of a golden brown sun.
Over hills and mountains comes the sensation of the summer sun.
The green grass grows.
The summer sun disperses burnished gold,
And with it, the true beauty of nature's corsage emerges greeting all,
Liberating those in rest.
The green grass grows.
With a low dimming fade of the rainbow moon, fall intercepts.
A battle of the breeze strikes upon the world.
But with this war, arrives a beauty in all shades and color,
Showing to the world,
The green grass still grows.

Blake Dittman, Grade 7
Rolling Hills Country Day School

Last Thought

Sitting on the steps, looking across the street
Wondering of all the people in my lifetime I will meet
But in that second it took me to just think
I realized my life could change all within a blink

This is the reason why we should always cherish
Not knowing when loved ones might suddenly perish
Living every day, like it was our very last
For our days could be long or go by very fast

So I'll love and take nothing for granted
Not say things that shouldn't be chanted
If this is the last day I have on Earth
I accept it for all it's worth

Kacee Forrester, Grade 8
McCabe Elementary School

Hikari

You shone so brightly
You gave me hope and happiness
I was hoping you would never give out
But once you said those
Dreadful words
"Goodbye"
You went out of my life
I couldn't get the chance to tell you mine
"I love you…" I wanted to say
But all there was between us
Was words…
So how could I love you?
But how could I not love you?
That was the real question
It was impossible for me not to love you
It might not have been real love
But you made me feel special
And that's why I loved you
But now…you have burned out like a candle
And I am no longer in the light
All there is now is darkness…

Angelica Silva, Grade 8
Madrona Middle School

Flight

If I were flying
I would look down
at the people in the town
and my eyes would be filled with pleasure
and dominance
I would strike the citizens
with fear and joy
a feeling
never felt
My wings would be filled with
happiness

Alex Garcia, Grade 7
St Timothy School

Falling in Love with You

I never thought I'd fall in love with you
I thought someday of course I'd fall in love
But what it felt like, I just never knew
That it would be you…

That day we were walking home
It felt like we were both alone
But what little did I know…

You held my hand
I wished that it would have lasted
You took a glance to see who would pass
I smiled, and my friends laughed…

It was that time
When we had to say goodbye
Something held me back
I think it was the love that he brought back…<3

Alexandra Moreno, Grade 8
Alondra Elementary School

Blinded

You came in and turned my life around.
I love you so much
But I guess you're just blinded
You can't see the real me.
I guess I'm just blinded by your looks.
In my head I'm like "What the heck am
I doing with him?"
I realized it's because I see something in you.
I guess you don't get it.
Well all I can say is "I love you"
And I wish you can love me back.

Kayla LeGree-Taylor, Grade 9
Regency High School

Determination

I feel a burning desire. It burns like a wildfire.
An urge of knowledge, wanting to go to college.
Some say do your best. Others want me to fail that test.
That desire still burns. It cries and it yearns.
"Be diligent and succeed, knowledge is all you need."
It tells me to keep on going. Never stopping but still knowing.
No matter how long it takes.
I will be there.
In this place where all my hope and dreams will come true.
This place is known to all as my future.
I will strive.
I will drive.
Until I get there.
So lead, move, or get out of my way,
Because I'm coming through.

Adrian Toscano, Grade 8
Alondra Elementary School

Bird

I am Bird
Flying higher and higher
Flying away
From this intelligent guy

He has these laws
That you must follow
Since I am a bird
I can defy his laws

I am Bird

I am lucky to be a bird
Instead of a bear
As I can fly
Bears can't

Higher and higher I fly
Lower and lower as the bear dies
Still to this day
The laws of physics can't catch me
I am Bird

Alex Littaua, Grade 7
Santa Rosa Technology Magnet School

Simple Thought

Nature's wonder
May never be known,
It is all accident,
Or God's divine intent?
We will never know for sure,
How
A rose bud gets its scent,
Why
The fruit has its taste,
Or how
The mightiest of redwoods
Could have such minute cones,
And finally,
How it all
Came to be.

Nicholas Bowers, Grade 7
Bethany Lutheran School

Because of You

If it weren't for you
I would be nothing.
I wouldn't be the same.
I wouldn't be the person
I am this very day.
You made me who I am.
It's because of you
I am the woman I am
Today.

Jezzica Sunga, Grade 8
Corpus Christi School

Beloved

I've been searching, searching forever.
Now that I've met you, I know we're destined forever together.
When I look into your eyes, I see a light, bright as the stars at night.
You are God's perfect creation and everyone's inspiration.
I look forward to see you all day, from Monday to Sunday.
My love for you is undefined.
Any guy would be crazy to dislike you in their mind.
It is fate for us to be together.
Nothing could stop us from meeting each other, even bad weather.

Darien Gee, Grade 7
West Portal Lutheran School

Like Any Other Day

"Start on the top!" he yelled, frustrated because no one is listening.
Colorful swimsuits leaped in at once, with a big splash that always followed.
Once you jump in, no matter what mood you are in,
the water always makes you feel worse.
Jumping into the water when you've had a bad day,
feels like a million daggers striking your whole body at once.
But there is nothing you can do about it, one arm after the other,
you just have to keep moving.
As you continue the long and always unexciting warm up,
you can't help but to reflect on your day, whether it was good or bad.
How you're going to tell your mom that you bombed the math test,
or how you just barely got an A on that 160 point history test.
Then you think about your friends,
and how the blonde haired boy doesn't seem to notice you and who you really are,
even though you've gone to school with him for what seems like your whole life.
But then you think, it's just another day at swim practice,
I'll be doing the same thing tomorrow.

Christyne Eck, Grade 8
Robert C Fisler School

Along the Sea Ranch Trails

As I walk along the Sea Ranch trails I look beyond the bluff
I see some seals lying there basking upon the rough
I walk a little further and sure enough I see
A sign with a picture of a mountain lion that reads "Beware of me!"
I look around in caution but there's no danger to be found
So I stroll across the wooden bridge and then I hear a sound
I'm sure it's a hungry lion but I get the courage to look that way
I'm hoping its something small and cute that won't harm in any way
It's only a white tailed deer that was trudging through the leaves
She had a small fawn that was looking up at me
I keep along the path where there isn't much light to be seen
I look up in search and I see a bird oh so serene
It chirped for me a few times and then it stopped its song
So I went back to my walk where there were steps; wide and long
I walk up each step and there is a woman and her dog
I say hello to him and her who shiver from the fog
The dog gives me a big wet kiss so I stroke his golden fur
The woman waves goodbye to me so I wave goodbye to her
I've come to the end of the Sea Ranch trails I hope I can come back
To see my fellow furry friends along the Sea Ranch track

Whitney Gould, Grade 9
La Reina High School

Life

Oh the days we live in
The joys we've been given
The happiness we face
The mistakes we trace

We enjoy the good times
and struggle through the bad
Still appreciating every moment that we have

Life is only mortal
So live life best you can
Before you enter death's portal
And find yourself at the end!

Kevin Park, Grade 8
Citrus Hills Intermediate School

Ode to Sky Bar!

Oh how much I crave your taste.
For your idea of having five flavors at once.
For I will compliment your idea of taste.
Your chocolate is delicate
as frozen water that came out of the freezer.
Your peanut butter is like a jar of honey.
Your vanilla is like a cup of milk.
Your caramel is as thick as syrup.
Your mint is delightful as a lollipop.
Oh how much I love your taste
I would cry and beg to get you.

David Dinh, Grade 8
Presidio Middle School

Goodbye to a Good Friend

Do you remember that day way back when we first met
and then we were friends
about the time we set, until the end
always be there cause we were friends
how we caused a lot of trouble
but when mom found out
we would get quiet managing a mumble
and when what's her name asked you out
you told me, and I laughed
the teacher got mad and kicked us both out
Yeah, we were great friends
Side by Side
until the end
but what we didn't see
and wished it didn't come
was the day you would leave
and our laughter was done,
Surely you're someone I'll miss
so to a Uso, a brother a friend
I wrote you this

CJ Tauala, Grade 8
Jefferson Middle School

Christmas

Chimney stockings
Reindeer droppings
Having a blast
From my childhood past

Cookies on a plate
With some cold milk on the side
Hope the reindeer like the carrots
Because they were supposed to be a surprise

Michael O'Connor, Grade 8
McCabe Elementary School

Choosing Schools

When we turn 14
We all have to choose
Where we spend our next four years

Canyon Crest Academy, or Torey Pines
Are both great schools
But no one likes to choose

The school with football and cheer or
The artsy school
Hard decision

Picking which school to go to
Is very hard
If we didn't have to pick it would be a lot easier

Everyone wants to go where their friends go
But sometimes that is not what is right
Go to the school that you want to

If only we didn't have to choose
That would solve all the issues
Of choosing a high school

Avery Anton, Grade 8
Carmel Valley Middle School

Pandas

Pandas, pandas, big and small,
Pandas, pandas, standing tall,
Pandas, pandas, through the day,
Pandas, pandas, all the way.

Black and white,
They do not fight.
Cute and furry,
Never in a hurry.

Pandas, pandas, always a friend,
Pandas pandas, even in pretend,
Pandas, pandas, even a Panda Express,
Pandas, pandas, you could beat them in chess.

Riley Clark, Grade 7
Long Valley Charter School

Spring

Birds are flying
In the clear blue sky
Bees are buzzing
Over their honey-filled hives

The kids are playing
In the green, green grass
Dads are fishing
Where the bass are swimmin'

All the flowers are blooming
In the fields, in the meadow
All the smells of spring
Are coming to be.

Elisha Lawrence, Grade 7
Packinghouse Christian Academy

Joan of Arc

It is dark
The sound of gunfire louder than a bark
England and France manned
Fighting over the land

Blood falling to the ground
Armor over twenty pounds
A young female to change the war
Born to poverty, raised with the poor

Swords clashing, blood rising
The site of blood is undying
From poor to general
She does not go feral

She leads her army to the field
Where they fight but never yield
The English think they're using witchery
She leaves the field with the victory

Surprise attach her troops attacked
She was not killed but kidnapped
Then she was burned in the dark
We will never forget young Joan of Arc.

Nicholas R. McCabe, Grade 9
Lucerne Valley Jr/Sr High School

Alone

Alone is
Trying to be someone else
Alone is
Not having a best friend
Alone is
Not being chosen for the team
Alone is
Not having anyone there for you

Jasveen Singh, Grade 8
Citrus Hills Intermediate School

Road After Rain*

I am a fence made of wood running along a lonely road.
I was alive once, now I am here to create a barrier.
I was put here as a surrounding border to watch over and protect my home.

I have been here many years and have come to enjoy the neighboring area.
Every day I spend time socializing with my close companions.
Mornings I wake up to the breeze brushing against my sides.
I smell the trees' wonderful scent throughout the day.
Every once in awhile, a car will drive past and I kindly say hello as it slips away.
I love where I live and would not trade it for anything.

Although I love living and don't want to give it up,
I feel like my time here is coming to an end.
I am very worn down and have a few broken pieces scattered around me.
Every day I grow older and weaker.
Whenever there is a strong gust of wind blowing by,
Splinters of my wood break off and travel with it.

I know now that my end is drawing near.
After I am gone, I hope to return to the soil,
To be with friends who have already passed.
It is so hard for me to do this, but it is time I say goodbye.
Farewell to my home and my beloved friends.
I release my Earthly strength, but my spirit remains strong.

Olivia Pimentel, Grade 9
Salinas High School
*Inspired by Ansel Adams' photograph "Road After Rain"

An Ode to Sweaters

When feeling cold in a world where hugs come of few to you
It holds your arms, it has your back
And it soothes your heart
It secures the pale and raw skin
To which is too vulnerable to free, into our shattered atmosphere
It clings snug to your frailty like a warm breath out of a shy whisper
And yet you say you are alone
When you have a kindred spirit all along
A skin to your irresolute conscious
That second coat of paint you can't do without
Or you and your personal bubble won't feel just right
It closes itself around you, buttoned tight, to shield yourself
From things in the world that only scrape at the ice, that won't melt on its own
But not to fear, for it is something easy to find
In fact you have it, or maybe have them
A place not too far, from where you open your spirits,
And let your personality fly like a liberated eagle
Look in the place where you hang what covers your fragile skin
And where you are most indecisive
Just open the door, or the wooden drawer
Go through the disarray, and put it on

Ana-Paola Laveaga, Grade 8
South Lake Middle School

An Ode to My Grandpa

My grandpa was a very wholehearted man,
He would always try his greatest,
In all that he did,
My grandpa was always by my side through thick and thin,
He was my grandpa.

My grandpa would always take care of the
Three-piece children whenever their parents were out,
Whenever it was my grandpa's birthday,
We the three-piece children's would always write him a letter.

But now I may not be able to write him letters
But in my heart he is always there forever by my side
As I was by your side when you entered Paradise
He was my grandpa…

Vanessa Park, Grade 8
Robert C Fisler School

Dad

I love you more than words can express,
Through everything, you've stuck by my side,
You're my coach and my best friend,
Losing you would be like losing my heart,
Silent and painful.
You make me laugh when I'm sad,
And you calm me when I'm mad,
You're my rock and supporter,
I swear to never disappoint you,
And always make you proud,
Until the day you walk me down the isle,
I promise to always be your little girl.

Jillian Vasquez, Grade 9
Fountain Valley High School

Quest for Friendship

What is a friend? Oh, tell me, what's a friend?
— A friend is one that stays with you through woes
And trials, worries, straight through to the end.
A friend will stand by you in all sorrows.

Oh, tell me more, I pray, about a friend.
What traits would a trustworthy friend possess?
— Look for a will that is not quick to bend
But being wrong, is not slow to confess.

Say on, wise man, say on; enlighten me:
— A friend knows you like the back of his hand,
Knows you better than the waves of the sea
Are acquainted with the shore's golden sand.

Then tell me, how can I find such a friend?
— To others, do as you would have done to
Yourself. Then surely the heavens will send
A true, invaluable friend to you.

Cindy Tay, Grade 9
The Harker School - Upper Campus

Hand in Hand

Black hair, brown eyes
When he walks by my heart flies.
Emerica shoes, Etnies hat
There's not one better than that.

Dark skin, beautiful smile
I steal a glance as he walks up the aisle.
Tall; muscular
I pray you won't go far.

You were cool and I know you care,
But seeing you was something rare.
I got distracted.
I overreacted.

I wasn't thinking and I needed someone who could be there.
I never imagined it would be a burden I needed to bear.
It hurt you and it crushed me.
I will never forgive myself, I will never be free.

Although you don't talk to me,
I love you even if you'll never see.
Maybe one day you'll understand
So once again we can be hand in hand.

Maggie Ollry, Grade 8
Abiding Savior Lutheran School

Transitioning Days

Blue skies melt into yellow,
As daylight slowly fades away,
Cold air chills the retreating day,
While the lingering light is aglow.

Invading darkness swallows the sun,
Bringing a black world without light,
Streaks of yellow have gone to leave none,
Making a city darkened by night.

Rabbits scurry into their holes,
Bees swarm into their hive,
Raccoons and bats sneak out with moles,
As nocturnals need night to survive.

For several hours the sky remains black,
Until the sun overpowers the night with its ray,
Surrendering night needs to go back,
Everyone awaits a brand new day.

Dawn rises over the somber sky,
Shades of pink and yellow dominate up high,
Getting rid of our worry and strife,
Daylight rushes into our life.

Aswini Krishnan, Grade 7
Challenger School – Ardenwood

A Strawberry
If only I had silver nickel
To buy a juicy red strawberry
Brilliant red and pink tinge
Making it stand out
In the small fruit stand
Resting near the curb
Expelling an aroma
Beckons all that come across it

The salesman sits
On a cracked leather stool
Beside the stand
Reads the paper that crinkles
He looks up
Gives me a beaming smile
He notes the hunger in my eyes
And hands me a strawberry

As I take a bite
Its juices spill out over my tongue
I close my eyes
To relish the perfect flavor
Yet at the end I still hunger for more
Shayna Gersten, Grade 8
Emek Hebrew Academy

Alone
I try to fit in with everyone,
I go out and buy fancy new clothes
But that still doesn't seem to help.
I try to be funny but nobody likes me
There is nothing I can do,
I am too small and I am
All alone,
In this great big world.
Kyle Brown, Grade 8
McCabe Elementary School

Spring Rain
When spring rain falls
I smell the freshness in the air
The precious pitter, patter
Over and over again

The rains causes mud
I love to ride my motorcycle in mud
The engine and the rain are harmony
Making beautiful music to me

After riding I play with my dog
He is so vicious
But after the rain stops
You can hear the birds outside.
Shyanne Mitchell, Grade 7
Packinghouse Christian Academy

Flowing Beauty
Waterfalls falling,
Falling through — out the air ways,
The sight of beauty.
C.C. Cummings, Grade 7
Santa Rosa Technology Magnet School

Confusion
The only word I can think of.
My body is numb
Skin pale
Heart beating faster
His words are unclear at first
How can this be?
I am certain I am awake
Worried
What will happen next?
Things will never be the same.
My mind is like a puzzle
Except the piece scattered everywhere
His voice repeats
Over and over again
I want to run and hide from the world
Emotions thrown at me
I begin to feel pain
Scared at a loss for words
Our friendship is broken.
Alyssa Gutierrez, Grade 8
St Alphonsus School

Lost
I am but a mere being
Lost in the sea of eternity
In the vast wonders of the universe,
I am but a mere being
Trapped by the necessities of others
In the worries of the simpleminded,
I am but a mere being
Lost in the anger of everyone around me
In the destruction of peace,
I am but a mere being
How will you find me?
How will you find me?
Jorge Carbajal-Kelly, Grade 8
McCabe Elementary School

A Wave of Freedom
Beyond the horizon
and beyond the sea,
I spot a wave,
but not from the sea,
the wave I spot waves proudly in the sky,
showing courage and freedom
and no disguise.
Isabel Miranda, Grade 8
St Cyprian School

The Face on the Door
Behold the wrath,
Of those victim eyes,
Fearful,
To ponder what's inside,
To gaze,
It is dark,
And you're struggling immensely,
To the dark alley…
Tony Ng, Grade 9
Purple Lotus International Institute

Heartbroken
You broke my heart;
it is shattered into pieces.
My love and your love
are gone.
My heart is broken;
my soul is lost.
My spirit and my heart —
you've taken both away
from me.
We don't have anything
that connects us
anymore.
Amy Zhou, Grade 8
Corpus Christi School

I Love You
As time goes by,
I start to
worry
I think about the
time
we have left
together,
the laughs we
still get to share,
and
the smiles we still
get to exchange…
So before I leave
and say my
goodbyes,
I'd like to end
with:
I Love You
Faye Tan, Grade 8
Corpus Christi School

Fear
Fear, it's what's near or,
Is it me, running from the
Truth of life ahead.
Joel Garcia, Grade 8
Richard Merkin Middle Academy

Fraud

Save the new President from assassination
So the government won't have to take over the Nation
Save us from being Democrats, save us from being Republicans
They say curiosity killed the cat,
But what about the war? Did anybody think about that?
Low budget schools. Kids these days think doing drugs is cool
What's wrong with our generation? Is that a serious question?
Have you seen the sick children living in the streets?
These kids are influenced by drugs and are being beat.
You think it's the government? Maybe Democracy?

Can Barack Obama bring us to peace?
Will it get worse before it gets better?
Or will it get worse to the point where it's at?
Economic problems, global warming
And all these residents giving up.
What have we done?
I guess we were wrong.
Will this world last for very long?

Frida Aleman, Grade 9
Regency High School

Moonless

"Do not be afraid"
Do not be afraid of the night
'Cause I will be your light
Your knight
Your moonlight
"Do not be afraid of opening your eyes"
'Cause next to you I always am, forever you and I.
"Do not be afraid of opening your eyes
And see that I'm not here"
'Cause I always will
And you will not fear.

Mariana Lopez, Grade 8
McCabe Elementary School

Be the One…

Be the one who says "I love you"
Be the one to secretly stash notes in my pocket
Be the one to make me pancakes in bed
Be the one who plans surprises
Be the one who makes me forget my worries
Be the one to never let go of my hand
Be the one to make me feel pretty while wearing no make-up
Be the one to steal my first kiss
Be the one who lets me take yours
Be the one who knows everything about me
Be the one who makes my heart flutter when you smile
Be the one to give me a ring
Be the one who says "I love you"
Be the one to say "I do"

Erin King, Grade 9
Calvin Christian School

Summer

Stepping outside for fresh air to breathe
the sun gleams in the eye
as the puddles start to seethe.
Fresh light and free birds
it can't get any finer than this.
This is the season
we all can't miss.
It's ten o'clock,
and I'm not late.
Homework's not on my list today
and there's no due date.
Laying down, hands behind the head
no more lessons that need to be read.
Summer is here, but I must be a fool
to forget that tomorrow starts summer school.

Samantha Tolentino, Grade 8
Robert C Fisler School

Humpty Dumpty

Humpty Dumpty fell on his head.
And children laugh when they hear of him dead.
Presidents typically fall on their face.
But only the media leave their place
To jeer at
Laugh at
Tease as they please
To finally realize
And see through their eyes
That nothing
Will remain
Many will come, and many will go
Some will serve one, but some will serve two.
But one thing will stay
While everything goes
We the people
Of the United States
In order to form
A more perfect union
Are leaders.
All of us

Seung Jo Yoo, Grade 8
Fairmont Preparatory Academy

Best Friends

Some friends are like birds and drift away
But mine are here to stay
I have five best friends
Who will always be with me till the end
Even though we get in fights
I always know it will be all right
They always make me laugh when I am down
When I am with them I never frown
My five best friends mean so much to me
More than anyone will ever see.

Brenna Hardaway, Grade 9
McCabe Elementary School

New Season
Grey skies over our heads,
Blue skies on the horizon,
A new season arriving,
A season ending,
Times are changing.

Days become longer,
Nights become shorter,
Sleeping animals will awake,
Flowers will bloom,
Things are changing.

A new time,
A time of changes,
A fresh beginning,
A different way of being,
A new season.
Maria Luisa Fabregas-Iglesias, Grade 7
St John's Parish Day School

Liars
funny when things never change
even when you say they will
but while you're off with her
my life is standing still

you tell me that you love me
when I go to leave
you tell me I'm your only one
and I let myself believe

I know that you are using me
but you never let me go
I know that you don't love me
I know I'm just for show

I don't know if I can stand
to see you love another girl
you know that you broke my heart
you know that you're my world

but while your standing by my side
I'll believe your lies forever
cause everything seems so perfect
when we are together
Stacy Larson, Grade 8
Natomas Charter School

Charm
There once was a girl named Charm.
Who fell and broke her arm.
She slipped on rice,
Not once, but twice.
Please, don't do her any harm.
Griselda Izarraras, Grade 7
Yolo Middle School

Serenity
I stare into the ocean, as it seems to go on forever.
I hear the waves crashing upon the shore.
The moon's reflection shines onto the water.
I look up at the beautiful sky, and observe the breathtaking stars.
I wonder how things could get any better then this.
All my worries seem to disappear into the night sky.
I feel the slight breeze, as I walk through the sand, as it mashes between my toes.
Thoughts travel through my mind, but nothing seems to bother me.
Samantha Smithers, Grade 7
Santa Rosa Technology Magnet School

Obama Made History!
We have a new president, that has made history,
For being the first African American president as we can all see.

BARACK OBAMA is his name,
But we call him Mr. President so we show respect and no shame.

He plans to bring change to his country,
And does all his work and without ever being silly.

He lives in the White House, as we all know,
Leading the country and also making lots of dough.

He works in the oval office with a lot of stress,
And with all that he leads us without even a little mess.

Did great at his inauguration,
And were millions of people there watching until he was finally done.

So this is our new leader,
Who loves his people and is most popular breaking the meter.
Aakash Kadakia, Grade 8
Thornton Jr High School

My Sister Loves Her Makeup
As I peek into the lion's den to see if she's asleep
I hesitate to wake her up although I know she's late.
For once her eyes awake, Godzilla takes her place
To rush to the bathroom and take a look
At her crazy bed head and smeared makeup.
The devil takes a look at the clock, 6:45
15 minutes until we depart.
I am smart and stay out of the demon's path, because she needs to rush.
As the monster cleans up, she puts on the mask of glamour
And there she stands as good as new
The beast is now the beauty.
Only I will always know what lies behind the mask
And just for now I will not tell
For if you see the truth, you may stand in horror.
We leave for school, 7:00 and arrive a little late
Although in a hurry she is again, the mask will do the trick.
Many are fooled by the elegance of the mask that hides her face
For only I will always know what lies behind that mask.
Holly Matsunami, Grade 8
John F Kennedy Middle School

Civil War

War was declared.
Entire nation split into two.
Emancipation Proclamation was created.
Slaves fled towards freedom.

Free slaves fought for the North.
Demand of slaves increased in the South.
Cannons sounded like thunder.
It felt like a constant earthquake.

Smoke covered the sky.
Taste the blood of your enemies and allies.
Brothers fighting against each other.
Many had fallen.

The smoke had cleared.
The war had ended.
The slaves were free.

Donovan Herndon, Grade 9
Lucerne Valley Jr/Sr High School

Grandpa

I would always be bad
You would always get mad
I would always get yelled at
But I know you never mean it
Cause I know how much you loved me
I always go to your house
To see you and grandma
But now I can't
I wish you were here
And not there
But I know you're happy there
I miss your hugs
I miss your kisses
I miss your face
I miss you yelling my name
I wish you were here to tell you how much I love you
I hope you know how much
Our whole family misses you
And I just want to say that
I love you and I miss you so much

Ashley Galindo, Grade 8
McCabe Elementary School

My Gift

If I wrap a toy
And give it to someone
But to the wolf
I have no spare gift
I don't want to take this power to the rose
There is rain in my life
Inside me
Don't forget to take my gift

Juri Thomas, Grade 7
Katherine Michiels School

In a Bird's Eyes

I wake up to a rooster's song,
And look around my nest.
I see the twigs and leaves
Aligned to give the very best.
I hop out of my nest
And scurry along a promising branch
Which opens into a meadow.
And then all I see is paradise.
I open my wings
And take flight to the endless skies.
As I soar through the air,
The beauty begins to rise.
I glide over hills and rivers,
And I gaze down upon the sea.
I see trees as small as shrubs,
And lakes shrinking to ponds.
Then, the meadow flashes.
I find myself in bed.
I long with all my heart to be in paradise again,
So I close my eyes,
And I'm in a bird's eyes once more.

Courtney Rawda, Grade 7
Rolling Hills Country Day School

The Paintbrush

A paintbrush sits in the old studio,
looking at the bare spots on the wall,
where its masterpieces once hung.
It longs for the good old days,
playing with its love, paint,
and dancing though the canvases together
hours upon hours.
It remembers traveling to the most exotic places,
and capturing their beauty with the stroke of its brush.
The paintbrush wells up with envy,
never forgetting its enemy, the camera.
All it took was one click,
One flash, and now…
A paintbrush sits in the old studio,
lonely
abandoned
forgotten.

Katherine Workman, Grade 9
La Reina High School

Liberty Is…

Liberty is freedom for my country
Liberty is soldiers fighting for their country
Liberty is the red white and blue flying high
Liberty is speaking my mind
Liberty is colorblind
Liberty is the United States of America.

Alex Bock, Grade 8
Mary P Henck Intermediate School

Absent

I look upon a black wall with thousands of engraved names of men and women that without them life would not be the same.
As I read sadness and anger take over my mood making me forget about all the good in the world
because I feel the pain and suffering as they did.
I continue to read the wall thanking God that one name is missing for if it wasn't I would not be here.
As tears roll down my face my angel wipes them and picks me up and blesses me.
I begin to walk away and hope that someday I will be someone's hero and soar to heaven the second I pass.

Elizabeth A. Remick, Grade 7
Holy Family Catholic School

The Studio

You step in, and a whirlwind of heat floods your face
The familiar scents of wood, sweat, and sticky hairspray are inhaled
Surrounding you, the high-pitched chatter of perky dancers fills your ears
You set your bag in front of the mirror, and sit down on the wood floor
The satin of your pointe shoes is a peachy pink
The ribbons are elastic and clingy
You tie them deftly and hurry over to the rosin box,
Daintily dipping your toes in, as a cloud of amber powder whooshes into the stuffy room
And the piano music fills the air, the notes wafting in one by one as
Mozart's concerto plays throughout the studio
The pins in your hair dig into your scalp
After pliés it's your favorite part, across the floor
Time for the whirling and the spinning, the spotting and sweating
The arabesques and piqués, the waltzes and the, "Beautiful arms, girls!"
You take a few graceful steps, and leap into a grand jétè.
For a second, you almost feel like you're flying.

Madeline K. Zimring, Grade 8
Lindero Canyon Middle School

The Solution or Question

Do not tell me of glory, of liberation, if you do not also speak of pain and illusionment;
Do not believe for an instant that the world is *either* wholesome or sickly.

Think not that man is greater than creature of subservience,
for in the end, I will avow that the greatest crime of life is *to be* human.

But answer this: When you at journey's close reflect upon the workings of this world,
what think you?

Alas, if you will say that existence is drear and dark!…
Bless you, jubilant soul who shall never be brought down!…
Now, at last, we meet the one who stands undecided, torn between them both…
Hear this voice, this pitiful attempt at reasoning in a context that inevitably renders *all truths false and all lies true.*

Have a care, for sorrow and joy are but two halves of a transparent circle, one that dictates only those who fall to its thrall, and that is, essentially, we who do feel and comprehend this place of ours, this pocket of the universe that we only are part of.

So our simultaneous curse and blessing is truly, or falsely, knowledge — knowledge that can destroy, but knowledge that can also bind and nurture.

Sandra Vadhin, Grade 7
George Ellery Hale Middle School

An Ode to a Great Flutist

Oh, her flute
Sounds great when it toots,
Major and minor scales
Tricky tones when she exhales.

Practicing the Circle of Fifths
Makes her fingers move very swift,
She masters the trill and vibrato
Oh, wow! She's really a virtuoso.

She plays each note to connect
That creates a Doppler effect,
Double or triple tonguing
Surely makes her more intriguing.

She plays Sonatas in Vivace, Largo and Allegro
People clap and say bravo!
A bow compliments a standing ovation
She performs with great passion.

Creative artistic technique
Her signature for being unique,
A musician with immeasurable dedication
She truly is an inspiration.

Khadija Ashley Aguinaldo, Grade 7
St. Joseph School

Racing Through the Night

The velvet dusk
Seems to say goodnight to me.
I climb into my four-poster bed,
Draw the bed curtains,
And they encase me in warmth and safety.

I lie down and stare through my skylight;
The moon and stars shine and twinkle faithfully at me.
I gaze at the moon
And the zillions of stars
Shining like diamonds around it.

I close my eyes,
As angels whisper to the stars,
"Fall,
Fall."
Then boom!
A star falls,
And lands in my mind.

Now,
The dreams begin!
They race through my head like a horse drawn carriage.
And, I awaken to the brilliant light of a new day.

Morah Geist, Grade 8
Rolling Hills Country Day School

Sandy Expectations

The bay so beautifully bountiful who knows where it began
As I walk near the water I see a tame wave roll by
On the sparkling sand a stunning shimmering shell shines
Seals seem to make a seat upon the reef
Their destination defended until they must descend
The lovely lapping shore, brings waves to my feet
Time to tend to other tasks, to bed until tomorrow

Stephen Linam, Grade 8
Dehesa Charter School

Confusing Graduation Dance?

You asked me to the dance last week,
And I shouldn't have said, "Yes."
Because now there's someone else I want,
And this is so much stress!

We were going to go to the mall,
To buy something that's matching.
So when we walked onto the dance floor,
We would be very eye-catching.

But everyone tells me you like me,
And I shouldn't lead you on.
But I can't randomly say "No" to you now,
Because that would just be wrong.

Now, I think I'm just going to go alone,
So I won't lead you on or hurt you.
And I'm sorry that I got your hopes up
I hope you find another that deserves you.

Amelia Pinto, Grade 8
Madrona Middle School

Ode to the Yellow Circle

Oh yellow circle how you shine so bright in the sky
How you bring me light each and every day
Though I wonder how you keep from falling
Perhaps the sky has been your calling
Stalling
For a few hours every day
To give the white donut a chance in the sky
So grateful you are oh yellow circle
Giving, sacrificing

Where have you been oh yellow circle
Hiding beneath the Earth I see
Stalling
To give the white donut a chance in the sky

I wait to see you again oh yellow circle
For I must sleep
Brought upon the spell of the white donut
I drift
Only to dream about the awakening of the yellow circle

Shantice Wells, Grade 8
Madrona Middle School

Flight

Whenever I feel like I
Have become
Something I'm not
Shunned away into darkness
With me and maybe my iPod
I can always take
FLIGHT
And become something I am
Art music
FLIGHT
Love truth
And when I am ready to go
I can pack up my
Memories
Feelings
FALL
Into society and back into
Art music love
FLIGHT
But still
Grounded

Sadie Goff, Grade 8
Aveson Charter School

Love

Love is so sweet
It is like a treat
I think of you night and day
Wondering how I look in every way
When I see your eyes
I think of snow
Just like the moon's glow
This is my love

Jesus Vera, Grade 8
McCabe Elementary School

Oh How I Wish I Could Be Free

Trapped in a place I don't want to be
Wanting to escape and run free
Wishing to feel the sunlight on my face
Holding back tears
Trying to be strong
Not letting the fear of death overcome
Even though it's knocking at my door
Closing my eyes
Pretending to be somewhere far
Only there I can be free
No pain, no sorrows, no good-byes
Everyone is happy
But this is only in my dreams
Once my eyes open, I'm back
My little body trembling in pain
Can't sleep, the night is full of screams
Oh how I wish I could be free

Christina Quintero, Grade 9
Kearny High Educational Complex

Seven Years Ago in the Park

Cherry blossoms flutter in the wind,
Your hair releases the scent of your sweet-smelling shampoo.
The might sun shines gently on this day,
The blush on pale soft cheeks is revealed.
A cool breeze comes and goes.
I watch you as you inhale the fresh passing air and sigh upon its leave.
As I hold our ice cream cones,
You are bent down,
Feeding the white puppy with some of our leftovers from lunch.
I steal a bite from your ice cream cone,
And smile happily at the scene in front of me.
The owner of the cute puppy arrives, and sadly,
We are leaving,

I will always remember the cute pout you gave me
When you noticed the difference in your vanilla cone.
I will always remember your expression
When you were demanding a new ice cream cone after that.
I will always remember us laughing in the end.
That was seven years ago in the park.

My last memory of you.

Juan Carlos Ng, Grade 9
Purple Lotus International Institute

Soaring Through Water

After placing my hair in a pony tail, I secure my goggles on my face.
I mount the platform, wait, then hear the crowd cheering with excitement.
Fierce competitors position themselves while spectators wonder who will set the pace.
As the buzzer sounds, I dive into the icy pool hoping the race brings self-fulfillment.

All swimmers speed down the lanes displaying their stamina and endurance.
Striving to reach the finish line first, each pushes himself to the fullest.
While some support a competitor, most onlookers are cheering on the fence.
Determined to win, each individual drives forward while being put to the test.

At first, my body shivers but then grows overwhelmingly energized.
My adrenaline increases while my heart starts palpitating.
Compelled to win first place, I strive as the trophy is well prized.
Imagining the reach for the finish line, I focus my efforts on stroking and kicking.

Stroke after stroke, I smoothly glide through the surface of the refreshing water.
Feeling an exuberant, energetic rush of great exhilaration.
My face, hair, and entire body propels like a dolphin underwater.
Completely exhausted, I persevere through sheer determination.

With the end of the race in sight, I sprint and touch the finish line.
The crowd applauds in an uproar while I bask in total jubilation.
Stepping onto the winner's platform, I realize the trophy is finally mine.
Full of pride, I accept the honors with complete self-satisfaction.

Ashley Wong, Grade 7
Challenger School – Ardenwood

Volleyball

The game is not played with skill;
It is played with passion.

Passion does not come from talent,
It comes from the love of the game.

To win you must have passion,
To have passion you must have a desire,
To have a desire you must have a dream,
A dream, a desire, and a passion
For volleyball.

There is one team, one coach, and a dream to succeed.
You have to be good,
For there are many people fighting for the same spot
But you must have heart to achieve.

Volleyball is not a sport,
It's a way of life!

Courtney Robledo, Grade 8
Holy Family Catholic School

At Night

At night I see things I
Don't want to see.
Ghouls, ghosts, monsters.
When I turn on the lights, they disappear.
At night, I go to sleep, finding
Myself in a nightmare I want
To wake up from. At night I
See aliens invading my house
And abducting me and looking
In my guts. At night, I want daylight to come.
It the morning, I felt better.
"What a night! Good thing it was only 14 lines!"

Daniel Medellin III, Grade 8
Robert C Fisler School

Umbrella

Your love is like an umbrella; it shields me from the rain
And even though you're not close, I know you'll never go away
Your love is like an umbrella; I always feel protected
We might have our hard times but I never feel neglected
When I'm under that umbrella I know you'll never leave
And in my heart I know we were always meant to be
But when that umbrella isn't there it's like you never cared
I'm standing in the rain alone
Away from the love you haven't shown
Is your love still like an umbrella, of that I have to think
And when I think of that, maybe then we shouldn't be
I wish that wasn't so because maybe then I should know
That this love won't always be, not forever nor eternity
Your love is like an umbrella
But I know it won't always be.

Ashley Kayombo, Grade 8
Blessed Sacrament School

Ars Poetica?

What is poetry?
Thoughts that are visible,
Or is it nothing at all?

What is poetry?
Something that is temporarily thought,
Or strong and meaningful?

What is poetry?
A touch?
A thought?
A silence?

Or is it an emotion?
The true meaning cannot be described in words,
For what is poetry, no one knows.

Zha'Nera Maloy, Grade 8
Madrona Middle School

You Come Again

Take your hand and let it fall
Return your own for once and all.
Golden fury, blackened earth,
Here be all tears, with no mirth.
But hope at last shall come again,
When with healing you come in rain.
The world is gone in fire and hail
The humble ris'n, the proud derailed.
Out of nothing you did make,
Again to ashes you do take.
And though deserve we not your peace,
From justice, Lord, we implore you, cease.
And in your mercy, let us ascend,
And live in sight of you till end.

Joshua Aaker, Grade 9
St Michael's Preparatory School

Are You the One?

Are you the one who will always
Be there for me through good and bad times?

When I fall,
Are you the one who will catch me?

When my heart breaks into pieces,
Are you the one who will help me put them back together?

When I cry,
Are you the one who will wipe my tears away?

Are you the one…
For me?

Jasmine Anzora, Grade 8
Corpus Christi School

Due Dates

Due dates aren't my thing
Never do my work on time
It is always late

Amanda DeSimone, Grade 7
Santa Rosa Technology Magnet School

I Don't Understand Why…

What I don't understand is…
  …Why there is no balance
  That holds us all together.
  …Why there is no scissor
  That breaks the hatred tether.
  …Why there is no end
  To those who toil forever.

But most of all…
  …Why there are the screams
  Of those who have to die.
  …Why there is the crisis
  That causes us to cry.
  …Why the crippled bird
  Will never touch the sky.

But what I understand most is…
  …Why some of us are brave enough
  To keep others strong.
  …Why there is forgiveness
  To purge all that is wrong.
  …Why the crippled bird
  Can still sing its song.

Curtis Haist, Grade 8
Dorris-Eaton School

The Forgotten Orchard

Sitting in this car,
I imagine once more…
a sea of green,
lush green trees.
Nimble branches,
swaying in the breeze.
Heavy with fruit,
the fruit of cherries.
but wait there's more,
a fruity galore!
It's not just cherries,
but apricots too,
stretching for miles
and miles, over this sea.
A sea of green,
lush green trees…
and now I stare
at this single, solitary orchard.
All alone.
Where did the others go?

Serena Lau, Grade 8
Sunnyvale Middle School

An Ode to a Mother's Love

An ode to a mother's love for it is like a rose.
It never fades. It never goes.
It'll keep on loving you till you're old.
Its thorns keep danger and fear at bay,
Till you're safe from harm's way.
An ode to a mother's love for it is like a snowflake.
All soft and white like purity.
It cleanses you from your sins.
Its softness makes you feel safe and warm.
An ode to a mother's love for it is like the sea.
All calm and still when she is at ease,
Knowing that her child isn't in jeopardy.
But she is like a tempest when,
She knows that she has been wronged.
All violent and fierce and the stillness all gone.
Her love is like the vast expanse of the sea,
Rolling and rolling on forever more.
An ode to a mother's love for
It'll love you, cherish you, and protect you for an eternity forever more.

Mai Nguyen, Grade 9
La Quinta High School

Palm Leaves Burning Flames

Palm leaves burning flames…
Kissing in the dark, killing in the light
Making dreams die
Wish upon a blue star, crying on the broken pages of dreams
He's got the voice of an angel kissing a bright bird
Marry me he says
Yes, but not until you promise to never leave me
I promise darling…
You kiss at your wedding, he breaks his promise
Palm leaves burning flames at your first child's fingertips
Brightly colored paper stares you right in your eyes
Your cat-like eyes die…you scream for help…but help never comes
You cry out in silence…
You're blinded by the love you thought you had
He comes back with a child in his hands
The child looks up at your eyes…nothing happens
You laugh in sadness, he cries in happiness
You both turn away
He cuts the vine and you fall…sleepy
The hurt is finally gone
Because of the palm leaves burning flames…

Alexandra Forté, Grade 8
Palm Desert Charter Middle School

Love

Love is something that a mother tells a son or daughter.
Love is when a man buys a woman flowers for a birthday.
Love is when someone tells you "I love you" and means what they say.
There is another type of love, that kind is what God did for us,
Giving us His one and only son, to die for us and take our sins away.
That is real LOVE!!!

Becca Shuebruk, Grade 7
Holy Family Catholic School

I Can't Take It

I can't bear it any longer
Too much pain and sobbing

You can't see how I feel
Even though God made it so

I cry every night
While you wear blindfolds on your sight

Your misconception is what you think is right
Don't blame me about my size or height

I'm a person just like you
And I deserve my rights too

Samiira Hussein, Grade 7
Islamic School of San Diego

Dinner Time

As I sat around the table
Eating potatoes with my friends
We were having a good time
And wishing the day would never end
In spite of living in such a small house
Our room was always clean and never had a mouse
We picked our potatoes from the round-shaped bowl
We bowed our heads in grace for the sake of our souls
In spite of the house having a dim light
Our souls felt happy and our futures bright

Jared Smith, Grade 7
Daniel Savage Middle School

The Dying of the Light

The place where the sun enters the sea is golden clear
even through its depths
as the shining disk sinks into the crystalline water
the air sizzles
the ocean froths
spurts and flares of golden flame
rocket through the air
plumes of steaming fire
erupt into the purpled horizon
as everything twists into and onto
under and beneath the world's eye
calming but smothering it's golden depths
until the hostile eye is drowned
the day destroyed
but held together by the rising of the night
the brimming tears silenced by the dark
calm, serenity of the new world
contrasting with the energy
of the dying of the light
the beginning of the night.

Zachary Freier-Harrison, Grade 9
Palo Alto High School

Dreamland

Dreamland is a wonderful place to be.
No one, but you can see.
Dreams are always there new, fresh and different.
The key to enter Dreamland you find it here.
As you're tucked in your bed…
Waiting to fly all over the Milky Way.
This is why,
When time is right
Your key will open Dreamland.
Sometimes dreams can be bad, sad, happy.
'Specially, is thy whose dreams are high
And fly to the sky
Cause they dream day or night.

Paula Soto, Grade 7
Blessed Sacrament School

What Is…?

What is the moon without the sun?
A pair that simply can't be undone.

What is fire without water?
A horrible element; a reckless disaster.

What is day without night?
What is darkness without light?

Incomplete; not yet full.
And same for darkness; very dull.

What's the reason for all of this?
Why, oh why do they exist?

For inspiration?
or simply admiration?

To make you think and to make you wonder.
To make you question and make you ponder.

Austin Chavarin-Ramirez, Grade 8
McCabe Elementary School

Gratitude

I'll rely on you,
In my time of need
I'm sorry to say,
I need so much
I will try to repay the debts,
I heap upon myself

That is,
A matter to be settled between you and me
Depending on,
A number of variables
That should already be
Crystal clear.

Rebecca Chhay, Grade 9
San Diego High School of International Studies

Kids/Adults

Kids
Mysterious, loving
Learning, starting, sharing
Toys, games, books, report cards
Working, drinking, changing
Long, awesome
Adults
Dan Erdman, Grade 7
Kadima Heschel West Middle School

All the Little Things

I hear
The pat-pat of the maiden's feet,
Running through the meadow
Misty from the morning dew
Which dampens the weather.
She climbs up the gnarled limbs
Of the elegant elm,
Old and wise from years bone by,
Strong from age and toil.
She perches on a "y" branch
Looking out beyond
At all the living creatures,
Beautiful and strong.
She watches the red rose buds
Bursting into bloom.
She sees the baby mouse
Taking its first breath of life.
She keeps note of all the little things,
The ones that no one sees.
The ones that are significant
To nature and her beings.
Lindsay Salem, Grade 7
Rolling Hills Country Day School

Little Raindrops

A teardrop sounds like
little raindrops
falling down
from the dark midnight sky

A dark cold day, wet, sad

At home tucked in my blanket
I drink a cup of hot chocolate

So delicious, so warm

The day passes by
as quick as a baby
becomes a teenager

Not much time is left
Maor Swisa, Grade 8
Emek Hebrew Academy

Love Is…

Love is a fire.
It burns with such intensity.
It might just cause propensity.
Love is dire.
It kindles the heart's eternal flame.
It's not something you can tame.
If love is your desire.
You can't retire,
From your search.
It's important.
That you don't.
Play with it.
Or just like fire,
You might get burned.
Robert Reynoso, Grade 8
La Joya Middle School

Sunlight Hold

Light splashes away
the nightly gloom,
it dashes and bashes
away at the dark
It covers the land
with a longing gaze
and then it goes down
at the end of its trip
And then the cold moon rises
giving us a shallow bath
just giving us a bit of pale moonlight
it sits there and stares
a blank and empty stare,
looking down in disgust
at what is down below
Then light creeps up
in twinkling twilight
not quite in the dark
not quite in the light
Then at dawn's first light
we feel light's soft caress
Tim Ruiz, Grade 8
Madrona Middle School

Missing You!

I miss you I really do,
I hope and pray
you come back someday
to relive those days
I spent with you

I know you're out there
somewhere safe,
up there above us
in heaven's sake
Karen Gomez, Grade 8
McCabe Elementary School

The Wonders of Nature

When I sit outside and listen,
I hear some wonderful sounds.
The birds are chirping loudly.
The leaves are rustling in the wind.

When I sit outside and watch,
I see some wonderful sights.
The deer are chasing each other.
The squirrels are climbing trees.

When I sit outside and smell,
I smell some wonderful scents.
The scent of soil fills the air.
The scent of pine fills my mind.

When I sit outside and touch,
I feel the wonderful textures.
The moist feel of soil,
The soft feather of the bird,
The rough touch of the bark.

It is, the Wonders of Nature.
Sarah Pashby, Grade 7
St Victor Elementary School

If

If you don't know me,
Don't talk about me
If you don't know me,
Let me have a little respect
If you love me,
Show it by understanding me
If you love me,
Know I'll love you back
If you hate me,
Don't talk to me
If you hate me,
It's okay, I won't get mad
But just tell me.
Susana Gomez-Barajas, Grade 8
Richard Merkin Middle Academy

Mother

She's kind and thoughtful
And pretty and sweet
She gives hugs
And kisses
And fixes "booboos"

She fixes meals
With chocolate milk
And helps with homework
What would we do without Mothers?
Katt Larson, Grade 8
John Muir Middle School

The Power of the Dream

I have a dream that
N o one can stop
S upport is all we need
U rgently needing change
R unning together both black and white
G enerations together, my father before me
E veryone needs to stand for what is right
N ever underestimate
T he power of a dream

Mazelle Etessami, Grade 7
The Mirman School

Honeysuckles

Do you remember in third grade
When we ate those Honeysuckles growing on the fences
Seemingly reaching out to us,
Telling us, pick me, pick me
Of course, like always
We would pluck them off their vine
And slowly, carefully
Pinch off that small green bud at the bottom
As we pulled it out we would guess
How big a droplet would come out
And then the moment we were waiting for
A nice, luscious drop
And as we put it into our mouth
We tasted sweet, savory, heavenly goodness
After that we would immediately look for more
Ranging from white to yellow
We would eat and eat them until we were full
And all that was left were a bunch of Honeysuckle flowers
Left on the bench for someone else
To see what we had been up to

Emily Chou, Grade 8
John F Kennedy Middle School

A Never-Ending Winter

I have not seen a red rose in ages
Nor heard a single bird's heavenly song
I can only see the brown dead branches
Alabaster snow has been here for so long

One morning I feel brave so I step out
Only to my dismay I chill my skin
In this weather I cannot go about
I cannot let that Mother Nature win

I waited for winter to be over
And superb spring to appear in its place
The shining sun shining on a flower
To see the smiles on little kids' faces

Summer fades into fall the cold is here
Is that a pale leaf oh no winter's near

Isabella Freeman, Grade 8
Carmel Valley Middle School

Where Were You?

You left when I was a baby.
You left me with my mom for thirteen years.
She struggled to take care of me
While you were gone, going out with someone else.
You missed all my birthdays, my First Communion,
All the special occasions that happened in my life.
You missed…everything.
And now you're trying to get to know me?
I'm thirteen years old.
What kind of person are you?
All I can say is,
Stranger, where were you all my life?

Mark Caramat, Grade 8
Corpus Christi School

As Lightning Strikes

Its fiery rage strikes the Earth,
With a beautiful glow
That twinkles in the sky
That crackles and blows

It was as bright as a spotlight,
It gleams like the sunlight,
It enlightens the starlight,
When over, it's as dark as black light

The darkness comes as the daylight goes
The moonlight shines as the cold wind blows
The clouds roll in as the thunder booms
And lightning comes back for its once more,
Strike of doom

Victoria Garcia, Grade 8
Madrona Middle School

Traffic Lights

Green is what everyone wants to see,
they go fast as they can worry free.
They honk their horn if you do not go,
everyone wants the traffic to flow.

Yellow sometimes makes people go faster,
which often turns out to be a disaster.
Nobody wants to have to wait,
wherever they're going they might be late.

Red is when people slam on their brakes,
like an airplane that stops and the power it takes.
They pound their car 'cause they didn't make it,
the car who did nothing just sits there and takes it.

Sometimes you're lucky and other times not,
it won't always turn out the way that you thought.

Kaleb Tapp, Grade 8
Madrona Middle School

She

She is as young
as a newborn deer

And as sweet
as the morning dew

She looks
as pretty as a flower

A special baby
All mothers would love

Renad Awad, Grade 7
Islamic School of San Diego

John Deere

In life,
there is this little thing
called hope.
People build it up,
thinking they can
make the world greener.
Then,
the people I call
Lawnmowers
slice it down
right when you reach
your full height.
The "lawnmowers"
slice it down with
their anger blades
thinking it will
bring them up.
But it won't.
It only brings
everyone down,
and shortens the grass.

Ronnie Watkins, Grade 8
La Joya Middle School

The Commute

I'm on my way
To see my family
From a busy day
Of six to ten,

I'm on the highway
Seeing the gleam of cars
Front and back
Their enlightened ends,

Now stuck in traffic
Like a caged beast
I wonder if,
I'll ever get home.

Layne Rudisille, Grade 8
Madrona Middle School

What Love Is

Love brings happiness, love brings loneliness
A whirlwind that leaves you dazed, a smile, a laugh, a kiss perhaps
Those precious moments that you want to last
Comfort and security that everything will be OK
A dream in your head that they'll be there every day

But it's always the same tale
A tale we don't tell 'cause we're all scared of the truth
Clinging to our falsehood to escape the ruins of losing hope
But reality eventually finds us
It lasts for a time and then it slowly fades, love has never changed

Contentment once brought, now boredom and is this what love is?
A lie to wash the insecurities away, a charade that we all must play?
Heartbreak that we endure continuously
To find this dream everyone is seeking
Has it always been this way?

Love is all these things and more, a rush of feelings, our heaven on Earth
And yet we all lie to ourselves
Never finding the true love we yearn for inside
All we find is comfort
What love really is, is a lie.

Melissa Strows, Grade 8
Jefferson Middle School

My Grandfather

My grandfather was a big man
small in size, big in heart
he was like a ringleader, like a referee
My grandfather held my hand
through the scorching sun
and the pouring rain
his coarse, wrinkled skin never left me

My grandfather died on Saturday morning
he'd told me only days before he'd never die
I should've known then that it would be a lie
My grandfather's death left me alone
he took his loud whistle with him
and his cracking whip with him, up to the gates of Heaven above

My grandfather died at 5 am
it's funny how the compass broke then
and the ship stopped then
and the Earth froze in place then
My grandfather told me he'd take me everywhere
told me he'd keep me by his side
but the thought never occurred to me
that he'd someday have to leave me behind

Rachel Lee, Grade 8
Robert C Fisler School

Waiting Room

In the waiting room
Nothing to do so gloom
All the magazines are whack
Dying of hunger with no snack

The television is on some kiddy show
Even if I wanted to listen the volume is still too low
The girl next to me is asleep
The guy across is a creep

When will they call my name
It's driving me insane
I have been here for an hour
If only I had the power

I should have brought something to do
I feel like throwing my shoe
It's like they're calling everyone but me
I almost jumped up when they called some marie

"Mary" I hear from the door
I run up and almost slip on the floor
In and out and all done
"Patience is the key hon"

Mary Fitzpatrick, Grade 8
Robert C Fisler School

Could It Be You?

Could you be the one
The one I've been looking for?
I saw you last night in my dream
I couldn't help but wonder if you feel the same way I do
Could it be you?
I'm not sure
Can you tell me please?
I've always wanted to know who my true love is
I'm glad I found you
Could it be you?
Yes it's true that I found my soul mate
I love you now and forever

Lauren Guzman, Grade 8
Walter F Dexter Middle School

Summer Time

After sitting in the blazing hot sun
You have a tendency to go have some fun

When you are playing you start to feel you are burning of steam
Then you want to get something cold like ice cream

At the end of the day you want to rest
Then tomorrow you are going to have to be your best

Justin Warren, Grade 7
Santa Rosa Technology Magnet School

Normal?

Normal? What is normal?
Is it normal to eat a PB&J sandwich?
Is it normal to live in a single story house?
Is it normal to like to drink malted milkshakes?
What is normal?

Who is normal?
Is it your neighbor across the street washing the car,
Your dentist asking you if you've been brushing your teeth,
Or your friend who eats pizza every night for dinner?
Who is normal?

No one is normal.
Everyone is different in his or her own way.
Like dancing waves on the beach, each is special.
Like handmade pottery, each is unique.

Me? I'm not normal.
You? You're not normal.

Normal? What's normal?

Amber Fong, Grade 8
Rolling Hills Country Day School

The Quickness of Life

This time of year has finally sprung up
The leaves turn golden and fall to the ground
My life is slowly leaking from my cup
The weights I can lift go down pound by pound
Yesterday I was young, how can this be?
Decades have gone by in just a flicker
Oh, the quickness of life, I did not see
Why had I wished that it would come quicker?
As I weep and mourn, I remember thee
Your beautiful eyes, your uplifting smile
Just me thinking of thee brings me much glee
Thoughts of you lift my spirits many miles
    But after my great joy, I remember
    When we just met, it was still the summer

Tiffany Sin, Grade 8
Carmel Valley Middle School

I Am Your Dream

I am your dream
I hear you whisper in your sleep
I see myself in your fantasies
I say, "OH MY!"
I cry because it's beautiful
I am your day dream
I am here when you're not sleeping
I feel your breath next to mine
I try not to wake you from your divine sleep
I dream but I am a dream
I am your everything.

Jamie Douville, Grade 8
Robert C Fisler School

A Storm to Remember

It was a Friday evening late on a day to remember.
The prevailing winds passed through the streets as the clouds came out behind the mountains.
As the grey, powerful clouds moved in, I felt a chill of pride that reminded me
of the country I lived in where so many memories are present.
The streets are quiet and the trees are blowing increasingly
as I watched the magnificent clouds in their greatness move towards me like a wolf stalking its prey.
I hear a distant thunder and the clouds light up with Earth's fireworks.
A rain starts to fall and engulfs me in Earth's oasis.
The last ray of light disappears on the horizon and the sky darkens to a cool grey
like the strong goddess Athena's noble eyes.
This storm reminded of my life in the country I love and was truly…a storm to remember.

Christopher Baldwin, Grade 9
Temecula Valley Charter School

Freedom

Feel the wind pass by second after second and day after day, feel the butterfly flying near your heart, have the warm feeling you always wanted and tried so much to gain. The cool air that your lungs breathe, taste victory in your hands, have the will to go where you want. Fly in the air and reach the ends of the Earth. It will be time, time for freedom.

Dante Johnson, Grade 7
Grace Christian Academy

Wonders of the Moon

Such a wonder…
I watch the moon. It is glowing with might, some sight I can't fight
The luminous rock flying high conquering the midnight sky
Rugged craters encircle the surface and the enormous ball travels day by day, week by week,
moving slowly and in silence. What a mystery

As I stare at the moon. It overwhelms me with extraordinary delight
I no longer dwell in misery and woe, my bitter emotions and unpleasant regrets are forgotten
I rest myself under the elegance of the moon
Stealing the life in me piece by piece I relax and I feel as smooth as silk
And my body and soul has reached its divine peace

I wonder what I'll spot there, the wondrous Earth gazing at the moon
Millions of dazzling stars ring the white orb
And the black endless night fulfills the limitless beauty
of the glorious, sparkling moon

What if the moon was no more?
There is no point to gaze at the black yonder
I wonder, what a wolf would howl to
This dilemma is like a spare light bulb unused in a dark room
No twinkle in the forest to guide me through the
unwelcoming frigid hours of darkness
What a wonder…

Jonathan Bautista, Grade 7
St Victor Elementary School

Clouds

A cloud passes by the window. There one minute, gone the next, much like faces in the crowd. The cloud brings with it a sudden dampening of light, but only for an instant. The cloud reminds me of a ship at sea, always seeming to have somewhere to go. The cloud is alone in the spring sky, yet it seems to be at peace with itself. The instant I saw it was very short but it caught my attention. A peaceful moment in a busy day.

Martin Sabonis, Grade 7
Holy Family Catholic School

At a Distance

At a distance,
Is the way we view the world
From an airplane or a ship.

At a distance,
The Earth is clean.
A soldier in a war-torn land
Is nothing but another office worker,
And a starving child
In a country stricken by famine,
Is just like you or me.

They say the best view is at a distance,
Where you can shut it out
And focus on the distractions.
But some things
Can't be seen at a distance,
Like a lonely scarf in an abandoned bazaar,
Or a single flower
In a bombed-out garden.

Hannah Seymour, Grade 8
Aveson Charter School

Smile

Oh so bright and oh so helpful
Make me happy when I'm blue.
A smile is powerful,
Especially when it comes from you.
Makes me laugh and makes me smile
Won't you please smile a little while longer.

Rebecca Chavez, Grade 8
Robert C Fisler School

Home

There's a piece of my heart residing in
a two room condo on Antigua Drive.

Now I live on a street called Whitney.
I left home and it didn't come with me.

I woke up every morning feeling whole.
Now I've got a big black hole.

I'm older now and I understand
my dad felt how I do and jumped
at the chance.

The chance to go to the place you call home.
To the place you feel whole, but just like him
I'll have to wait for the chance to go to the place
I call home.

A two room condo on Antigua Drive.
To claim the missing piece of my heart

Alexander Barreto, Grade 8
McCabe Elementary School

A Dream of Dreams

A dream, of all dreams, this one came true.
And. If you want, I'll tell it to you.
It all started, a bright, sunny day.
A day that took my breath away.
I went outside, to play a game.
That's when I heard you call my name.
Its sound, so faint, yet loud and clear.
I called out, to you, "I'm here! I'm here!"
You ran to me, arms, smile, so wide.
Our happiness wasn't able to hide.
We spun 'round, the dreamful field
I had to take a moment, to steal,
a final glance at this glorious land.
I've never dreamt a dream so grand.

Ebony Ellison, Grade 7
Odyssey Charter School

A Girl's Sorrow

I am just a girl with a broken heart.
Can't you see that my life is being torn apart?
I have a dreadful sorrow
that may last more than today and tomorrow.
This sadness is so hard to explain
and it's a sadness that I can't contain.

Oh Lord, it would be a great help if You were at my side,
so my sadness won't come over me like a huge tide.
I'd love it if You could keep me nice and warm,
so my pain will begin to transform.

When I feel better, I will want to rejoice
in a very loud voice,
"Thank You Lord for this glorious day
and I pray every day would be this way."

Victoria Rodriguez, Grade 8
Palm Desert Charter Middle School

The Love I've Always Dreamed Of

You my love I think about you at night.
It is hard to stop thinking about you,
I can't even stop with all of my might,
With your beautiful eyes so very blue
And that grin spread across your face so wide.
Your joyful spirits lift towards the blue sky.
For all I want is to be by your side.
You walk with your chin help up very high,
For you have succeeded in quite a lot.
But you are still kind and caring to all.
To put a person down is not a thought.
You pick me up when all my outlooks fall.
It is not a lie and it is no myth,
You are the one I would want to be with.

Natalie Grabowski, Grade 8
Las Flores Middle School

Maturation

This year I will grow
into a beautiful young girl,
put the past behind
focus on the future.
This year will be all mine.

I will change from a child,
to a woman
delicately, elegantly
like a white baby dove
spreading its wings for the first time

I'll go through real problems,
real pain.
My heart might ache,
but will not break.
For I am a woman

I am ready to wander the world.
Sheer Dadon, Grade 8
Emek Hebrew Academy

Intellectual Capacity

Intellectual capacity,
    exceeds with its audacity
    bravery is lost…
    and your soul is what it cost.
  Society is poor in choosing,
in its mind
    it's great on fusing…
  tighten the bond
    that separates me
  from:
the norm of the people,
  I'm one out of three.
  The rest are facetious,
I think more factitious…
    so I play ferocious,
  but I'm not all vicious.
Isabel Gil, Grade 8
Walter F Dexter Middle School

Fine

I try to make it look like I'm,
fine,
I hate that word,
fine,
It's not good or bad it's,
fine,
to me,
fine,
doesn't sound very,
happy.
Emily Csabanyi, Grade 8
Buchser Middle School

Ode to a Dragon

Ode to a dragon,
They are filled with might.
They drink out of a flagon,
And fill others with fright.

Ode to a dragon,
They scare people just by sight.
They could flick away a Kraken,
They can kill aliens that bite.
They're creatures of the night,
With superior might.
Luis Calderon, Grade 7
Yolo Middle School

Dusk

The sun goes down
As a velvet dusk falls.
It's melting lemon sherbet
In a brilliant burning ball.

A singing breeze
Brushes away,
The traces of the day,
With a navy blanket.

The star-laced night.
The reflecting river and cricket strum,
Only adorn,
A diamond mirrored moon.

When night is at its blackest,
The stars are at their brightest.
The iridescent night shies away,
And a dusty dawn is reborn.
Life is a truly glorious awakening.
Daisy Jacobson, Grade 8
Rolling Hills Country Day School

He Loves Me, He Loves Me Not

To sit and hold a flower
Is the task she will do
To answer a simple question
And find out if love is true.

She pulls upon a petal
Just one pull at a time
And asks herself the question
If he or is he not mine.

At the end of the petals
When she is down to the stem
She picks another flower
And starts all over again.
Lauren Hall, Grade 7
Santa Rosa Technology Magnet School

Open Mic

Because of you I thought
I'd never see the sky

Because of you I thought I'd
Never see another year with you

Because of you
I was meant to be on this earth

Because of you I have two parents
That love me a lot

This is all because of you
Laquttea Wilson, Grade 8
Richard Merkin Middle Academy

Love

Love,
What does it mean?
Something tangible,
or nothing but a dream.

A strong hand to hold,
or loving embrace.
Such a bold feeling
with a smile on their face.

It seems odd
how most people think
love is unfathomable
something on the brink.

I believe love
may and can be touched,
you just can't look
or think of it much.
Alexis Arancibia, Grade 8
Holy Family Catholic School

Valentine's Day!

It's Valentine morning
There's love in the air
Anxiously waiting for your roses
From someone special
Knowing they're arriving any second
The doorbell rings —
Guess who it is
Your secret admirer
Standing there
Holding chocolates and roses
"Happy Valentine's Day,"
He yells,
From your secret admirer.
Sabrina Barajas, Grade 7
St Alphonsus School

The Power of Music

Music is the force that holds us all together
Getting us through even the worst of times.
It is important, incomparable, and included in out identity,
It shines through our life with much needed clarity.

Music is not just an enigma of sound
It is a composition of anger, bliss, and melancholy;
Music speaks no particular language
Every note, every word forms its own story.

Music is the thread that connects us all as one
It pulls us in until we become intertwined.
Music emotes more than words alone possibly can
It is the epitome of passion and unity.

Songs are written for the whole world to hear,
To comfort and stifle everyone's fears.
And here we all stand, with a song in our hearts
All of us waiting, to share our little parts.

Tiffany Chen, Grade 9
Gretchen Whitney High School

My Brother

My brother has been there since the beginning
he's been by my side always
since childhood and growing up
he's always been there for me
through the years we've laughed and cried
together and forever
our memories are priceless
but mean the world to us
we'll always remember our times together
when we stood up for each other
we'll keep on growing up
our love stronger within the years
soon we'll be going our separate ways
no matter how far away we get
we will always have —
our memories, our laughs, and our cries
in our hearts we will always be
together and forever

Nathalie Silva, Grade 8
McCabe Elementary School

Assignment

Today I sit in class just thinking
Not about school but maybe drinking
A cool glass of lemonade as I sit outside
I make the effort to listen, God knows I've tried.
And when I am dismissed and I am safe inside,
I will soon find, the thought of the assignment,
Is no longer in my mind.

Nick Alvarez, Grade 8
McCabe Elementary School

Where Do I Go from Here?

My heart hurts deep down inside
It's like I'm in this world by myself
All I do is cry every night
I'm stuck on a three way street in a big thunderstorm
I feel so far away and I can't find my way home
I don't even know what is home
I wish I could just say I can make it through the rain
I can stand up once again on my own
But it's just too hard to deal with, too heavy to bear
I just keep falling down

I feel like I don't belong anywhere
I don't know if I can lift my head if it's another day
Where do I go from here?
I'm lost and looking for directions.

Mayra Garrido, Grade 8
Madrona Middle School

I Am Focused

I am focused
I hear my conscience say quit over and over again
I see my work that I have to do
I say don't quit over and over again
I cry only at the difficult problems
I am on task
I am working
I feel my grip of the pencil become lighter
I try to keep going, and I do
I dream of a day without work
I am determined.

George Bushala, Grade 8
Robert C Fisler School

Rebellion

It resides in the heart and soul
you can fight it but you'll lose control
it comes up when oppression begins
so you fight and hope you'll win
it strikes with a red hot fury
it burns harder than spicy curry
it flames up in your veins and mind
you will fight for the sake of your kind
your anger is ready to burst
but your enemy has faced worse
your blade will but scratch his skin
you must trample him for it to cave in
you can move mountains with your deeds
so all rebels take my words to heed
your foe is colder than hard steel
he does not care about how you feel
he is a demon of all torturous sorts
he hits hard and shows no remorse
the peaceful outside, the beast within
you've heard my words, so the battle begins.

Selene Cheong, Grade 8
Whittier Christian Jr High School

Book Firsts

When you open a book
Your feelings attack you
Love, hate, joy, grief
All the words in the world can't
Describe the feeling you get when you
Sit down with a book,
Turn on the light, and
Flip to the first page,
Read the first word,
The first sentence,
The first paragraph,
But the feeling doesn't
Go away.
And then you find yourself
Finished with the book
And you flip back to
The first page,
The first word,
The first sentence,
The first paragraph,
And begin all over again.

Waverly Tseng, Grade 8
Palm Desert Charter Middle School

Love

Love, love is sometimes peaceful
Love is sometimes stressful
But most of the time love is meaningful.
Love is a feeling and an emotion.
I know because my mom loves me.
I feel loved when I am happy.

Anthony Michael Kahnis, Grade 8
McCabe Elementary School

The End

Your heart beats very slowly,
Again again we pray
Tears are filling in our hearts,
Each and every day

Our hearts, our hopes are fading,
Though many times we cry
But God alone in with you,
His love will never die

The pain, the suffering, the sorrow,
All has gone away
Although we wish you well,
We wanted you to stay

Your golden heart stopped beating,
Your gentle eyes at rest
God took you in His arms,
To prove he takes the best.

Lauren Clesi, Grade 8
Holy Family Catholic School

I Have a Dream

These were the words spoken by Martin Luther King
Leader of the African American Civil Rights movement and Peace movement
He helped everyone make self-improvement

Equality was the purpose of Martin Luther King
He inspired our nation "To let freedom ring"

Martin Luther King made a tremendous impact in history
He was granted the Presidential Medal of Freedom in 1927
He was assassinated on April 4, 1968
He died at age thirty-nine in Memphis, Tennessee

"Free at last, free at last, thank God, Almighty, I'm free at last."
Segregation is now in the past!

Maribel Munoz, Grade 9
Lucerne Valley Jr/Sr High School

I Am…

I am red like a firecracker bursting with light
I am blue like a blue jay about to take flight
I am green like many leaves relaxing on a branch
I am brown like a horse running free on a ranch
I am red, white and blue like an American flag, rippling in the sky
I am white like a plane drifting, passing by
I am silver like a trophy shinning, showing off
I am tan like a human sitting on a loft
I am purple like the glow of moonlight stars
I am orange like the dirt lying on Mars
I am a rainbow smiling, having fun.

Julia Callow, Grade 7
Solvang Elementary School

Just One More Time

Tell me a story Papa,
just one more time.
Tell me of places far away,
and long ago.
Fill my mind with the hopes you have for me,
and the places I will go.
Just one more time.
Let me learn from your mistakes,
and laugh at how stupid you were.
Show me a way to make the room brighten the room with a smile,
or tell the perfect jokes.
Just one more time.
Let me imagine you meeting my nona,
or saying goodbye to her before War.
Fill my mind with your memories of watching my mom grow up,
and then walking her down the aisle.
Please, show me a way to live my life full of love and joy,
and to be the person you see me as,
and tell that you love me and will always be there.
Just one more time.

Megan Fraser, Grade 9
Central Catholic High School

Game Day

I love the sport of hockey. Occasionally, I do get cocky.
I love scoring goals, but I despise hitting the poles.
We train hard and we run. It's not all that fun.
But when it is game day. I show up ready to play.
We are surely having fun. The score remains zero to none.
Matt shoots the puck, too high as I must duck.
I hear the colliding pads. And screaming moms and dads.
I wind my stick to fire. Before my time expires.
I look for the perfect spot. I quickly take my shot.
Silence fills the air. The audience jumps from their chair.
I open up my eyes. And to my surprise.
My coach tells me well done. Now, the game, we have won.
Merrek Peters, Grade 9
Fountain Valley High School

Ode to the Wind

During the winter
You bring in a blizzard of white snow
Which makes winter time very cold, you know
During the spring
You hide leaving the sun shining bright
Making the temperature rise to great heights
During the summer
You bring wind to the beach
Making it hard to collect seashells, one of each
During the fall
You knock leaves off trees
With your gentle breeze
You are the wind, that blows every hour
It's amazing how you blow with all that power.
Jonathan Cenica, Grade 8
Robert C Fisler School

Music

Music comes from various instruments;
Big and small, heavy and light
All with different sounds.
Some sound better with different songs.
Some sound good put together
Making musical hurricanes of notes and
Chords and contagious beats that can
Change moods from the ear splitting silence
Of being alone to deafening laughter of being with friends.
Music can be the power of a secret or
The adventure of telling someone
Something only you know.
It can be described in many ways,
And it can describe anything in any way
From last year's trip to the Grand Canyon
To this year's trip to Disney world.
Music can make the worst day
Seem like one of the best.
It can also make the happiest person
Understand someone else's problems.
Justin Hardin, Grade 8
Rolling Hills Country Day School

Speed

My car is as fast as the speed of light
It goes vroom, vroom
On its front show 2 lights very bright
As it passes all the other cars, it cannot be seen by an eye
When this car hits the road, boom!
They all shout look at that car go!
My car is as smooth as silk and shiny as a star
This car has a polished red coat with sparkling rims
Where is it going?
It is going to a place where man hasn't been
It can race like a person on a track
When it hears the gunshot, it's gone
Abdirashid Abdella, Grade 7
Islamic School of San Diego

Helen Keller

Helen Keller, her world black like a cellar
She accomplished the impossible, and changed the world
No sound or sight, lost in the deepness of night
By a terrible illness, that robbed her sound and sight

All alone, yes all alone
Until Anne Sullivan came and opened her world
Anne became her best friend, who was always there to lend
A loving helping hand, forever they were together

Helen's fingers talk, to some it was a shock
That this little girl could talk all day, Helen spelled and learned
To school she went, it was hard to hint
That she was once alone in the abyss of darkness

Graduated she did, and now she was not hid
In darkness grasp, so she told her story
She died, which is everyone's fate, on June 2, 1968
To all she is known, and Helen changed the world
Krystia Hanson, Grade 7
Vista Verde Middle School

Mysterious Feline

In a blackened peaceful house,
a mysterious feline roams.
Always on the prowl
tense hunting her prey
her black fur turns lavender
under the moon's faint creamy glow.
Guarding her territory
steadily swinging her long slender tail
sharp yellow eyes scanning every corner.
Soon, morning's golden shine peeks through the window.
Curled in her bed,
she slowly drifts off
to sleep.
Melissa Marquez, Grade 8
Bethany Lutheran School

My Horsey and Me

My horsey and me, cantering
through leaves, having fun
on a warm spring day
My horsey and me galloping in
meadows with love so deep and
mountains so steep.
With wind in my hair and sun in
my cheeks as happy as ever my
horsey and me
My horsey and me walking
through trails pounding with
spring hail with hills so high and
birds flying by.
My horsey and me running
through flowers upon the hours
with plants so green I bet I'm
imagining.
My horsey and me, my horsey
and me is all I want to be is my
horsey and me.
Katie Beasley, Grade 7
Monte Vista Christian School

Sunlight

Every day the sun awakes
And shows us its beautiful rays
It brightens the sky
Almost all the time
Except for when it rains

It keeps us warm
While we're having fun
Or just sitting and talking indoors

But at the end of the day
It slowly fades away
And waits 'til
Dawn of the next day
Kristen Reyes, Grade 8
Madrona Middle School

Xbox 360

Oh, my great source of war and guns,
My parents say my eyes will rot.
But I just laugh and run
And say "they will not!"

I like to play all sorts of games
Except for Halo 3
Because I think the game is lame.

But tonight my eyes turned red,
Therefore, I think I'm going to bed.
Justin Thompson, Grade 8
Citrus Hills Intermediate School

The Moon

On a hazy night
A spooky light,
Comes from the moon

In a mysterious bog
A light shrouded by fog,
Comes from the moon

In a pitch black sky
A pearl shall lie,
That is the moon

Surrounded by dark
A sole light will embark,
That is the moon

Seen by the sun
Without it, it is none,
This is the moon.
Grant McPherson, Grade 8
Madrona Middle School

Football Is

Football is
Huge men blocking
And their fans mocking
Face painted fans
Screaming from the stands
Starting on Sunday
And ending on Monday
The Super Bowl is waiting
And the teams are debating
Kyle McCarthy, Grade 8
Citrus Hills Intermediate School

Together

Her eyes are crystal clear,
and she rarely ever sheds a tear,
she sleeps so sound at night,
only to wake at morning's light;
Her hair like silk shining in the moon,
Her smile enchants the afternoon,
The wind carries her heart through,
and it always comes back to you.

A lot of people will never see,
what drew us together, you and me,
even if life is just a game,
my heart will never be the same,
You make me smile every day,
my heart's a song that you can play;
my heart is locked, but you have a key,
that will never separate you and me.
Kaytie Strait, Grade 7
Citrus Hills Intermediate School

Tide

The tide comes in
And the waves foam and crash
Pounding the rocky shore
Into fine soft sand
The tide goes out
And the waves turn meek
Caressing the golden shore
The soft sand that tickles your feet
The tide comes back in
And the limpets cling to rocks
For dear, sweet life
The sand becomes softer still
Oh, what a perfect beach!
Katya Kramer, Grade 8
Lindero Canyon Middle School

He's

His eyes are vivid rivers
in a secret enchanted land
His hands like trees filled
with growth from age
His feet lead to love
His touch as warm as the sun
His voice as frightening as thunder
and as beautiful as a bird's song
He is strength and he is weakness
He is my spring in my winter
Anna Maldonado, Grade 8
Raymond A Villa Fundamental School

God

G ood in every way
O mniscient and powerful
D eliverer

S trong, he's my Shepherd
O mega

L oves you no matter what
O mnipotent
V ictorious
E verlasting love
D iligent

T ender
H oly one
E xcellent

W onderful counselor
O ne and only God
R ighteousness
L oving
D efends the feeble
Andrew Burdick, Grade 7
Monte Vista Christian School

The Hike

Our life is a hike.
We travel high and low,
Bushes and trees block our way
Confusing us where to go.

Cliffs and mountains we must climb.
Nothing can ever stop us.
Some people choose to complain and whine,
But others refuse to make a fuss.

Don't forget to bring a buddy,
When you go on your hike.
Sometimes you need a comforter,
When that bear brings you fright.

There are many mountains to climb,
Different courses and trails,
Don't be afraid of not reaching the top,
'Cause you achieve even when you fail.

Our life is a hike.
We travel high and low,
Bushes and trees block our way
But somehow, we reach where we want to go.

Amy Wong, Grade 8
Robert C Fisler School

Why Are Writing Poems So Hard?

Why is writing a poem so hard?
Makes me think endlessly
I have no more ideas to write about
But I still have two more poems to go for a project

After I finish writing this
What topic will I have to choose
Why can't writing poems be easy
Like the regular rhymes we think of daily

Alliteration always are used
Onomatopoeia made my brain snap crackle and pop
Imagery of me standing on a bed of papers
Writing till my death came

Figures of speech are used
"No time to lose" is so true
I never should procrastinate like old
Oops I forgot the rhyme

It doesn't mean I have to start
All over again, but
It means that I have to use some devices
Free verse is always the easiest

Andrew Y. Lee, Grade 8
Robert C Fisler School

Someone Special

This poem is for a special friend.
It's great to have someone like you around.
We always like being in the same trend.
We are a hot newspaper strongly bound.
A best friend stays with you until the end.
You are the medicine to my whole life.
You are the only one I can depend.
Days and years go by and summer arrives.
We splash and play in the dark deep blue sea.
Waves tried to get us but we still survived.
The hot bright day arrives setting us free.
We were all scared but thank God we're alive.
You were the one who made my love so strong.
That love which seems to fill our hearts so long.

Jessica Escobar, Grade 8
Henry T Gage Middle School

My Best Friend

My daddy was always my best friend
Until his life came to an end.
It was really hard to have him part,
But he is always and forever in my heart.
I'll never forget his calming goodnight kiss,
That now I forever truly miss.
Whenever I see a shooting star,
It makes me think of where you are.
Knowing you're gone makes me sad,
It's even harder not getting to say the word 'Dad.'
So rest in peace my best friend,
I'll love you always til the end.

Kelley Tessier, Grade 9
Fountain Valley High School

When the World Is Yellow

Today the world is yellow
Stars shine
The sun is bright a summer day
Canaries sing the joyful melody of peace
They are at rest
Gray skies after weeks of pour
Clouds grayish blue open up the lemon sun sparkles
See the world calm just sitting
Daisies flowing by the wind's side
Sunflowers grow a child's first step
Mothers at ease
Wars finished people reunite to loved ones
Hmmmm
The world hums to the melody of growth
Child born healthy pure
A glow pops out like lightning from in his harmless topaz face
Tears roll off cheeks
The world is new, calm as the aqua lake
Peaceful a soldier coming home unwounded
Pure a baby's smile

Sarah Badreau, Grade 8
Emek Hebrew Academy

I Don't Understand

I don't understand
Why we pollute our Earth
Why we destroy our future
Why we don't work together

But most of all
Why we constantly fight
Why we always complain
Why we don't change

What I understand most is
That we will try
That we will struggle
That we are the difference.

Nina Fairbairn, Grade 8
Dorris-Eaton School

Fear

Blue sweater running to class
Afraid of being scolded by a teacher.
Or bullied by an older kid.
One who doesn't fear you
He's just frightened
Of getting in trouble.
Maybe the other blue sweaters
Feel grief
For the one who fears tomorrow.

Korissa Baeza, Grade 8
St Alphonsus School

Ars Poetica

What is poetry?
Not the picture, but its beauty.
Not the house, but the inside.
Not the body, but the heart.
What is poetry?
Not the writer, but the words.
Not the school, but the teacher.
What is poetry?
Nor the roses in the field
Or the birds in the sky.

Leslee Olson, Grade 8
Madrona Middle School

Tossed

The stone remembers
when you punted it
tossed
and dropped it.
Gunned it across the water.
Cast out
from the rest of the group.
The stone shall
always remember.

Ryan Klika, Grade 7
Bethany Lutheran School

The Smile of an Imperfect Girl

There she goes with her perfect face, her perfect hair,
her perfect life, and her perfect boyfriend.
But here I am with my nose slightly crooked, my hair out of place,
my annoying parents, and my cocky boyfriend.
Yet I'm the one wearing a smile.
Why is that?
Maybe, because I don't have to act like someone I'm not.

Taylor Mestres, Grade 8
Rio Vista Middle School

Forever

I walk this Earth
lost and confused
I do not understand…
why do things always turn out how they're not supposed to?
Why do people leave and never return?
This life has a lot of things I do not understand
I turn to those who I know for help
answers to my question
but sometimes the ones I know
do not know the answer I am forever searching for
does that mean I give in?
No it means I keep searching
one day I'll find the answer I am looking for
and that is the day I will wait for my entire life probably
but one day everything that happens and has happened will make since
the people who hurt me and the things they did
will be just a small blur of the past
I will once again walk this Earth with my head held high
when I find that answer I am searching, forever searching for.

Brittney Gleason, Grade 9
Hesperia High School

Barack Obama's Inauguration

He came in a time of chaos, amidst war, poverty, and hate.
Through ignorance and fear, helplessness and confusion,
He came.
He came with a promise of hope,
And offered his condolences to Americans everywhere.
He was different, but not in appearance, voice, background, or race.
But in his ambition, and understanding of the everyday suffering
Of the average middle class family.
His plans to put an end to the harm being set on our planet,
And his knowledge of the long years that lie ahead.
The years spent repairing the great nation,
And the rest of the world's outlook on it.
Let it be known that the United States of America is and forever will be
A nation of hope, peace, and diversity.
A nation where we can.
Yes we can.

Gene Wang, Grade 7
Lawson Middle School

The Elegy of Mary O'Donnell

Mary, you always were quite merry.
You could cheer up anyone with humor.
There was no such a soul you couldn't carry.
But as your life crumbled from a brain tumor.
You still held your head high with joy.
Your faith in God and your faith in humanity.
It was something everyone could enjoy,
The roots and morals of Christianity,
You always held them with you,
If I grow up to be even a mere shadow of your stand,
I would be greatly honored along with others too.
To you Mary O'Donnell you really were grand,
As my aunt you taught me morals
Which are still inherent in me and will forever be engraved,
If you led this world it would be covered in laurels
Your thoughts and memories will always be saved.

Jack Conway, Grade 8
Carmel Valley Middle School

My Summer Day

Spring says goodbye.
Summer greets me with is bright colors.
The sun shines overhead
As I walk into the sea.
It is a time when I can enjoy the beach
As the water calls to me.
The sea's power and grace team up with summer
To create freedom's space.
Summer smells like potpourri.
It feels like heaven and
Tastes like ice-cream.
It sounds like dolphins splashing
And looks like a rainbow.
As the tide travels out,
I return to my towel and
Admire the beauty of summer.
Lemonade trickles down my throat
And I quench my thirst after a long day.
But I know not all can enjoy summer
Because an early winter is already in their lives.

Jane Tsui, Grade 7
Rolling Hills Country Day School

Home

Home? What is home?
A place you go to when you're scared?
A place to go when you have nowhere to go?
What is home?

A home to me is somewhere quiet and secluded,
A place to escape from the world and its problems.
Somewhere safe, a place with no worries.
There is where my home lies,
Somewhere quiet and somewhere safe.

Cheyenne McDaniel, Grade 7
Santa Rosa Technology Magnet School

Dusk and Dawn

When the sun starts to set
When the moon becomes visible to the naked eye
When people get tired and owls start to rise
Dusk is coming
Dusk is coming

The clouds turn rose to violet
The wolves start to howl
Dusk is here
Dusk is here

Though the night is dark
A speck of lemon can be seen
Dawn is coming
Dawn is coming

A mouse wakes to drink dew
A rooster crows
A cow moos
Dawn is coming
Dawn is coming

The sun springs above the horizon
Dawn is here

Xavier Prunty, Grade 8
Bethany Lutheran School

Soccerphenom

Soccer is my way of life.
Soccer is my obsession.
For me, my friends, even my dad's wife
It's like my favorite possession

A feeling that matches no other
Stepping on the field hoping for your very best
Standing side by side, with your best brother
The next sixty minutes will be the toughest test

Kicking, running, trapping, and heading
Using all of your body and soul
Against all odds you are better
Your main motivation, scoring the winning goal

A superstar in the making
A *Bend It Like Beckham* wannabe
It's mine for the taking,
If only the future will bring it to me

I am going to be a pro
I will thank my soccer mom
I am going to grow
Into a soccerphenom!

Brendan Johnston, Grade 8
Madrona Middle School

Paths

I was a lost traveler; I sought for a path to walk on
But I was a lousy traveler, I was lost
You were also a traveler, but you weren't nearly as lost as I
You said, "Walk with me," so I did
We found a marvelous path to walk; a path of glittering gold and sparkling silver
But then you did the most bizarre thing, you fell
Not a fall like when one trips, you don't even know you fell
You fell in such a way that you stopped traveling, and followed
I tried to reach for you, but the path got in my way
I tried to shout for you, but you couldn't hear me
You just kept following, following the path of glittering gold and sparkling silver
When I looked down to my feet I saw a darker path, the path we walked became a path of mud and dirt
You haven't checked the path you're walking, is it still the path you thought it was?
You haven't checked in days, weeks, months, even years
I stepped off that path long ago, "Whose path are you following now?" you might ask
What a silly question, I don't "follow" anyone's path
I am traveling my own

Jacob Parisse, Grade 8
Madrona Middle School

Home at Last

My eyes open to the bright glowing sun, I jump from my bed and hop to a run.
On my way out the door I grab my jacket and gloves, go to the barn door shooing away the fat turtledoves,
And step into the warm barn, as it is weathered and worn, is perfect for Penny and the newly harvested corn.
I pat her cheek, she shakes out her mane, on goes her saddle and we head down the lane.
She kicks up the dust then picks up her feet, she is now going at a flying, galloping beat.
The forest flies by and quails so shy, waddle back to the bushes maybe they are camera-shy.
We get to the field where atop a lone hill, there stands a tree so sturdy and still.
I let her graze as I sit on my perch in the tree to gaze, at all the beauty posed around me illuminated by the sun's gentle rays.
After our nice rest overlooking mountains and lakes, we get ready and reside from the break.
My horse bows down and I climb aboard. I kick her to start out to the shore.
The silken shiny surf splashes and rumbles, the rough rocky realm crashes and crumbles.
I am calm and alive I know as the sun sinks away, I am here to stay.
As I sit on the pebbly beach where the moon shines its cast I realize, I am home at last.

Sydney Lindquist, Grade 8
Sacred Heart School

Before I Leave This World

I shall experience at least an inkling of the wonders life has to offer me
I will climb the Eiffel Tower, and view the pinprick heads of people bustling about below me
I will ride in a gondola through the canals of Venice,
and watch the graceful ripples that oars make as they cut through the water
I will bathe in the sun-soaked beaches of Jamaica, and bring home a bottle of sand to show my grandchildren
I will struggle through the wildlife of Yellowstone, and breathe in the warm spring mist that emits from Old Faithful
I will visit the pyramids of Egypt, and touch the crumbling stone sphinxes glaring down upon me
I will glimpse the many marine creatures dwelling in Sea World, and feel the velvety, silky-smooth skin of a dolphin
I will scuba dive through the Great Barrier Reef, and count every pore in the corals residing in the sea
I will embark on a Serengeti safari in Africa, and perhaps I will even get close enough to touch the spotted fur of a giraffe
And I will fly on a plane back to Nanjing, China,
and walk inside the hospital where I first entered this world
Before I leave it

Alice Yin, Grade 8
John F Kennedy Middle School

Lock and Key

A mirror is mounted on the wall
And I'm standing in that empty hall
But who is the girl staring back at me?
What I feel's not what I see

Her smile is fake, not warm and true
But when it's real her soul shines through
That's the smile I want to see
It's in there somewhere with the rest of me

It's under the thoughts that aren't her own
With her real feelings she's never shown
'Cause she cares too much about what others see
Hiding her real self under lock and key

But someday someone will find that key
To unlock and find who she really can be
A person who understands is what she needs
Who can stop seeing her and start seeing me.

Theadora Kwan, Grade 8
Buchser Middle School

Letting Go

Holding on to this balloon of bad dreams
Prying fingers slowly coming clean
Quivering, shaking, heavy breathing
The heat was mind wheeling
Close my eyes and count to ten
It was like the world was going to end
Soon I saw a radiant light, pure and bright
My mind was taking flight
The last little finger breaking free from this string
I let go of this balloon of bad dreams

Brooke Rosenblit, Grade 8
Jack Weaver - Oak Grove School

Endless Love

I love you, will all my heart,
Even though we're far apart,
I miss you so much,
I want to feel your touch,
Kiss me, hug me, and play with my hair,
When we go out, spaghetti we'll share,
Your eyes are brown and my eyes are blue,
But no matter what our love is true,
You want to hold me when I cry,
I never ever want to say goodbye,
We spend hours on the phone,
The whole time speaking in a soft tone,
You whisper you love me into my ear,
And for the rest of my life, that's all I want to hear.

Shannon Lucey, Grade 9
Fountain Valley High School

My Journey Ends

I write about you in vocab. each week.
You are my Edward on and off the screen.
Your charming mane of hair is almost neat;
If I possessed a lock I'd be a queen.

When shy, you grin oh so adorably;
I will melt even if I had a choice.
It makes my heart beat uncontrollably,
When I hear your attractive English voice.

You must get tired from so much running;
Running through my mind all day can be tough.
Someday you'll propose, your eyes so cunning;
At last you'll be mine, for me that's enough.

My lifelong journey ends when we become:
Mr. and Mrs. Robert Pattinson.

Madison Mittleman, Grade 8
Las Flores Middle School

Oh Palestine

Oh Palestine
When I heard you call
I think of home
The place where my grandparents once lived
The land of the prophets…
The land of the golden dome…
Your olive trees are
So alive and beautiful
Oh Palestine
How much I love your land

Ziyad Albahri, Grade 8
Islamic School of San Diego

Wonderland

my land of make-believe where the little children fly
where the animals speak and the mothers never cry
and the streets are safe, and the schools are fun
for this life, no one knows how far I would run

in this land of the wonders and the wonders beyond
there are creatures of which we are extremely fond
and these creatures, kind of mysterious, each one
we can acquaint with each other and fly up to the sun

and the citizens of this super spootylicious place
are amazingly zen, but insane to the face
they are skinny and fat, short and tall all combined
for appearance has no effect on the mind

but if only you could experience my wealth
my fantastic life and my incredible health
but I can only sit and play in the sand
and dream about my glorious wonderland

Clarissa Shultz, Grade 8
McCabe Elementary School

Monsters

Little boys
Play with scary toys
They touch worms
Contaminated with germs
They eat their boogers
Make a mess
Oh all the boys
I wish there were less

Cass Aiello, Grade 8
La Joya Middle School

Ode to Music

Ode to music
the many rhythms
the beats
Ode to music
that drowns out the noise
that keeps me
safe and fills the
silence
with blaring
screams or
screeches of guitars
pounds of drums
Ode to music
that can
send a message
and maybe
one day
unite the
world

Mallorie Diaz, Grade 8
La Joya Middle School

Global Warming

Global warming is
the heating of this planet
shall it never end

David Flores, Grade 8
Richard Merkin Middle Academy

Perfection

They say that no one is perfect.
They say you shouldn't even try.

I say that to even attempt
To cure your faults
Is perfection.

It matters not if
You fail or succeed.
To me,
To try
Is perfection.

Oishi Banerjee, Grade 7
The Harker School - Middle Campus

My Heart and Soul

My heart is ready to show all the secrets it has kept
My soul is ready to give the love that you deserve
I am ready to feel

I'm giving in to love it has won the battle
It is time for my heart to pour,
All its feeling and truth

My soul is ready to love, it knows how it feels
My soul is ready to express its deep emotion
It is ready to tell about its love

My heart wants to speak, no longer will it stay silent
My heart will say what it wants, and it wants you
Forever you shall be my heart and never anyone else

My soul is ready to declare it is yours for the keeping
So please don't mistreat or break it, I love you is what I want to say
For it is really true!

That my heart and soul to stay and forever they are yours

Simone Everett, Grade 8
Temecula Valley Charter School

Bomb of Life

Life is like a bomb that can go off any second
So when you have a chance to be with someone
Be with him/her because not everyone gets to have a very special friend
And when that bomb does go off at least it exploded with a feeling called…love.

Edith Velasquez-Mancilla, Grade 8
Willow Grove Elementary School

Ode to Football

It was that day
When my dad threw a football
And a lasting love
That would never go away
The rubber — rough, gear — heavy
Kept me going through the game
When it was early, or deep into the night
I always got tackled, But always got up
The QB yelling
26, 27, 8, 14, 31, HIKE!!!
The coach would teach how to play
How to tackle, How to catch
And suddenly I would do, what I would learn
There were times when I gave up, and there were days I would cry
But even so I made it through, my football skills began to rise
Injuries have pulled us apart, I was separated from the field for miles
Truly, the only thing that keeps me going, Is the love I have for this game
This is an ode to my favorite sport, the sport I love
I will always play
Ode to Football

Jonathan Farraj, Grade 8
Robert C Fisler School

Family

Family is supportive.
They give you advice.
They are there whenever you need them.
You have your parents,
who love and care for you.
You have your sisters.
The youngest looks up to you.
The older sister cares for you.
You may have a brother.
He's protective of you and cares for you.
He loves you very much.
You also have your wonderful grandparents.
They're always there when you need them.
They are kind.
Family is a very precious treasure.
Even in your ups and downs,
You're still united.
Family is the best.
Forever and ever family you'll be.

Gabriela Rosas, Grade 8
St Helen Catholic Elementary School

Home

Mom and sister in the kitchen
Making dinner for the family
This doesn't happen often
But they cook together happily

They sing aloud and out of tone
But I've got to admit; this is what I call home

Brittany Bartholdi, Grade 9
Bella Vista High School

To Overcome

I was born premature and really weak
Not knowing my life span was thought to be bleak
As I grew up I started to see
My twin sister was so much taller than me
I thought to myself some day I'll be the same
Not realizing my height has already came
However many obstacles arose because I'm SHORT
It's okay cuz I find a solution and can honestly report
That top cupboard that holds my favorite treats
I stand on a chair and there is no defeat
Then when pictures are taken and I get lost within the tall
I stand on my toes, head high and never withdraw
To those of my friends who make fun of me
I laugh out loud but with a tear no one can see
I'm always trying to stand out and always reaching
Knowing that everything I overcome is just a teaching
I know my life's obstacles are just a small challenge
Try to live in my world where sometimes its hard to manage
However, I know being small will never define me
I have so much to offer not just the SHORTY you see

Syrena Hernandez, Grade 8
Los Coyotes Middle School

Time Flies By

Today is a day of reckoning,
tomorrow is a day of wonder,
yesterday was a day of knowing;
the life in you will go by if you stick to a day-by-day plan.

Anywhere you go,
everyone you see is there,
anyone you saw was there,
everyone you will see will be there.

Remember: You must not wait for opportunities to pass,
don't let life go by,
don't wait until you die,
live life happily,
because time flies by.

Kate Mook, Grade 8
Palm Desert Charter Middle School

Forever Alone

The night is empty, dark and cold.
As it hears the howling of the wind below.
It feels the iciness all around,
and the smell of pine trees on the ground.
Breathing in the cold midnight air.
Wishing hard that someone was there.
It dwells and waits for the bright morning sun,
until the dead silence of the night is done.

Kendahl Hawkins, Grade 8
Bethany Lutheran School

Speechless

Covered in the moss of the dark, tinted forest,
You're feeling at your poorest.
You wish there were some other way,
To turn around and say what you want to say.
You think it through,
But no new thoughts come to you.

Drenched by the pouring rain,
The numbness kills the pain.
Tears fall from your eyes,
But you can't figure out why.
Lost by the color that the world chooses to see,
You suddenly realize why you can only see me.

The sun rises, the sun falls,
You're still confused by it all,
You doubt yourself and question why,
You feel so blind, you feel so nigh.
Forever seems like such a long time,
But with you by my side, all I want is more time.

Chanel Nye, Grade 8
Sonrise Christian School

Song Birds of the Night
Some crickets chirping
Hear their songs filling the air
Listen to night's birds

Angelique Therrien, Grade 7
Lakeside Middle School

Iraq War Memorial
As they run through the mud
They think of the blood.
That will be shed,
And all of the dead

The soldier's retreat
To the navy's fleet
They all started to run
Soon they would be done.

All the widows weep,
As the bodies go in deep.
As all the children cry,
They think of the lone lie

They told their dad,
When he got mad
The cries all added
They yelled I am sorry dad!

Nicholas Watamura, Grade 8
Citrus Hills Intermediate School

Hues
Deep in the city
Where the lights never slept
She slipped on her shoes, coat
Out the door, she crept

For the pretty blue Hue
Continued to make her eyes glow jade
Made her hair glisten violet
On the grass where she laid

The park was translucent
Beneath where she stood
Breathing into the dead of the night,
As she pulled on her hood

The rain fell soggy and fast
Running through her long hair
The droplets quickened
Dampening the air

But the lights never faltered
In the cool of the night
And even as it poured
The Hues glowed bright

Laura Farris, Grade 8
Holy Family Catholic School

Nature Is
Nature is green forests
Nature is dew on the grass
Nature is the reddest leaves in autumn swaying in the wind
Nature is the sound of wolves baying at the moon
Nature is the thunder and lightning pounding the ground outside
Nature is

Nature is the blackest of nights
Nature is the crashing of water on rocks
Nature is sun shining down on an endless desert
Nature is

James Fowler, Grade 7
Santa Rosa Technology Magnet School

Rain
Darkness falls over the land and skies are not bright
Now the day is as dark as the night.
The weather becomes colder and temperature starts to decrease,
The sky is the color of white piano keys.
The wind whistles through the trees,
And gives the classrooms a little breeze.
The clouds cover what used to be a blue sky,
And people say rain is just like God's cry.
I hope the rain won't be here the next day,
I just want the rain to go away.

Daryl Ann Dela Cruz, Grade 7
St Cyprian School

The Traveler
I was walking a dusty road, on the way to Galilee,
When I met a mysterious man, who had lived along the sea.
Wanting to converse, I asked an interesting question,
"What is love, good sir? What is your definition?"
He turned to me and smiled, a simple, but genuine smile.
"Good sir," he replied, "Why don't we debate this for awhile?"
I turned to him and said, "I really do not know.
I have heard once though, that love was all for show."
His response though really shocked me; his voice was clear and strong.
"Good sir," he replied, "I think you have it all wrong.
I know something about love, and it is unselfish and does not boast.
It never leaves you and does not care if you have the most."
Shocked as I was, I managed to say,
"Good sir, where are you planning to stay?
I want to ask you more questions today.
But night seems to be closing fast,
And yet I want this conversation to last
Because it seems like you have been sent to me from above."
He turned to me and smiled, as gentle as a dove.
Then to me he said, "Good sir, *I am love*."

Laraine Chan, Grade 9
Valley Christian High School

Broken Haven

Imagining for the wonder she longs for
Wishing, hoping, and believing for its arrival
Before her eyes appears a gate that shows more
Of a world, welcoming you to visit for eternal

Stepping in, a big dimply smile drew across her face
Just for once, finally being treated with utmost respect
In a magnificent land, without a single trace
Of any horrendous past you can ever expect

Feeling as if finally treated as the supreme
Such a wondrous place for any soul's desire
Until being swept away by some force, she tried to scream
Her voice grew coarse, not believing her land she admire

Has vanished away as the sounds grew violent and dark
Shadows fading away screeches coming from afar and near
With all the surroundings making such a horrific remark
Surrounded in toxic fumes of darkness, seeing her worst fear

She finds herself trapped in the dark depressions
Of reality once more, haunting her life
From all the devious eyes building tension
With the teacher's scolding, like a stab with the knife

Eizyl Tanedo, Grade 7
Challenger School – Ardenwood

Elegy of a Dying Dove

Struck down by a cruel arrow
Replaced by a black crow
Who now sits on the gray, dead tree
Which used to be full of light, and as big as the deep blue sea
The olive branch is far from sight
Trapped in a deep dark pit
Without the sight of the bright light

What happened…
…to the white bird that used to *live?*
…to the bright sun that used to shine?
How has…the world fallen under the spell of *evil?*
I'll tell you how, greedy men were not satisfied
They wanted more than they were looking for

And so, the beginning of the end, started up again
Leaving the black crow, to sit on his perch and enjoy the show
And to this day
The forgotten dove lays
Trapped in the darkest pit
He is tortured by Hate
And his never-ending followers
Wondering…If this is his true fate

Hannah Kaplan, Grade 8
Carmel Valley Middle School

What Can Poetry Be?

Poetry can be everything,
like the bottoms of our shoes
or like shadows drifting across the floor.
Poetry can be anything,
like the fingernails on our hands
or the smelly old gym sock in your locker.
Poetry can be a smell,
like the scent of a rose.
Poetry can be a touch,
like the touch of a ghost
sending chills down your spine.
Poetry can be a sight,
like the sun slowly setting down.
Poetry can be a taste,
like the sweet taste of chocolate
melting in your mouth.
Poetry can be a sound,
like an explosion of a bomb.

Daniel Chong, Grade 8
Madrona Middle School

Why War?

We fight, we fall
We yearn for peace
The war brings pain and sorrow
Mixed emotions fill our minds
As all hope is washed away with tears

Friends lost, families separated
All for the selfish benefits of others
What do we do when our heroes fall?
And haven't the strength to rise?

All want peace, but few have faith
That this sorrow that haunts us will cease to exist
No good comes from fighting.
No good comes from war.
So why fight?
Why war?

Hagen Lendewig, Grade 7
Holy Family Catholic School

Never Love Again

Love was the most painful thing ever in my life.
When he appeared my eyes started to lighten up.
He made me enjoy love,
He told me that you can lose sadness, but never happiness.
By that time my life was full of happiness.
Until he…dumped me.
My heart was broken into thousands of pieces.
My love and happiness had slowly evaporated into thin air.
He was the first one to make me feel love.
And now he would be the last one.
After all this happened love would never exist in my life.

Shirley Lin, Grade 8
Presidio Middle School

Fans

NBA
You hear the NBA fans
Screaming, yelling, cheering, and
Booing the teams.
The arena where they can have fun
And just enjoy the
Fun and
Excitement.
We all love
The action and
Performance during
Half time,
But we know that once
The excitement is over we will
All be sad or tired.
Just to let all
NBA fans know
That when the
Excitement is gone
We will remember
The cheering in the NBA.

Alexander Tang, Grade 8
Purple Lotus International Institute

Waiting

A dreary place
Chilly winds
And the cold shiny snow
Covered
My heart
The beautiful grassland
Waiting for the sun to come out
Melt the snow
And see the beautiful grassland again
But
When is the sun
Going to come out?

Shinn Pek, Grade 9
Purple Lotus International Institute

Friend

A friend knows how to comfort.
A friend knows what you like,
And how to get it.
A friend knows how to make you happy
Or sad.

A friend knows how to build you up
And how to bring you down.
A friend knows how to tease
And how to respect.
A friend knows how to help or teach.
A friend just knows.

Tanner Pruett, Grade 7
Yolo Middle School

My Friends

M arvelous
Y ou are always here

F unny
R andom
I rreplaceable
E nergetic
N oisy
D rama
S arcastic

Mary Ann Montalbo, Grade 7
St Mary of Assumption School

Over Two Thousand Years Ago

Over two thousand years ago,
Jesus died for our sins.
He gave His life for us
we should have been on
that cross, not Jesus.
Jesus I thank You
for dying for our sins
and I want to follow
You more and love
You with all
my heart.

Miguel Sepulveda, Grade 7
Our Lady of the Rosary School

Soldiers in the Sky

When you look across the midnight sky,
What do you see?
Shiny objects floating,
Floating overhead

There are millions of tiny ones
But only one big one
It is the protector of the night
Defending with its army

The soldiers are the stars
The leader is the moon
Together they protect us,
Protect us while in bed

They have been here for an eternity
Protecting us and guiding us
They led the slaves to freedom
And guide the Marine Corp. home

So the next time when you gaze,
Gaze across the midnight sky
If you're lost and injured
Follow the night army toward victory

Ken Williams, Grade 8
Madrona Middle School

The Light of Life

Everything begins with sunlight
Rising from their beds

Very soon comes daylight
Activity is everywhere

Off the horizon comes skylight
Fading off in the distance

Approaching last is moonlight
Nighttime's own light bulb

Brent Saito, Grade 8
Madrona Middle School

BSA

Skills of survival,
Friendships that last forever.
Boy Scouts of America.

Where do boys become men?
Where do circles of cloth become pride?
Where does a group become a family?
Boy Scouts of America

You make lifelong friends,
Learn to fend for yourself.
Troop 434
Boy Scouts of America

Scouter and Tenderfoot
1st class and 2nd class
Star and Life
Eagle
BSA

TJ Hughes, Grade 7
Holy Rosary School

Irreplaceable

Born crippled in body and spirit,
He changed the world.
Among all the hearts he broke,
He ended this life far too young.
He lived in a place of terror and fright
And helped lead people into the light.
He united the world together
And always fought through hard weather.
He ended war.
He will be remembered forever more.
Even after he is gone
His soul will live on.
May he find peace
For he is forever
Irreplaceable.

Patrick Rin, Grade 7
St Cyprian School

The Abovelands

Run along the pipes, through the door
Find the rock marked 'E' and press it
To open the door of steel
and press the buttons on the edge of the moors

And behold the boats with moving light
That has the matches to light them
But do not fright, they are bright
Enough to lead you through the stream

Push to the top of that hill
Follow the dim lights in the cave
Navigate through it to find krill
Take the boats, and do not be afraid

The water will take you to the cavern
Which will show you the small ledge
That will lead you up the stream
To help you find the Abovelands

Avinav Rao, Grade 7
Challenger School – Ardenwood

Birds That Don't Fly

They are black and white,
They have wings but they don't experience flight,
They swim around with glorious might,
They fish in the daylight,
But be careful,
They do bite!

Samuel Lay, Grade 8
Robert C Fisler School

Soccer

It is Saturday morning…again
As I prepare for the highlight of my day,
My soccer game.
When I arrive, my coach says,
"Go play, I know you can do it,
I'm counting on you."
As I go out onto the field,
I can feel the hot sun beating down on my back.
As I hear the loud blow of the whistle,
I run as fast as I can down the field.
My teammate boots the ball down the field to me.
I get the ball and start dribbling as if I were a bolt of lightning.
Past the defenders I go,
Towards the goal,
Closer, and closer I get,
Until finally, I take a shot
And hear the "pop" of my foot pounding the ball.
Into the net it goes.
I hear the deafening roar of cheers
Coming from the sidelines,
And then the game is over.

Tara Leeds, Grade 7
Rolling Hills Country Day School

Enslaved to Love

My Forever Lost.

A walk down the beach
Would be nothing without you
The way we were was something new
Through the fire and flames we prevail
Through a day of holy grail
The childish things we have done
Shall never be undone
As we would never be apart
Under breaking dawn we caress
As if we just met
A day that would never be let
A moment of everlasting ecstasy
But all went over
As I remember the pain
Like a day of disdain
Because forever is just a word
A word of overstatement
And with time has stricken judgment upon us
Making us two-apart

Brandon Tran, Grade 9
Fountain Valley High School

Self-Portrait

My hair is thick strands of dark chocolate.
My hazel eyes are like bottomless pools of infinite light.
My fingers are long pencils, pointed at the ends.
My legs are spotted with black and blue, worn from work.
My heart holds forgiveness,
Patching up the wounds, and moving on.
I live in the goal.
I eat flying soccer balls, and players that get in my way.

Abigail Perry, Grade 8
Citrus Hills Intermediate School

My Eternal Sun

Sharp winds do blow; fierce slashing rain does chill,
A day of endless darkness spent alone,
Vast clusters of harsh boundless clouds do spill,
And the swaying trees let out a low moan.
In my tattered, frayed home, far from divine,
I gaze, longing for sun, out the glass pane,
Through dreary blackness, a light seemed to shine —
A young man walking, in spite of the rain;
Gravitation moved us forth, we embraced
With the warmest of hugs, gladdest of smiles;
The large dazzling sun gleamed, the clouds erased;
He had found me after traveling miles.
Flawless and bright, he was the only one;
He was my very own eternal sun.

Caroline Pohl, Grade 8
Las Flores Middle School

Midnight Is the Brightest Hour

I've lost myself
My heart beating
Under black velvet
Enveloped in the deep
Blackness of lies
The enemy here
My devotion
Shreds each piece of
Reason I had before
You arrived.

Because whenever I see blue
I bury it deeper
In that midnight cloth
But you hold on
So I break away.

With every glimpse
My heart climbs a mile
But I won't let
Their beauty be my death
Or my light.

I'm in deep water.

Stephanie Renteria, Grade 9
Woodbridge High School

This Game

It hurts so bad
We knew it would happen
We knew someone would get hurt
Is it supposed to hurt this bad?

We bet a lot
Maybe too much
Now I am shattered
And broken.

This is what happens
When we play this game
Called "teenage love."
A game of lies and deceit.

It hurts so bad
We knew this would happen
We knew someone would get hurt
Is it supposed to hurt this bad?

Daniela Acosta, Grade 8
McCabe Elementary School

Iraq

There to protect us
The army of our country
They won't let us down.

David Martinez, Grade 7
Corpus Christi School

Superstar

Your heart's pounding a million times, you're thinking,
you're shivering, you can't stop thinking of mistakes.
You try to keep your mind on the game. You're thinking,
still shivering. I'm going to be okay, coach says I'll be okay.
You get on the field, team's down by six
on the twenty-yard line with zero point, twelve seconds left on the clock.
You change your attitude once you get in the huddle.

It's all up to me.

The ball hikes, you take two steps, sweat dripping from your helmet,
you're breathing hard but you know that you can do it.
You release the ball. Should I have done that? You think.
The ball's in slow motion, high in the air, soaring like a bird.
Then it drops like a rock. You close your eyes, it's pitch black.
You hear nothing but the sound of the wind.
Then you open your eyes, you see people screaming,
but you can't hear it. Soon your ears pop.
The referee says, "Touchdown!"
The receiver caught the ball. He caught it in the end zone.
The field goal kicker comes out — he makes it! The game's over!
We won! We won! The crowd screams my name.

I said to myself, "I did it."

Marceles Clash, Grade 7
Odyssey Charter School

Flying Free*

I remember the day you became sick,
Though with the news you were as solid as a brick.
We all felt the heartbreak and tears,
We all shared the same fears.

You were happy for such a long while,
But though you might have been in pain you always warmed us with your smile.
You were the brother I never had.
Our families came together to deal with the sad.

On that devastating night
We couldn't overcome our fright.
Before we knew it you were gone.
The memories we tried to remember were so fawn.

The day came and all I saw were people in black,
Then on came the realization and panic attack.
We handled our grief with shared hugs and cries,
But we knew in our minds it was time for our final goodbyes.

Now you are not in pain,
The special memories we will always maintain.
Now that you are watching over from up above,
You fly free like a beautiful white dove.

Dakota Matiko, Grade 8
Citrus Hills Intermediate School
*R.I.P. Ryan Sorensen

Tired and Uninspired
To feel so isolated
What am I supposed to think?
Here, with no one to explain.
The world goes round and round,
Friends come and go,
Homes come and go,
Cities come and go,
Who am I to complain?
All those endless hours sulking,
Finally when time has come for me to smile,
Something changes.
The feeling I can't explain.
Lately,
I've been tired and uninspired.

Ingrid Kim, Grade 8
McCabe Elementary School

Ode to Friends
You bring great joy into everyone's lives.
When we get one,
We are filled with much happiness and joy.
When we lose one,
We are depressed and strive for one.

Once we have one,
We never want to lose them.
When we don't have one,
We are lonely and envy those who have one.
Having one could lift our spirits and
Make us feel as bright as the sun above.

So having a friend,
Just one friend,
Could change us around and
Bring much happiness and joy into our life.

Hana Chyun, Grade 8
Robert C Fisler School

My Little Cutie
I know my little brother
Baby whining, Toys flying
Food throwing, Height growing
I know my little brother
The smell of dirty diapers,
Watching Dora and Diego save hurt vipers
The taste of chewed up corn,
The sound of a little bike's horn
I know my little brother
"Nope" and "Nigh Night"
"Wuv Voo" and "Vroom! Vroom!"
I know my little brother.

Demi Allen, Grade 8
Citrus Hills Intermediate School

Season's Greetings
Through the window the seasons approach,
Summer at its end, dry and damp like an old cockroach
Fall on its way,
The leaves began to sway,
Halloween is near with scary masks and a candy ear,
Now winter is around the corner, some people are a mourner
Jingle bells and Christmas trees,
People praying on their knees
Now the cold has past, spring is here,
Children running around with cheer,
School is out, time for a break
Time for rain and to barbeque the steak
This isn't winter or is it fall
It's the season we all like, the one we call
That season is summer the hottest of all
The school bell rings indicating it's over
Little kids playing, finding a four leaf clover
This is the time we all get together,
Around the campfire, praising this amazing weather

Allie Ramirez, Grade 7
Santa Rosa Technology Magnet School

Friends
Those we lean on, to listen and play
Friends is their name
We hear what they say.
Laughter and tears, times of pure joy,
Our friends are our friends,
Without any ploy.
Maybe just one or maybe a few
We all need our friends
No matter what — we just do.
They start out as playmates when we are so small
We keep those that care
As we grow so tall.
And maybe in life,
A few will remain
Close to our homes or our hearts just the same.
Time may pass
Without "Hi — how do you do,"
But true friendship will last through and through.
Friends are a blessing from our Lord above
For my friends I am grateful
And for my friends I do love.

Lennon Webb, Grade 8
Holy Family Catholic School

Driven to the Forbidden
C ome a little closer, hissed the gleaming snake
A n apple entices her, it hangs so daintily by the stem, a
J ewel among fruits, the epitome of temptation
O nly a fruit, yet a symbol of damnation
L ustily she bites, though she knows it's forbidden
E ternal punishments, banned from the Garden of Eden

Bree Iskandar, Grade 7
The Mirman School

Love Is…

What happens when you get left heartbroken does it hurt, does it sting, does it feel like someone has shot a dart through your broken heart? Or does it just occur to you that it wasn't meant to be, I'm just trying to be free from these feelings you can't see, it's impossible to know why I would rather kill to die, why do we say such things that just make us want to sin, I had shed too many tears, I can't bear to see you anymore, why don't we just face reality, what I'm facing is insanity, you can call it a sickness sure, but I just cannot find the cure, God gave me the strength to face this thing I never felt before, I mean I just don't care, for my heart would never feel love forevermore.

Miguel Sarabia, Grade 8
Richard Merkin Middle Academy

Thank You

When I was exhausted or frustrated, crying uncontrollably, you gave me a hug and told me it would be all right
When I was alone in the darkness your gentle voice pulled me out of my depression
No matter how emotionally distraught I was you were always by my side, comforting me
When you're around me I can smile the prettiest smile

I will never, ever forget the things you've done for me
The things that helped me become a stronger person, the helping hand you gave me that pulled me from the darkness
I will never let go of them

I run up to you, seeing you off to your next journey, knowing we won't meet again for a long time,
I say with gratitude, "I will be stronger and won't be ashamed
I will persevere with no regrets no matter how far apart we live
I will never let go of the memories we had, but most of all, I will never forget what you did to help me
Help me become the person I am today, until we meet again,
Promise me that our dreams may be achieved," you nod and we pinky swear

As I walk away from the platform your figure become smaller
I turn around with tears shining in my eyes and I whisper, "Thank you"

Emily Liu, Grade 9
Gretchen Whitney High School

Alone

I packed my suitcase: my leather shoes, black striped jacket, Bible, and even my favorite underwear.
I gave goodbye hugs to my friends and goodbye kisses to my mom and sisters.
Dad solemnly drove me to the airport and we quietly ate our last bowl of Kimchi and rice together.
I gave dad a bear hug and a firm handshake and entered the security area.
The guards swirled a sensor around my body, and verified my passport.
The bald guard let me through and escorted me to the terminal.
We walked and walked and walked, and finally I boarded the plane.
It was my sixth time to fly on a plane, but the first without my parents.
I was ok, even though I felt like crying.
I read my Bible, skipped dinner, slept and watched the movie overhead.
Twelve hours is a long time for a thirteen-year-old boy
to watch the same movie over again and again.
Suddenly, the plane started to shake.
Descending…
Descending…
Descending…

Landed!
I stumbled off the plane, weak from sitting so long.
A black-skinned guard spoke to me in English,
But I didn't understand, so I handed him my passport.
He smiled at me and said, "Welcome to America, kid."

Danny Yoo, Grade 7
Linfield Christian School

A Best Friend

Best friends will be with me forever and never let me down.
They are there, when I need a hand.
When I am sad, they are sad with me.
When I am mad, they are mad too.
When I am happy, their spirits are lifted.
A best friend will tell me when I'm a stick in the mud,
Or when I did something wrong.
But no matter what, they are there.
They can get through to me when I'm a wall.
A best friend is like a present waiting to be opened.
A best friend goes through the good times and the bad,
The silly times and the sad.
I'll hold on to my best friend with all my life.
My best friend and I will always be two peas in a pod.

Phyna Samson, Grade 7
Rolling Hills Country Day School

Bugs Bunny of Course

Bugs Bunny the looniest tooniest looney toon there ever was
With his catch phrase, "What's up Doc?"
He is the undisputed king of comedy
Always outsmarting his opponent
Into just giving up…or blowing up
He has never lost a battle (with the exception of the tortoise)
He is cunning, quick-talking, and above all funny
He helped us get through World War II
So I heard from a talk show in the car
What our world needs now is this looney tooney cartooney
To help us get through our war and recession
He'll end our depression
Cunning, quick-talking, above all funny
Bugs the Bunny.

Johnny Biller, Grade 8
Holy Family Catholic School

Free

The cold breeze blows
Slowly as it softly speaks,
Free.
The bounds of the mighty seas
Is life and purities,
Free.
The blue sky towers with majestic pride,
Clouds roaming in wonders,
Free.
The uncontrollable songs of the birds at dawn
And the lovely ones that rest when light sets,
Free.
The patience of the life meant to be —
Its called destiny, that one day leaves you,
Free.
The fight for life and never giving up
Eventually the beginning ends,
Free.

Laura J. Lujan, Grade 8
Walter F Dexter Middle School

Capture the Flag

I have the flag
The blue team on my tail
I race back to the alpha base
I hear gun shots in the background
I race on
Trying as hard as I can to get back to alpha base
The gun shots are getting closer
I know I don't have much time
A bullet penetrates my leg
I begin to limp
I must pass on the flag
There is no time!
Suddenly…
A turret sounds
In the distance I see my team with a Jeep
Then the sounds of bullets stops
My surroundings are silent as the grave
I slowly recover
My teammates recover the flag
We win!

Hunter Dobson, Grade 7
Santa Rosa Technology Magnet School

Ars Poetica

"What is poetry?" people ask
Poetry is no slight task
It takes feeling emotion and heart
Most people don't know where to start
Poetry is a dream that comes to those who are awake
Poetry is a song, that only your heart can make
Does poetry have rhythm or rhyme,
Is it a story, do you have to say it in time?
It is the language of the heart, a breath from the soul
Poetry is free, it takes no toll
It only takes toll on your mind, makes you think
All you need for a poem is a though, paper and ink
So what is poetry in a nutshell?
It is not a toy you can sell
You can't wish one up from a well
It is love, thought and meaning
In a story you can write
Poetry cannot be wrong
It can only be right

Ashley Lawson, Grade 8
Madrona Middle School

I Have No Home

This is life, cars going by.
This is life; homeless people on the street,
they have nothing to eat.
No pets, no home, just a life on their own.

Stephen Figura, Grade 7
Odyssey Charter School

Drift Forever

"Crash! Whoosh!"
the sea cried out
as it swooped down
on the terrified sailors.
"Splash!"
the sea exclaimed
as it sent the sailors
soaring through the air
like ragdolls.
"Smash!"
went the sea
as it smacked down
into an underwater grave.
Finally, with one last wave,
the sea crawled away
from the ships and sailors,
leaving them
stranded and shipwrecked
out in the middle
of the cold, dark sea.

PJ Martinez, Grade 7
Bethany Lutheran School

Hope

Don't give up hope,
For everything is possible,
Unless you work hard.
Don't give up hope,
For if there's no hope,
The world will be in chaos.
Don't give up hope,
For it is the brightest star,
During a dark, moonless night.
Don't give up hope,
For everyone deserves it,
To start a new, wonderful day.

Thet Chen, Grade 8
Thornton Jr High School

Ode to Childhood

Soaring high above in the sky,
You are an eagle, king of the air.
Flying home, you retreat to your lair,
You hope this moment will never go by.

Awoken by this adventure,
Your mom calls you in for lunch.
You run inside beaming,
Your stomach growls; it's time to munch.

But one day you realize,
There is no time to play.
The eagle has been shot down,
It lies peacefully on the ground.

Alex Reynolds, Grade 8
La Joya Middle School

Sandbox

In the comfort of my sandbox,
My friends and I build sand castles as large as dinosaurs.
We laugh and play together,
Wishing that the day warmed by the comforting sun would never end.

The day goes on.
My friends edge away from the sandbox.
As they run quickly to their glowing red tricycles,
They leave me there sitting in the dark isolation of my sandbox.

They incessantly beg and beg me to leave it and go with them,
But I robustly refuse
For it has given me the joy of one-thousand burning suns.
Soon, they stop begging and leave me as they get ready to play once more.

The sun fades into the sky, and
My friends go home smiling knowing that they had a good time.
But, I still lie in stupor in my sandbox as the rustling wind blows the sandcastles
And the faded footprints that once marked peace and joy.

I get up and take in everything;
The park — an emerald forest, the smell of the fresh breeze.
Time passes, but I still remember the comfort of my sandbox.
I wish my life were sandbox-simple now.

Ryan Nguyen, Grade 7
Rolling Hills Country Day School

Rose

With every moment we spend, a rose is at hand.
Each color has a meaning but all in all, it just means one.
A lavender rose will enchant her with its timeless hue,
Capturing her heart and imagination.
It speaks of true love at first sight, a love that always seems to be right.
Wrap her in bright warm smiles with a sunny, yellow rose from your heart.
And hopefully, you'd be more.
Hand her an orange rose and show her that she's more than special to you.
Tell her that like the message of the bloom, she means the world to you.
Gentle like a pink rose is she, so tuck one down in that corsage.
Hope she gets the message and maybe her lips are as tender as petals.
Show her how beautiful and charming she is
With a deep-honored blood red rose.
The symbol of an undying love like the one you two have.
And when you're finally down that aisle, a white rose will flawlessly say,
"As I start this new life with you, I promise:
No matter what happens; I'll always love you."
With every moment we spend together, a rose is at hand.
From the tiny buds within the sepals
To the dying roses entwined forever.
Which rose would you give her?

Stephanie Ha, Grade 8
Citrus Hills Intermediate School

Video Games

I returned from school
Found everything real dull
I needed something cool
What could amuse me?
It might be some technology…gy…gy…gy

Got myself a video game
Picked up one DVD
So I would see nothing called boring…ing…ing…ing

Then I turned to my computer
Surfed the net
Found the information I needed
Watched the video I wanted…ted…ted…ted

Ahmed Almodares, Grade 7
Islamic School of San Diego

Ode to Peanut Butter and Jelly

Buttery and sweet,
After a long school day
It's you I want to eat
I get so high, you should be an illegal treat

Without it, we would reside
In a dark, summerless place
We wouldn't have PB and J on our side
And the smile would be wiped from my face

PB and J is the snack of winners
It fuels the smartest student
It's also a way to get thinner
And makes you smart and prudent

Andrew Maneval, Grade 8
Carmel Valley Middle School

The Real You

Are you the right path I should take,
Or the wrong one to follow?
Are you my best choice to pick,
Or the worst selection ever?
Do I know the real you,
Or are you hiding behind a mask?
How will I know the answers to these questions?
Would I know if you are telling the truth,
Or just telling lies?
I could search the whole world for the answers,
Yet not find the right one,
Because I know where the true answers are —
The answers come from you.
They may never be revealed,
But will always be true.

Allison Balocating, Grade 7
Corpus Christi School

I Know Basketball

Players sprinting, coaches screaming
Nice shot, how many points, a lot
I know basketball
The feel of the basketball, and everybody so tall
Everyone screaming, new basketball shoes gleaming
I know basketball
Giving the ball away, the kid running the other way
Teams that lost the game, and then sharing the blame
I know basketball

Myles Moore, Grade 8
Citrus Hills Intermediate School

The Tale of Rumbling Hearts

A love that was forsakenly untold
A tale of two rumbling hearts
Forced to depart
Though they parted
Their love was true the love never died
Though thyself was no more but pain
Know thyself as if it were true
Heart weeping tears streaming
Never to bare arms
Unknowing of the future ahead
Thy no one may know
Banishing them
They never to cross paths
Never to see the light of day
Only the darkness of others
Ripping at thy souls
Though their hearts may never cross onward to others
Thy might take their rights
But not thy heart
What should I do?
The one that thy love?

Angelic Ramos, Grade 8
Royal Oak Middle School

Dance, Like No Other

The music begins to play,
The spotlight on her and all the rest gray,
Nervous, but that she does not display,
The lights glowing just like her,
Energy surges as she dances without an err,
No one in the audience dares to stir,
Passionately prancing along,
Perfect form, brave yet strong,
Her soul escapes into the song,
And with such inspiration in her eyes,
The song slowly dies,
Presently, the dark swarm begins to rise,
The applause booming all around,
Making such a satisfying sound,
The spotlight on this artist, so profound,
As she takes a bow.

Tara Rezvani, Grade 8
The Bishops School

Waves

Out in the wide blue ocean
Stretching out from any direction
Waves kicking back and forth
along the long shore

Working very hard
To keep its home clean
Because of the intoxicant waste
Thrown into the harmless sea

Sakariye Mohamed, Grade 7
Islamic School of San Diego

When I Am with Her

When I am with her,
I don't know what to do.
When I am with her,
I just freeze.
When I am with her,
I get so nervous.
When I am with her,
my heart beats faster and faster.
When I am with her,
she is the only one I can concentrate on.
When I am with her,
I love to make her smile.
When I am with her,
I love to make her laugh.
I love the days
When I am with her!

Aaron Padrones, Grade 8
Corpus Christi School

My Sister

She's the person I wish to be
When I look up she's all I see
I can't believe
That soon she's gonna leave
And be eighteen
On her own.

Each day she strives
To be a success
And unlike all the rest
Confident and strong
With such grace
She always puts a smile on my face
When in doubt I go to her
She knows the best is what I deserve.

Without her I couldn't breathe
Her life to me means everything
When I am weak she is my voice
Sisters by blood
Best friends by choice!

Kendall Henry, Grade 8
McCabe Elementary School

Why?

I have many questions in life,
But I will only ask two?
Why must we live in a world where there's always war?
Not just between nations,
No, between families and friends.
This is no war to always be fighting and arguing.
We were born to love one another,
Not not to hate one another.
We fight for the meaning of less things;
Property and money.
Why? Why war...
Why are books judged by their cover?
The outside doesn't matter,
It's the inside that matters.
People always judge other people by the way they look, and where they come from.
You judge a person for who they are
Why can't we all be friends
And live in peace and harmony.
To love one another for who we are.
Why?

Gisela Aguilar, Grade 8
St Helen Catholic Elementary School

Tired

Stuck inside a horrible place, just trying to escape.
I want to break down and cry. I understand my mistakes.
I'm thankful you took care of me, but stop throwing it in my face.
I understand you had a lot of responsibility at such a young age,
But I'm thirteen now so just give it a rest.
I'm tired of being annoyed day after day; you say it's how you show your love,
But sometimes it feels like hate. It just makes me feel like running away.
I understand the things I've said, but I'm trying to change.
I have no one to blame, so I'll take blame for my mistakes.
You put me in shame, blaming me for your mistakes.
I won't take fault, because you have no one to blame.
I'm tired of you trying to act like my father; won't you just give it a rest?
Don't think you're responsible for me, because to you that's only stress.
I'm tired of being so sad, like a kid without cake.
I'm tired of all those heavy streams, falling down my red face.
I'm tired of hearing those drops go clank, clank, clank.
My heart tells me it's tired from all this pain.
I wish we could travel back in time to when we were little kids,
When we where like best friends.
But then you grew up, and I grew up, and everything changed.

Genesis Cuevas, Grade 7
Colonial Heights Elementary School

What Is Love

Forever, you and him even forever has to come to an end.
You thought it was love at first sight, but what's with all the fights.
You want the boy you fell in love with then, but all boys turn into men.
You'll always have the love for that one, but right now you're just done
Love him for as long as you can. But maybe there's another man.

Taren Ortega, Grade 8
Robert C Fisler School

Why!
Why oh *why* am I in this world?
I feel as if I'm following the path
Of some unknown girl,
The way life goes,
Makes me want to know
The true meanings of what
I am REALLY here for,
I try to do my best and, nevertheless
Everything I do, I do it to PERFECT
I haven't been through it all no, not YET
But I ask God *why I MUST* go through this
MESS
Nobody can judge me because no one knows
My STRESS
You may come close but you haven't felt my
Paint YET,
Yeah you can talk to me, and be on my side
It'll make me feel better but it still won't
Answer my question which is WHY?

De'Jornae Thomas, Grade 8
Elmhurst Community Prep School

The Light
I feel the impact over my body
Being sucked into the frigid depths below
Struggling for my survival

As if the water was stealing my only air
Leaving me helpless, vulnerable
Against the vast blue

Then I see a luminous light
Like rays shining down from the heavens
Calling to me

Following this serene light
To the swift surface above
As fast as I possibly can

I see the searchlight
Knowing they have come for me
Saving me from the monstrous sea

Kaley Kubokawa, Grade 8
Madrona Middle School

Spring Wonders
As the sun glistens in the sky,
The birds rise and start to cry,
As blossoming flowers begin to sprout,
The bees buzz and fly about,
As water splatters on stream rocks,
A bear awakes and hungrily stalks,
As spring becomes nearer and nearer,
The Earths wonders become clearer and clearer.

Meagan Hoffman, Grade 8
Bayshore Prep Charter School

Fall in Love
I am a little kindergartner boy,
who saw a little girl play hide-and-seek with her friends.
When she smiled, she was like a sunshine.
When she laughed, she was like a little puppy.
I think I am falling in love.

I am a little ten-years-old boy,
who saw a little girl riding swing with her friends.
When she smiled, she was like a sunshine.
When she laughed, she was like a little puppy.
I think I am falling in love.

I am a sixteen-years-old boy,
who saw a girl chitchatting with her friends.
When she smiled, she was like a sunshine
When she laughed, she was like a little puppy.
I think I am falling in love.

I am twenty-years-old and I am all grown up.
I saw a girl who proposed to a guy.
When she smiled, my heart cried.
When she laughed, my heart cried again.
I think my love is gone.

Greene Shin, Grade 8
Robert C Fisler School

Shattered Glass
My dreams and hopes shattered
Without a single word being uttered.
The windy tempest of my soul
Lashing out, sharp and cruel.

A black hole of sorrow and misery,
Sucking me in and engulfing me completely.
A vortex of chagrin and despair,
This feels like a never-ending nightmare.

My heart feels heavy and torn apart by jagged teeth,
Dragging me down beneath,
Threatening to drown me in my fears
And in my very own tears.

Carried by a tiny pest,
The cause of my distress
Has made me a mental wreck
With a huge burden resting upon my neck.

I've caught the infection;
No longer do I recognize my reflection.
Inside me I feel a great clamor
As I gaze into the mirror.

Alix Rousselière, Grade 8
Madrona Middle School

My Best Friends

My best friends always are
the ones I can count on.

Through bad times,
they're the first ones
to be here for me
when I need a shoulder
to lean on.

Without them,
there would be a vast
empty space within my heart

Thank You,
My Best Friends!
Jazzel Nguyen, Grade 8
Corpus Christi School

Watch with Me

Loud explosions
  in the air.
    I knew
      it was time
        for them
          to soar.
Up in the air
  they will go.
    I wonder
      how they fly
with so much beauty
  like an aurora
    in the night
      I wonder
        how they fly.
Steven Riggert, Grade 8
Bethany Lutheran School

Win or Lose

We win some.
We lose some.
But at the end it's all done.
Some keep their heads up.
Some put their heads down.
But we all shouldn't frown.

Some are happy.
Some are sad.
But at the end we shouldn't get mad.
Dads are mad.
Moms are happy.
But they should be glad.
At the end it's just a game.
Brandon Mulligan, Grade 7
Odyssey Charter School

Hidden

We hide and we hope
In hidden walls of wood
The sounds of bombs we heard
Our ground we stood
A loud bang on the wall
It's just a false alarm
The sound of screams and calls
Our ground we stood
An unwelcomed guest
Breaks down our secret door
Our hope laid to rest
Our ground we stood
Our family torn apart
Gassing chambers ahead
Together at heart
Our ground we stood
Terrified, brown eyes of an old friend
Separated by a fence
Near my dear sister's end
Closing my eyes with tears we reunite
Our ground we stood
Desiree Walker, Grade 9
Lucerne Valley Jr/Sr High School

I Love You

You made me cry.
You made me sad.
You made me die inside.
You lied and lied,
You laughed at my sadness.
You hurt me all the time.
And the worst part is,
I love you.
Although words can't describe how I feel
I feel that I must say
I love you.
Alexandra Mendoza, Grade 7
Citrus Hills Intermediate School

My Dog Ginger

  Ginger oh, Ginger
You are so loving,
  You are so fast,
You even leave ruts in the grass
  You're a good pal
A man's best friend
  You cheer me up
When I am feeling down
  You even protect me
When something's wrong
  You're the best dog
I have ever had
Nathaan Ohland, Grade 8
McCabe Elementary School

Moonlight

On cold and white winter nights
  one gleaming light
jumps through the dark sky
like a rabbit hopping around the grass.

Slowly, and peacefully
goes around the world.
Giving people brilliant shine
with happiness and love.

Slowly, and silently
circles the world.
Giving people glorious dream
with hope and wish.
Kanae Nabeshima, Grade 8
Madrona Middle School

The Ocean and Sky

Cool blue ocean
As a sweet as sugar
As blue as sky
But sometimes
They challenge you
With waves
But sometimes
It's peaceful
As the bright blue sky
And the planes
Glide like there's nothing
And sometimes the sky
Tests you too
Andrea Miller, Grade 8
Daniel Savage Middle School

Ars Poetica

What is a poem?
A poem isn't a knight,
But is a knight in shining armor

A poem is not a cat,
But a black cat stalking its prey
A poem isn't the night,
But the moon and the stars

A poem isn't a rainbow,
But the colors in the rainbow
A poem isn't a cloud,
But a cloud floating through the breeze

A poem isn't one color,
But is many vibrant colors
A poem can be anything.
Joseph Lassak, Grade 8
Madrona Middle School

Forever in My Dreams
Take me away to a place we belong
Where shadows blend to hide every fright
We'll stay away for our love makes us strong
You're my hero, take me away tonight
We will stay forever, just me and you
In our picture-perfect secret place
Never again will we ever feel blue
I'll smile softly as I see your face
You smile too as you gently touch my cheek
Thunder roars as I begin to feel fear
I look up as I see the sky turn so bleak
Our perfect world starts to disappear…

I slowly open my dark eyes and see
You are forever with me in my dreams
Irene Refuerzo, Grade 8
Madrona Middle School

Hermia's Huge Decision
Should I listen to my dear father?
Or be with the one who I want to be with?
My dad has all my ideas put together
Or should I go with the complicated myth?
Demetrius is a worthy gentlemen
Lysander is a loving person
My dad wants me at the ceremony to say amen
What should I do before this problem worsens
But my heart should tell me where to go
And it says to be happy with Lysander
My dad won't let this but he won't know
I'll hurt my dad but my heart is an aider
   So until death splits us partly
   My heart will be knit unto his smartly
Carla Torres, Grade 8
John Adams Middle School

I Don't Understand
I don't understand
How the wind begins to blow
How a butterfly can lift off the ground
How rain dries children's tears

But most of all
How Love's flower can blossom from a tiny seed
How waves doodle in the sand
How clouds can hang in the sky

What I understand most is
That Love creates the world
That once you are under It's spell you can never escape
That once you try to leave It, your heart never stops throbbing
Natalie Venezia, Grade 8
Dorris-Eaton School

I Regret
I regret the things I did wrong to you.
I regret breaking your heart.
I regret hurting your feelings.
I regret almost ruining your life.
But what I most regret is…
ever meeting you.
Joshua Seno, Grade 7
Corpus Christi School

Just Because…
Just because I have scoliosis
Doesn't mean I am a cripple
Doesn't mean I'm incapable of doing things like others
Doesn't mean I'm cursed
Doesn't mean I'm pitiful

Just because I have scoliosis
Doesn't mean I can't succeed
Doesn't mean you can look down on me
Doesn't mean I don't have feelings
Doesn't mean I'm useless

Just because I have scoliosis
Doesn't mean I don't have a life
Doesn't mean I can't help others
Doesn't mean I can't influence people

Just because I have scoliosis
Expect me to understand people's feelings more than most
Sophia Takashima, Grade 8
The Dorris-Eaton School

The Last Time
There had to be a last time
I played hopscotch, or ate raw corn.
There had to be a last time
I would go outside in my pajamas.
Or a last time I would ride my dog
Even though I didn't care that I always fell off her.
There had to be a last time
When I would ride on a Merry-go-round.
Or watch the Wiggles or Blue's Clues.
Or the last time I would hear
"Harvey Potter's Balloon Farm" before I fell asleep.
And there had to be a last time
I would have no homework.
And come home and lie on my bed,
And take a nap before I ate dinner.
And there had to be a last time
That I would play in the mud,
Because I didn't care about getting dirty.
Or the last time I would ride on the
Baby seat on the back of my mom's bike.
I have done so many things for the very last time.
Hallee Haygood, Grade 7
Linfield Christian School

The Only Person I Can Be
The wet sand of the beach
is the color of
my light brown skin
that people
assume of my race.
The wood you put
into the brick chimney
is the color of my eyes
that I use to see
my world.
My height of 5'8"
is the advantage I use
to help others
who have too short
of arms to reach.
And my red heart
like the one everyone has,
I use to place
everyone I care about
in.
Marissa Leal, Grade 8
La Joya Middle School

I Hope My Dream Never Ends
The sun rose above,
High in the sky,
Warming the sand below.
I stood there on the sand,
Soaking in the warmth.

As the ocean,
Further down the beach,
Made grumbling noises at me,
I thought to myself,
I hope my dream never ends.

The peacefulness of it all
Put me in a sort of trance.
But just to turn another bend,
Would make my dream end.

But eventually I would wake up
And realize it was just a dream.
But until then,
I hope my dream never ends.
Alicia Flynt, Grade 8
Holy Family Catholic School

Summer
Summer is summer
The end is a bummer
Summer at the beach,
Not listening to teachers teach
Summer…the end is a bummer.
Miranda Andrews, Grade 7
Packinghouse Christian Academy

Lord of the Flies*
The boys fighting for power. One kills the other.
The sad air of death blows by, and there Ralph sits all alone
The hunt, not only for animals anymore,
Jack had gone crazy, out of control just killing
The littluns were frightened,
They did what the older children did
If Jack told them to kill, they killed

Ralph, just wanting to get rescued, helped many people
Jack then turned his back to Ralph, and a big competition began,
Jack had taken all the people from his group
Ralph was on his own and didn't know what to do

Simon went out of his mind talking to a pig, being on his own,
He did not know what to do
Poor Simon poor Simon,
Tried to explain that there was no beast,
But instead he was just killed

Piggy always tried to help, but no one paid attention
He was just trying to do it for the good,
But still no one followed what he thought
Slowly slowly Ralph paid attention,
And then at the last second, Piggy was gone.
Roee Hezi, Grade 7
Kadima Heschel West Middle School
*Inspired by "Lord of the Flies"

The Moonlight
I walk under the light
that will guide me through all the pain and sadness.
I feel alone in the darkness of what I lost…
I miss all the happy times I had before.
All my happiness just had blown away
as the ocean waves come and go.
All my smiles are gone
as I heard more bad news each day.
Everything starts to disappear
as I began to lock myself into darkness…
But then…the moonlight shines through my life,
showing me what's important and what matters most.
The moonlight shows me my smile that was inside of me,
shows me the right path, shows me the meaning of "friend" again.
Though the moonlight is not always next to me,
I know somehow the light will always be with me.
I've begun to treasure what's close to me.
I wish…the moonlight will stay with me forever…and forever
As it is, the moonlight is always there to make me believe
I am not alone anymore…
Vivian Lee, Grade 8
Joaquin Miller Middle School

Dia de los Muetros
Day of the Dead
Favorite food and drinks being brought.
Praying to them.
Praying for them.
Parades with festival music.
Musicians and dancers dressed as skeletons,
In honor of the people who died.
They walk through the cemeteries
Blowing a horn to awaken the dead.

John Torres, Grade 7
St Alphonsus School

Samurai
I have an estate where people live
I have two swords a long and a short
I have leather armor as well
Do you know who I am
I'll give you some hints
I care for four things
The first is my honor
The second is my pair of swords
The third is my family
The fourth is the estate along with the people
But most importantly, my honor
Here is the answer to who I am
The most important thing to me is
Honor, my Samurai honor

Servando Avila, Grade 8
Daniel Savage Middle School

Under a Willow Tree
Walking in a park by your side,
Looking at the moonlight shining in your eyes.
I didn't know it could be this way,
I never knew that one day,
You would be in my heart,
And I would be playing this part.

As we pass a willow tree,
You come very close to me.
You gently take my hand,
And tell me in all the land,
There's not another girl like you,
And this is what I must do.

You close my eyes with your fingertips,
And rest your hand by my hair.
Next you give me a gentle kiss,
And tell me I'm so fair.

I open my eyes to look at you,
Lost in your eyes so dark.
I wrap my arms around you,
Right there in the park!

Kayla Judd, Grade 9
James C Enochs High School

Ferrari
My Ferrari is fast like the wind
It's small but stronger than a mountain
It's brighter than anything you've seen and
Zoom! It whizzes by

My Ferrari is a wind stream
And it zooms by everywhere
My Ferrari is the diamond that
Lives in my garage, and
Zoom! It whizzes by

My Ferrari is the car
That can zoom past everything
And my Ferrari is the car that is rarer than gold, and
Zoom! It whizzes by

Yousuf Soliman, Grade 7
Islamic School of San Diego

Old and Wise Is Beautiful
A woman's face
as old and worn as ancient mountains,
her hair
long and thin like ivy on an old brick wall,
her nose
perfectly curved like the Golden Gate Bridge,
her mouth
smooth and petite, carved by the master's hands,
her eyes
they seem vivid and wise like a grandfather clock,
ticking forever;
old and wise is beautiful.

Austin Musson, Grade 8
Odyssey Charter School

Some Days
Some days I remember,
The times that we shared
And some days I still wonder,
If I could ever go back.

You're getting so much older,
And I know you're changing.
But please, don't change the way
You're acting towards me.

I've been thinking,
About these memories, and how they change.
But they're always the same in our minds.
Exaggerated.
To make them sound cooler than they really are.
Than they really are.

James Taylor, Grade 9
McCabe Elementary School

Confusion Eating Away

Confusion is getting into my mind and eating it slowly as if my mind were to be dipped in burning acid.
Inch by inch, it being dipped in, then taken out for me to just suffer the burning flesh eating pain over and over again.
The acid just keeps eating at my mind until I'm just finished, there's nothing left of me and I have just gone into total craziness.
My mind stays speeding in every which way as if there were a line in my head that's nonstop going every direction possible.
Left, right, horizontal, vertical, up, down.
My mind is continuously trying to follow that line. That line leads to the right path
Of how to stop all this confusion in the human brain. But no, the line keeps going in every direction but the right one.
My mind has to find that door that's there to stop the flow of "confusion!"

Shall I just "try" to forget about it all? Key word: may it be Try? I have tried
But as soon as someone brings up anything that has something to do with the confusion I have
"It" starts happening again and again. The constant dip of the mind being slowly dipped in the acid.
As constant as you breathe. One Mississippi, dip, two Mississippi, dip, and so forth.
I have a silent cry that lasted a matter of anywhere between 10 seconds to a minute.
I pick up that pencil and write down the story of "it" all. Just picking up that pencil brings down a lot of confusion.
It's like the fact of having your own psychologist at your hands.
It's like the mind, that's twisted, tangled in a gigantic knot and all the above gets unraveled step by step.

It's like a parent trying to teach a baby to walk. Tiny step by tiny step, an accomplishment is being made.
Unraveling a new start to a fresh beginning. Back to the start where your mind is clear of all thoughts but still have memories.
Back to when the clearness here you can just sit back and ponder about anything,
Instead of lying down and ponder of questions that have no answers which build more questions to the answers that have no
Questions.

Babbette Jackson, Grade 8
Visitacion Valley Middle School

Imagine

Imagine world peace.
Imagine no war.
Just people talking verbally.
No children crying, no parents lying, no people dying.

Imagine a green world,
Happy people, lots of trees, no waste, no distaste.

Imagine no hunger.
Full stomachs, no potbellies, enough food for everyone,
No hunger would be great.

Imagine no hate.
Maybe that's the problem, maybe it's the hatred inside that makes these so-called problems,
Or maybe that's the way it should be, we must always have them.
Maybe the world could not go round if there was nothing bad.
Or perhaps there is no bad maybe it's all good,
Maybe it's the way it should be,
And that will get us out of this so-called misery.

Imagine a perfect world,
But wait, what is perfect?
Maybe it's whatever you make it to be maybe that's what's worth it.

Aine Gallahue, Grade 8
Dehesa Charter School

Loneliness

A lonely bedroom with many pictures
of the man living in that bedroom.
The owner of the bedroom must be lonely
living by himself.
It looks like he has chairs
for the people that visit him
but the room looks like
there haven't been any visitors in a long time.
It's a very small bedroom
so it looks like the man
doesn't have any kids or a wife.

Ramiro Torres, Grade 8
Daniel Savage Middle School

Where I'm From

I am from dark blue jeans, from Bounty sheets,
and Snuggle fabric softener.
I am from the plum tree out front,
tall, purple, and strong.
I am from Christmas Eve at Aunt Rosaline's,
and dimples from Grandma, and Uncle Mikey.
I am from the home-cooked meals,
and the warm cozy fires at night.
From cloud factories in Maui,
and reindeer on my roof.
I am from the blood on the cross,
and the nails in His hands.
I'm from California, Armenia, and Mexico,
Napoleon, and enchiladas.
From the nosey nosey song at night,
and the skinny man in my sister's room.
I am from mementos on the mantle,
and all the family stories shared throughout time.

Madison Mason, Grade 7
Linfield Christian School

Pain and Love Come Together

I ever more did love you, believing in love.
We so happy together; like love birds.
Until, you hate me; what happens to my beloved?
Why did everything have to brake into thirds?
Until now I know that love is painful like death.
I offer you everything and you deny me.
The only thing you can do is take my breath.
It's so sad that I am as naive as thee.
But, love can be as joyful as spring.
We come together as an eternal couple.
I am ever more glad, we share a ring.
Could love ever be so beautiful and supple?
Love can ever be scary and dreadful.
Love can ever be pure joy and beautiful!

Mary Rivas, Grade 8
John Adams Middle School

Silver Mist

Clear skies the day before
No one could ask for ever more

But then the silver mist came
Nothing on the pier was the same

Sun fighting and fighting
But slowly fading and fading

I'm sure he will return someday
For now the silver mist is here to stay

Anna Santoro, Grade 8
Longfellow Spanish Immersion Magnet School

He Was a Musician

He was a musician
That once played the trumpet
He was a jazz player
They also said he was a singer

With his distinctive gravely voice
He came to the prominence in the 1920's
He was a foundational influence
Nicknamed Satcho or Pops

His pride and glory was jazz
Where the beat went smooth
Behind the lyrics and music
His songs were for expressive purposes

Some say his music was elegant
He was born in New Orleans, Louisiana
His name is forever known by his fans
His name was Louis Armstrong

Carl Wittmann, Grade 9
Lucerne Valley Jr/Sr High School

Stars

The stars are diamonds in a black seamless cloth
They are fires that shine bright at night
They are glowing silver lights in the mine
Twinkling softly, twinkling softly

Pictures of heroes imprinted in the heavens
Suns in a far off world
Lions in bright majesty
Twinkling softly, twinkling softly

Souls in heaven
Battles of great ferocity
The birth of new worlds?
Twinkling softly, twinkling softly

Morning has come and they are gone.

Paula Quach, Grade 7
Jefferson Middle School

Flowers
The life of spring,
They bloom and bring,
Vibrant colors to a dismal scene.
Cherie Gambino, Grade 9
University Preparatory School

Seasons
Rainy day
The rains are falling
As the clouds weep in sorrow,
At passing of spring.

Summer beach
The pounding of waves
Breaks all the serenity
On the peaceful beach

Autumn dinner
As everyone sits,
The autumn wind blows outside,
And good food is served.

Winter wind
The snow is piling,
As saplings bed from the wind.
O, how the wind howls!
Mayank Tiwari, Grade 7
Challenger School – Ardenwood

My America
I thrashed and screamed,
Not wanting to go
Elders said sorry.
Didn't change anything.
I came with reluctance school every day
Hard to comprehend
Hard to communicate

Years later, a reflection of myself
1 year older than I was
1st grade, seemed like forever
Like her, I had resisted
America
Freedom
Everything.
Months later, I gave in
A far away place, a different language
Culture and Meaning

Now I know the why in my stay
Longer than half my life,
Loving it, embracing it

My America
Nahoko Hashimoto, Grade 8
Jane Lathrop Stanford Middle School

Ode to Music
There is a beat in my mind, a song I cannot find,
The words are at a miss, I don't even know if it exists!
It dances out of my reach, a wall I cannot breach,

I hear snatches of the melody, will someone please help me?
I am becoming desperate, I can't rest yet,
Until I find this song, I've waited so long,

As the day begins to fade, still no one has come to my aid!
And it keeps playing again and again, all I can do then,
Is to take out a pad and pen, and write down the words I repeat over and over again.

Wait I remember what it is! I have beaten my personal quiz,
It is so simple and easy, except a little cheesy,
As I remember more and more, to think I couldn't have thought of this before?
Anna Tobin, Grade 7
Santa Rosa Technology Magnet School

First of My Day
I hear the ringing of the bell.
Immediately, my nose is hugged by the coffee smell.
Walking into the colorful class,
I am welcomed by the teacher full of sass.

I sit down, grab my box of Tic Tacs and can't help but smile.
Because I haven't seen Melissa or Muñoz in a while.

In one ear I hear, "Pencil, not pen," and, "Clicking, tapping done."
In my other ear I hear, "Did you watch the Lakers game last night?"
And, "Do you want some lotion?"

As the clock strikes 8:54,
I quickly rush for the big, heavy door.

But wait! She has one last thing to say. It's, "Peace out, have a rad day!"
Maianh Huyen, Grade 9
Fountain Valley High School

Misery
Loneliness feels like walking barefoot on deep shards of glass
A shark planting its teeth into your skin

Loneliness sounds like the never ending echo of your own voice screaming
The wind screeching through a hollow cabin

Loneliness is the fearsome look of families quivering from the cold
People shivering in a bombed shelter waiting to be released

Loneliness smells like rotten eggs infesting your small crowded bedroom
The fresh fertilizer on the newly cut grass

Loneliness tastes like sour milk on a cleanly brushed tongue
It is the feeling of gloominess on a dark rainy night
Rachel Abucasis, Grade 8
Emek Hebrew Academy

I Don't Understand

I don't understand
Why there is a loss with life
Why with downhill there is uphill
Why with progress comes sacrifice

But most of all
Why there are people hungry when I'm full
Why there are people sleeping on the streets while I'm in bed
Why there are kids with no one but themselves

What I understand most is
Why when one door closes, another opens
Why with death comes life
Why humans have two hands and one heart

Sara Jensen, Grade 8
Dorris-Eaton School

The Legendary Tony Hawk

I saw how one man could become such astonishment
A difficult stunt could turn him into a legend
Conquering such a strenuous achievement
Only he could start such an ongoing trend

He had a family that he loved with all of his passion
Skateboarding was his career for life
Started a clothing company with lots of fashion
Tony has lots of compassion for his wife

Even though he had to retire
Everything turned out perfect in the end
He is now greatly admired
Tony will always be a legend

Now that he is teaching his four sons how to skate
He will always be a mystery
Who knows what new stunts he will create?
Tony Hawk will always be remembered for making history

Cheyenne Lujan, Grade 9
Lucerne Valley Jr/Sr High School

From the Darkness

As the clouds consume the towers above us
and the darkness overcomes the light
we are left in the darkness
now as cold drops of rain falls upon my face
washing all hope away
water starts to swell up in my eyes
and burst to acid tears dissolving my soul
as I open my eyes to see
a light coming from the darkness
your arms reach out to me
to embrace me as love and warmth takes me in
slowly putting my broken heart back
making it whole again

Priscilla Pascua, Grade 9
Miguel Contreras Learning Complex

If We Had the Power

If we had the power to change ourselves,
Would we use it?
We do the same things every day.
Same gang colored rags, it's a war that
Never ends but we only feed.

If we had the power to help others, would we?
It's amazing how we expect others to give
But we never return the favor.
This world is full of scandals and greed,
But we all take part of it somehow.
Nobody's perfect.

Most of us wish for fancy cars and diamonds
When in reality we can't even spend $20.00
Without owing someone else!

If we had the power would we use it
To do good or to make things happen
I have this problem where when people judge me,
I tend to judge them back, and that's something
I would like to work on.
But I don't know if I have the power…
I probably do, but will I use it?

Kimberly Kaufmann, Grade 9
Regency High School

Wondering About You

When I think of you,
I do a lot of wondering.
How did you look,
or what was your personality.
I was only one or two when you died.
My mom talks about you,
how you had purple hair and loved to cook.
I hope you know she misses you.
If only you had held on a little longer.

You sound like you were fun
and very caring.
It makes my heart hurt
when I realize I didn't know you.
I want to thank you for my mom
and the way you raised her.
I'm sure you were just as good as her
and would be proud of her.

But now you're gone,
and you're living with God.
I can't wait to see you in heaven,
but for now you are watching over me.

Krista Harvey, Grade 7
Linfield Christian School

Tomato

We grow in bundles from
the ground beneath the ground
We stay strong together, but
splatter alone

Roll on and on as a tire
beneath a yellow school bus;
We are red as Rudolph's nose and have
Green hair like a punk rock kid

You can find me in any of my forms,
even if you don't know I'm there.

Marcos Vega, Grade 8
Packinghouse Christian Academy

I Solemnly Swear…

"I Barack Obama, solemnly swear…"
The world is changing,
And so must we.
Time to join together,
So we can be free.
Of war and terror,
And families starve.
We must change, we must change,
Let our prayers be carved.
Let hope and virtue,
Be alive and true.
An old nation dies,
And a new one cries…
"Yes we can! Yes we can!!"

Bianca Agard, Grade 8
Citrus Hills Intermediate School

Ish…

I loved my goldfish
his name was Ish
unfortunately he died
because I thought he was a land fish.
I kept him in my pocket all day long
we were such good friends
I can't believe he's gone.
When we used to play dodge ball,
he would laugh when I would fall.
Then I would get back up
and hit him with the ball.
Even though we had our ups and downs,
we had mostly smiles and never frowns.
Sometimes, I would come home
and tell him about my day
and then he would say
"OMG like no way!"
I will remember the good times
and the not so good ones too
BFFs forever…Ish I love you!

Ciera Martinez, Grade 7
Holy Family Catholic School

Best Friends?

You and I, have been through so much and have made it through,
we've grown stronger and smarter together.
Remember when, I would cry on your shoulder and you would stand up for me.
We would sing crazy songs and would create our own lyrics.
We would talk about everything, and nothing at the same time.

Me and you.
Everyone was jealous,
we knew all each other's secrets,
from crushes, to breakups I knew of them all.
We would do absolutely everything together,
no one could separate us.

Until one day,
she came around you guys automatically clicked,
you started to call each other 'best friends'.
I felt completely abandoned,
with no one by my side,
I finally decided to do the same thing you did.

I found new friends,
and a new person to call my 'best friend.'
Just like you and her did, we got along perfectly.
But there was still something missing and it didn't feel right.

Sheldin Seminario, Grade 8
Robert C Fisler School

No Shelter, No Hide, No Soul

I have two ears, two eyes,
Four legs, muzzle and fangs
I sleep among the stars, howl at the moon
This is my story…
We got our kill, eat, CRASH!
Two legs destroy our land with a Metal Monster.
Grizzly is angered, my pack discouraged.
Robins search for new nests
Rabbits out of their burrows
Pack is confused and frightened of two legs, but we forgive.
Then a pack of two legs with weapons shot my pack friend
I whimper to ask if he is okay he growls to run
I should have, I feel numb and drift away…
Wake and whimper at animals…hides?
I realize the two legs take hides for show this disturbs, confuses and angers me.
I SNAP at two legs but fangs practically float through flesh.
I am bewildered, and feel light.
I am floating! See a light my Pack Brother is there
I hesitate finding my own hide on the floor.
I sprint towards the light tribes heaven engulfs me
I give one last howl and grunted saying goodbye to this world.

Jazmin Solorzano, Grade 8
McCabe Elementary School

Time Is Precious

Each morning I wake up to my mom,
"It's time to get up!" I don't make a peep!
I often think it would be better
If I curl up under the covers, and go back to sleep!

Then my mind wanders,
And I start thinking about my day.
I would miss my friends at school,
Have to do make-up work instead of play!

Each day I stay in bed, I would miss a lot.
The sunshine, birds singing, and soccer outside.
I would also miss TV, Gameboy, and reading inside.
My mind and body would be on vacation!

I smell bacon, eggs, and French toast cooking,
I jump up and get dressed.
I rush downstairs and my family is seated,
Ready for breakfast.

Dad says, "Where are you going so fast?"
I realize it's Saturday, I have the whole day ahead.
Time is precious and I don't want to miss a minute!

Cody Spoon, Grade 7
Holy Rosary School

Imagine If…

Imagine if, I was a butterfly
Evolving into a kaleidoscope of colors
Shedding my cocoon behind
Fluttering freely in the azure sky
Enthralled by an optimistic future

Imagine if, I was a puppy
Modeling a glistening coat of fur
Utilizing an iconic, keen sense of smell
Mimicking the idea of love with true devotion
Acting as a man's best friend

Imagine if, I was free
Embarking on harrowing adventures
Fulfilling my inner purpose
Ignoring what is bequeathed upon me
Seeking my true identity

For now, I can only imagine,
And stay content with my reality
But maybe one day, someone will hear my diminutive voice
And finally take the ponderous chains off of my back
Then, I will be free.

Jackie Adelsberg, Grade 8
Lindero Canyon Middle School

Love Can Do Anything

Love gives me courage
You make my fears disappear
Love can do anything as long as you're here

When I'm sad and dreary you come
And lighten my world
And for all this I love you

I truly love you with all my heart
Even when times are good and bad
I can truly love you for everything

May we grow apart and move
There will be a part of my heart with you
That will not move

From the day I saw your beautiful face
To the day we became best friends
And the day we move I will always love you

Ryan Ruthel, Grade 7
Daniel Savage Middle School

Red

Red reminds me of my first bed covers
Red reminds me of my first blanket.
It was the color of the apartment I lived in
My bouncy ball was red
    The stairs,
        The carpet,
Even my stuffed animal was red.
Red is the vision of my past.

Mauricio Menjivar, Grade 7
St Cyprian School

An Offbeat History Over Drinks

What could you learn?
Would a thousand snapshots fly
out of the walls?
Each a picture
of a loved one?
A house with broken shutters
and cracked ribs?
Pictures of Gold?
Revolution? Coffins?
The cold rigor mortised people resting inside them?
Did they have conversations with their daughters,
Sipping beer or wine
At a table?
On a couch?
The voluptuous contours
Of the bottle
A key
To the words locked up in a chest.
Cheers.

Sofie Werthan, Grade 7
Prospect Sierra School

The Pear
It is plump and inviting
Yellow and soft,
Tasteful and enticing,
As it hangs aloft

Tasty in salad,
Or on the run
Good with friends, or
While in the sun

Some prefer them juicy,
Some prefer them firm
The pear is sure to please,
Even down to the worm.
Neil Markley, Grade 8
Packinghouse Christian Academy

Struggling Sisters
Without welcome
You yakked
About allowing
Different decisions
That I have thought through.

Seeing only some
Part of the picture. Please,
Reign in those rabid rationalizations.

Will we ever win? "Whatever,
Yes," you yield.
Finally, fate.
Eloise Bacon, Grade 8
Lindero Canyon Middle School

Joy
I feel joyful about Legos
They make me excited
My pieces shapes and colors
Built with imagination
All from me

I feel joyful about my cat Mozart
He head-butts me and makes me laugh
Purry furry rambunctious cat
Taken care of by me
He is special

I feel joyful about life
I have all I need
Friends family pets and toys
Surround me at all times
I am lucky
Austyn Sedler, Grade 7
Daniel Savage Middle School

Broken Escape
My eyes start to water
As I say, "Forget me not"
And I always seem to ponder
On the very thought

These qualities I admire
"It's the thought," he says, "that counts"
My feelings have retired
But he won't let me out

It was me that wanted him to stay
But now he won't go
I feel the sharp sun rays
On my now bitter soul

I see him and he's holding me back
But the mirror never lies
It suddenly turns black
And so does the skies

For the person restraining me
Was never really him
It was me, and only me,
And only me…again
Elexis Alford, Grade 9
La Quinta High School

Our Song
Our song is that special song
We sing and practice
All the time.
Our song —
It's the song
I can escape to
When my day is going bad.
Our song is the song
I can't get out of my head,
or out of my heart…
our song.
Allan Guintu, Grade 7
Corpus Christi School

Amelia Earhart
Whatever happened to Amelia Earhart?
Bound by determination
Driven by passion
Solo flights
Setting records
Only to disappear in
The Pacific blue
Leaving behind
Not one clue
Jamie Williams, Grade 9
Lucerne Valley Jr/Sr High School

The Pain of Losing Your Mother
The pain is enormous
You feel like you want to give
Your whole life for her —
Instead of it being her,
It would be you

I would do anything
For my mother
Because I love her more than
Anything on the face of the Earth

So painful, losing someone you so love
You feel like your life
Is nothing without her,
And nothing can replace her.
Salvador Gomez, Grade 7
Corpus Christi School

Life
Life is a road
You keep going on
It goes up, it goes down
But you keep moving on

Life might be sweet
Life might be bitter
But no matter what it is
You have to hold on

A life starts
A life ends
Life is a road
That's full of surprises
Hoda Barhoush, Grade 8
Islamic School of San Diego

Icebergs
An iceberg, a mountain of the sea
Staying still to you and me,
But moving by wind and waves.
They carry all different aquatic colors,
White, blue, and green
Suddenly, everything is quiet.
Splash!
A chunk of ice falls,
Shattering the glassy water.
This will not stop
The monster from moving on.
The birds rest on top
Only five feet above the water
While fish surround the iceberg
One-hundred feet under sea level.
Rakin Talukder, Grade 7
Islamic School of San Diego

New Years

The night's winter air chills the crowd,
A few stars light the pitch black night,
A perfect night without a cloud.
Though the moon was clearly in sight.

A crystal sphere slowly descends,
And with each second passing by,
The crowd started to blend.
Then rockets filled the night sky.

The orb had touched the ground,
And the crowd was cheering and jumping.
New York was filled with sound,
And the beautiful night sky was booming.

Let's hope this is a good year,
And we'll soon see that crystal sphere.

Arian Cano, Grade 8
Thornton Jr High School

It's Spring

Walking along the road on a bright sunny day.
You look to the right and see kids are at play.
The scent of flowers surround you as you pass by them.
But sometimes you might have allergies, ahem.

The lake is warm.
Bees do no harm.
Butterflies fly in a passel.
Waking up is a hassle.

It's the time of year when flowers bloom.
When the sun will loom.
When bees fly in a ring.
That's when you knows it's spring.

Kenny Fernando, Grade 8
Robert C Fisler School

The Tree Cycle

Green leaves frolic to all branches as spring begins,
Giving shade to everyone passing by,
And a home to any bird flying through.
With roots that go far beneath the surface,
It is strong.
As summer rolls around it endures extreme heat.
Time goes on and its beautiful green leaves
Begin to fade into a bright maroon.
It is now autumn,
And the tree's gorgeous leaves fall off.
Autumn goes by and it is now winter.
The tree is now cold and bare.
It is no longer flowing with vibrant colors,
Or blowing in the wind.
Three months go by, and the cycle repeats.

Brandi Boulay, Grade 8
Holy Family Catholic School

This Road I'm On

This road has taken me to places,
Places I never want to go again.
Sometimes the road is covered by footsteps,
And following them often hurt me.
Surrounded by parties and beer,
I was blind to those who really loved me.
The road often led me to the beach,
Where the salty spray of gossips and betrayal,
Was splattered all over my fragile heart.
When I finally chose to leave the beach,
And turn towards the empty forked road,
I was lost, not knowing what to follow.
Hoping to find one who can help my numb heart heal
Finally, loving myself let my heart able to feel.

Catherine Qian, Grade 9
Gretchen Whitney High School

Love of My Life

When you walked into the room, I was amazed,
Your eyes shined so brightly under the light,
Whenever I see you, I feel very dazed,
I will always love you with all my might,
Your beautiful hair gleams below the sun,
I want to spend the rest of my life with you,
When you're around, life is so much more fun,
My love for you will forever be true,
Your personality is stupefying,
Your smile is delightfully pretty,
Your laugh is very electrifying,
You are as cute as a little kitty,
You are always looking as sharp as a knife,
You are the absolute love of my life.

Tyler Allen, Grade 8
Las Flores Middle School

Fly Away

Sometimes I want to fly away
Not think of my worries of the day
Go all the way up to the moon
And hopefully I will get there soon.

I want to see Venus, Saturn and Mars
And then go catch some falling stars
Go far beyond the Milky Way
And not hear what people have to say.

Stress is the part of life that we dislike
It makes us feel like you were on a ten mile hike
If you cope with it in the right way
You won't feel like you want to fly away.

Jennifer Garcia-Lopez, Grade 8
Palm Desert Charter Middle School

Christmas
Everybody is happy
Christmas is coming.
People wait
To open their gifts,
The houses are covered
With a blanket of snow.
A time of chills outside and
Cheer inside.
The smell of pine in the air,
The sound of children trying to convince
Mama to go to the mountains to play.
Ivan Camacho, Grade 7
St Alphonsus School

I Wish
I wish I could fly,
up into the sky.
I wish I could run,
as fast as the wind.

I wish I could hear,
the sounds far away.
I wish I could see,
as far as the eye can.
Reuben Vijayakumaran, Grade 8
Robert C Fisler School

Dreams
A place where I can get away
A place where my troubles are gone
A place where everything is right
And nothing is wrong
This is my Dream Place
The place where I want to go
Daniel Viray, Grade 7
Corpus Christi School

Love
Love, is like a song
It repeats itself all day long
It never fails and never seeths
It is something beautiful to me

Love, is like a dream
It never seems real
It is sweet and blissful
It is something magical and mystical

Love, is a thing
That can't be suppressed
It is a feeling that everybody needs
It is an action that everybody sees

Love, is the key to the heart
Lauren Dewiggins, Grade 7
Citrus Hills Intermediate School

Elegy of Africa
She has died been killed by our own kind
how could this happen, how could this happen
her ghost haunts all who leave her
it is a tricky ghost it is
it does not put its victims in sheer terror
it is guaranteed, she'll be remembered for sure
so when something makes us think of her
and, in the past, how things were
she makes sure people are missing her and just reminiscing
For some she can be seen like she's a real human being
for some, this happens on a yearly basis,
and they realize something and they have to face this
that they have left heaven behind
others are just too blind to see that they left behind
for what some believe, is part of the basis of mankind
What I speak of is not a woman, it cannot walk, speak, or run
it is what I left behind, such a beautiful place
my family and friends I had to replace
it is a large region of land that reaches from the beaches of sand
through the desert, no man's land
to southern Europe this whole continent is grand.
Jesse Mandell, Grade 8
Carmel Valley Middle School

I Want It All
When I wore a younger, spryer man's clothes,
I owned the simple, sweet blessing of a strong family, friends, and a home,
But like a poison of hemlock, poverty soured my happiness.
Opulence, wealth, finery, luxury,
I wanted it all.
Each day, month, and year I plotted my rise to a higher station.
A portfolio of stocks, a cluster of bonds, the wills of many
Were the only things that existed in my life, my winding path to my goal.
My wife wanted back the love that money took away.
She was a melancholy ghost when she left.
My children grew up not knowing a caring father.
With their silvery voices they called for me, but I ignored them, thinking of wealth.
To cut the pain that bound them to me like a rope,
They dissolved our fading bonds.
Still I wanted it all, even as they disappeared like autumn leaves.
Later rather than sooner, I got what I wished for,
Opulence, wealth, finery, luxury.
But I was too withered and aged to enjoy these spoils
I lost my health and happiness to what I thought had mattered.
Now, in an empty mansion with the grey wind tormenting me,
I want my life back.
Rachel Pak, Grade 7
Rolling Hills Country Day School

Storm Waves
As the waves of fear come crashing down, I can barely hear a sound
I look around time and time again just to realize
I'm surrounded by the black night tide again
Della Stroh, Grade 8
Palm Desert Charter Middle School

I Am

I am a guitar never played,
I am words unspoken,
I am a dandelion in a garden of daisies,
I am the missing piece to the puzzle,
I am a book with the last page ripped out,
I am the soundtrack of your life,
I am a single shed tear dropped in the Pacific Ocean.

Nicole Tucay, Grade 7
St Mary of Assumption School

Spring

She walks in
Smiles…sees…smells
Sunflowers shining like the sun

She smiles as she sees
A daisy shimmering like the rarest ruby
A tulip shining like the bright sun

Butterflies flutter their beautiful wings
Cats brush against their fellow cattails

The tulips become dark…the daisies become dull
The fluttering of the beautiful butterfly wings stop
The cat rushes under the bench…she runs inside

Drip, drip, drop…rain
Brushes against
Tulips…daisies…cattails
It stops

She walks in
Smiles…sees…smells
Sunflowers shining like the bright sun

Zainab Umarji, Grade 8
Al-Huda Islamic School

Ode to the Jonas Brothers

What a band,
What a show,
That I watched in the stands,
In the front row.

And as I watched them for hours and hours,
My love for them was more outrageous,
I started to scream louder,
When one jumped off all of the stages.

He grabbed my hand,
Then sang to me,
And in my land
We are meant to be.

Courtney Holt, Grade 7
Yolo Middle School

Ode to the Jonas Brothers

The Jonas Brothers are the reason I'm alive
I was super excited as their new CD arrived
As I plug in my headphones and press play
It felt like I was at their concert just yesterday

My friends say that they're not the best
I don't care what they say but I do admit, I am obsessed
With their new 3-D movie that is out now
First thing I said when I saw Joe's abs was, "WOW"

With their appearance on the cover of Rolling Stone
I kissed all their faces and glad that I was alone
An "I Heart Jonas Brothers" pin is what I wear every day
As a symbol for my love that won't ever go away

So basically, they are my life
I will be glad if I end up being Nick Jonas' wife
They are the only boys I will ever love
The three angels from up above

Colleen Vuong, Grade 9
Fountain Valley High School

Ode to Trees

The breeze blows through your leaves.
Because of you man is given air,
and the way you are repaid does not seem fair.
We chop you down, which is an abuse,
we seem to forget your mandatory use.
You provide us shade, as well as food,
and to use you for toilet paper is really quite rude.

Tillie Greco, Grade 8
Robert C Fisler School

I Don't Understand

I don't understand
    Why people judge.
    Why people assume.
    Why people stereotype.
But most of all,
    Why people can't work together,
    Why there is no harmony; no balance,
    Why hatred plagues the air of the world.
What I understand most is
    Why people laugh,
    Why people hug,
    Why people love,
Because there is barely joy,
    Rarely happiness,
    Little care.
Because there is barely magic,
    Rarely miracles,
    Little strength.
Because people understand
    Why life must be lived.

Kiren Singh, Grade 8
Dorris-Eaton School

Born Again

Renewing the visions of old, through many generations, being retold.
Those nightmares coming alive, tearing you apart with thrive.
Giving you no second change, not even a second glance.
No hope whatsoever not thinking you to be a good endeavor.
You shall be nothing forever different always and sever.
Those shadowy figures against the wall smiling gleefully from their brawl.
Waiting to feast on all your sorrow, knowing there is no morrow.
Waiting for you to dismiss your pleasure, when you're aware you've turned away from leisure.
Those allusions of the past, that will remain unsurpassed.
The remembrance of those days of agitation. Oh! That period of frustration.
Then I remember I'm never alone. and I can never be on my own.
There are others, who have suffered hardships as well, and I'm not the only one, being wished farewell.
We must remember there was a redeeming time, and we have been cleaned of our crime.
And always Remember, faith is giving us that advance,
Hope is giving us that second glance, and, most importantly Love is giving us that second chance.

Cathryn Gowen, Grade 9
Harvest Christian Academy

Water's Phases

Water is a transparent, odorless, tasteless liquid
That is a compound of hydrogen and oxygen.
Water is a little, bland, blue bird that has a mother and a father,
And is trying to build up his character by experiencing new things.

Rain is water that is condensed from the aqueous vapor,
And falls to earth in drops of a small amount.
Rain is a cute and curious child that is growing constantly,
And is learning how to dance like a swan.

Hail is a showery precipitation in the form of irregular pellets
That falls from a cumulonimbus cloud.
Hail is a touchy and timid teenager that always stays close to her friends,
And is teaching herself how to play an instrument.

Snow is a precipitation in the form of ice crystals,
And forms directly from the freezing of water vapor in the air.
Snow is an average and amiable adult that is starting to settle down in life,
And is becoming a businesswoman like Meg Whitman.

Flood is a great overflowing of water onto normally dry land
That is usually caused by a large water source.
Flood is a generous and grateful grandparent that is beginning to appreciate things more,
And is giving gifts to all her grandchildren.

Claire Chen, Grade 8
Carmel Valley Middle School

Silent Confusion

My world is like two diverged roads by reality and fiction. I took the wrong path and now I stand here confused. Why did I take this road when I just walk all my life and never stop? There is no end, just problems and anger; I thought love would help me heal my heart. Fill the empty space that this road gives me.

It's always quiet, I wonder how it must be in the other world. To live a happy life, with a happy family, and a great job with no problems. Not ever silence. I realize that I hate the quiet because it screams the truth.

It helped me think and say I do live in a real world. There is no perfect life everyone has something to complain about. And once I did this…my road finally stopped and I lived on.

Angie Zavala, Grade 8
Richard Merkin Middle Academy

High Merit Poems – Grades 7, 8 and 9

Inspiration

My blessed muse, whisper in my ear,
All of the secrets I long to hear.

Are star-crossed lovers never meant to be?
My personal muse, whisper the answers to me.

The world unveiled I may never see,
If my muse doesn't open the door for me.

I have become solely dependent on you,
To take your leave, I give you your cue.

My cursed muse, leave my ear,
Your toxins I no longer care to hear.

I was made by someone's creation,
To be my own blessed inspiration.

Taylor Partin-Majerus, Grade 7
Dorris-Eaton School

Growing Up

I've known them for the past nine years.
We've been through everything together.
They are like my brothers and sisters
And Carden is like my second home.
But now it is time to leave,
Time to say goodbye.

I knew it was coming.
The end of a chapter in my life.
It came too fast;
I don't think I'm ready to leave.
But I have to.
It's all part of growing up.

It's time to go out in the rest of the world.
To meet new people; to see new places.
But I will never forget them.
They will always be in my heart.
The graduating class of 2009.

Kayla Barkell, Grade 8
Carden School of Sacramento

Believing in Him

Even though my future is unknown,
The path I take, I'm not alone
Even though my path is not always clear,
I always remember that you are near.
I believe in Jesus who died for me,
It's because of Him that I am now free.
His gift is for me today,
As long as I follow Him to my dying day.
One day I will go to the place I long to be,
And see my Father who believed in me.

Chris Acosta, Grade 8
Chino Valley Christian School

The Hunting Game

The little brown whippet,
With his little brown eyes,
Chased the white cotton ball,
With its long, floppy ears.
Running through the big, brown poles,
With their green, painted fingers hanging low,
All the while, casting big, black pictures,
Large enough for all to see.
Where did the white cotton ball go?
Into the big, green thicket,
Its dull knives sticking out,
Its beautiful, pink sculptures grasping its arms.
After it is gone,
The white cotton ball,
That little brown whippet,
Sees another,
And off again he runs,
Like a bullet out of sight,
Into the big, dark forest,
With all of its thickets,
Standing guard.

Brianna Gardner, Grade 7
Alta Loma Jr High School

Want

I want the world's common
Language to be
Laughter

I want to gather all of the green plastic soldiers
And rip the guns from their
Arms

I want to find all the hidden puzzles
And fit their pieces back
Together

I want to cook dinner
For a million at one
Time

I want to mix all of the paints
And blend them into one united
Color

I want every child
That was created to be
Born

I want to change the world

Kailin McFadden, Grade 8
McCabe Elementary School

My Little Monster

I have a little monster named Loo,
when he sneezes he says "Ka-choo."
He likes to say "hi"
His favorite food is pie
He lives in my closet in my favorite shoe

He always loves to dance
He doesn't walk, but prance
He has one sharp tooth and green fur
when he is scared he lets out a 'grrr'
You will love him with just one glance

Lauren Stafford, Grade 7
Citrus Hills Intermediate School

The Void

Space
   the blank void
waiting to be filled.
Exists everywhere
vast
   stretching for miles
cold
   waiting to be discovered.
Space
   could be
an unwritten piece of paper
   or our sky.
Places to see
people to find
millions
   of stars
to explore.
This space
could exist
   anywhere.

Taylor Fields, Grade 8
Bethany Lutheran School

Greatest Dream

My greatest dream
My greatest hope
Is something I might never find

It is to find someone
Who is just like me
To find someone who I can
Completely be myself with
A person who I can laugh with
Or to talk about my problems with

A person who won't call me
"weird" or "stupid"
When I am just being myself
That is my greatest dream

Theresa Nguyen, Grade 8
Daniel Savage Middle School

Severing the Soul

Train wreck
There's blood splattered across the rails
But it's not my blood; it's yours
Yet I feel the pain as if it were mine, maybe even worse
The floodgates open and I can't hold back
The salty tides they once contained
"Just tough it up. Dry your eyes," you command
But I am physically incapable
It's too horrible, the chains binding you too thick to break
You're tied to the tracks and I can't release you
"I made my choice," you say, head held impossibly High
But I don't want that to be true
And I can't leave you alone to face the oncoming train ever again
And I can't lose you to the pain no matter how far gone you might seem
Forgive me, but I'll hold on until the bitter end
Blinded by your light which severed my soul
Leaving me with nothing
Nothing at all
But bloody train tracks
And a broken heart

Goodbye

Maya R. Pilevsky, Grade 8
Carmel Valley Middle School

Christmas

Christmas is a time of joy,
It is also a time of cheer
The smells of home cooking fill the air

Children play in the streets
As they await Christmas morning
Christmas Eve is passing by quicker
As the air gets chillier

There are presents to open
And trees to decorate,
Sometimes there is snow, if you are fortunate.

When you are with your family, the love spreads fast
The nights are cold, but you feel the warmth within
Even dogs and cats feel the love and warmth that flow through the air
They sing and dance as the carolers sing their tune of delight,
Everyone feels the love and joy on this Christmas night

However it is not about the presents or gifts
It is about the love and bliss
Of your family and loved ones you share this day with.
MERRY CHRISTMAS!

Irma Zuñiga, Grade 8
Alondra Elementary School

Thanks

Thanks to my parents
I have an opportunity to go to a laptop programmed school
Thanks to the teachers
I got an excellent result in tests
Thanks to friends
I got used to the school
Thanks to my dog
I learned patience
Thanks to God
I got a life that is too good for me

No thanks to my parents
I am always pressured
No thanks to the teachers
Sometimes too much homework
No thanks to friends
We argue a couple times and get into a fight
No thanks to my dog
I have to take up time to take responsibility of her
Still thanks to God
To put me in a wonderful world with helpful people.

Su Kang, Grade 8
Robert C Fisler School

I Know Babysitting

I know babysitting
Babies crying, children lying
First they're huggin', now they're buggin'
I know babysitting
I'm about to doze, boys picking their nose
She wants a treat, man I'm beat
I know babysitting
"Just calm down…" "Did you steal her crown?!"
"Hey! Use your spoon!" "I hope your mom will arrive soon."
I know babysitting

Paige Truman, Grade 8
Citrus Hills Intermediate School

Dreaming

Your heart is pumping harder and harder.
In your head you think you're going to explode.
Blood is running through your veins.
You think you can't hold no more.

Trying to yell and nothing comes out.
Trying to open your eyes again.
Thinking it's just a dream.
You are imagining lots of things that are fantasies.

Wanting to get out struggling, while thinking there's no way out.
Knowing the floor is moving wanting to hide.
Thinking you might die.
Yelling was this all of my life.

Angelina Herrera, Grade 8
Jefferson Middle School

Friends

F orever and for always
R ight there when you need them most
I n our hearts forever and ever
E ach has a secret to tell one another
    but shhh…you're not allowed to tell…
N ever any negatives and always positives
    about each other
D own to earth, always dependable
S uper sweet and caring

Kaytlyn Villegas, Grade 8
Jefferson Middle School

That Low-skied Day

Crisp, crunchy grass beneath our feet.
Water wailing at us from a sprinkler.
Bright, beautiful sky above our heads.

The sun is shining,
My grandma's loud, likeable birds are
Screaming, and lunging at their cages,
Wishing to be set free on such a vivacious,
Low-skied day.

My sister's screams echo (echo, echo)
Up to the wooden, suntanned porch.
"SNAKE!" she yells, as she runs for the house.

She runs with fear,
But we quake with laughter.

Summer Hays, Grade 9
Mount Whitney High School

Pain from Inside

I feel so much pain inside of me,
Knowing that my love would never come back.
Realizing that soon my heart has to know,
But in what way would I break it up to my heart?
Can my heart handle it?
Without having to make any sacrifices?
In the meantime my love is playing tricks on me.
I see him come and go beside me,
But I know he has no temptation of coming back with me.
When he passes by I try to look into his brown eyes,
But he never turns and looks into my direction,
It hurts so bad inside, wouldn't it hurt you?
However, I have to keep on living with or without him,
It would hurt, but my life has to go on.
Having fake laughs is no joke, but it helps me out,
Making people think that I am feeling happy,
While I know deep down it is not true.
Why would it matter to them or even to him?
So it doesn't matter if my laughs are real or not!
This got to be the last time; I'll fall for an unreal love.
And if luck is on me, I would never feel pain inside of me again!

Karla Parada, Grade 8
Richard Merkin Middle Academy

Could It Be a Dream?
Lightning flashes.
Then just white.
Black clouds and thunder
Roll right on in
Could it be a dream?

Flying over the city, the country
You fall, but don't get hurt.
It feels good somehow, almost like
Hitting a pillow.
Could it be a dream?

Fun in the sun at the beach.
Being there all day with a loved one.
They float into the sky—
Out of sight,
Is it only a dream?

Why is it only a dream?
Is there a reason?
It makes me wonder.
Emma Sherwood, Grade 7
Citrus Hills Intermediate School

Your Smile
Every time I see you smile,
I melt and die inside,
I want to spend forever with you,
Always be by your side.
I love you.
Nothing can change that,
Not even time!
Justin Perez, Grade 7
Corpus Christi School

Friends Forever
Friends forever, all as one
Jump and skip having fun
Us friends have to stick together
We will be friends forever and ever

Friends forever, all as one
Playing and singing in the sun
Together forever we're all having fun
We all love each other a whole ton
Friends forever
Erica Zavala, Grade 7
Santa Rosa Technology Magnet School

The Sunset
Watching the sunset
Oh! It shines upon the roaring waters.
Now the sun has gone down,
The ocean calms down to sleep.
Veronica Jardeleza, Grade 7
Corpus Christi School

A Child's Perspective
Oh child of war, child who is scared
Child please speak to me about the lifestyle of war
    I'm scared to go outside, I'm afraid to go to sleep
    I'm worrying about who next the militia will keep
Oh child in poverty, child without food
Child please speak to me about this terrifying condition
    I wake up hungry, I beg to eat
    I have no home, I sleep on the street
Oh child of gratitude, please tell me
About the thoughts that occur to thee
    I may live humbly; I may live on a battleground
    But that doesn't take away from my being sound
    I don't follow my dreams, I chase them
    The pursuit of knowledge is my life
    Not only that being without it is my number one strife
    I may not have an ideal life, but I've learned to be thankful forever
    And most importantly, no matter how I live,
    I've learned to be arrogant
Never
Suleekha Musse, Grade 8
Islamic School of San Diego

My Last Breath
I used to wake up thinking about you
I used to always have someone to talk to
I used to see beauty everywhere when I was with you
My heart used to drop every time I saw you
My heart used to want you by my side at all times
But now since you're not with me, it's harder to breathe
My heart is now split in two
I have nobody there for me, as were you
It's almost as if you took my last breath
Because now it feels harder to breathe the love I used to breathe
Michael Saidawi, Grade 8
Corpus Christi School

Barack H. Obama
Martin Luther King Jr. had an American dream
He wanted all Americans to "Let freedoms ring!"
Regardless of race, color, or creed
Martin was willing to give his life for what he believed

The man was born August fourth, nineteen hundred, sixty-one
Graduated from Columbia University and Harvard Law School; his education was done
Elected to the US Senate in 2004; political career had begun
Ran for President in 2008; Barack Obama won!

From the steps of the Lincoln Memorial
To the steps of the Oval Office
Martin Luther King faced a bitterly divided nation
Our first African American President what a celebration!

"Free at last, free at last, thank God, Almighty, we are free at last"
Daniel Jauregui, Grade 9
Lucerne Valley Jr/Sr High School

Light and Darkness

Bad times and good times are like autumn and spring
completing the cycle of life, rotating in a ring.
Bad times and good times are lightness and darkness
completing the cycle of day, a setting sun moves west.

You can be spring, and I'll be autumn
you can walk in the light above the clouds,
with my head hung low I'll be the darkness down below
because bad times require tears and sorrow.
They cease and crush the dreams of tomorrow.

Forget lifelong wishes
and limitless desires
bad times will do away with them all
like paper in a fire.

Tomorrow we'll switch places and you'll be depressed
while I'll blissfully climb the ladder of success.

Misbah Khan, Grade 8
Madrona Middle School

Apart

As I walk on this day
the wind blows my way.
Though my soul tells me we need to be apart,
you're still holding my heart.
Where do I start?
This love is falling apart.
I think to myself,
How could you not see,
I thought we were meant to be?

Natalie Kardous, Grade 8
Holy Family Catholic School

My Big Sister

My big sister who I truly adore,
Is my big sister who couldn't take life's pain anymore.
My big sister who I thought had it all,
Is my big sister who I thought would never fall.
My big sister who did better than me in school,
Is my big sister who thinks she's a fool.
My big sister who was throwing her life away,
Is my big sister who I looked up to every day.
My big sister who fell on her knees crying,
Is my big sister who is now on her feet fighting.
My big sister who looked for love,
Is my big sister who knows there's not only us,
But a loving God up above.
My big sister who is now stronger,
Is my big sister who now can hopefully live a peaceful life,
Much much longer.
My big sister who I truly adore,
Is my big sister who I will love,
Always and forever more.

Kyanna Dagdagan, Grade 8
McCabe Elementary School

Power of Friendship

No one was there to see her slowly fade.
Her laugher was a sound yet to be found.
To them she was invisible; they did not see her scars.

Her cries for help were unanswered.
She felt useless, worthless, and afraid.

She ended her journey alone and in pain.

Friendship was what she needed.
It would have been the thing that saved her.

If they had taken the time to listen to a broken soul,
Taken the time to know,
This story would never be told.

The power of friendship is something unknown;
Everyone has it, if they use it right.
You never know,
They might be the one who listen,
Who takes the time to know,
And be the one who saves a life.

Darian McClure, Grade 8
Lucerne Elementary School

Ode to Freedom

Freedom, the gift to be free,
with no one telling you who should or should not be.
Restrictions, refusals, to go to a different place,
are not denied by the appearance of your face.

Freedom, the moral thing to possess,
shall not determine a man greater nor less.
Dignity, respect, are qualities that we all have acquired,
when used properly, we shall all be admired.

Freedom, the right that you hold,
should not make sadness, hatred unfold.
Righteousness, belonging, two words we have gained,
will not be stifled, ignored, nor chained.

Freedom, the item that you crave,
will show forward, will make you brave.
Perseverance, ambitious, words that we seek,
will forever be reached, will not make us seem weak.

Freedom, the way of life,
should not be hidden, or bring strife;
but should be loved and cherished
for all and all time.

Lauren Williams, Grade 9
Redlands High School

My Paycheck
Every day is my payday
A big puff of suffocating smoke
If this continues,
I will never go broke

If this is my paycheck,
I don't want a raise
Not even a 'thank you'
Not even praise

I am constantly hurt
Pain of all kinds
This is something no doctor can cure
It is caused by mankind

I would expect better treatment
From people I support
I am everyone's shelter
Don't I deserve a little more respect?

I have been supporting life
Since the first humans' birth
Been here through joy and pain
Through crying and mirth
Take care of me…I am your Earth
Yasmeen Alhomsy, Grade 8
Islamic School of San Diego

America
United people in America
Pride in themselves,
Many people in America
With suffering lives
During war,
Others living in freedom,
In America
Different cultures,
Religions and lifestyles
We judge people differently.
Although different —
We are all united as one.
Candrice Hernandez, Grade 7
St Alphonsus School

Christmas
A cold, snowy day,
A time for family gatherings
Full of fun and games,
Gazing at your Christmas tree,
Filled with beautiful bright lights,
Drinking your cup of hot chocolate,
Glad to open presents.
Crystal Banuelos, Grade 7
St Alphonsus School

Him
She can't stop thinking about him
He doesn't know she exists
She talks to him
He doesn't hear her

She calls him
He hangs up
She walks over to him
He turns away

She smiles at him
He looks away
She has a party
He doesn't show

But no matter what
She loves him
He will never know
Allison Schafer, Grade 8
Holy Family Catholic School

Ice Cream on a Cold Day
You don't eat ice cream
On the coldest of days

You don't drink hot cocoa
When there's the hottest of rays

You don't go swimming
With a winter freeze

You don't go outdoor ice skating
With a pair of sweaty knees

But whether red or blue
I know it is so true
That I'll always
Always play with you
Katie Bang, Grade 8
Robert C Fisler School

Elegant Sunset
Beautiful, quiet, serene
peaceful like an endless dream
Birds flying in the air
freedom roams everywhere
Wonderful, radiant joy
waves crashing ashore
Orange, yellow, red
harmony in the air
Brightness, darkness, happiness
evermore
Marjillaine Santos, Grade 8
Our Lady of the Rosary School

The First Day of Spring
Sky is clear
Grass is green
Birds are singing
Sun is shining
Kids are playing
Day is warm
Love is in the air
It's the first day of spring!
Kyle Hipolito, Grade 8
Corpus Christi School

The Perfect Guy (For Me)
The perfect guy, for me, would be:
smart, not self-centered, kind, cute,
a gentleman, and respectful, but
I should stop there, because I don't
think that any guy in the world
is that perfect, except for
you
Marcela Alvarez, Grade 7
Corpus Christi School

A Hole of Darkness
I'm falling into a hole of darkness.
It seems like it's never going to end.
Just a pit of nothing.

I'm falling into a hole of darkness.
Nothing to look at, nothing to do.
I just have to keep on falling.

I'm falling into a hole of darkness.
I hope it's going to end.
Hold on, I see a light.
Jocelyn Schmidt, Grade 7
Yolo Middle School

Freedom
America
the free land,
always taken
for granted,
until the
Vietnam War,
when 17-year olds
were drafted.
The draft lasted
four years,
and when the war
was over,
all that was left
were tears.
Daniel Jimenez, Grade 8
Grace Christian Academy

Totem Pole

I am a totem pole,
Not knowing what will come next,
I am a tall worthy totem pole.

When people disrespect me I will haunt them,
When I am loved I will please them,
I am a tall worthy totem pole.

When I am being carved I stand tall,
When I am being admired I feel meaningful,
I am a tall worthy totem pole.

When I am standing in the rain I feel alone,
When the sun is shining I feel complete,
I am a tall worthy totem pole.

When the tourists come around I look the same,
When my creator comes around I change,
I am a tall worthy totem pole.

When war is made I cry,
When peace is made I cheer,
I am the tall worthy totem pole.

Taryn Sall, Grade 8
Palm Desert Charter Middle School

Bravery

Bravery is strong and fierce,
Bravery is what it takes to take the blame,
Bravery is what it takes to take the stand and give it your best,
Bravery is not trying to be something
You're not.

Bravery doesn't stand alone,
Bravery is toughness and strength,
Bravery is a weakness overcame

Bravery is achievement,
Success,

The heart of courage is,
Bravery
Bravery is like a superhero,
Saving people's lives and being a friend,
Face life through bravery,
Overcome every fear you have ever had,
When you do this you will be,
Happy

Bravery is what I am.

Nick Julier, Grade 7
Santa Rosa Technology Magnet School

My Dream

My dream is something that I have every night
My dream is different all of the time
Sometimes they're happy,
Sometimes they're sad,
And with my dream
I am unique.
My dream makes me more unique than any other person
So, therefore I like my dream.

Erik Montierth, Grade 7
Sierra Charter School

Basketball

Faster than a speeding bullet
Stronger than a powerful mullet,
I charge my way through defenders
The only way to lose is to surrender.

With the basketball alternating in both hands,
A triumphant march is heard from the band
With the crowds expressing their joy with cheers
I have played my heart out for so many years.

I have loved basketball from the bottom of my heart
From the end of the games all the way to the start
This game's all about speed and agility
The sport's given me my inner resting ability.

Ever since I've joined I've been much stronger,
And the endurance to keep fighting longer
Now I say good-bye to all the memories; disappeared and dead,
And I tilt my head upward and await the journey ahead.

Richard Lin, Grade 8
St Victor Elementary School

Darkness

The darkness consumes me in its madness
I scream with fear and terror
But no one can hear me
And now the dawn is breaking,
But to me it's blinding
To land among the roses
Would be a dream come true
But in my world there are no flowers
There is only darkness and sadness
Mirrors to reflect
My pain upon the world
Darkness has taken my soul
And locked it in these mirrors
You are the key
To unlock my dreams
To unlock my happiness
And self-esteem
And when the sun shines;
It's time to fly free.

Kelsie Shumard, Grade 8
McCabe Elementary School

Just the Same

Every night I keep dreaming.
I wish you were here.
Every day I keep thinking.
What am I to fear?
I know I haven't been honest.
I haven't been quite true.
I know I'm not perfect.
But neither are you.
You're definitely no better.
You see, we're just the same.
I want to say I love you,
But somehow I'm just afraid,
Afraid to be rejected,
Afraid to look like a fool.
But I can wait no longer…
I have to tell the truth.

Jan Kip Sison, Grade 8
Corpus Christi School

Veterans' Memories

A victory after war
Veterans cheering
Red-faced veterans
Come back after hard work
A veterans' parade dedicated to
A family brings bouquets of flowers
People screaming and cheering
Veterans' memories
Of their friends killed in combat.

Vincent Abbas, Grade 8
St Alphonsus School

Family

My family is everything to me
Family is always going to
Be there for you
Family is the people
You trust
Family is the kind of people
Who cares a lot about you
Family is the first people
You come to if
You have a problem
Just remember that
Family is going to
Be there no matter what
In tough times
And in easy times
In you could think of
Everything so family
Is going to be there
No matter what so
I just want to say
"I LOVE MY FAMILY"

Michael Nwaogu, Grade 8
Richard Merkin Middle Academy

My Dream Boy

Boy,
Do you know that I really like you lately?
Because every time I come around
You seem to be around
Is it a sign or are my dreaming designs of Love.

Do you know that you are my dream boy?
Everything I say and do is about you
Hershey Kisses, cotton candy, or even chocolate cookies
I fantasize my feelings and I realize that I'll soon make you mine.

I remember when I walk past you, you glance at me and smile
I look straight into your eyes
We had that silent communication
It was like taking a vacation in paradise

If I had one wish I would express my love for you
You would know that I am the right girl
I am honest, faithful and you'll see that you will never have a girl like me

Theresa Massaquoi, Grade 9
Vallejo High School

We, Have a Dream

If American history is a long river
Today, is the dazzling wave that splashes the shore
If American history is written in a book
Today, is one of those pages that truly reflects the meaning of the United States

Looking through them, historical moments flashing before our eyes
We saw Abraham Lincoln, drafting "Emancipation Proclamation"
We heard Martin Luther King, delivering "I Have A Dream"
We felt the battles of race, of faith, of value

Today, as we celebrate the new leader of our nation
We are living history with our votes and beliefs

Yesterday, you yearn for democracy: spoke about hope
Today, you may stand on the giant's shoulder: overlook your nation
To see the struggles, the crisis, and yet, potential
The road pointing forward, is long, curly, and faint
You shall not be worried, as we are all walking with you

Let others recognize America, as a nation
Who despites how different we are
Just cares how much we share
Common needs, common deeds
And the same prayer we say silently in our hearts

We, have a dream

Lixinbei Jing, Grade 8
Jane Lathrop Stanford Middle School

Encouragement

Encouragement is getting an A
Your parents have faith in you
Winning a basketball game and
Knowing you put your mind to it.
Encouragement is the color yellow
Of a bright sun
A thought and feeling
We see in people's eyes
Hidden but visible —
In people we know who are here for us
Clap! Clap! Clap!
The excitement of crossing the finish line
Encouragement…we can see and it touches us.

Jessica Aparicio, Grade 8
St Alphonsus School

Gone

My grandpa's not here now
At least not by my side.
But I can sense him in my heart
And see the impact he's made on others.
He was always gleeful,
Never downcast or pessimistic
Always thoughtful and just.
When I think of the fact that he's not here
I bow my head
And weep inside.
I see his eyes
Greeting,
Comforting,
Strengthening.
I'm not the only one who still grieves a bit
But, I'll be with him one day.
Then we will be
Together
Again.

Kenny Bakken, Grade 7
Bethany Lutheran School

The Two Lovers

There's a story of a fair maiden and a man
He and her were madly in love
But her father did not like this one plan
The fair maiden and man got tired of
This undelightfulness, so to runaway
To runaway was their only fate
Now her father was out of their way
But the love for each was no more great
He now changed and loved another women
There love again was tested once more
Their love was as sour as a lemon
But like magic their love was like before
He again loved her with all his heart
Now nothing more can tear the two apart

Raphael Reyes, Grade 8
John Adams Middle School

Friends, Friends, Friends

Going out, sleeping in, late nights
Eating Craisins, dancing crazy, and flying kites
Of all the friends I've ever met,
You're the ones I won't forget
When we were younger all we could talk about
were our cool new toys
Now all we can talk about are those boys
I know that I can trust you,
And you can trust me too
Friends is what we are,
Forever friends we will be,
Friends until the end,
Together, forever

Nikki Dimeck, Grade 9
Fountain Valley High School

Rainbow Emotions

What do you see when you look
deep inside your soul?
A rainbow of colors is what I see
A splash of angry red
Spots of blue sadness
Stripes of orangey happiness
That fade into yellow in gleefulness
Waves of purple jealousy
with green splattered across
Maybe a hint of pink for love
Sometimes light pink, dark pink, or just normal pink
Tiny lines of brown where they all blur at the border
And an orb of darkness, pitch black darkness
centered around my heart
filled with dark, nasty emotions
That threaten to destroy
the rainbow of my soul.

Hitomi Fujiki, Grade 8
Madrona Middle School

To My Love

Your personality is so bright you'd make the heavens shine,
You'd be any girls dream, but only fate to say you're all mine.
Your heart could warm the coldest ice age,
You're like a book something good on every page.
Your charm and good looks make me go insane,
After your presence, warm flickers still remain.
Your smile is as radiant as the sun,
Ever since the start I knew you were the one.
To me you're a treasure in every way,
Finding you might have been my luckiest day.
I just think of you and I'm filled with dreams,
I love the way your form suits your jeans.

Jhoanna Carrera, Grade 8
Henry T Gage Middle School

Light?

How is there light?
It is seen when delirious, but also when, you are most serious.
What is the light?
It's still quite mysterious.

When is the light?
It is between the dusk and dawn, when the light goes out, the whole world will yawn.
What is the light?
A great phenomenon.

Where is the light?
It is in space, the sky, as well as in your heart, it has played a part, in making this world start.
What is the light?
A piece of vivid art.

Now, why is the light?
To give guidance, hope and peace, with it, all Earthly pain will cease.
But what is the light?
From life, an essential piece.

Light will reach out and show us the way,
it will not let us weaken and sway or let us go amuck and astray.
Light, our light, is here to stay…

Kevin Kim, Grade 8
Madrona Middle School

It's Time

"It's time to grow up now," my parents used to say; time to give up your toys and all that child's play
Time to expand your mind and start your knowing; it's time to be an adult and start your growing

It's time to sleep late in that empty bed and study all the answers in your head
These are the times you will always stress; to try to achieve that personal best

You can't have naps and no more times to relax
There's only time for work; cause the rest of high school will drive you berserk

"It's time to move out now," my parents used to say, time to part and go our own separate ways
Time to sleep in very strange places and it's time meet some very new faces

Now it's time for you to go get a new job and there's no time for you to sit there and sob
You need to make money to pay that pricey rent and pay for those groceries with your every last cent

"I've grown up now," I told my parents one day; I forgot all my toys and all my child's play
I studied with great passion galore; I even moved out of your very front door

I got a great job and bought great books; mom and dad, I even got your great looks
I've had fun and I've learned a lot, but there's this one little thing I've almost forgot

When I look back to my childish days, I remember the warmth of the sun's beautiful rays
My life passed in one simple daze and all my childhood had gone in a haze

Sheila Sadr, Grade 8
Corona Del Mar High School

Forgiving Warmth

Frozen wasteland, covered in absolute ice,
Vanished into the forgiving warmth of the sun.

Slick squirrels slide across the slippery ice,
Rapid rabbits return to their burrows for refuge.

Suspended on an adjacent limb,
A cacophony of cranky crows.

Gold droplets from the heavens,
Fall flawlessly upon our innocent bodies,
The golden rays of life.

A cloud or two that disappear,
The coming of a brand new year.

Emerald leaves gleam in the sunset,
The calm, silent nature does not pose a threat.

The world is so different, the world is diverse,
This new, vibrant season, will reverse the curse.

Justin Dunn, Grade 7
Dorris-Eaton School

Fall

I look out my window while I lay in bed
All that I notice is bushes, trees and the land
And watching the leaves change from green to red
I see a nice white band
Stretch across the deep blue sky
Watching it close but without a stare
Unknowing why I should care
I look into my yard and see my mother
For I don't say a word
Because I don't want to be a bother
And then on my window sill lands a tiny bird
I watch her rake the multicolored leaves
As they fall so endlessly from the tops of the trees

Andrew Keller, Grade 7
Yolo Middle School

You

I went to the park and there you stood
looking at the stars, just waiting to be understood
I wished all my life that I would be the one
to keep all your secrets and warm you like the sun
and now I worry that I cannot
for there is another star that I forgot
so now as I sadly lay in this field,
I make a new wish that I hope will be fulfilled

Now I want to be your sky,
always with you, always by your side
but it's up to you to look at me
but remember that I will always be there
just in case you forgot

Joan Park, Grade 8
Robert C Fisler School

What a Friend

My "best friend" smiles at me across the lunch table,
I smile back, trying to show how I feel inside.
She has turned her back from the good side.
How could she have done so?
I tried to keep her from the dark side,
But she never listened.
She betrayed me, not knowing she did.
She just left me standing there.
I can't even confront her like a real best friend would,
I've tried,
It's never worked.
She thinks the arguments we've had mean nothing,
She thinks she's still my best friend.
But how could I trust her anymore?
She had and still does spread my secrets,
She gossips about me…
I'm speechless…
What a friend.

Racquel Gonzales, Grade 7
Holy Family Catholic School

Me

My eyes are as blue as the bluest ocean.
My hair is as soft as a feather flying through the wind.
My head is filled with intelligence.
My hands are as soft as calm water
My heart beats with every breath I take
I live in a house
And I eat perfect food

Nathan Grismer, Grade 8
Citrus Hills Intermediate School

One Wish

If I had only one wish
I would make us more than friends
Cuddling and holding hands
Loving each other till the end
If I had only one wish
I would make you my whole life
I would make you my wife
For my whole entire lifetime
If I had only one wish
I would always promise to trust you
I would never stop loving you
Because there's no one like you
If I had only one wish
I would give you everything
That makes and keeps you happy
So I can see your loving smile every day
If I had only one wish I would make you my sweetheart
And I would be happy if I were also yours,
And I would be glad if you were mine
Because you and I were both created
To love each other till the end of time

Allen Lucas, Grade 8
Corpus Christi School

I Am the Betrayed

Sad.
    That's one way to define the hurt,
That's been built up inside.
    Lonely.
That's the way I feel when they
lie…
    Cheat and talk.
        Passive.
That's the way I feel when they really
don't understand what they did to me.
I picked my name.
I am the BETRAYED!!

Erica D. Acosta, Grade 8
McCabe Elementary School

Football

Running down the field!
Anticipating a hit,
Hearing my breath against the wind!
Gripping the threads,
Tightly in my palm,
Hearing my cleats glide.
Running down the sideline,
Hearing the crowd roar,
I reach my goal, diving over the pylon,
Touchdown!

Peyton Cotto, Grade 7
Citrus Hills Intermediate School

Love

I'm giddy, I'm sweet,
Not taking defeat,
I run true and free,
And you think you have me

But you don't know,
What love really is,
I'm the wintry snow,
I'm the summery bliss

You think that I'm yours,
For you and you alone,
For your friends and family,
And for everything you own

But I'm also for the beggar,
The hurting and the sad,
The hopeless and the hungry,
And the ones who have gone mad

I'm for the hated lonely,
For the ones that hate themselves,
But you won't show them they are loved,
If not you, who else?

Bethany Porter, Grade 9
Dehesa Charter School

Ode to Dogs

Dogs are wonderful creatures, loyal, obedient and bold
They'll love you if you're young or growing old
Whether you're rich, or whether you're poor
They'll look at you through those admiring eyes, all while sitting on the floor

They'll watch you at night with their amazing smell and sight,
Protecting you from any form of fright
For their courage is not based on height
It's based on what their soul is like, this for sure is right!

Dogs are loving, dogs are graceful, dogs are pure
If you're feeling down and in the dumps, they're the cure
Giving you that look, the one that makes them so allure
You know they're thinking of something, but you're not so sure

Dogs will always be there, sitting on the floor
And you'll just smile at them, while you walk out the door.

Mark Rimensberger, Grade 8
Robert C Fisler School

Tired

When I close them, I have no eyeballs.
I always sleep through breakfast.
I wear only blankets and PJs 'cause I hate waking up.
I took Lazy on a date because we match up, but I missed it.
My favorite color is black because that's what you see when your eyes are closed.
My biggest secret is that I was hyper once.

Jeremy Sanchez, Grade 7
Odyssey Charter School

Flying

What would it be like to fly?
To just lift up your arms and soar through the sky?
I think that flying might be a breeze,
If you could just raise up your arms and fly as high as you please.
Maybe, in that moment, you would feel free.
Leaving all of your problems behind, you could just enjoy yourself and laugh with glee.
You could touch rainbows and brush past the treetops,
Just keep on going, with no one telling you to stop.
Just fly with the birds and float with the clouds,
You would never again have to be stuck in a crowd.
Maybe you would loop and twirl.
Throughout the sky you'd swoop and swirl.
With all this fun you'll be able to laugh and unfurl.
And again feel like a young, little girl
Yes, flying might be wonderful; it could be a ball.
Just flow with the wind and hope that you don't fall.
However it might not be fun.
It may not be such a great idea to fly as high as the sun.
I, for one, might have trouble flying
Throughout the days and nights,
Because I am terribly afraid of heights.

Celia Herreros, Grade 8
Robert C Fisler School

A Bear Nightmare

As I remember my nightmare
I was clearly aware
Of what I saw over there
Something big and fair
I was a bear.

It was black and gold
And really bold
And I was scared, scared that it would attack
And everything would be pitch black
I finally awoke huffing and puffing
To realize that it was only a dream.

Isaias Rios, Grade 8
Palm Desert Charter Middle School

My Enlightenment

Sometimes, when life seems to quiet
into paralyzing silence
like the breaking dawn
an inspiration comes

When the cold black darkness
suddenly awakens
like the leaves of a rose
my eyes open to the world

Left alone with
pieces of my dark past
will I open up my soul
and my pen dances across the page

As I reach the end of this poem
I read it aloud to see if it makes sense
satisfied, I set it down then frown
for this makes sense, but my life does not.

Merlin Llamas, Grade 8
Madrona Middle School

Rain

Drip-drop, Drip-drop
The water falls to the ground,
You hear the cars whoosh by as they hit puddles of water.
Some people are sad because the rain has ruined their plans,
Their emotions, as well as the skies, are gray,
But for others they find the rain as an opportunity,
An opportunity to explore new life,
Study how the temperature changes,
Or even get a free car wash.
Their attitude is gay and joyful,
They learn to explore the wonderful works of the world,
The darkness that had once fallen over the land
Disappears into a rainbow and brightens the world,
Like a baby's smile brightens your day,
As a reminder of God's promises to the world.

Lauren Johnson, Grade 7
St Cyprian School

Who Am I?

Am I here?
Or am I there?
Am I me?
Or am I you?
I guess the only one who can explain this to me is me
But beyond this hollow cast, who am I?
I try to answer that question frequently,
I am a girl who is 13 years of age,
Am I that young to already be all that I can be,
Or something in between?
I try to act older than I am,
This side of me I cannot stand,
A combination of races from my family tree,
American, Hispanic, and Indian all in me,
Many things I still can't grasp,
Like how the now was the past,
And if I am me and you are you,
Is my identity true?
Am I really who I know I am?
Yes, I am me,
Confused and still searching for my inner beauty.

Alyssa Hernandez, Grade 8
Los Coyotes Middle School

Orange

I am orange

I am not the orange you think I am.
Not the one you see at the store
Or in a fruit basket
But a color with little hue.

I am orange like the sunrise sky
That brings light to your day.

I am orange like a leaf on a tree
That opens up the season of autumn to you.

I am orange like some Golden Poppies
That have a beautiful glow in the sunlight.

I am the orange that flickers in that pumpkin
On that dark, scary Halloween night.

I am orange like the sunset sky
That takes away light from your dark nights.

I am orange.
That is who I am

Zaria Lovelace, Grade 7
St Cyprian School

Best Friend

Dear Best Friend,
It's been so long,
since I've talked to you,
It's been so long,
since we linked, just two,
It's been so long,
since you've made me smile,
It's been so long,
since you've sat a while,
But that's okay,
and that's all right,
You're my best friend,
and our friendship will always be bright,
So if I die,
Before you do,
I'll go to heaven,
And wait for you.

Hannah Lee, Grade 8
Robert C Fisler School

WWII

In the wide ocean
Men are split into motion
Planes flying overhead
American soldiers leap out of bed

The guns rapidly shooting upward
The planes on fire coming downward
The green salt water
Changing to a bloody slaughter

The sinking boats
Men losing hope
The rising smoke
Men cough and choke

Pain in the men
After they tried to swim
Bigger guns they bring in
This gives advantages; they pray to win

Dropping bombs, exploding boats
Let's pray that men float
Finally the planes retreat
The soldiers go back to sleep

Steve Rosales, Grade 9
Lucerne Valley Jr/Sr High School

Brothers

Dirty, messy, stinky,
lots of meanings for brothers
pests, brat, dirty, messy but whatever
Brothers are Brothers
and you love them any way they are.

Abrianna Marchesotti, Grade 7
Tenaya Middle School

Different This Year

School will be different this year because
I'm sure to work harder in writing
Remembering always that showing possession needs apostrophizes
And never forgetting a comma when listing.

School will be different this year because
I'm sure to play better handball
Impressing the little kids and the bigger kids too
With incredible back lines and super low slices.

School will be different this year because
I won't have to take the fitness test again
I wont' have to study the solar system once more
I won't have to eat at the old worn out table
AND I won't have to deal with all kinds of different trouble.

School will be different this year because
I'm sure to practice my trampoline jumps
And I'm sure to master that 360 back flip
Who knows? Maybe in June, I can definitely do it
And someday I might be able to post it on YouTube.

Josh Husen, Grade 7
Citrus Hills Intermediate School

Gloves of Glory

I catch a whiff of the freshly cut green glistening grass,
As I quickly run to my outfield position.
The warm sun tickles the back of my neck while the cool breeze gently kisses my face.

One out to go and the game is over.
The batter steps towards the worn and dusty plate.
She towers over the catcher like a skyscraper and swings the bat with absurd energy.
Yikes — I hope she does not hit the ball over my head!

Ping! The aluminum bat strikes the neon yellow ball like lightning.
It soars through the jeweled blue sky.
Mine! Mine! I got it!

My outstretched arm reaches high,
While my worn and trusty glove anxiously waits for glory.
Thunk!
A tiny glimpse of yellow catches my eye as I peer into my brown glove.
Yes — I did it!

My team leaps for joy while running to high-five me.
A smile stretches across my face, and I enjoy the fleeting but memorable moment.

Game over, Game won!
I wish life were this easy.

Kaitlin Leimbach, Grade 7
Rolling Hills Country Day School

The Reunion of Dawn
Time passes slowly as I wait for the light to come,
The sun seemed lost forever when I left it behind me,
For years has lived this terrifying night,
I long for the glorious light,
Is it its radiance I remember,
Or its kind and gentle nature?
I remember how it used to glow with joy and happiness,
Selflessness, apparent in its beautiful rays,
But I am still consumed in shadow,
Morning approaches slowly,
And I know that the light has come near,
But now as it rises,
I have nothing to fear,
For I have seen once again,
My sun.

Sarah Winstead, Grade 9
Faith Christian Jr/Sr High School

I've Got a Question for You!
Beauty speaks of populated city streets,
I see in the lights of your eyes,
I sway with the seaweed through all the oceans,
I moved to the beat of the clicks of keys,
I walk through repeated mirrors' dreams,
My body moves the way of her bouncy curls,
I'm off in a beautiful daydream,
I refuse to come back to life,
For I like to be lost in the midst of something else,
Intertwined in the telling of a magical fairy tale,
My name is whispered through the words,
As I lie on the railroad tracks,
Movement stirring all around me,
I begin to see the real me,
A life filled with the glass half full rather than half empty,
As restless nights pass on by,
I'm still left with that one thought,
Am I giving enough or just too much?
All I know is that I am left with the silence and only one choice,
You know my meaning and where I am heading,
But if it's not what you like why don't you stop me?

Ciera Rose Carter, Grade 8
Palm Desert Charter Middle School

Cheeseburgers
Cheeseburgers,
Let their scent fill your nose,
Watch the ketchup drip to your toes,
Hear it sizzle on the grill,
Touch the sesame seeds, they feel like a wrinkled dollar bill.

Cheeseburgers,
So tasty and mouthwatering,
Its juicy patty gives it a kick,
Its assortment of cheeses give your taste buds a click,
Its zesty blend of sauces so sweet,
Oh, the cheeseburger cannot be beat.

Keane Virola, Grade 7
St Cyprian School

Your Love
Your love will last for a lifetime,
That's why I praise You.
In the midst of a storm, You comfort me,
That's why I trust You.
When I'm all alone, You're there,
That's why I have faith.
When I pray to You, You answer,
That's why I seek Your guidance.
When I am thirsty,
You fill my cup.
When I am hungry,
You replenish me.
When I'm filled with anger and hatred, You calm me,
That's why I seek Your peace.
When I'm sad or feeling down, You're there,
That's why I'm happy.
You gave me this life,
That's why I won't take it for granted.
You accept me, flaws and all,
That's why I love You.

Alexis Washington, Grade 8
Chino Valley Christian School

Faded Glory
This is to the great men who stood at their stations.
Who fought off the British and protected our nation.
To the men who prevailed through the revolutionary fight.
And to those who were lost in the perilous plight.
I praise all soldiers who had volunteered and served,
For if we had lost, the American future would be curved.
I will always honor your tag,
Because of the fact that you saved our flag.
For this, I thank the strong and the brave.
To this day, we still remember and honor your grave.

Hunter Finley, Grade 8
Citrus Hills Intermediate School

Fear
Fear is staying home alone
Hiding under the blankets while
Watching a scary movie
Hearing sudden noises around every corner
Like the thump, thump on the door
Or the pitter patters of the rain
Afraid of walking into the darkness of every room
Not knowing what could be hidden
It is the monster hiding under your bed
Just waiting for you to fall asleep
In order to devour your flesh
Fear is the animal camouflaging into its scenery
Waiting to pounce on its prey
It is the color red
The blood that drips down to the floor
From your body.

Christopher Munoz, Grade 8
St Alphonsus School

I Am a Girl Without a Father
I am a girl without a father
I hear his voice
I smell his scent
I see his face
I am a girl without a father.

I am a girl without a father
I hear his laugh
I smell his happiness
I see his smile
I am a girl without a father.
Jakaya Miller, Grade 9
Regency High School

Song
A song in you
A song in me
What shall we do?
Set it free

Everyone has
A song of their own
In the way they act
Is how it is shown

Some are jazz
Few soft rock
If you listen hard
Your song will knock

A ballerina's song
May be from the Nutcracker
A young punk teen's
Might be by a hard rocker

But all have a song
Some soft some loud
Your song's who you are
Points you out in the crowd
Alison Clifford, Grade 7
Monte Vista Christian School

Silent Lightning
Jagged scars flash in the sky
like long fingers of light.
Grasping buildings and touching trees
with fingers of destruction.

Streaking across the night
with thunder in its wake.
Bright pulses of light
soundlessly blinding the eye.
Marshall Reid, Grade 8
Madrona Middle School

My Mom
She is of stunning beauty,
She is of stunning grace.
She is one mother
Who cannot be replaced.
She gives me hope,
She gives me light,
And before bed we pray at night.
She has shown me love like no other,
I thank God in Heaven for my mother.
Erick Celis, Grade 8
St Vincent Elementary School

I Am…
I am the wombat
that walks the earth
I am small, cute
I have stubby arms and legs
I am the wombat
Who on warm, sunny, happy days
goes around looking
for adventure
I am the wombat
Who on cold, rainy, sad days
burrows a hole in the ground…
Hides
I am the wombat
that roams the earth
Nick Terry, Grade 8
La Joya Middle School

Missing
Sunday morning
I was going to wish him
Happy birthday
But
He's missing

With Dad and JJ
Mom and Paige
And me on my bike
All frantically looking for him
I'm still kind of confused
I just had woken up
But I knew what was going on
I was scared
We looked for 45 minutes
Still nothing
I had almost given up
When
I saw Mom pull up
With my missing bother
Found
Mike Donato, Grade 8
Bethany Lutheran School

The Saguaro
I am the Saguaro
Lonely as I speak
A young baby armadillo
Make a small squeak

This tall Saguaro
Holding only three arms
Each one takes time to grow
one by one

I see an owl return home
To see its family
My fruit and shelter help grow
Its hungry little babies

My needles are powerful
For which they can seize
Any harmful predator
For it wishes to feast

I am not afraid of the summer storms
Nor the drowning monsoons
I am not scared of lightning strikes
That could kill me soon
Joshua Heitzman, Grade 7
Presidio Middle School

The Refugee
He was once a wealthy man
With a grand, golden life.
He had private schools for his children
And servants for his wife.

When everything seemed perfect
War came and took it all.
He had to get his family out
As he watched his country fall.

In the fateful year of 1975,
He took his family and fled,
Grabbing only papers,
To escape from the bloodshed.

Praying to God for protection,
He went straight out the door,
To begin his journey with his family
As he fled from war.

He must start a new beginning
In a world he does not know
However he is strong and ready
For a long way he must go.
Dahlia Pham, Grade 7
Rolling Hills Country Day School

The Lost

We are driving in silence
my world is spinning
what had happened, where did the love go?
did I do something?
I am shaking
my sister is crying
and the babies are sleeping
I get out of the car
my sister in hand
my bag's on the sidewalk
no goodbyes, no kisses, no hugs
the car drives
away
she doesn't
look back
what just happened?
will I see you again?
so many questions wondering my head
standing there cold
confused,
alone.

Gabby Medina, Grade 8
La Joya Middle School

Baseball

The season starts and I beg my dad to get tickets.
He finally gets them.
I wait impatiently for the game day.
I can't sleep the previous night.
We are driving, and I see the stadium from miles away.
We don't buy VIP parking,
so we walk a mile from the car.
As we enter the stadium, I smell the freshly cut grass.
We walk to our seats and the game soon begins.
The game is intense.
One team scores a run, and then the other team scores two.
It is halfway through the game,
and my stomach grumbles.
We wait in the elongated line for our food,
nachos and garlic fries.
It is the seventh inning stretch in no time.
At last, the game is over and my team won.
While driving home, we stop for some ice cream.
That night, I dream about the game next year.

Dave Parikh, Grade 8
John F Kennedy Middle School

Christina

My hair is like chocolate ribbons flowing down my back.
My eyes are like crystal sapphires sparkling in the night.
My fingers are like long little tentacles on a baby octopus.
My loving heart holds infinite amounts of compassion
that is forgiving as true love.
I live in an emotional world and eat love and hatred.

Christina Devitt, Grade 8
Citrus Hills Intermediate School

The Chocolate Bar Whispers

The chocolate bar whispers as you stroll by
The chocolate bar, it even starts to cry

It lets you in on its secret. It says it's very lonely
It wants you to buy it, so it will have a friend
The chocolate bar whispers

But as it relates its story, let it be known that the story's a lie
A lie that towers like a small hill
A lie, a deep pit which hypnotizes you and draws you near
The chocolate bar whispers

If you are strong, then you'll resist its pull
Going to look for something else
Something honest, something worth it
And leave the whispers whispering
While you leave the aisle

But if you are weak, then woe upon you!
Buy it, eat it, and leave it grateful,
But once it's down your throat, you'll be regretful

The chocolate bar whispers
Temptation is to be denied.

Sohaib Kazmi, Grade 7
Islamic School of San Diego

The Show

All the world is a stage,
Everyone just reads their lines,
Everyone lost in a star struck daze.
The script is far too wrinkled and old,
But no one dares to rewrite it,
Because no one is that bold.
The audience is too faceless,
The actors stumble through their lines,
And all their cues get missed.
The stage lights are too bright,
Focused directly on the actors,
They cannot see through the light.
For this play the lead is unequipped,
He forgot to memorize his lines,
And his makeup is too thick.
At long last the final act closes,
The actors take their bows,
And the audience throws them roses.
Backstage the actors wonder what might've been,
If the audience had wanted an encore,
If they'd had a chance to do it all again.

Amber Riley, Grade 9
University Preparatory School

Above in the Sky
The great ball of orange light
reports the morning
when it peeks over the hills,
it may decide
to play a game
and hide behind a cloud,
it keeps us warm
with its scorching glares,
its bright face shields itself
from our many glances,
in the evening
as it precipitates towards the ground,
it paints a perfect picture in the sky
of magenta,
violet,
and creamy orange,
then it falls asleep
waiting to meet and have fun with us
the next day.
Dean Miller, Grade 8
Bethany Lutheran School

A Flag's Country
Flap, Swish, Flap, Swish
Goes the flag
With fifty stars each brighter
Than the other
Making an infinity of energy,
Thirteen stripes both red and white
The red stripes stand
For those whose blood
Has been spilled
This blood alone will not do,
The white stripes
Are the memories of those
Who have fallen
Giving the nourishment
To the heart
Of those who believe
In the memories of those
That have given their lives
To the home of the brave and the free,
The country this flag here
Goes Flap, Swish, Flap, Swish for.
Moses Aguiniga, Grade 8
Robert C Fisler School

Spring
S hining sun
P retty hot
R un outside
I ce cream melts
N ever go inside
G o outside
Arturo Montealegre, Grade 8
Walter F Dexter Middle School

DNA
This is what causes you to look like you
It has genes and chromosomes too
This molecule's in every adult and kid
The name is Deoxyribo Nucleic Acid

The DNA starts mitosis with interphase
All that DNA looks like is a double helix maze
The DNA is very complex from its sugar-phosphate to cytosine
It also is composed of guanine, adenine and thymine

DNA controls heredity with its chromosomes
The mystery of genetics was even too hard for Sherlock Holmes
Until a man named Mendel discovered genetics with garden peas
He experimented with slightly under 30,000 of these

Some of Mendel's pea plants were short, others tall
But in their second generation all were high with not one small
In the second generation the peas grew in multiple sizes
This major scientific breakthrough allowed many microscopic surprises

Now we know about heterozygous, phenotype and the Punnett Square
We know about mitosis and mutations which are rare
It all goes back to DNA for our looks and our size
It also is what chooses whether we are girls or guys
Jacob Story, Grade 8
Linfield Christian School

The Root of All Good
The root of all merriment, good will, and delight,
Is the same feeling which makes many faces shine bright,
Wherever you choose to look, you will see beatitude and bliss,
Because happiness is a one-of-a-kind sensation you can never miss.

A light in the darkness, the warmth in the cold,
Happiness is a necessity for your success,
It is always more precious than twenty-four karat gold,
Since it shows in every moment of life, and no less.

Happiness can be the result of one's hard work,
Or, when cheering someone else up, you become joyful,
It could be because of your best friend's joke,
Or the comical side of an object recently awoke.

Happiness is contagious, and you can pass it along,
To any person who needs a smile on their face,
Then, gaiety will they also embrace,
And pass the good cheer to another sullen case.

When you are happy, you feel glowing and warm inside,
Like a candle's flame which cannot disappear no matter who tried
When you are happy, you can accomplish the tasks beyond,
And you will keep trying, never even attempt to despond.
Shivani Chandrashekaran, Grade 7
Challenger School – Ardenwood

Mistake

I miss you.
My words cannot describe the way I feel.
I miss you and you don't know that.
We haven't talked in months.
Without you my life has fallen apart.
You were always there, day and night.
When I needed someone to talk to or to hang out with,
You were there.
With the snap of a finger, I made a mistake.
You have changed.
I try to talk to you but you just nod.
It's as though we were never friends.
You talk to my friends as though there's not a problem,
But when I come into view you stop talking.
Were you talking about me?
I am an outsider.
I am an outsider.
I blame myself.
I never wanted this to happen.
I miss you.

Natalie Makhoul, Grade 7
Rolling Hills Country Day School

An Ode

Domineering master,
intelligent composure —

He owns many servants, slaves.
They feed him, praise him,
accompany him on morning strolls,
provide the endearment he deserves.

Occasionally one of them carelessly
casts away a treasured possession, say,
but he, in most graceful poise,
pursues it, claims his prize
before its fate — there is no leftover grudge!
the unpredictable follower is still
entrusted with the treasure.

He is wise in laws; he knows truth;
he persuades with conviction;
he forgives all wrongs, and
approaches with loving grace —

I stroke his head,
his tail flickers back and forth;
the dog licks my hand,
succumbing to my affection.

Crystal Moon, Grade 9
Troy High School

What Is Love?

Love is pink,
it tastes like chocolate,
it sounds like birds chirping,
and has a sweet aroma smell,
it looks like the beauty when you gaze in her eyes.
It feels warm when she is around.

John Meehan, Grade 7
St Mary of Assumption School

The Life of Sin

The life of sin is short but has long highs
The way it lives, the way it dies

The life of sin inside is in your heart
The same as gloom, and cold, and dark

The dying sin begins another's life
So free the cold, the bloody knife

The jaded wheel of sin can birth its kind
As long as death, the golden find

The funeral of a sin a living vent
Thus creating when not meant

Though While the end of sin is yet unfurled
It is the cause of this dead world

But while even still the sin's alive
Or to the least the way it lies

Johnnie Crockett, Grade 9
Fortuna Union High School

At Bat

Dropball. Strike. Fastball. Strike.
I look into the pitcher's eyes.
She knows this one's important.
It's 4-3, runner on third, seventh inning.
Last out, and the pressure's on me.
I stare down the bulky pitcher, and
I have a gut feeling it's going to be a screwball.
Which is bad.
'Cause I couldn't hit a screwball for my life.
I'm going to bunt, so it's good I can sprint.
She pitches the screwball,
and I bend down for the bunt.
BAM!!! I hit too hard.
Turns out to be a hard grounder.
I know I can't make it,
unless there's a miracle.
I'm in luck.
Short fumbles the ball,
and I make a sliding finish. SAFE!!!
WOW. That's the first time I've ever made a screwball.

Ipsita Dey, Grade 8
Hopkins Jr High School

When We're Old

When we're old we'll live together, once our husbands are gone forever
We'll dance under the stars, and late at night we'll swim in rivers by moonlight
We'll cook and bake delicious foods and always be in happy moods
We'll wear ribbons in our silver hair and have trees and flowers everywhere
We'll sing in our crackly old lady voices and make dumb but funny choices
We'll wear bare feet and flowy things and friendship bracelets and wedding rings
We'll buy super-tall Christmas trees and sing Christmas carols on the streets
We'll sleep in one big bed at night and comfort each other when we shake with fright
We'll go out in the rain in our bare feet and get muddy and never be neat
We'll read aloud by firelight and share the poems and stories we write
We'll go to the beach and feel wind in our hair and swim in cold water and taste salty air
We'll string a clothesline across the lawn and hang in the house the pictures we've drawn
We'll put vines on heads and flowers behind ears and be there to lean on and catch each others' tears
We'll travel around to different places, learn different languages, and see famous faces
We'll laugh and cry and talk and sing, what other people think we won't care a thing
As long as we're together we'll go wherever, it'll be great, finally together forever

Maddie Adams, Grade 8
Medea Creek Middle School

I Write and I Sing

I write of the epoch, of the newfangled blue moon,
The people, like sand in a dune
I sing about the lenient lands, merciful mountains and far forests
The glorious sounds they keep, what a beautiful chorus
I write about hope, the fealty and skepticism of the common man,
Of empathy and sympathy, and the world's most astonishing plan
I sing of colors, fragrant beauty, the masking of morality
Walking forwards and walking backwards, a nice duality
I write about decadence, the infamy, the sorrow, and being ensnared
Looking to the heartened side, letting freedom find you but acting scared
I sing as regards to my feelings and others outlooks
The skirmishes of the protagonist and the antagonist and the sly crooks
I write about the problematic solutions, the scorching desires
Possible lifetimes consumed in days, dispersing like fires
I sing about who to blame for the world's faults, who or what did all these things and why
The riddles of old, universal hypocrisy, why people must die
I write about the silvery stars in the sky, about this creation
The purview of the galaxies and the era of salvation.

Gregory Lobzakov, Grade 9
Campolindo High School

I Am Anne Frank

I am a bright star trapped in the darkness around me
I hear the bitter cries of anguish
I see a bittersweet, long road ahead, yet no end
I feel lost like a lonely bird who can't find its own kind
I say that people are truly good at heart though on the outside they may seem cruel
I cry when the flames of hope start to diminish
I am strong and courageous, my dream will never shatter,
I am shielded by love and anchored through hope and faith
I am powerful for I believe that everyone should have a chance to speak and live in this world together
I dream to be free, to be under the beautiful blue skies and have nature surround me
I am Anne Frank

Joyce Wang, Grade 7
West Portal Lutheran School

Uneasy Love

The course of love cannot always run smooth.
Love sometimes flies away like a balloon
It disappears like a falling loose tooth
Turns cold as it gets closer to the moon.
Lysander and Hermia's love faded.
He fell in love with another lady.
As a result, their love was shredded
Made the entire world sad and shaky
But the course of love can run easily.
Inside of them their love runs sweet
Their problem was solved very peacefully
Everyone and love changes very neat
    Love is very valuable and precious
    And lasts until the death of the venous

Karina Dominguez, Grade 8
John Adams Middle School

Predator

I am rage as fierce as a lion
I hunt when the sky is painted black
I could see through the thickest fog
I can hear a mouse scurry in the distance
When I see my prey
I stalk and I chase
The smell of blood and flesh
Means success
I am what I am
What I am is a predator

Steven Mojica, Grade 8
St Alphonsus School

My Mommy and Me

I remember Princess
Books, dolls, and dress-up.
I remember wearing my favorite
Princess dress about the town,
With my mommy smiling at me.
She'd help me brush my teeth.
Side to side, up and down.
Making my smile ever so pretty.
I remember her doing my hair
For kindergarten picture day.
With lots of hair ties, ribbons, and bows.
Every day was a surprise on
What color bow was today.
I remember going to the zoo
The beach, and the park.
Anywhere we'd go I just remember being happy
With my mommy next to me,
I remember getting ice-cream,
With extra sprinkles on top.
We'd eat our ice-cream
Happy as can be…my mommy and me!

Madison Pledger, Grade 7
Linfield Christian School

Awakening from Despair

Crying in my sleep
Dreaming — going ever so deep
This longing, this yearning my desire is burning
Deep down inside of me it is trying to break free
Trying to reach the middle of it all; this is where it starts
Running, falling, running
Still it follows me; this wave of darkness
I want to give in but I'm trying to get out
Running, falling, running
It is coming closer everything is closing
Darkening — this is the end of everything
Waiting, standing, watching
I hold my breath and let it come
Slowly it is overshadowing me
Beautiful in its silent destruction
Just when it's almost over
Something begins to stir
Light is flooding in
I am awakening from this nightmare
I am breathing the now fresh air
I live for another day I live for you

Alexia Estrada, Grade 8
Thornton Jr High School

Could This Be True?

I stared deeply into his hair-covered eyes.
He looked back at me, lovingly and affectionately.
I didn't understand what I was feeling.
He was the imperfect person I saw perfectly

We were walking along the sea blue water shore,
Each of us leaving our footprints in the sand.
We saw the shining sun beginning to set.
I knew this meant forever, as we walked hand-in-hand.

We sat upon the soft baby blue towel.
He looked at me lovingly and froze.
I wondered why he turned away from me.
He looked back, said, "I love you," and gave me a single rose.

I smiled shyly but brightly,
And I whispered, "I love you too."
I leaned against him, hugging him, as we watched the sunset.
I knew somehow this couldn't be true.

I woke up abruptly that starry, silent night.
My perfect dream was too good to be real.
I guess the love that I truly wanted from him,
Was something I would never, ever feel.

Tiffani Ruiz, Grade 8
St Victor Elementary School

I Don't Understand
I don't understand
Why laughing feels good
Why laughing at others feels better
Why being laughed at feels awful

But most of all
Why we laugh at others
Why people laugh at us
Why something good can be so hurtful

What I understand most is
Why we laugh
Why we hurt
Why we learn to accept the pain
Annie Marggraff, Grade 8
Dorris-Eaton School

Death of Light
As the darkness
Drags the sun down,
Drowning it in the ocean.
As it shoots its last
Beam of color to the sky

The moon creeps up,
Smirking at the sun's
Horrible fate,
As it covers the land
In its cold unfeeling hands.
Gabrielle Carmona, Grade 8
Madrona Middle School

A Full Time Friend
I love you
Like how kids
Love to eat cake
Like how
Grown ups
Love to drink coffee
Like how old
Timers love to
Play Bingo
You are the
Cheese to
My macaroni
You are the
Peanut butter to
My jelly sandwich
You are the best
In the words
Best friend
You're a part-time
Lover and
A full-time friend
Serena Flores, Grade 8
St Helen Catholic Elementary School

Global Damage by Vehicles
We humans, being very lazy, have created many ways to travel.
To identify all the ways of traveling would be hard to unravel.
So, we will focus on the most commonly used vehicle of all —
This one has definitely caused the largest environmental downfall.

This commonly used vehicle comes in many different types.
One that we use is a large diesel truck which has no tailpipe.
Instead, the dangerous polluted gases spilled out at its top,
And, it has created many tons of soot up on the mountaintop.

Next are the automobile and the one we used the most.
We humans like driving the car from every coast to coast.
The car is the main transportation for many people.
But, it has been used so much that it creates a carbon ripple.

Notice that for vehicles, we only focus on two main types.
But, these two have caused the largest worldwide carbon hypes.
This is because gases are not filtered when released into the sky,
So, the pollutant increases to a dangerous level in our air supply.

As you can see, what we have done to our former great world —
Our many different ways of traveling have caused it to unfurl.
Please, even though it seems extremely convenient to ride and drive,
We must change! The damage to the earth will affect our lives.
Mark Chen, Grade 8
Challenger School – Ardenwood

Under the Lamppost
Out from under the lamppost the electricity rises,
Causing surges to engulf the people all around. Everybody electrified.
Very shocking
Don't play around with electricity or you might hurt those around you.
Listen to your elders they have lived longer than you.
Much smarter
You stupid fool, you don't pay attention to those around you.
Maybe you deserve those burns. From under the lamppost.
No love
Why don't you love me, my son? I'm so sorry for yelling at you.
Why don't you have any respect? For Mom?
I'm sorry
It's all my fault. For the way I've brought you up in this world.
All a waste of time, isn't it, son? I should have had a much better son.
You agree? Of course not you won't agree that you are a mistake.
It's common sense to not wish you were never born.
Common sense
I will have to raise you up to be a good kid because I'm your mother.
And that's what mothers do, right? Am I correct?
So don't play around with electricity, my beloved son. You may hurt those around you.
Thank you for listening to me, baby. I love you too.
Bill Lebbin, Grade 9
Calvin Christian School

Beginning and End

That golden desk was where
I used to write
Letters, homework, and memories.
That black chair was where
Grandma used to sit,
Knitting.
That round table was where
We all sat down for dinners.
That small backyard was where
I found my other world.
That yellow and brown lawn was where
I cooled off from countless summers,
Leeching off the sprinklers.
This white, peeling, tattered, and ancient
House was where
Everything started.
Underneath that cool, old tombstone was where
That sweet, smiling face,
full of dimples and shine
That made everything possible,
Lay.

Katie Khuu, Grade 9
La Quinta High School

Seasons of Football

The leaves are falling
The sports are changing
Football is calling
As our heroes take the field
We rejoice with friends
The excitement will not yield

The plains are now white
The season is changing
The season of football is nearing its height
The men in the armor have taken their route
They are almost finished
It may well be their last bout

The flowers are nearing their bloom
You can guess nothing but excitement
With the Super Bowl soon
The men we can call knights
Play for it all
In the playoffs it may be their last fight

It may not be America's pastime
But you can bet there's nothing but excitement
As we near game time

Jeremy Valdecanas, Grade 8
Thornton Jr High School

Bravery and Courage

As I curled into a little ball in a corner with fear
Cornered by a bully ready to beat me
I stood up to face him face-to-face and eye-to-eye.
Life a knife slicing through butter that blocks my way.
My heart of stone can be seen only be looking at my hard fists.
Just so full of anger that gasping for air was difficult
The anger pounded like a hammer it was too much —
I began to cry.
I was filled by anger head-to-toe.
Flames burned in my eye.
I felt my heart pound like a drum
As I yelled with anger and hate
I made fists with my hands, they turned red
As my blood rushed to my hands
The anger spread like blood through my body
He has gone now
I feel calm and relaxed
Anger now sleeps waiting to be awakened again
Now my heart beats slower than the minutes that tick by.

Nicolas Roman, Grade 8
St Alphonsus School

That Perfect Someone

When it comes to love it's always a mess
Family and friends tell you what's the best
It ends up the same since you always stress
Everything becomes bad and it becomes a test
You begin to think that love is not true
That the course of true love never does run smooth
You begin to have obstacles in your way
But one day you meet somebody new
And now this time you know what to do
You pay attention to people you know
They begin to know something is different
That nothing could mess up this time
This you know that everybody knows
That love can be found at any given time

Isabel Torres, Grade 8
John Adams Middle School

You and I

As days went by,
You were my first crush,
Talking about you every time,
I always ended up being shushed at,
I always sat and stared,
Thinking of the moments we once shared,
I never thought we'll end up together,
But now I see that there's always a chance,
That maybe someday we'll be together, forever.
I've never felt this way,
But it definitely feels good,
I love you and I think I always will.

Gaby Gonzalez, Grade 8
Richard Merkin Middle Academy

Love

It is the butterflies in
your stomach and the
sweet kiss on a first
date.
The scent of perfume on
a shirt or the scent
of cologne on a skirt.
The walk on a beach on a movie screen.
the coziness by the
fire on a cold day.
The "I do" on a
wedding day and
the "Happy Anniversary"
on your 50th.
It is the warmth of
a hug and the
laughter from your
family.
The shoulder you
cry on and the
advice you use for growth.

Madison Campbell, Grade 8
La Joya Middle School

Summer

Summer is…
Feeling the sand between my toes
Letting the sun hit my nose.

Playing by the beach
Having no teacher to teach.

Eating ice cream by the bay.
It's such a nice day.

Getting a tan
Standing by the fan,

Sitting outside watching the stars
If you look in the telescope maybe
You can see Mars

Erica Romero, Grade 8
Citrus Hills Intermediate School

Love Story

Her hair is so golden brown and soft.
Her skin is the color of my favorite fruit.
She is beautiful in every way.
I just wish I had a chance with her.
I love her like crazy
I finally understand "Romeo and Juliet"
It's a love story.
It's just that I don't know
if she feels the same way.

Tony Rodriguez, Grade 7
Citrus Hills Intermediate School

Barack Obama

He was the Junior United States Senator
Is a graduate of Columbia University and Harvard Law School
Worked as a community organizer in Chicago prior to earning his law degree
Practiced as a civil rights authority in Chicago

He was the first African American president at the Harvard Law School
Taught law at the University of Chicago Law School
He was elected to the United States Senate in November, 2004
Whoever wins in November will face enormous challenges at home and abroad

First African American to hold the Oval Office
Is the 44th President!

And he is the brave, the only Barack Obama!
Obama! Obama! Obama!

Avery Casillas, Grade 9
Lucerne Valley Jr/Sr High School

Summertime

Summertime is a time to have fun.
We have no more school, but we have book report books to read.
Summer means visiting a place where I have never been before.
Summer is having more time to play with my friends,
Staying home most of the day, and
Doing absolutely nothing but sleeping.
Summer is seeing kids who are just playing video games, reading, or
Grabbing their water guns to have water fights with friends.
I can also smell millions of wonders.
The weather may be as hot as a sauna,
And the sun may sizzle like a barbecue,
But I can just go to the beach and cool off for a while.
Summer is tasting lemonade a zillion times a day.
At night I can hear and feel the cool wind whistle through the area.
Summertime isn't going to last forever.
Soon it'll be over and I'll have to go back to school.

Saburo Nakano, Grade 8
Rolling Hills Country Day School

Sweet Innocence

As I gaze upon this boy
Indifferently splashing, thrashing through the waves
I think of this other me
And try to recover that wisp,
That whisper of the distant past
That time at which that world was in my youthful grasp,
That time at which life would ever-last,
That time at which my mother would always be a constant unsurpassed
That time of sweet innocence,
Running about the waves, as down they came, like a harmless ripple in the blanket,
That is the great blue sea
That time, oh that time,
Of everlasting peace.

Owen Hardee, Grade 8
John F Kennedy Middle School

Rosa Parks

Rosa Parks a leader for rights
Parks refused to obey bus driver, James Blake
Blake ordered that she give up her seat for a white passenger
Park's declination sparked the Montgomery Bus Boycott
Her actions were not the first of its kind

Parks was secretary of the NAACP
Attended Highland Folk School
She organized and collaborated with the Civil Rights Leaders
She was the mother of the Modern Day Civil Movements

She was a woman of courage and didn't fear anything
She was brave and dauntless
Rosa Parks

Yaritza Carlos, Grade 9
Lucerne Valley Jr/Sr High School

Go Green!

The Earth is getting warmer,
Global warming has arrived.
Icebergs and glaciers are melting,
Animals are losing their homes.

Kids across the world can help,
Just by turning off a light or recycling.
When kids go green,
They are helping to make a difference.
A difference that could save our Mother Earth,
It is a simple task.
Go green!

Madison Hopper, Grade 7
Ralston Middle School

Growing Bloom

the yearn for caring,
is something that should be given,
it is a plant,
searching for the soul,

waiting desperately,
wishing for the care and tenderness,
without it it is a dry seed,
that does not know where to go,

dying slowly and shamefully,
as each day goes by,
cannot live,
practically throws its life away,

give it the care, time, and compassion,
it rises proudly,
shining its growing bloom,
to feel whole you need the care from those who surround you.

Elizabeth Santos, Grade 8
La Joya Middle School

Dandruff

I skydive from the top of a very high place.
I slowly drift weightlessly down
to a large and mysterious base.
Others begin landing besides me.
I now feel like living in a town.
I begin meeting some of the others.
Some were big,
and some were small.
We talked till we were no longer strangers.

Next thing I know
a mysterious force attacked me.
Again,
I began to slowly drift weightlessly down
Only this time,
I have some company.
We eventually land,
in a group,
all together.
What's gonna happen next?
Well at least I do know
it will not take forever.

Patrick Yu, Grade 8
Presidio Middle School

Breakfast

Every day she woke up early
Turning on the kitchen light,
Preheating the pan, ready to cook

I would wake up from hearing
The sizzling of the egg
Its first moment on
The scorching pan
The bubbly, hot soup
Cooking the elusive noodles

After all the flips, turns, and stirs
It is ready to be displayed
A work of art, a masterpiece
A magnum opus

I'd always thank her
For a wonderful, rich, and plentiful meal
In reply, she would always say
No need to thank me, it is my job,
But I knew a "thank you" would always suffice,
After all, what is better than
An appreciative son

David Cheuk, Grade 9
Purple Lotus International Institute

Barrels

Dirt under my boots
Becomes dirt under his hooves
Excitement rushes through me
And he feels it too
In the arena
First work through circles
Walk, trot, lope
Then clear the arena
The competition begins
All I can think is
Have fun, try to win.

Chelsea Webster, Grade 8
McCabe Elementary School

America

A variety of cultures
Where people unite
And friendship is found
No matter the color.
Love is found in every place
Where hate is dishonored
And happiness is appreciated
The sound of freedom
Is heard near the soldiers
A feeling of pride
Within their souls
New presidents are elected
Every four years
New laws, new actions
A time when everything changes
America filled with many dreams
Most importantly
We are all equal
No matter the color
The actions
Or characteristics.

Denise Briseno, Grade 7
St Alphonsus School

Fighting Desires

Walking up to the table
I sighted a brand new PSP
I wanted to take it, but I couldn't
Yet I really had been craving one
It was just sitting there all alone
It called me to snatch it
I thought about pocketing it
I started to walk away, but came back
And took that PSP
I started to walk calmly from the table
But realized it was wrong
Then I carefully put it back

Subair Mahamoud, Grade 7
Islamic School of San Diego

A Goal to Have: A Beautiful Soul

I see you on the cobbled road,
Every day I see you there.
How I wish that instead of you,
It was me just standing there.

I can see your words are only kindness,
Your eyes are full of bliss,
How I wish that instead of you,
It was me just standing there.

I can see you are no hypocrite,
You gossip about no one,
How I wish that instead of you,
It was just me standing there.

I can see you speak no arrogance,
Your boasts are but not there,
How I wish that instead of you,
It was me just standing there.

I see you on the cobbled road,
Every day I see you there.
How I wish that instead of you,
It was me just standing there.

Medeeha Khan, Grade 7
Islamic School of San Diego

Sing

You can clip a bird's wing
And encage it forever
But if it has the will
If it chooses to
It can still sing

You can handcuff my wrists
And lock me in a prison
But I have the will
And I will choose to
Sing

Let my song be heard
Let my spirit live on
So I will survive
Even if I die
I will sing

Have the world join hands
Sway left and right
Each mouth singing
This incredible song
The song of acceptance

Rebecca Kuan, Grade 8
Carmel Valley Middle School

One Hit Wonder

The game was on the line
sweat dripped from every player
fans watched in stress
I was up to bat
It was me
and
the pitcher
it was extra innings
the game was tied at three
there was a runner on third base
the pitcher wound up his throw
the first pitch came in fast
he had thrown a strike
he threw again
a strike
once more he threw
it was a hit
in an instant
I was lifted off my feet
and off the diamond

Andy Arant, Grade 8
La Joya Middle School

Holiday

Colorful lights in the sky,
My heart skips a beat.
Sitting side by side with someone
You'd like to meet
Shiny stars
Glimmering lights
What do you know,
It's fourth of July!

Alyssa Garcia, Grade 7
St Alphonsus School

i'll always love you

you were the light
that made me shiny and bright
i couldn't believe
for i thought it was all a dream
i wish you knew
how much i loved you
but our time has gone
its all said and done
it hurt me bad
i was so lonely and sad
it should be a crime
for people to say
that everything heals in time
oh, how i wish that you were still mine
and i know that i'll always love you
you were my dream come true

Alicia Zamora, Grade 9
River City Christian Academy

His Audition

He waits in line, trembling under the pressure
Scared of the four judges who could change his future
The door opens and a girl creates quite a stir
Crying and sobbing she leaves seeing failure

Realizing that his journey could end the same way
He lets his head collapse in his arms
And here is his chance to shine about to walk away
For now he can run from the farms

The door opens and it is his turn to sing
He walks slowly, so tense so afraid
Seeing the four judges watching what he will bring
He takes one last deep breath and he quickly prayed

An unexpected voice echoes in the room
The song so brilliantly sung
A star that is about to bloom
Gets four yeses from the judges tongue

And his father standing outside waiting for his son
Hoping that he will definitely go far
Cries for joy, seeing what his son has done
For he arrives with a golden ticket as a star.

Aniket Saoji, Grade 8
Challenger School – Ardenwood

Lazy Days

Leaves flutter by in the breeze,
Everything and everyone is at ease.
Lazy days bring no guarantees,
The rumbly, bumbly sound of bumblebees.
Today no one disagrees,
All listen to the whisper of the trees.

Petals gather on the ground,
Standing on the pitcher's mound.
Everyone is fooling around,
Don't you wish this was year-round?

All the flowers are in bloom,
People stretched out with enough legroom.
Nature's sweet scented perfume,
Fills up the entire classroom.

But, nobody is there today,
Everyone has gone away.
That is the best part of a lazy day,
But, sadly tomorrow is a school day.

Kaitlyn Mastin, Grade 8
Madrona Middle School

I Wonder

I wonder if I can see, the way it was meant to be
Also, I don't know if someone is watching over me
To see what it is meant to be,
To see the way they look at me

I wonder if someone can change the way they live,
How they can change the way they see things,
For what I have been through,
It feels as though the pain can't seem to go away

The pain that I went through
I can't bear to feel the pain again,
It's hard for a child to feel,
To feel, again and again

Though my road will be rough
I will finally find a rest,
For when that rest comes,
I will feel better, for it will be for the best

For I will be in paradise,
With my family, once again,
The way I felt before,
The way it always was, again

Myedith Damba, Grade 7
St Victor Elementary School

Coffee

You are the coffee of my life,
You comfort me when I am weak,
You provide me warmth when I am cold,
And when I need a break, you are there on my gray
Marble counter waiting for me.
Without you I would go mad
And end up living in a shoe with nineteen cats.
Thank you
My delicious, sweet friend.

Milan White, Grade 7
St Timothy School

An Adventure of a Lifetime

The time has come to pack again
We're headed off to Czech Republic.
We will see some deer and not have fear.
Na sheldanou and Dobry Den is
Just as normal as hearing hens.
Camping out is always fun
Especially out in the nice warm sun.
Midnight is good playing hide n' seek
While the bats come out and take a peek.
Now time to leave the months flew by
Back on the plane flying high,
And looking at the dancing sky.

Jessica Vana, Grade 9
Fountain Valley High School

Memories

So many memories
In so little time
Life went by fast
Like a bullet,
Spinning,
Our lives go by fast.
Memories are formed,
Memories are reminded,
Memories will be made in the future.
People come in our lives,
But then again leave.
Deaths are memories
Birth's are memories
Death,
I wonder if dying
Will be the last memory
A human can have
Birth will be the first,
Memories.

Grace Han, Grade 9
Calvin Christian School

Untitled

You wish for the best
But that's not what you get
Only some things come true
When it all comes down to you
The pressures up to you
If you want it all to be true
So choose what you want
And give it all you got

Celeste Mendoza, Grade 8
Robert C Fisler School

Frozen Face

seeing my mother's face
that day
that's one of the things
I couldn't face.

"Grandma's Gone." she told me.
my face frozen with fear.
"No! She can't be." I groaned with agony
Why her! Why now!

bursting through the door
to a house I once knew
as I ran down the street
with tears pouring down my face.

I couldn't help but think
why didn't she stay
for me at least
to say goodbye.

Lyssa Arzola, Grade 8
La Joya Middle School

Chaos

Much of everything is chaos at the moment
I don't know whether or not if I should keep asking questions
I promised myself I wouldn't have such a negative sentiment
On things that would probably never make sense

Esther Kim, Grade 8
Robert C Fisler School

Four Walls

I was leaning on one of the four walls,
Surrounded by the rest, as I thought how I got here.
Two days before I was sitting with all my family at dinnertime.
Except my father.
I asked where he was at, they said not here yet.
I wasn't four or a year old, so I didn't understand.
I saw my mother crying next to the Virgensita saying:
"Please, please, mi morenita don't take him from us."
I didn't understand who she would take from us.
The third day came, October 15 and my father had not come yet.
I wasn't four or a year old, everything was so confusing.
Nobody remembered it was my mother's birthday.
I told them but nobody listened to me.
As waited for an answer to what was happening,
My mother came with her face down and said:
"Your father is dead."
I couldn't cry, I couldn't imagine how it would be without him,
That's how I got to these four walls
Leaning on one, surrounded by the rest
Watching the chair where he would rock me,
Every night he came home.

Alexia Landa, Grade 8
McCabe Elementary School

My Unknown Brother

I remember that awful day
It was the day you were taken away.
You were brought into this world and taken away; only after one day.
I wish you would've stayed a little longer —
I wish the doctors would've tried harder.
If only I could see your eyes.
If only I could hold you so tight.
I imagine you here with me.
I can only imagine how you'd be with me.
I dream of the day when I will see —
Your glorious face looking straight at me.
If you were here, I'd always be there for you,
I'd be there to care for you.
I'd watch you grow so big and tall,
I'd probably even take you to the mall!
I can only imagine how those days would've been,
And I would've been your big sister.
I miss you so much. I wish I could've tucked you in at night.
I can't wait for the day, I see your face again.
I want to tell you how much I love you,
I want to let you know how much I miss you my unknown brother!

Aimee Castro, Grade 8
St Helen Catholic Elementary School

A Day at School

Beep, beep, beep! My alarm wakes me up at seven o'clock
I can barely get up or even talk
I roll out of bed to start the day
Which will be filled with work and not enough play

I stumble to the bathroom to wash my face
I'll probably be last in this big "race"
When I'm done getting ready and say my goodbyes
I get in the car and buckle up, which is wise!

Vroom, vroom! We hurry to school
And hope we're not late and made into fools
After assembly, we have three classes until our first break
And I hope they're not difficult, but rather a piece of cake

After recess we have two periods and later a luring lavish lunch
Throughout this time, all you hear is munch, munch, munch!
After lunch we have two periods more
And most of the time they're not a bore

At three o'clock to home everyone leaves
Sometimes having to stay longer is my "pet peeve"
I finish homework and find myself about to fall asleep
Before I know it, I hear beep, beep, beep!

Ramah Awad, Grade 8
Sacred Heart School

Dogs

Dogs are great friends.
They run and play.
Some sit and stay.

All they need is to be walked and played with.
Otherwise your dog might run away.
It'll jump cars and hitch a ride on a train.
Just imagine when it rains.

No real food to eat.
No real home to live in.
Hopefully it will find its way home.
Where it will get a big backyard where it can roam.

Christian Dudynski, Grade 7
Holy Family Catholic School

Death

Dying I've found the heart of this,
all of the evil that lingers about,
the scariest thing is it lingers without a sound.
Dying, I've learned that the inside is
the craziest of all, that when all the other people
fade or drift away —
that when I'm by myself —
I see my TRUE COLORS.

Franchesca Caliwan, Grade 8
McCabe Elementary School

Spring

The wind is singing a new song
It tells me that after all of the long cold days of winter
Springtime is finally here
At long last, the barren Earth is coming back to life
Rain pours down upon the land giving plants new life
New buds in vibrant greens sprout up everywhere
And the animals start to reappear
The bear rises and blinks the sleep from his eyes
Deer teach their shaky-legged fawns to take a first step
Squirrels run joyfully through the new leaves on the trees
Rejoicing in the ripening nuts that are growing
All of the animals are shaking off winter's cold touch
Running through their greening homes
And teaching their newborn young about the world
Everything is growing, just like the animals new to life
As the birds start to sing their joy of spring
Flowers of every hue bloom into being
Thick carpets of flowers fill the air with their scent
Bringing the beauty of the Earth back to life
This rebirth has a name that all should know
Spring

Russell Huang, Grade 8
Alternative Family Education School

When We Think of You

When I think of you, I see a sweet little lady
Living in an old house with her husband.
I remember all those lunches I've had there,
With you, and Papa, my cousins, and my family.

When I hear your name,
I see that little old house,
With green land around it.
I remember picking plants and berries,
And asking you what they were,
And if I could eat them.

When I speak about you,
I see us going to your house, Nana, playing in your yard,
While you, Aunt Teresa, and Mom watched us,
You were laughing and smiling,
With two of your granddaughters.

When Mom talks of you,
I see sadness in her eyes.
It hurt her to not be there,
The day you were buried.
I will never see you, my great-grandmother, on this Earth,
But I can't wait 'till the day I will see you again, in heaven.

Malia Rickards, Grade 7
Linfield Christian School

My Safe Place

Many people have their own special place where they feel safe
It may be in their bed with a book
It could be in a tree away from you and me
Or it may be at the beach where you can have some time to beseech
But for me there is only one safe place where I always feel safe
In my mother's arms
In my mother's arms I know that I am always safe
I love my mom so very much and I love her soft touch
She keeps me safe in her arms, she is my magical safety charm
I can cry in her arms all day and she'll just say that it will all be ok
My one and only safe place is in my mother's arms

Alexis Perez, Grade 8
Coronado Middle School

Friends

The secrets I have cannot be known,
for I am afraid they will be told to everyone.
The stories I have cannot be told, for they bring the tears I had once shed.
The memories I have cannot be remembered, for they bring the sadness back to my life.

But my best friend can be known, told about, and remembered,
for she is worth that much and more. Many people can bring out the worst in us,
but the people worth fighting for are those who bring out the best in you.

Life isn't about traveling to find and make real friends but it is the journey
you make while traveling with those friends.

Real friends are those who make us think that they are really our guardian angels
who are just watching over us, helping us fight for what we believe in.

Our best friends are those who can be trusted with our secrets, stories, and memories.
They help us to get off our knees and stand up to fight the fight of our lives.
They help us to knock down the walls that were holding us back.
And for this we owe them everything.

Morgan Robledo, Grade 8
Holy Family Catholic School

Social Change

Division, not just an operation in math, but an obstructed vision leading us to a collision
There are many things that create a barrier
These things blind us. They obstruct our vision
There are colors, race, and religion
Division is not just created by a pencil on paper, but by the expression being unequal
A barrier obstructing our vision can be dangerous
However, once it continues and ceases to end it can be lethal
    We must not allow such division by color to blind us with black, white, yellow,
and brown, our minds must not be feeble
    We must unite past our differences and solve the equation of social and ethical
justice and rise over the colored mountain and look down upon the valley of unity
    We must as a whole knock down the barriers of division by multiplying our force
We are one community
Over color, race and religion we must find unity
Then only we can solve the problem.

Neal Nathan, Grade 8
Carmel Valley Middle School

My Best Friend, You Are Always There
A bad day. I feel crushed,
so mad, so sad at the same time —
Could this even be possible?

I come to talk to you...

I say simply, "Hello."
Then you say things that make me laugh.
I can say anything that's on my mind.

You always turn my whole world inside out!
You make me smile (my first smile all day).
You make me laugh (my first laugh all day).
When my heart was cold, you warmed it up again.

You are always there, so wonderfully.
You trust me,
and I trust you.

My Best Friend,
I am right here for you, as well!
Dana Estipona, Grade 8
Corpus Christi School

Original
There are many things I'd rather be called,
But "normal" is not one of them.
How boring, how dull,
It must be to be "normal."

Like another star or another cloud,
Or a dream, stopped before lived.
How horrible it must be to live life famous,
But die and be forgotten.

Another famous actress, another singer,
Only to fade after death
I'd rather be abnormal,
Strange, quirky, unique.

I'd rather be mistreated for being me
Than to wear a mask in society.
I'd rather be an unpopular original,
Than a famous fake.

How ironic that the world
Strives to be normal.
While the few of us
Choose the other path.
Kristen Shim, Grade 8
Carmel Valley Middle School

What Our Flag Stands For!
Red represents strength,
As men fight for great length.

Blue is for courage
As our liberty will flourish.

White is for the heavens,
For our people who died on 9/11.

A red stripe stands for a fight,
And white is for the light.

The blue that hugs the stars
As our government gives us peace in our hearts.

As for the tassels that surround the flag,
They are for when America gets mad.

When put together,
They represent why we stand beside her.
Alex Larsen, Grade 8
Grace Christian Academy

Who Am I?
Who am I to deserve life's greatest gift?
Who am I to get to be loved?
Who am I to even take a part in that?
I'll walk alone in my silent movement.
Sit in corners alone.
And stand alone so no harm is done.
Scared of hurting him, so I'll let him go.
Even though my real desire is to keep him close.
But I can't risk hurting him.
Who am I to cast my feelings upon him...???
Bianca Jones, Grade 7
Spring Grove Elementary School

Man
What is man?
In the beginning he is a tiny drop in a mother's womb.
What is man?
He is but a creation of perfection and beauty!
What is man?
Man is but a divine structure which is too complicated!
What is man?
Man is everything at once — sorrow, happiness, grief, and joy!
What is man?
Man is a creation
A work of art
And simple beauty
A divine structure of equations
And he is but a creature
And a mystery.
Kousar Buul, Grade 7
Islamic School of San Diego

Love

Love symbolizes eternity
Deletes all sense of time
Destroys all memory of dismay
And takes away all fear of a kiss

Elizabeth Pineda, Grade 8
McCabe Elementary School

What You Are to Me

You are my rising sun,
You are the light when I am in the dark,
You pump the blood into my heart,
You are the missing part to my soul,
Without you I cannot live my life.
If I lost you, I would go to
The bottom of the earth to find you!

Andrew Pineda, Grade 7
Corpus Christi School

Spring Is Here

Flowers begin to bloom
Grass grows green
Streams start to run smoothly
Children prepare to run outside.

The bright sun emerges
Birds return and sing
Bees set to work
Dogs shed their fur.

The Earth is warmed
Animals come out of sleep
White clouds fill the sky
And spring arrives.

John Carter, Grade 7
Packinghouse Christian Academy

I Don't Understand

I don't understand
  Why our hearts must beat
    With the rhythm of a drum
  Why our lives depart
    Just as sudden as they come
  Why our minds must fail
    Despite a living world
    A living heart

I don't understand
  Why our hearts must beat
    But cannot beat as one
  Why our lives must stop
    But time forever run
  Why our minds remain closed
    Despite an open world
    An open heart

Lexie Burton, Grade 8
Dorris-Eaton School

Poem

We all know that a poem is just a fancy word for a writing piece.
We all know that a poem is just a bunch of words that rhyme.
But what *is* a poem?
No one really knows.
They just assume they do.
I bet their definition just popped into their head.
I guess it's just a matter of opinion.
But I say only a poem knows what a poem is.
I bet a poem knows everything about poems.
But how do you know what they're trying to say?
That's the hard part.
I bet they're just trying to confuse you by making you think
They're talking about one subject.
If they would only stop talking in riddles.

Leann Barth, Grade 7
Odyssey Charter School

Best Friends

They know all our secrets, swearing not to tell a soul.
They finish our sentences and
Laugh at our jokes, even when they stop getting funny.
They are the ones we go to when our heart is broken.
For they are always there with a clean shoulder to cry on.
They know what to say when our worlds have fallen apart.
They are the ones we call for advice
And the ones that will be there with us 'till the end.
They are always encouraging, even when they know the worst is to come.
They are the type of people that you dance like maniacs with in PE.
The type of people that stick up for you, even when you're wrong.
They are the people that want the best for you.
They want you to be happy, loving to see you smile and not sad.
They help you cope with all the lies in your life.
They protect you from rumors,
But most importantly,
They are our sisters, our second half.

Rachael Wix, Grade 8
Robert C Fisler School

The Fish That Screamed

I could not believe what happened one day!
It was in the month of May.
It happened so fast, I thought it was a dream.
How could a fish, which was swimming in a stream, let out a loud scream?
Was the water too cold?
Was the fish too old?
Did the stream have lots of mold?
Then I saw the magic of it all. I was not dreaming the fish was screaming.
The stream was diluted and polluted with cans and bottles, oil and gas.
People had dumped their waste and trash.
Who could be so mean to a little fish in a stream?
We all must do our part and keep our creeks and streams clean
Because you never want to hear the painful scream of a little fish in a dirty stream!

Katie Fiffick, Grade 7
Holy Family Catholic School

In Memory Of

When I think of you I wonder a lot of things.
Like why you had to leave so soon.
I remember us playing Monopoly together.
And going to movies.
Seeing you dying in that hospital bed
Was the hardest thing for me.
You were always the one that could make our family laugh.
The one who was never afraid to talk at anytime,
And the one we called the "Game Girl."

But all those things happened three years ago.
When they called Code Blue,
I knew you were then with God.
When I visited you, you weren't with me.
You didn't even get to say goodbye,
When you took your last breath it killed us all inside.
You were so strong,
We thought for sure you were going to pull through.

In April we will be going on four years,
Separated from each other.
I really hope you're having a good time in heaven,
I know you're watching over me.

Makala Phillips, Grade 7
Linfield Christian School

Destiny

I pray to God
My destiny is with You,
so please stay,
I want to feel You.

Dear Lord, You are mine,
stay a little while,
hold me and keep me in Your mind.
My life is afraid when You are not around.

Supreme Being.
I don't know what to do without Your love.
There are days I feel sad and scared.
You are the water that dries my thirst,
The mind that makes me fly
And lets me rest.
Without You, I AM LOST.

Casey Linares, Grade 7
Blessed Sacrament School

Gilly Gillasarus

Gilly Gillasarus giggle gaggled around gamble gam gam gallery.
Gilly Gillasarus only eats gummy garlic grapes.
Gilly likes germs, gold, and glimmer glam dancing.
Silly Gilly dislikes gory gorillas and germy Germans.
Gilly Gillasarus once grabbed my gummy Grammy.

Alexis Corral, Grade 8
Citrus Hills Intermediate School

If Only…

If only we could take in Earth's beauty
If only we could stop war's fury
If only we could help all the needy
If only we could sign a world peace treaty
If only…

If only we could create cures
If only we could mature
If only we could restore the Earth
If only we could stop things from getting worse
If only…

If only we could enjoy the small things in life
If only we could stop all the fights
If only we could start over again
If only we could make everyone a friend
If only…

If only we could erase our mistakes
If only we could stop the hate
If only we could make everything right
If only we could make the future bright
If only…

Gabriella Medina, Grade 8
Walter F Dexter Middle School

My Prayer

My prayer is that the world is a happy place
People smiling all the time
Their smiles like great vibrant sunbeams

No more wars or fighting
Just love, peace, and understanding

No more debt or foreclosures
Just people who have self control

As I pray and pray
It seems as the Lord is mocking me

Because it is all getting worse and worse
And the Earth's final blow is coming soon

So every night I have this prayer
Over and over again
Over and over again

But will my Lord answer me?
But will my Lord answer me?

Matthew Canalez, Grade 8
McCabe Elementary School

AZN

I am said to be smart.
Is it that or is everyone just stupid?
I am said to be yellow
Is it that or is everyone just too white?
I am said to have squinty eyes.
Is it that or does everyone have big eyes?
Am I really all these things?
Or is everything just a stereotype?

Kevin Wang, Grade 8
Carmel Valley Middle School

Living Life

You start from a nut
It drops from another

The nut turns into a seed
It gets nourished and watered

It starts sprouting
and growing

Growing into a twig
and strengthening

It's growing into a small tree and
keeps growing

Eventually it is a massive pine tree
and growing massive branches

It drops seeds on the
ground

And the cycle continues
on and on

Gabriel Mata, Grade 8
La Joya Middle School

Perfect Pitcher

P ractices all day long
E ats healthy food
R eady for the game
F ans batters down like 1, 2, 3
E ffective pitches
C onfidence
T ry to help the team

P ut hitters in a slump
I ntense
T ry not to walk batters
C heck mechanics
H igh velocity
E mbarrasses good hitters
R eady to rock

John Angel, Grade 7
Monte Vista Christian School

How I Feel About You

You're the first boy I ever truly loved.
When I see you I run out of words to say.
The first time I looked into your eyes,
I knew the love we shared was true.
I didn't need words to describe you
Because all the words in the dictionary
Aren't nearly as precious as the way I feel for you.
When I see you, I forget all my problems and think about you,
Your smile, your eyes.
I love you. Forever will you be in my heart!

Alice Saidawi, Grade 7
Corpus Christi School

The Journey

In the beginning, a journey began. My journey.
I took baby steps towards achieving greatness.
I've been pushed around, demanded of, and left to fend for myself.
People left me, people ignored me,
Leaving my mind a swirling mass of melancholy and hatred.
Then, I found hope.
I was discovered, frightened and small, and taken to safety.
And for two years, I stayed there, content and happy.
But then my life took another dramatic, emotional crash.
I was moved to another place,
Now just recovered from weakness and loneliness.
I was frightened at first.
Why was I moved again? I felt betrayed.
I loved and trusted those people. How could they reject me?
But I soon adapted to the new environment, and settled into my new lifestyle.
I battled my fears, and locked away the ghosts of my past.
I am a different person now.
With wild brown hair, walnut eyes, and an unstoppable personality.
Still battling the hardships of life, facing obstacles and emotions,
But I'm in a better place now.
And whereas I'm still destined to do great things, my journey ends here.

Christopher Velasquez, Grade 7
Grass Valley Alternative Charter School

Rain Rain

People have always loved the rain
But for many years, it just stopped and made nature insane!
The deserts dried up and the wet weather disappeared.
The sprinklers running and spraying…
hoses being pulled out while they were turning.
All these were alternatives to the rain, but none could be
as invigorating
and wholesome
and satiating
and wonderful
and fresh.
The plumerias, birds of paradise, and pansies cried for the rain's goodness again.
They were tired of water shooting out from the ground times ten!
So we promise we'll NEVER sing again,
"Rain, rain go away. Come again another day."

Lauren Kim, Grade 8
Robert C Fisler School

Touching Spirit Bear Island

Frigid water against my beaches,
Fertile, green and cold is what I am,
The spirit bear walks all over me,
Fish swim through my lakes and streams,
Trees, grass and rock cover my landscape,
The squawking of birds and the splash of water,
Makes my nature's song.
Smoke fills the skies above me,
Trees smash to the ground,
As wood is being nailed to build a cabin,
Birds are losing homes,
Cole mauled by the spirit bear,
Totems being carved on my ground,
Makes up my nature's song.
Boulders are rolled down my hills,
And crash at the bottom with a loud bang,
Boats come and go to my lands with more men,
Fires are lit at night,
Spirits are felt everywhere in the air,
Sunrise comes from the mountain ranges far away,
Makes my nature's song.

Blake Oligney, Grade 8
Palm Desert Charter Middle School

Ode to Erasers

What you find on top of a pencil
is a fascinating thing:
as soft as the morning,
as wonderful as spring.

Really, erasers are a necessity to me.
It's a problem I will never address
It's my knight in shining armor,
coming to save the damsel in distress.

Erasers are always there
to correct my every mistake
I could ever make.
Except when I'm using a pen…

Pen's ink, dark as midnight
intoxicating a page with errors.
For pen's mistakes cannot be undone
and rewriting is no fun.

So turn away from evil's followers!
Walk away from the midnight meet!
Step into the beautiful new light of day,
and see the stationary store across the street.

Sally Cai, Grade 8
Carmel Valley Middle School

Hockey's Intensity

Third period, tied at one.
Faces filled with determination —
"One minute left in the period, one minute!"
Last line change of the game.
The home team's D-man starts the drive with the puck,
Skates through the neutral zone.
Passes to the winger.
Odd-man rush, two on one.
Skates past the other team's D-men,
Shoots rebound, another shot from the other winger —
SCORES!
Victory for the home team's win column!

Luis Wright, Grade 7
Corpus Christi School

Friendship Is Special

What could be more special than a friend?
You shop, and you talk
It's like the day never ends
You can go to the beach
Or take a dip in the pool
A bite of a sweet peach
Or a long day at school
Friendship will protect you forever and always
Your friends will always be there
For all the tragedies did they bear
So thank your friends
For never letting your friendship come to an end

Falak Jandga, Grade 9
Fountain Valley High School

A Shoulder to Cry On

My heart will never mend itself together again;
After losing a person that meant everything to me
My mother was the only person to comfort me
A part of my heart will always be in sorrow
Until the day I'm gone
She was the only person that held me together
I was always shunned from everyone;
Even when I was little.
I always tried to get attention;
But always ended up paying the price
My mother was the only person
That I could cry on.
But in time my life got better
By making my first friend
She is part of the family to me
I treat her as if she were my sister
I would sacrifice myself
To save her from anything
My heart is still in sorrow
But I have a close friend;
And my mother to cry on.

Sabrina Weeks, Grade 7
Heritage Oak Private School

Grandmother

Mi Reina, My Queen
her words still echo
as I lie to sleep
I slowly let go

I enter the house
the sweet smell of perfume strikes me
I look around and spot my grandma
staring right back at me

I run over to her
give her a hug and a kiss
she hugs me back,
but something seems amiss

I turn to my grandma
she's seeming to fade
I scream her name
but all she does is smile and wave

Mi Reina, My Queen
her words still echo
as I lie awake
I try to let go.
Haley McCormack, Grade 8
McCabe Elementary School

Shopping

Shopping is my thing
And I mean bling bling
I can shop for days
Prepare to be amazed

I want to buy it all
I spend most of my time at the mall
I buy a lot of stuff
So my chauffer is buff

I live for trends and fashion
It is my passion
When there's a sale at the mall
I know I'm going to have a ball

I have a bad shopping habit
I see something and grab it
I love to buy shoes
But it's so hard to choose

My friends say what's the matter with me
I'm just helping out with the economy
I love to sit and tell you more
But there's a sale at my favorite store
Ashley Barragan, Grade 7
Monte Vista Christian School

Poetry Is Life

Poetry is a blooming flower,
A bumbling bee,
A leaf rustling in the wind.

Poetry is a crashing wave,
A crab scuttling in the sand,
A shell washed up on shore.

Poetry is a child's laugh,
A family's joy,
A parent's happiness.

Poetry is a musician's music,
An actor's lines,
An artist's creation.

Poetry is life.
Jessica Cole, Grade 8
Madrona Middle School

Friends and Enemies

Friends
Nice, honest
Loving, caring, sharing
Family, sister — antagonist, opponent
Backstabbing, annoying, disturbing
Mean, unreliable
Enemies
Margarita Guzman, Grade 7
St Mary of Assumption School

I'm Sorry*

I stole the cookie
From the cookie jar.
I thought you were outside,
unloading the car.

Forgive me
For my mouth began to water.
A seductive smell filled the air,
If only I had known better.

I am sorry
That I ate it so.
To my room
I now must go.

Sorry that I ate it,
Sorry for my folly.
Now I am filled
With melancholy.
Jaycob Jalomo, Grade 8
Madrona Middle School
*Inspired by William Carlos Williams

Who I Used to Be

Innocence sounds like
The care-free laughter
Of a small child

Innocence feels like
Cold, muddy sand at the beach
Oozing through my toes

Innocence tastes like
Caramel ice-cream melting
In my warm, sticky mouth

Innocence smells like
Barbecued chicken on a grill
At the park

Innocence looks like
A girl smiling
Eyes wide, pure
Pumping legs up and down
On a swing
Enjoying the moment
Me
Who I used to be
Tzivia Raboy, Grade 8
Emek Hebrew Academy

A Stormy Night

Thunder is mean
An angry man
Yelling all night
At his dear young children

Lightning is yellow in color
And frightening in sight
When their forces join
They become
A great stormy night

The children start to weep
For they have to go inside
They huddle together
In a dark cold room
Afraid to go to sleep they are
Because all they hear
Is yelling and yelling
Electricity kept off
With fear of being zapped

A stormy night
Is dark and heartless
Like the deep, deep ocean
Hamza Saleem, Grade 7
Islamic School of San Diego

Have Hope in Life

Life is a journey, up and down, it is a rollercoaster,
Challenges are faced, frustrations are met,
Those are the times not to fret.
Babies are born,
People mourn,
Lives are lost,
There is a big cost,
To live with luxuries and turning down love.

Then one day, bang! Tragedies hit and all is lost,
Some cases differ, and have troubles through the cold winter.

Believe, achieve, receive, is a good motto to live by,
Sometimes it's not so easy.
Sad Sallys solemnly sit scared,
Wondering what wishes will wane,
But, they never do give up hope.

Then boom! Their prayers are rewarded,
The winter is now not so cold.
Life is a gift you can't find in a store,
So treasure it, and have hope,
And all will soar.

Erin Casini, Grade 8
Sacred Heart School

School

School is for learning, not playing around,
throughout time the benefit of hard work
will help you when you grow up,
even though you might think classes are boring,
but those classes might be the key
for you becoming someone in the world.

Jose Fuentes, Grade 8
McCabe Elementary School

Ernesto and the Space Chimps

Ham III went up into space.
He wore a big helmet that covered his face.
All the chimps saved the planet
And met a pink alien named Kilowatt.
Space Chimps is the worse movie I've seen
But with Allison it doesn't matter.

I'd never laughed so much in my life.
But then we bought those hats;
The smiling hats that make me giggle.
Remember Ernesto that odd man?
The one who wouldn't let go of the
Popcorn from his hand?

All the good times Allison and I have had
Has only made our friendship stronger.

Lindsay Bebout, Grade 9
Fountain Valley High School

Waiting

If you lived in the ocean,
I will have this one wish,
I'll exchange my legs for fins
So that I may become a fish.

If you inhabited the air,
I'll become an eagle and fly,
I'll spread my wings and soar
To meet you in the endless sky.

If you lived in the darkness,
I'll willfully leave the lights,
Without fear, I'll become a shadow
To wander even the darkest nights.

I dwell on the days that were granted to us,
Memories are blurs of something grand.
As your voice fades in the echoes,
I long for the warmth of your loving hands.

I will wait for you to come back in my arms,
I am wishing for that day till I finally do.
Hopefully, our love will serve as a guide
So that I can finally be with you.

Camille Ong, Grade 8
Chino Valley Christian School

My Lie

He came to me a month ago
Asking if I would represent him in court.
I knew he was guilty
But the pay was just too good.
I told myself time after time
Not to think too much about it.
But this wrong I've done
Weighs too heavy
For me to just ignore.
At the time I figured
We'll find the evidence
To support his case
But that evidence never came.
Instead we told lie after lie
To the judge, to the jury.
To the deciders of fate.
I never thought I'd be saying this but
I'm just too good at my job.
Because of the lies I told,
On that what seemed to be victorious day,
An innocent person is sitting in jail wasting their life away.

Megan Mendoza, Grade 8
La Joya Middle School

A Cast

Feeling hard and cold
Painful but not
Near the end you smell like you'll rot
To see the saw, to get it off
Hearing the noise, it's just a lot
But the reward: a sweet-tasting lollipop
That's all I really want!

Marcedia Strangio, Grade 7
St Cyprian School

Words

A few words can't hurt,
Right?
Awaken by Mom
And still sleepy by sight.
"Wake up, wake up, it's time for school,
Wake up, wake up,
Or you'll be late for school!"

Mother always woke me up like this.
I was young and naive,
And grumpy then,
I mumbled two words back to her.

On that morning those words
I said affected her.
I heard my mother's tears
She shed.

For I have sinned
I cannot say
Those two words
Forever will stay.

Melissa Vang, Grade 8
La Joya Middle School

Ars Poetica

Poetry is a mailbox,
It has all the thoughts in it.
Some are happy, some are sad.

Poetry is a bicycle wheel.
It rolls and rolls,
And never meets its end.

Poetry is not a song,
But it's a melody.

Poetry is math.
There are always ways to solve.

Poetry is caffeine.
You have it, and have it again,
But you're still wanting.

Caroline Kim, Grade 8
Madrona Middle School

Lucy

In the blink of an eye it happens, you never see it coming,

In this neighborhood we worried
in this neighborhood we scurried,
And the pounding of our hearts could be heard,

No other way home, but the outbacks of town
no other way home, but the alleys we followed,
Lucy and I walked hand in hand a barrier to the danger around us,

And the pounding of our hearts could be heard,

Every car that drove passed every person we saw, we ducked at the sight of it all,
I looked to Lucy no fear in her eyes, and the pounding of our hearts could be heard,
When the shot rang out there was no one in sight,

And the pounding of only one heart, could be heard that night.

Jasmyn Day, Grade 8
Ruth Paulding Middle School

His Eyes

His eyes
They are so beautiful
Sometimes even at the thought of his perfect golden, I hyperventilate
When I see his eyes set on his perfectly godlike face, I hold my breathe
In my time alone I can't help but think how unhealthy it is for me to do that
Then I ponder over what life would be without his sweet scent and face and sweetness
I don't think I will ever live without him
How I did before I do not know and I hope I never will know again
Just thinking about life without him makes me want to cry and scream
If I think about it I will become depressed and I think I shall surely die
And then…
I stop reading…

Viviana Ruiz, Grade 8
Coronado Middle School

English Honors

An eerie room, yet at a convenient one,
One glance at our grades, and the Asian parents shun.
Look around, at all of the poor, underaged victims,
As the vicious and frosty room temperature nips them,
We are all under ward.
But why, oh why, is this so hard?

Oh, but the horror begins here,
LQ High, room 205.
All the homework given, even on weekends, by Mrs. LaPera,
Makes us groan, for it would be more fun to hang at Bella Terra.
When we think a-yonder, back in the day,
Junior High, in English, where we usually get A's.
But now, he or she probably ponders:
'Why am I in English Honors?'

Jocelyn Le, Grade 9
La Quinta High School

Superhuman

It's when you think that all hope is lost,
when you think that it's hopeless,
to love love when it hates us.
Until you find that one person,
that makes your heart feel warm again.

They're the one that makes you laugh when no one else can,
the one that can break your heart;
but can mend it again.
They're the one that cares when no one else does,
Listens when no one else is around.

They understand like no one else can,
We make mistakes but they remind us,
it's not a mistake unless we learn from it
We make them mad,
but they forgive like no other.

We're the plane,
but they're the ones that make us fly.
If the plane goes down,
they still remember where the love was found
Superhuman,
they are.

Michelle Han, Grade 8
Robert C Fisler School

Haircut

Pulling open the drawer, I
Take out the scissors,
Make sure my dark brown locks are brushed,
Decide on a decent length,
Bring the scissors to my hair,
And chop.

As I watch the strands fall to the floor, I
Smile at the change only I can notice,
Run my fingers through my tresses,
Watch as a bit more drops,
Bring the shears up once more,
And chop.

Snipping more and more, I
Ignore the mess on the floor,
Shake out some of the hair that I haven't brushed out,
Add some final touches,
Bring the scissors up again,
And chop.
I've gotten a haircut.

Casey Tsen, Grade 8
John F Kennedy Middle School

This Dream

I look around and see nothing
    For darkness encompasses me
        I start to run, why? I don't even know
Minutes pass
    And I remember why I'm running
        It's the same reason I ran all the other times
I look back and there it is
    A monster of red with chains draped across it
        Never ceasing, only chasing, me — again
I see a bright light and start running towards it
    The monster comes closer and closer
        And before I can reach the light, it grabs a hold of me
The monster — is my heart, wanting to be unlocked
    Wanting to have a second chance in finding love
        And as I'm about to free this heart of mine
I awake from this dream

Theresa Pasion, Grade 8
Holy Family Catholic School

5 Cents

My favorite coin is the nickel.
Believe it or not, it's true.
Of course you can have your own opinion,
But this is my view.
My least favorite coin is the penny,
It has a strange hue.
And although the quarter has a substantial size,
It doesn't live up to its value.
The fifty cent coin is so overrated,
You can argue, but it's true.
The dime is rather small for my taste,
But others find it pleasing to the eye.
And now, that favorite coin of mine.
The nickel has no problems with its color, shape, or size.
You cannot find fault in the nickel,
No matter how hard a man tries.
Now paper money is another matter,
If you'd like to discuss which is my favorite
Sure enough I'll share,
I like the bill worth the most.
Argue if you dare.

Caroline Olson, Grade 8
Palm Desert Charter Middle School

Strawberry

The important thing about strawberries is
That they are big and red.
They are very juicy.
You bite them, and the sweetness goes into your mouth,
And the tasting of it is unforgettable,
And it grows out of the ground,
But the important thing about a strawberry
Is that they are big and red.

Elvira Sanchez, Grade 7
St Mary of Assumption School

Forever to Stay in My Heart

Life is mysterious wherever I walk, I step in new areas where I can talk talk talk.
I get to know you, and you get to know me, and the next thing you know, we are living happily.

We go out on dates and living our lives, and not even caring wherever we drive.
As long as I'm with you and you are with me, we can dive into trouble for all I can see.

One day I came up to you and I said what's up? You said do you love me and I said yup yup.
I was very curious and I asked why, you didn't even look at me and said goodbye.

I got very scared and talked to a friend. After we talked, she told me it was the end.
I didn't believe her and told her to leave. After she left, I was very relieved.

I called you the next day, to ask whether it was true. You picked up the phone and said we were through.
Before I said a word, you hung up on me, and I was by the telephone, falling to my knees.

Ever since you said we were through, I couldn't stop thinking of you.
I feel pain from every angle just trying to make it stop, but every time I try, I just feel my heart drop.

Life is mysterious in so many ways, love is a puzzle and is also a maze.
Although you are still in my heart, I know that my love for you won't be too far apart.

Christy Vong, Grade 9
Fountain Valley High School

Manufactured

To be manufactured, a product/mannequin,
is it really worth it to be with what's "in?"

Step out of your shoes and jump into fashion:
superior conformity; expression without passion

Following trends, abandoning friends; but "they'll" be sure to make it worthwhile.
Don't cover yourself in this abstract illusion and trade your devotion for a fake plastic smile

Kevin Kison, Grade 8
Robert C Fisler School

Handle with Care

This is for every little troubled piece you took of me. I was drowning so hard that I could barely breathe.
Because so deep in this love, I wasn't able to break free.
As I watched you take my heart and walk away. And paint every color the shade of gray.
My heart believing so much in you. That it shattered apart and broke in two.
So I was left with the tears you won't see I've cried, the smile I had to fake for everything I kept inside,
And every old and new scar you left behind. So don't ask if I'm all right.
As my heart sings another sad song I can't deny.
And I never knew how hard I would fall. When I put my heart on the line and risked it all.
But it never helped when you put up those walls.
So I stood there loving you and wished them all away. As my heart spoke the words you can never say.
I let you take every piece that was left of me. Breaking my heart, and all my worthless dreams.
But for some reason, I couldn't let you go, and that cut me to the core.
The worst part was, my heart longed for you more and more.
I didn't know if I could hold myself together any longer. I was so willing to fall apart, though I thought I was stronger.
I was so stupid to be relying too much on fate. But we're both going to lose if you keep playing these games.
So I'm writing this to the boy who was careless and unaware. Of the sign over my heart that says, "handle with care."

Adrienne Utleg, Grade 7
Holy Family Catholic School

Invitation

True Friendship, it lasts forever.
It's the people that you can trust.
Things that can love, cherish and appreciate you
For whom you are and not for whom you seem to be.
True Friendship never fades away.
Never lingers, then leaves,
It's always there for you.
Always wanting to help you.
Don't leave it waiting at the door.
Wanting, longing to come in, but can't.
Invite it in, let it stay.
Keep it close so it never goes astray.
It's something that at no time should be allowed to leave.
It's like the rising sun, bringing up a new day,
New warmth, new happiness.
It brings longing and wonder.
Brings patience and kindness.
But most importantly, it brings hope.
Hope that your friendship will be everlasting,
Never ending, strong, and true.
If it is then you truly have eternal friendship.

Angelica Bouzos, Grade 7
Bethany Lutheran School

The First President

I was the first president
Of the United States
I died from a cold because there was nothing to cure it
They put my face on the United States quarter
I had wooden teeth
I chopped down a cherry tree
I have a gray wig hat curls a lot at the bottom
Now I will tell you
My name
George Washington

Austin Meyer, Grade 7
Daniel Savage Middle School

Ode to Peace

When death hangs like a thundercloud
And everywhere grief does seep
A desperate wish resonates in the air
A desperate wish for peace.

Peace, the bringer of freedom and joy
Peace, the stopper of war
Peace, the universal concept
That warms the hearth of every door.

The planet is in a constant state
Of bombing, killing, and grief.
In these times of destruction
It'd be nice if we could have some peace.

Zayn Razi, Grade 8
Robert C Fisler School

Wolf vs Puppy

A puppy,
   Delicate as a feather.
A wolf,
   Gruesome like the frigid winter weather.
A puppy,
   Quiet and can hardly bark.
A wolf,
   Noisy and howls in the midnight dark.
A puppy,
   Adorable and domestic.
A wolf,
   Hideous and wild.
A puppy,
   Naive.
A wolf,
   Independent.
How cute lies a puppy?
How clever lies 'the' wolf!

Brandon Sevilla, Grade 8
Theodore Roosevelt Middle School

Blue

Blue is me when I am down.
When I am blue I tend to frown.
Blue are the waves that hit the shore.
The waves of the shore will stay forever more.

Blue is the color of my jeans.
Sometimes I wonder what blue means.
Blue is the color of the sky that will never end.
It is the color of the shirt I wore that weekend.

This color melts in my head.
Blue is forever, it is never dead.
But today I was not blue —
What color are you?

John Patrick Azurin, Grade 7
St Cyprian School

The Important Question

When they first met, he knew she was the one,
That beautiful day, burned into his mind,
Her smile: his own private shining sun,
His love for her, an unbreakable bind,
Her laughter is like an angel's singing,
When he's with her, he finds it hard to breathe,
It's hard to remember he's not dreaming,
Around the world, the wilderness he'd cleave,
Just to find her that certain blade of grass,
She holds in her hand the key to his soul,
His love has an immeasurable mass,
To be with her forever is his goal,
Will she please, as he gets down on one knee,
Answer his question: Will you marry me?

Tiffany Allen, Grade 8
Las Flores Middle School

Best Friend

I think about you all day
From when I wake up 'till when I sleep
You're even in my dreams
You're the sweetest thing in the world
You mean so much to me
You're my best friend
But yet so much more
Every day you're mad at me I cry
When you're sad I feel your pain
Everything you say makes me smile
When you say I love you too
I feel all warm inside
I love to read your texts
When I see your name
On the unopen message
I get so excited like
A kid on Christmas morning
You're my best friend
But yet so much more
I love you

Courtney Gamblin, Grade 9
Olympian High School

Grass

A beautiful scene
Full of green
It grows high in Eugene
Edible in types of cuisine
Probably thick under your trampoline
Relax on it after class
I love to lie in the grass

Cody Jacobs, Grade 7
Long Valley Charter School

Pushing Daisies

Raining, on an unholy night
Raining, as if the heavens were crying
Just as we were and will always be
When you were dying

Blind to see our undying love
That sorrowful night of dejection
Your despicable thought of rejection
As your heart beat softer and softer

Your blue icy lips of grief
Drowned eyes of ocean blue
Leaving us towards the clouds
So innocently young, you flew

There you shall lay, pushing daisies
Our worlds sealed off forever
Never to see each other together
There you shall lay, pushing daisies

Sarai Arreola, Grade 9
Santiago High School

Summer's Here

Summer time is very near
So let's go fishing at the pier
Summer summer here it comes
Get ready all you beach bums

You can play many sports
Even in your swimming shorts
Tanning is the way to go
Because you can't do it in the snow

When you're swimming in the dark
Beware there might be sharks
Let's go build a sandcastle
It's all the fun without the hassle

Splish and splash in the sun
Summer couldn't be more fun
And when you get back home
Don't forget about this poem

Sofia Valenzuela, Megan Baldenegro and Hannah Walters, Grade 8
Madrona Middle School

Hope

Hope is the memory embraced
on people's hearts forever
the picture taken
unable to be erased
travels from person to person
place to place
stays together
can be ripped, tugged on
and burnt, but stays strong
it allows you to experience,
remember and look through the past
yet pushes you towards the future
with just a glance.
Hope last forever.

Mariah Soto, Grade 8
La Joya Middle School

Meadows

In this meadow
I am looking at tall grass,
on a cold spring day,
I am feeling rich soil,
when I am walking
down this lonely way,
I am hearing wind roaring down,
this peaceful place,
I feel my soul flying around,
this meadow is so calm,
I wish I could live here.

Alondra Rodriguez, Grade 7
Our Lady of the Rosary School

Easter

I wake up
To the smell of delicious food
Waiting to be eaten
Walking to church
To celebrate the
Rising of Jesus Christ.
Helping my mother hide Easter eggs —
Filled with chocolate bunnies
Awakening past memories of my
Wonderful family
I watch the children run joyfully
Through the bright green grass
Seeking candy filled eggs.
Today is Easter.

Ariana Valdez, Grade 7
St Alphonsus School

The Sky

Stars shining in the dark blue night
The moon so round and white
The grass is wet where I lie
I look up to the beautiful sky
To think it's ugly is such a crime
The Lord filled the sky with love
So we would enjoy what was above
I took a breath to take it in
I looked up again with a grin
Its beauty is out of my belief
When I need to go, I'll be in grief

Jordan Mazza, Grade 7
Monte Vista Christian School

Twilight

The most beautiful
time of the day,
when in the horizon
the sun meets the ocean.

When they meet you can see it,
the reflection of the sleepy sun
in the water.

It is tired from the job it has,
giving light to people
all around the world.

But in the morning it will be rested
and ready for a new day to pass by.
And when the day ends once again
it'll fall in to yet another dreamy sleep.

This is twilight!

Arelí Navarro, Grade 8
Madrona Middle School

Ode to Legs

How lucky I am
They can carry me at all
They are my support
I use them every day
I have fun with them
What a blessing are my legs
They take me everywhere
To my favorite places I walk
Up and down the hill I go
To the end of the field I run
I am grateful for my legs
To the beautiful music I dance
With my friends I play
When I am excited I jump
At soccer, I carry the ball until I hear the goal!
What would I do without my legs
So every morning I give thanks
For this amazing gift
Our Lord has given me
And I promise I will take good care of them
Until the end of my days.

Eduardo Sanchezdiaz, Grade 7
Linfield Christian School

Ode to Riding

Riding through the valley,
feeling the wind in my hair!
Faster, Hagan!!
I cluck him on,
once, twice, then a third time!
I'm speeding like a bullet.
My heart races,
as I pass by the fresh cut grass.
The heavenly smell, of fresh air!
My mom, by my side.
I see a river, I go through it.
I hear trickling water,
pit, pat, pit, pat.
I stop, I enjoy life.
I think of what I'll do next.
I catch my breath,
my horse drinks.
It's like time stops,
right in its tracks.
I take a deep breath,
then ride into the sunset.

Kelly Trammell, Grade 7
Linfield Christian School

Index

Aaker, Joshua 121
Abarca, Francisco 48
Abbas, Vincent 176
Abdella, Abdirashid 133
Abiri, Arash 81
Abucasis, Rachel 160
Acosta, Chris 169
Acosta, Daniela 146
Acosta, Erica D. 180
Adams, Maddie 188
Adelsberg, Jackie 163
Afable, Akina 51
Agard, Bianca 162
Aguilar, Andrea 71
Aguilar, Gisela 152
Aguinaldo, Khadija Ashley 119
Aguinaldo, Marie 94
Aguiniga, Moses 186
Ahmed, Alina 31
Ahmed, Elaina 23
Ahn, Daniel 52
Ahumada, Cesar 79
Aiello, Cass 140
Akende, Tunde 45
Akiyama, Jessica 108
Alahmad, Asem 104
Albahri, Ziyad 139
Albillar, Alicia 62
Aleman, Frida 115
Alexanians, Jennifer 82
Alford, Elexis 164
Alhomsy, Yasmeen 174
Ali, Salman 35
Allen, Demi 147
Allen, Tiffany 209
Allen, Tyler 165
Allustiarti, Adam 50
Almodares, Ahmed 151
Alvarenga, Claudia 95
Alvarez, Marcela 174
Alvarez, Nick 131
Ames, Karl 67
Amirzada, Murtaza 68
Andrade, Lauren 90
Andrews, Miranda 156
Angel, John 202
Angeles, Karen 60
Anton, Avery 111
Anzora, Jasmine 121
Aparicio, Jessica 177
Apostu, Georgiana 27
Arambula, Edgar A. 80
Arancibia, Alexis 130
Arant, Andy 194
Archer, Megan 76
Arjona, Lillian 78
Armenta, Alejandra 55
Arreola, Sarai 210
Arzola, Lyssa 196
Ashdown, Christopher 29
Ashurst, Caleb 80
Atkins, Jazzmine 47
Attia, Sarah 40
Avila, Servando 157
Avila-Diaz, Alondra 29
Awad, Ramah 197
Awad, Renad 126
Ayala, Demi 100
Azizollahi, Ronnel 70
Azurin, John Patrick 209
Baciu, Matthew 84
Bacon, Eloise 164
Badreau, Sarah 135
Bae, Sukjin 23
Baeza, Korissa 136
Baker, Megan 54
Bakken, Kenny 177
Bala, Tristan 69
Baldarrago, Kimberly 68
Baldenegro, Megan 210
Baldwin, Christopher 128
Ball, Austin 100
Balocating, Allison 151
Banerjee, Oishi 140
Bang, Katie 174
Banuelos, Crystal 174
Barajas, Sabrina 130
Barhoush, Hoda 164
Barke, Hannah 85
Barkell, Kayla 169
Barragan, Ashley 204
Barreto, Alexander 129
Barron, Daniel 37
Barth, Isaiah 76
Barth, Leann 200
Bartholdi, Brittany 141
Bartholomew, Tori 106
Battle, Brooke 61
Bautista, Jonathan 128
Beasley, Katie 134
Beavers, Bryce 100
Bebout, Lindsay 205
Bennington, Shayne 67
Bernard, Eric 10
Biagtan, Kirsten 66
Bielke, Major 105
Biller, Johnny 149
Bitz, Christian 54
Black, Dafna 22
Bloch, Julien 34
Block, Madeline 100
Bock, Alex 117
Bolin, Gabriela 93
Boulay, Brandi 165
Bouzos, Angelica 209
Bowers, Nicholas 110
Bradford, Amanda 71
Brehm, Chasen 72
Brisbane, André 31
Briseno, Denise 194
Brogley, Max 90
Brown, Kyle 114
Brubaker, Alec 79
Brunson, KC 69
Bugarin, Chris 96
Bumacod, Kyle 100
Burdick, Andrew 134
Burns, Jonathan 30
Burton, Lexie 200
Bushala, George 131
Buul, Kousar 199
Cai, Sally .203
Caine, Darien 64
Caldera, Vanessa 101
Calderon, Luis 130
Caliwan, Franchesca 197
Callow, Julia 132
Camacho, Ivan 166
Campbell, Madison 192
Campos, Jessica D. 101
Canales, Kylie 81
Canalez, Matthew 201
Cano, Arian 165
Canterbury, McKenzie 46
Cao, Raymond 32
Caracoza, Daniel 93
Caramat, Mark 125
Carbajal-Kelly, Jorge 114
Cardenas, Ivan 23
Cardenas, Jason 97
Carlos, Yaritza 193
Carlson, Kellie 92
Carmona, Gabrielle 190

Carmona, Luis 22	Cosentino, Sebastian 21	Ellison, Ebony 129
Carrera, Jhoanna 177	Cotto, Peyton 180	Elmi, Layla 37
Carter, Ciera Rose 183	Craig, Keely 32	Engelhardt, Annaliese 33
Carter, John 200	Crockett, Johnnie 187	Erdman, Dan 124
Casillas, Avery 192	Cruz, Sir Lorenz 105	Erhard, Steven 24
Casini, Erin 205	Csabanyi, Emily 130	Escobar, Jessica 135
Castaneda, Blossom 101	Cuamani, Stephanie 77	Escobar, Stephanie 72
Castillo, Josefina 35	Cuevas, Genesis 152	Estipona, Dana 199
Castro, Aimee 196	Cuevas, Xavier 104	Estrada, Alexia 189
Casuga, Christian 98	Cullen, Fiona 41	Etessami, Mazelle 125
Cazel, Katrina 75	Cummings, C.C. 114	Evans, Jordan 87
Celis, Erick 184	Dadon, Sheer 130	Everett, Simone 140
Cenica, Jonathan 133	Dagdagan, Kyanna 173	Fabregas-Iglesias, Maria Luisa 116
Cervantes, Ignacio 36	Dale, Krista 55	Fairbairn, Nina 136
Chan, Constance 83	Daly, Daniel 20	Farfan, Julia 78
Chan, Laraine 142	Damba, Myedith 195	Farraj, Jonathan 140
Chandrashekaran, Shivani 186	Day, Jasmyn 206	Farris, Laura 142
Chapman, Elaina 93	De La Mora, Melissa 34	Farzan, Shayna 34
Chavarin-Ramirez, Austin 123	De La Torre, Nicole 90	Fazeli, Naseem 65
Chavez, Rebecca 129	Deckert, Zechariah 84	Feddema, Alexa 43
Chen, Claire 168	Dedenbach, Xavier 24	Feragen, Ashtyn 89
Chen, Mark 190	Del Rio, Roman 30	Fernando, Kenny 165
Chen, Thet 150	Dela Cruz, Daryl Ann 142	Fields, Taylor 170
Chen, Tiffany 131	Dela Cruz, Robert 28	Fiffick, Katie 200
Chen, Winnie 26	Dempsey, Jimmy 97	Figueroa, Stephanie 102
Cheng, Chris 34	Den Beste, Cody 99	Figura, Stephen 149
Cheng, Kim 70	Denson, Christopher 85	Finley, Hunter 183
Cheong, Selene 131	Deoudes, Allison 36	Fista, Jahmil 103
Cheuk, David 193	DeSimone, Amanda 122	Fitzpatrick, Mary 127
Chhay, Rebecca 123	Devitt, Christina 185	Flanders, Dylan 101
Chhum, Dustin 87	Dewiggins, Lauren 166	Flores, Alber 56
Cho, James 99	Dey, Ipsita 187	Flores, David 140
Chong, Daniel 143	Dhanani, Sofia 64	Flores, Kimberly 46
Chong, Samantha 93	Diaz, Lucy 45	Flores, Rut 23
Chou, Emily 125	Diaz, Mallorie 140	Flores, Serena 190
Christensen, Jennie 69	Dickson, Jack 39	Flynt, Alicia 156
Chu, Elizabeth 38	Dimeck, Nikki 177	Folena, Chloe 60
Chval, Andrew 54	Dinh, David 111	Fong, Amber 127
Chyun, Hana 147	DiStefano, Doran 33	Fong, Wendy 47
Cifu, Kelly 86	Dittman, Blake 108	Forrester, Kacee 109
Clark, Kayla 62	Doan, Christopher 51	Forté, Alexandra 122
Clark, Riley 111	Dobson, Hunter 149	Fowler, James 142
Clarke-Ball, Arianna 82	Dodge, Maryann 48	Fowler, Jamie 43
Clash, Marceles 146	Dominguez, Karina 189	Fraser, Megan 132
Clay, Joaquin 54	Donato, Mike 184	Fredrickson, Samantha 36
Clesi, Lauren 132	Dornadula, Apoorva 96	Freeman, Isabella 125
Clifford, Alison 184	Douville, Jamie 127	Freier-Harrison, Zachary 123
Cogan, Lyan 46	Drexel, Kayla 67	Frishberg, Charlie 85
Cole, Jessica 204	Driscoll, Riley 98	Fuentes, Jose 205
Colvard, Anthony 75	Dudynski, Christian 197	Fujiki, Hitomi 177
Cone, Jason 27	Dunn, Justin 179	Fusci, Annalea R. 22
Conway, Jack 137	Duong, Sally 108	Galindo, Ashley 117
Cooper, Ashley 62	Easton, Meagan 72	Gallagher, Kiersten 34
Cooper, Eddie 85	Echeverria, Cynthia 99	Gallahue, Aine 158
Corn, Katherine 29	Eck, Christyne 110	Gallegos, Natalia 44
Coronado, Juliann 44	El Newihi, Adam 106	Galyardt-Carr, Devyn 52
Corral, Alexis 201	Elliott, Gabriel 53	Gambino, Cherie 160

Index

Gamblin, Courtney 210
Gamboa, Jorge 99
Gamez, Brandon 43
Ganzorig, Sarangua............25
Gao, Amanda 58
Garcia, Aimee 106
Garcia, Alex 109
Garcia, Alyssa 194
Garcia, Anna Marie 34
Garcia, Brianna 72
Garcia, Celine 76
Garcia, Claire 11
Garcia, Joel 114
Garcia, Victoria 125
Garcia-Lopez, Jennifer 165
Gardner, Brianna 169
Garrett, Emily 21
Garrido, Mayra 131
Gates, Adam 50
Gee, Darien 110
Geist, Morah 119
Gentry, Hyrum 46
Geronimo, Jomari 102
Gersten, Shayna 114
Ghadiri, Darian 81
Gibson, Gabby 24
Gil, Isabel 130
Ginsberg, Alisha 50
Giron, Jorge 74
Glander, Sophie 82
Gleason, Brittney 136
Goff, Sadie 120
Goldberg, Weston 21
Goldsmith, Elizabeth 33
Goldstein, Shayna 31
Gomez, Karen 124
Gomez, Salvador 164
Gomez, Samuel 42
Gomez-Barajas, Susana 124
Gonsalves, Andrew 56
Gonzales, Racquel 179
Gonzales, Vanessa 89
Gonzalez, Arthur 89
Gonzalez, Gaby 191
Gonzalez, Iveth 50
Gonzalez, Juan 51
Gonzalez, Leslie 56
Gore, Analise 84
Gore, Ricky 26
Gould, Whitney 110
Gowen, Cathryn 168
Grabowski, Natalie 129
Greco, Tillie 167
Green, Sallie 79
Grismer, Nathan 179
Grover, Shannon 82
Guintu, Allan 164
Guitarte, Arthur 71
Guizar, Anthony 40
Gutierrez, Alyssa 114
Guzman, Lauren 127
Guzman, Margarita 204
Ha, Stephanie 150
Hacegaba, Mariah 86
Hahn, James 84
Haist, Curtis 122
Hall, Lauren 130
Halvorsen, Christian 31
Hamdy, Mohammed 94
Han, Grace 196
Han, Michelle 207
Hanson, Krystia 133
Hardaway, Brenna 115
Hardee, Owen 192
Hardin, Justin 133
Harned, Serena 42
Harrison, Bridgette 52
Harvey, Krista 161
Hashimoto, Nahoko 160
Hatter, Adrienne 60
Hawkins, Kendahl 141
Hayes, Tara 79
Haygood, Hallee 155
Hays, Summer 171
He, Ruby 55
Hearn, Kaitlin 12
Heim, Daniel 25
Heitzman, Joshua 184
Helmsin, Madaline 60
Henry, Kendall 152
Henson, Haley 27
Henson, Samantha 43
Hernandez, Alyssa 181
Hernandez, Amber 50
Hernandez, Candrice 174
Hernandez, Syrena 141
Herndon, Donovan 117
Herrera, Angelina 171
Herreros, Celia 180
Hezi, Roee 156
Hickerson, Tyler 26
Hicks, McKenzie 104
Hill, Tahirah 101
Hillendahl, Megan 92
Hipolito, Kyle 174
Hitchman, Drew 32
Hoffman, Meagan 153
Hoffmann, Jesse 84
Holden, Natasha 43
Holt, Courtney 167
Hong, Phebe 32
Hopper, Madison 193
Howard, Sierra 80
Huang, Russell 197
Hughes, TJ 144
Hunt, Devon 20
Hurtado, Jennifer 72
Husen, Josh 182
Hussein, Munazzil 63
Hussein, Samiira 123
Huyen, Maianh 160
Huynh, Daniel 20
Inga, Savannah 60
Iskandar, Bree 147
Izarraras, Griselda 116
Jackson, Babbette 158
Jacobs, Cody 210
Jacobson, Daisy 130
Jalomo, Jaycob 204
Jandga, Falak 203
Jardeleza, Veronica 172
Jasien, Chris 44
Jauregui, Daniel 172
Jensen, Sara 161
Jimenez, Daisy 49
Jimenez, Daniel 174
Jimenez Tapia, Janet 42
Jing, Lixinbei 176
Johnson, Briana 24
Johnson, Dante 128
Johnson, Jessi 73
Johnson, Kylie 86
Johnson, Lauren 181
Johnson, Nicole 41
Johnson, Sennuwy 89
Johnston, Brendan 137
Jones, Bianca 199
Jones, Kaelen 94
Jones, Mason 107
Jose, Shannon 77
Joson, Paolo 86
Judd, Kayla 157
Julier, Nick 175
Jung, Hee Jae 13
Kadakia, Aakash 116
Kahly, Yasmine 14
Kahnis, Anthony Michael 132
Kang, Su 171
Kao, Brian 83
Kaplan, Hannah 143
Kardous, Natalie 173
Kashani, Eilanit 55
Kathok, Natalie 38
Kaufmann, Kimberly 161
Kayombo, Ashley 121
Kazmi, Sohaib 185
Kearns, Allison 40
Kedzie, Elyse 25
Kelejian, Kathleen 82
Keller, Andrew 179
Keller, Brandon 44

Kelley, Quinten 22	Lee, Juliana 99	Mandell, Jesse 166
Khan, Medeeha 194	Lee, Lydia 82	Maneval, Andrew 151
Khan, Misbah 173	Lee, Power 57	Marchesotti, Abrianna 182
Khuu, Katie 191	Lee, Rachel 126	Marggraff, Annie 190
Kim, Caroline 206	Lee, Vivian 156	Marinelli, Patrick 69
Kim, Esther 196	Leeds, Tara 145	Markley, Neil 164
Kim, Ingrid 147	LeGree-Taylor, Kayla 109	Marquez, Melissa 133
Kim, Jae 106	Leimbach, Kaitlin 182	Marquez, Viviana 64
Kim, Janette 73	Lendewig, Hagen 143	Martinez, Adriana 52
Kim, Jennifer 61	Leon, Flor 57	Martinez, Ciera 162
Kim, Kevin 178	Lerno, Maci 43	Martinez, David 146
Kim, Lauren 202	Li, Fangfei 15	Martinez, PJ 150
Kim, Lily 84	Li, Natalie 37	Martinez Navarro, Tatiana ...54
Kim, Melanie 49	Liashenko, Caleb 104	Mascaro, Anna 35
Kincaid, Sean 54	Liberatori, Nanette 71	Mason, Madison 159
Kindrex, Alycia 47	Lim, Quincy Y. 72	Massaquoi, Theresa 176
King, Erin 115	Lim, Victoria 51	Mastin, Kaitlyn 195
King, Jesse 77	Lin, Richard 175	Mata, Gabriel 202
Kison, Kevin 208	Lin, Shirley 143	Mata, Yadira 52
Klerks, Mason 85	Linam, Stephen 119	Matiko, Dakota 146
Klika, Ryan 136	Linares, Casey 201	Matsunami, Holly 116
Kocalis, Cassie 91	Lindquist, Sydney 138	Mayfield, Morgan 86
Koval, Becca 20	Lingberg, Mason 74	Mayhew, Kelli 74
Kovary, Alex 53	Littaua, Alex 110	Mazza, Jordan 211
Kramer, Katya 134	Liu, Emily 148	McCabe, Nathan 27
Krishnan, Aswini 113	Liu, Vanessa 87	McCabe, Nicholas R. 112
Krivashei, Chase 54	Liu, William 68	McCarthy, Kyle 134
Kuan, Rebecca 194	Llamas, Merlin 181	McClintock, Ryan 56
Kubokawa, Kaley 153	Lo, Sharon 65	McClure, Darian 173
Kumar, Shreshth 63	Lobzakov, Gregory 188	McCormack, Haley 204
Kunde, Elizabeth 95	Lockwood, Chase 91	McDaniel, Cheyenne 137
Kwan, Theodora 139	Loh, Alicia 20	McFadden, Kailin 169
Lahammer, John 29	Lombard, Chase 96	McLean, Erin 95
Lalezari, Benjamin 50	Lopez, Jocelyn 25	McNeeley, Kelsey 77
Lamonte, Nathan 93	Lopez, Mariana 115	McPherson, Grant 134
Landa, Alexia 196	Lounsbury, Tessa 84	Medellin III, Daniel 121
Lang, Victoria 45	Lovelace, Zaria 181	Mederos, Jonathan 94
Larsen, Alex 199	Lowell, Tori 73	Medina, Gabby 185
Larson, Chris 62	Loya, Alex 103	Medina, Gabriella 201
Larson, Katt 124	Loza, Juanita 22	Medina, Jose 104
Larson, Stacy 116	Lucas, Allen 179	Medina Jr., David 54
Lassak, Joseph 154	Lucas, Justin 107	Meehan, John 187
Lau, Serena 122	Lucey, Shannon 139	Melara, Sarai 48
Laveaga, Ana-Paola 112	Luevano, Jorge 87	Melgoza, Daniel 51
Lawrence, Elisha 112	Luis, Carolina 67	Mendoza, Alexandra 154
Lawson, Ashley 149	Lujan, Cheyenne 161	Mendoza, Celeste 196
Lay, Samuel 145	Lujan, Laura J. 149	Mendoza, Megan 205
Lazo, Monica 74	Luna, Elisabet 57	Mendoza, Sarah 31
Le, Jocelyn 206	Mabanta, Alex 76	Mendoza, Yesenia 56
Le, Melissa 97	Macedo, Monica 26	Menjivar, Mauricio 163
Leal, Marissa 156	Macias, Myranda 91	Merrill, Katie 30
Leapley, Nicholas 62	Madarang, Janessa 21	Mestres, Taylor 136
Lebbin, Bill 190	Mahamoud, Subair 194	Mether, Ryan 40
Lee, Alex 74	Makhoul, Natalie 187	Meyer, Austin 209
Lee, Andrew Y. 135	Maldonado, Alexis 75	Meza, Mario 47
Lee, Hannah 182	Maldonado, Anna 134	Michalak, Hannah 75
Lee, Joseph 96	Maloy, Zha'Nera 121	Michel, Lucia 45

Index

Mikel, Tressa 87
Millendez, Cyril David 64
Miller, Andrea 154
Miller, Annaliese 22
Miller, Dean 186
Miller, Jakaya 184
Miller, Reed 34
Mills, Jack 58
Miranda, Isabel 114
Mitchell, Shyanne 114
Mittleman, Madison 139
Mittleman, Megan 53
Moalem, Eden 26
Modesitt, Jake 34
Mohamed, Sakariye 152
Mojica, Steven 189
Monk, Dani 106
Montalbo, Mary Ann 144
Montealegre, Arturo 186
Montierth, Erik 175
Monzon, Leticia 59
Mook, Kate 141
Moon, Crystal 187
Moore, Myles 151
Morales, Marco 37
Moreno, Alexandra 109
Moreno Jr., Daniel M. 65
Mosman, Jamie 40
Mueller, Jasmine 94
Mulligan, Brandon 154
Mun, Mike 25
Munoz, Christopher 183
Munoz, Maribel 132
Murillo, Kassandra 80
Murillo, Lindsey 66
Murillo, Natalie 47
Muros, Reginald 44
Musse, Suleekha 172
Musson, Austin 157
Myers, Roxanne 46
Nabeshima, Kanae 154
Nakano, Saburo 192
Napoles, Louis 32
Natanzi, Nima 54
Nathan, Neal 198
Navarro, Arelí 211
Nazaar, Salman 89
Nealy, Caylen 22
Neshovska, Lora 69
Ng, Bernardo 50
Ng, Ernesto 92
Ng, Juan Carlos 120
Ng, Justin 104
Ng, Tony 114
Nguyen, Allison 64
Nguyen, Amanda 63
Nguyen, Angeline 95

Nguyen, Anthony 73
Nguyen, Christine 38
Nguyen, Henry 65
Nguyen, Jazzel 154
Nguyen, Mai 122
Nguyen, Mai Khanh 21
Nguyen, Ryan 150
Nguyen, Theresa 170
Nguyen, Vincent 41
Norio-Tomasino, Veronica 56
Nuno, Tirzah 104
Nwaogu, Michael 176
Nye, Chanel 141
O'Brien, Cameron 79
O'Connor, Michael 111
Oberheim, Kara 80
Ohland, Nathaan 154
Olazo, Erika 105
Oligney, Blake 203
Oliva, Bailee 55
Ollry, Maggie 113
Olson, Caroline 207
Olson, Leslee 136
Ong, Camille 205
Ontiveros, Sabrina 74
Ortega, Taren 152
Ortiz, Alex 103
Ortiz, Jake 103
Osejo, Vanessa 44
Ost, Michele 102
Ostrea, Rheanna 44
Overcash, Adan 26
Padrones, Aaron 152
Pack, Jennifer 39
Pak, Rachel 166
Palomares, Angelica 39
Parada, Karla 171
Paresa, Kai 96
Parikh, Dave 185
Parikh, Karishma 59
Parisse, Jacob 138
Park, Joan 179
Park, Joanne 56
Park, Kevin 111
Park, Min-Woo 88
Park, Rachel 29
Park, Regina 92
Park, Vanessa 113
Park, Yuri 77
Parra, Benjamin 74
Partin-Majerus, Taylor 169
Parungao, Brian 61
Pascua, Priscilla 161
Pashby, Sarah 124
Pasion, Theresa 207
Patterson, Jason 69
Pek, Shinn 144

Peliz, Sebastian 83
Pereira, Samantha 61
Perera, Neomi 42
Perez, Aidee 50
Perez, Alexis 198
Perez, Brandi 36
Perez, Justin 172
Perez, Kimberly 74
Perez, Ryan 105
Perez, Stephanie 85
Perezgrovas, Nicole 34
Perry, Abigail 145
Perumal, Brinda B. 16
Peternel, Nicole 21
Peters, Merrek 133
Pham, Dahlia 184
Pham, Tu 70
Phan, Karena 30
Phillips, Makala 201
Phillips, Scott 33
Pilevsky, Maya R. 170
Pimentel, Olivia 112
Pina, Michael 35
Pineda, Andrew 200
Pineda, Brandon 89
Pineda, Elizabeth 200
Pineda, Flor 49
Pinto, Amelia 119
Pledger, Madison 189
Pohl, Caroline 145
Porter, Bethany 180
Powell, Alexander 105
Power, Brad 94
Pruett, Tanner 144
Prunty, Xavier 137
Pulido, Arturo 55
Qian, Catherine 165
Quach, Paula 159
Quezada, Andrew 95
Quijada, Janeth 105
Quintana, Santiago 36
Quintero, Christina 120
Quirante, Vence 91
Raboy, Tzivia 204
Racelo, Lynn 49
Raheeman, Rasheeda 45
Ramirez, Allie 147
Ramirez, Ismael Noel 99
Ramirez, Leandro 107
Ramirez, Vanessa 63
Ramos, Angelic 151
Ramos, Jeanine 20
Ramos, Nathan 70
Rao, Avinav 145
Rawal, Rachita 31
Rawda, Courtney 117
Razi, Zayn 209

Recendez, Nathalie 41	Salazar, Ivan 28	Smart-Abbey, Jonathan 53
Refuerzo, Irene 155	Saleem, Hamza 204	Smith, Drew 22
Reid, Marshall 184	Salem, Lindsay 124	Smith, Jared 123
Reimann, Keren Nichole 32	Sall, Taryn 175	Smithers, Samantha 116
Remick, Elizabeth A. 118	Samson, Phyna 149	Snook, Danielle 70
Renteria, Lauren 58	Sanchez, David 18	Soliman, Yousuf 157
Renteria, Stephanie 146	Sanchez, Elvira 207	Solorzano, Jazmin 162
Reyes, Kristen 134	Sanchez, Isabel 57	Song, Jenny 64
Reyes, Raphael 177	Sanchez, Jeremy 180	Sorey, Kasie 90
Reynolds, Alex 150	Sanchezdiaz, Eduardo 211	Soto, Mariah 210
Reynoso, Linda 27	Sandhu, Jugleen 88	Soto, Paula 123
Reynoso, Michelle 102	Santoro, Anna 159	Sovronec, Travis 49
Reynoso, Robert 124	Santos, Elizabeth 193	Spoon, Cody 163
Rezvani, Tara 151	Santos, Marjillaine 174	Squarcia, Brittany 75
Rhee, Annabel 27	Saoji, Aniket 195	Stafford, Lauren 170
Richardson, Randy 84	Sarabia, Miguel 148	Stanton, Hailee 94
Rickards, Malia 197	Sas, James 79	Stanton, Nicholas 36
Rickel, Evan 64	Sauceda, Zabreena 74	Steele, Taylor 77
Riggert, Steven 154	Schafer, Allison 174	Stogden, Dalice 87
Riley, Amber 185	Schafer, Ashley 101	Story, Jacob 186
Rimensberger, Mark 180	Schauwecker, Chelse 44	Strait, Kaytie 134
Rin, Patrick 144	Schmidt, Jocelyn 174	Strangio, Marcedia 206
Rios, Isaias 181	Schoff, Austin 35	Stroh, Della 166
Rivas, Mary 159	Schouten, Nicole 66	Strows, Melissa 126
Rivers, Kenny 104	Scott, Bria Marie 95	Stuck, Merilyn 59
Robledo, Courtney 121	Scoubart, Nina 104	Sullivan, Jessica R. W. 30
Robledo, Morgan 198	Scroggin, Madeleine 24	Sunga, Jezzica 110
Rocha, Brooke 88	Sedler, Austyn 164	Sussman, Ethan 37
Rodriguez, Alondra 210	Seminario, Sheldin 162	Suto, Amber 97
Rodriguez, Fabian 46	Sengchanthavong, Leon 62	Sutton, James 50
Rodriguez, Julia 45	Seno, Joshua 155	Suwa, Richard 90
Rodriguez, Tony 192	Sepulveda, Miguel 144	Swain, Molly 30
Rodriguez, Victoria 129	Sevilla, Brandon 209	Sweeley, Hailey 61
Romaguera, Juan Carlos 66	Seymour, Hannah 129	Swisa, Maor 124
Roman, Nicolas 191	Shao, Katie 28	Tadokoro, Bryce 103
Romero, David 84	Shapov, Sarah 83	Taira, Andrew 63
Romero, Erica 192	Shavers, Misha 42	Tait, Michael 93
Rosales, Steve 182	Shaw, Stephen 23	Takashima, Sophia 155
Rosas, Gabriela 141	Sherwood, Emma 172	Talukder, Rakin 164
Rosenblit, Brooke 139	Shim, Kristen 199	Tan, Faye 114
Rousselière, Alix 153	Shin, Greene 153	Tan, Mikayla 106
Rudisille, Layne 126	Shinmoto, Danielle 35	Tanedo, Eizyl 143
Ruggles, Katherine 44	Shuebruk, Becca 122	Tanega, Reginald 47
Ruiz, Cynthia 94	Shultz, Clarissa 139	Tang, Alexander 144
Ruiz, Tiffani 189	Shumard, Kelsie 175	Tapp, Kaleb 125
Ruiz, Tim 124	Silva, Angelica 109	Tate, Miranda 59
Ruiz, Viviana 206	Silva, Nathalie 131	Tauala, CJ 111
Russell, Andrew 64	Silva, Stephanie 44	Tay, Cindy 113
Ruthel, Ryan 163	Simmons, Lane 60	Taylor, James 157
Ryan, Timothy J. 17	Simo, Melissa 76	Tegen, Madison 94
Ryley, Olivia 81	Sin, Tiffany 127	Tennell, Breanna 61
Sabonis, Martin 128	Singh, Jasveen 112	Terry, Nick 184
Sacchette, Ashlyn 102	Singh, Kiren 167	Tessier, Kelley 135
Sadr, Sheila 178	Singleton, Gionny 65	Therrien, Angelique 142
Saidawi, Alice 202	Sinsioco, Matt 71	Thomas, De'Jornae 153
Saidawi, Michael 172	Sison, Jan Kip 176	Thomas, Juri 117
Saito, Brent 144	Sit, Brandon 29	Thompson, Justin 134

Index

Thompson, Mallory 80
Tiwari, Mayank 160
To, Kim 40
Tobar, Luis 83
Tobellah, Moody 107
Tobin, Anna 160
Tolentino, Samantha 115
Toro, Priscilla 97
Torres, Carla 155
Torres, Isabel 191
Torres, John 157
Torres, Ramiro 159
Toscano, Adrian 109
Trammell, Kelly 211
Tran, Brandon 145
Tran, Kimberly 97
Trejo, William 41
Truman, Paige 171
Tsen, Casey 207
Tseng, Waverly 132
Tsui, Jane 137
Tucay, Nicole 167
Umarji, Zainab 167
Uribe, Myriam 24
Useda, Delilah 86
Utleg, Adrienne 208
Vadhin, Sandra 118
Valdecanas, Jeremy 191
Valdez, Ariana 211
Valdez, Enoc 52
Valenzuela, Mari 57
Valenzuela, Sofia 210
Vallecillo, Wendy 102
Vana, Jessica 195
Vang, Melissa 206
Vargas, Ricardo 39
Vargas, Sergio 100
Vasquez, Jillian 113
Vasquez, Johnny 91
Vazquez, Jonathan 51
Vega, Marcos 162
Velasco, Tatiana 73
Velasquez, Christopher 202
Velasquez-Mancilla, Edith 140
Venegas, Juan 81
Venezia, Natalie 155
Vera, Jesus 120
Verdi, Marissa 83
Verma, Rithika 81
Vijayakumaran, Reuben 166
Villa, Daniel 75
Villa, Mayra 91
Villarreal, Lauren 53
Villegas, Kaytlyn 171
Viray, Daniel 166
Virola, Keane 183
Voelkl, Cierra 65

Von Tour, Kyle 39
Vong, Christy 208
Vrooman, Justin 39
Vuong, Colleen 167
Walker, Desiree 154
Walters, Hannah 210
Wang, Gene 136
Wang, Jeffrey 92
Wang, Jonathan 37
Wang, Joyce 188
Wang, Kevin 202
Wang, Susan 49
Warmerdam, Nicole 57
Warren, Justin 127
Washington, Alexis 183
Watamura, Nicholas 142
Watkins, Peter 70
Watkins, Ronnie 126
Webb, Ireland 103
Webb, Lennon 147
Weber, Katie 73
Webster, Chelsea 194
Weeks, Sabrina 203
Wells, Shantice 119
Wells, Xavier 90
Werthan, Sofie 163
Wheeler, Brian 59
Wheeler, Brigid 107
White, Milan 195
White, Rhad 53
Wilkerson, Cooper 96
Williams, Jamie 164
Williams, Ken 144
Williams, Lauren 59
Williams, Lauren 173
Willyoung, Marley 41
Wilson, Alex 33
Wilson, Laquttea 130
Winstead, Sarah 183
Wittmann, Carl 159
Wix, Rachael 200
Wollman, Troy 19
Wolman, Mira 44
Wolverton, Adam 54
Wong, Amy 135
Wong, Ashley 120
Wong, Jasmine 23
Wong, Josephine 78
Woo, Esther 67
Workman, Katherine 117
Worthington, Max 67
Wright, Luis 203
Yamaoka, Ryota 71
Yee, Isabelle 63
Yin, Alice 138
Yong, Stephany 66
Yoo, Christina 64

Yoo, Danny 148
Yoo, Seung Jo 115
Yu, Patrick 193
Yu, Vivian 76
Zamora, Alicia 194
Zamora, Mario 36
Zavala, Angie 168
Zavala, Erica 172
Zepeda, Carlos 50
Zhou, Amy 114
Zielinski, Alice 42
Zimmer, Sabrina 25
Zimring, Madeline K. 118
Zuñiga, Irma 170
Zuniga, Monica 33

Author Autograph Page

Author Autograph Page

Author Autograph Page

Author Autograph Page

Author Autograph Page

Author Autograph Page

Author Autograph Page

Author Autograph Page

Author Autograph Page

Author Autograph Page

Author Autograph Page

Author Autograph Page

Author Autograph Page

Author Autograph Page